Arctic Adaptations

ARCTIC VISIONS

Gail Osherenko and Oran Young

GENERAL EDITORS

The Arctic has long appeared to outsiders as a vast, forbidding wasteland or, alternatively, as a storehouse of riches ready for the taking by those able to conquer the harsh physical environment. More recently, a competing vision paints the Arctic as the last pristine wilderness on earth, a place to be preserved for future generations.

Arctic Visions confronts these conflicting and simplistic portraits, conceived in ignorance of the complexities of the circumpolar world and without appreciation of the viewpoints of those indigenous to the region. Drawing upon an international community of writers who are sensitive to the human dimensions, Arctic Visions will explore political, strategic, economic, environmental, and cultural issues.

The Arctic has always been a place of human and natural drama, an arena for imperial ambitions, economic exploitation, ecological disasters, and personal glory. As the region gains importance in international affairs, this series will help a growing audience of readers to develop new and more informed visions of the Arctic.

Arctic Politics: Conflict and Cooperation in the Circumpolar North, Oran Young, 1992

Arctic Wars, Animal Rights, Endangered Peoples, Finn Lynge, 1992

Arctic Adaptations: Native Whalers and Reindeer Herders of Northern Eurasia, Igor Krupnik, 1993

Arctic Adaptations

Native Whalers and Reindeer Herders of Northern Eurasia

Igor Krupnik

EXPANDED ENGLISH EDITION

translated and edited by Marcia Levenson

DARTMOUTH COLLEGE

Published by University Press of New England

Hanover and London

Dartmouth College
Published by University Press of New England,
Hanover, NH 03755

Printed in the United States of America
5 4 3 2 1
CIP data appear at the end of the book

Originally published as *Arkticheskaia Etnoekologiia* (Moscow: Nauka Publishing House, 1989).

This material is based upon work supported by the National Science Foundation under Grant No. DPP-9100711. Any opinions, findings, and conclusions or recommendations expressed in this material are those of the author and do not necessarily reflect the views of the National Science Foundation.

Contents

Illustrations

PHOTOGRAPHS (follow page 73)

FIGURES

Preface to the Russian Edition

My personal introduction to "Arctic adaptations" occurred in the summer of 1971. I had come to the Chukchi Peninsula, Siberia, as a member of an anthropological team led by the late Valerii Alekseev. I remember our first day in the Eskimo village of Sireniki, which figures frequently in the pages to follow. After we stowed our belongings, we set out for a walk from the village houses down to the beach. For the first time I stood on the shore looking out over the waters of the Bering Sea.

It was the middle of June. Walrus hunting season was at its height. In the light of the polar sun the beach gleamed red with blood. In long rows on the bare beach cobble, just meters from the water's edge, dead walruses lay in gray humps, their bodies still warm and lightly shrouded with steam in the cool, Arctic summer air. A few steps higher up the beach, men and women moved among neat piles of blubber, butchered meat, and eviscerated guts, in hip boots pulled up as high as they would go, grimy and smeared with blood from head to toe, the women's faces alive with excitement and pleasure. The sharp reports of more rifle shots still rang out over the sea before us. The air was filled with yells and calls as boats shuttled back and forth with fresh carcasses, and hunters sprang out onto the cobble, ready to heave the next huge carcass up over the shoal. All these sounds, smells, and human cries blended together in my mind as the apotheosis of Man the Hunter, Man the Predator, who must kill to survive in this harsh, rocky land on the shore of an icy sea.

In fact, no other event comes to mind that so clearly depicts the ambiguity of the human role in Arctic ecosystems. Popular and even scholarly writers often like to call the culture of the Arctic peoples "ecological." By this, they usually mean a certain kind of lifestyle in harmony and equilibrium with the environment and its local resources. By way of example, they point to the efficiency with which northern peoples use the game animals they catch, the specific nature of their hunting ethics and practices, or the deep respect for animals, plants, and other natural objects encompassed in the traditional worldview, folklore, and rituals. All of these points certainly hold true. But when I hear them I always remember that mid-June day on the beach in Sireniki and the faces of those men and women enthralled by the heat and excitement of a successful hunt.

Since that time, and more than once, I myself have had occasion to take part in that massive harvest of animals. I have set out in those same boats to go to sea with other hunters in search of walrus and seal. I have worked with reindeer herdsmen as they moved across the tundra with their herds. Time and again I saw native peoples in the various situations of their days and lives. I have seen and marveled at a hunter's infinite patience, yet lightening-quick explosions of courage and daring, at his keen powers of observation and capacity to endure in the harsh Arctic environment, and at his boundless exhilaration, yet sudden fatalism in confronting the ultimate dominion of nature and the elements over a mere human's strength and will.

This complex cultural and psychological identity was developed in the specific context of day-by-day adaptation, over many centuries in one of the most extreme inhabited environments in the world. At this point, in the late twentieth century, it is not feasible to claim we can describe in detail the mechanisms of this adaptive process for a prehistoric or even traditional society. However, it is within our grasp to assemble and analyze various historical models of human behavior in Arctic ecosystems. Based on such models, we can make plausible inferences and interpretations about the ecological anthropology of indigenous Arctic peoples in the distant, prehistoric past. For more recent times, our models are strengthened by the documentary evidence of books, archival records, and the memories of older generations among these peoples themselves.

The focus of this book is the unique historical development of Arctic societies and the role of ecological factors in their evolution. In addressing it, I have attempted not only to describe empirically but also to evaluate quantitatively the nature of human-environment relationships in the extreme conditions of the Arctic. Determining one's scientific criteria is one of the most critical tasks for Arctic or any other kind of "ethnoecology," in which the object of study is human behavior and cultural variations in all the locally unique corners of our world. Many factors are interwoven in the complex fabric of social and ecological processes among peoples of the north. One must responsibly choose a scientific goal, narrative form, and methodology which correspond realistically to the nature of the ethnographic materials at hand.

These considerations have shaped the focus of my research, which consists of subsistence, resource management, and ecological behavior. These three elements constitute the chief spheres of interaction between traditional societies and their ecosystems that lend themselves to quantitative description and analysis. They are not the only ones. It is in the nature of historical reconstruction that there will be gaps and omissions. In the present case, any major lacunae lie in the spiritual realm of human-environment relations—rituals, aesthetics, ethics and morality, upbringing and education. These are essential pieces of the picture, but I would do them injustice were I to address them with a similar cold algebra of quantification. They deserve their own, separate consideration.

The ethnographic data and personal recollections upon which this book is based were collected from 1971 to 1987 in a number of locations throughout Siberia and the far east of Russia. These include the Chukchi Peninsula in 1971, 1975, 1977, 1979, 1981, and 1987, the Kara Sea coast in 1974, northern Sakhalin Island in 1982, and Bering Island in 1983. Throughout these years and in tandem with such field investigations, I gathered narratives and records in central, regional, and local libraries and archives in St. Petersburg (Leningrad), Tomsk, Magadan, Petropavlovsk-Kamchatskii, Anadyr, Nar'ian-Mar, and Provideniia.

I want to note with particular gratitude the help and constant support of my closest colleagues, field partners, and coauthors in previous publications: Mikhail Chlenov, with whom I am connected by years of collaborative study of Asiatic Eskimos; Liudmilla Bogoslovskaia; Sergei Arutiunov; Sergei Bogoslovskii, whose drawings appear in this book; and Captain Leonard Votrogov (deceased). Russian colleagues—ethnographers, anthropologists, and archeologists—have rendered me immeasurable assistance with their commentaries, advice, and location of hard-to-reach research sources. These include: the late Valerii Alekseev, Galina Gracheva, Vladimir Kabo, Aleksandr Kozintsev, Vladimir Lebedev, Ol'ga Murashko, Aleksandr Pika, Viktor Sergin, as well as American colleagues John Bockstoce, Ernest Burch, Jr., Michael Krauss, Allen McCartney, and Linda Ellana. The factual data that form the basis of my study of traditional resource utilization were provided by native informants acknowledged in the respective chapters below. I want to thank each and every one of them for their invaluable assistance in my work.

The scope of this book is fairly large, and the reader will find in its pages the names of many indigenous Arctic nations. But it is addressed above all to the Asiatic Eskimos, a small group of approximately 1,700 people who live in the furthest northeast corner of Siberia on the coast of Bering Strait. It is with them that my acquaintance with the Arctic began some twenty years ago. It is also the case that among Eskimo people, who occupy half the Arctic from the Chukchi Peninsula to eastern Canada and Greenland, less research has been devoted to knowledge of this group and their world than to any other Eskimo community. If this book can serve to fill in some gaps in this knowledge, then I will be pleased to consider it an expression of my appreciation to the people to whom I am indebted for the brightest chapters in my life and in my development as an Arctic scholar.

Preface to the American Edition

In writing the preface to a translated publication is always a pleasure for an author. But in this case, it is also very difficult, because this book cannot be considered simply a translation. Not only has the title changed. Entire chapters have been rewritten and new sections added.

Most importantly, the intention of the book has completely changed. In the late 1980s, when the Russian edition was being prepared for publication in Moscow, it was destined to be a Russian audience's first opportunity to sample the language, ideas, and methods of ecological anthropology in general, and of its unique subfield, Arctic subsistence studies, in particular. At that time, there was simply nowhere a Russian reader could learn *what* hundreds of scholars in universities and research centers in western countries study when they study Arctic native subsistence, and *how*. Ideas of population homeostasis, cultural adaptations, and traditional community survival in a highly unstable environment were just beginning to penetrate Siberian anthropology. It was as though questions hotly debated in one-half of the Arctic simply did not exist in the other. Therefore, in the original book, my main goal was to introduce the theoretical framework of ecological anthropology into the huge expanses of the Eurasian Arctic and to cross-fertilize it with the classical tradition of Siberian ethnography and a wide spectrum of Russian research in the natural sciences.

The American edition required a completely different strategy.

More than anything, my western colleagues were eager for *concrete* information about Siberian subsistence systems and current patterns of transformation among them.

Throughout most of the twentieth century, the Russian Arctic and Siberia were closed to foreigners for field research. The "iron curtain" and the language barrier proved entirely effective in establishing a scientific schism. Lacking direct contacts, huge amounts of information were lost. In exploring new concepts, or even participating in entire theoretical "cycles," Russian anthropology lagged eight to ten years behind, sometimes farther. Some concepts that enjoyed great popularity in the West never appeared in Russia at all. Siberian anthropology has its own unique history, in which the curtains of such entr'actes not infrequently drop, a fact that the American is well advised to bear in mind. Only a few years ago, a trickle of foreign anthropologists began to reach into the formerly closed corners of Siberia. And it will be more than a few years still before new research data will bear fruit in monographs and dissertations available to the general public.

Against this background it is amazing how many similar researches and discoveries arose simultaneously and independently of each other on both sides of the scientific barrier. To give only a single example, in the summer of 1976, Allen McCartney and his colleagues began to measure whale bones in prehistoric Eskimo camps in the Canadian Arctic. In 1977, I measured forty skulls of prehistoric whales in the sacred Whale Alley Eskimo memorial site off the Chukchi Peninsula coast. With no knowledge of each other's work, we tentatively came to the same conclusion regarding the orientation of ancestral Eskimo hunters toward juvenile whales as a conscious ecological strategy. Ten years later, in the late 1980s, we finally confirmed our hypothesis when we met and compared our data in person for the first time.

There are many more such examples, which is why I feel this is, above all, a story with a happy ending. Two generations ago, the body of science was divided by its own private "Berlin Wall," leaving anthropological cooperation only a dream for decades. The trauma of this experience touched all of us to one degree or another. Through mutual efforts, holes started to appear in that wall in the 1970s. Now, it has tumbled down completely. I am glad to have had the opportunity to witness and participate in this. And I would like to convey even some part of these feelings to my American readers.

I must gratefully note the personal contributions several people made to this edition. Oran Young and Gail Osherenko suggested the idea of doing a translation, and put a lot of effort into its realization. Bill Fitzhugh and other colleagues at the Arctic Studies Center at the Smithsonian Institution helped me in many ways to make my work on the text productive. My translator, Marcia Levenson, deserves exceptional words of thanks. To an enormous degree the book's new image is the result of her labor, determination, and inspiration. And lastly, the love and support of my wife, Alla, were essential to this, as to every project I undertake.

In November 1991, when I had already started work on this edition, Valerii Alekseev died. It was he who first brought me to the Arctic with him over twenty years ago. For many years he was my teacher and senior colleague, and there is much in this text that bears the imprint of his character, our discussions, arguments, and talks. I would like to think of this book as a living dedication to him.

I. K.

Arctic Adaptations

CHAPTER ONE

Arctic Context and Research Design

Defining the Boundaries of the Arctic: Geography, Ecology, and Anthropology

The Arctic region is readily defined as the north polar (circumpolar) area of the earth, encompassing the edges of the Eurasian and North American continents, and the islands and adjacent waters of the Arctic, Pacific, and Atlantic oceans (Kratkaia 1960:130). Pinning down exactly where "the Arctic" begins and ends, however, is a more complicated matter. In the past, most people were content to draw the line along the Arctic Circle (66°33′N), a geometrical boundary setting off that area of the earth where the sun does not set during the summer and does not broach the horizon in the winter. Now, the geographical boundary of the Arctic is usually equated with the *+10° C (50° F) isotherm* during the warmest month of the year. Using that definition, the Arctic region measures approximately twenty-five million square kilometers. Ten million of these consist of dry land, split almost evenly between Eurasia and North America including its islands.

However, this is only one of the many ways one can draw the boundaries of the Arctic. Ecologists and botanists associate them with an actual natural frontier, *Arctic tree line* (Aleksandrova 1977, Roots 1985, Washburn and Weller 1986). This definition increases the land area of the Arctic somewhat, since tree line generally dips further south than the 10° C summer isotherm in both Eurasia and North America (fig. 1).

Sometimes the southern limit of *continuous permafrost* is used to delineate the Arctic (Stager and McSkimming 1984:27). This crite-

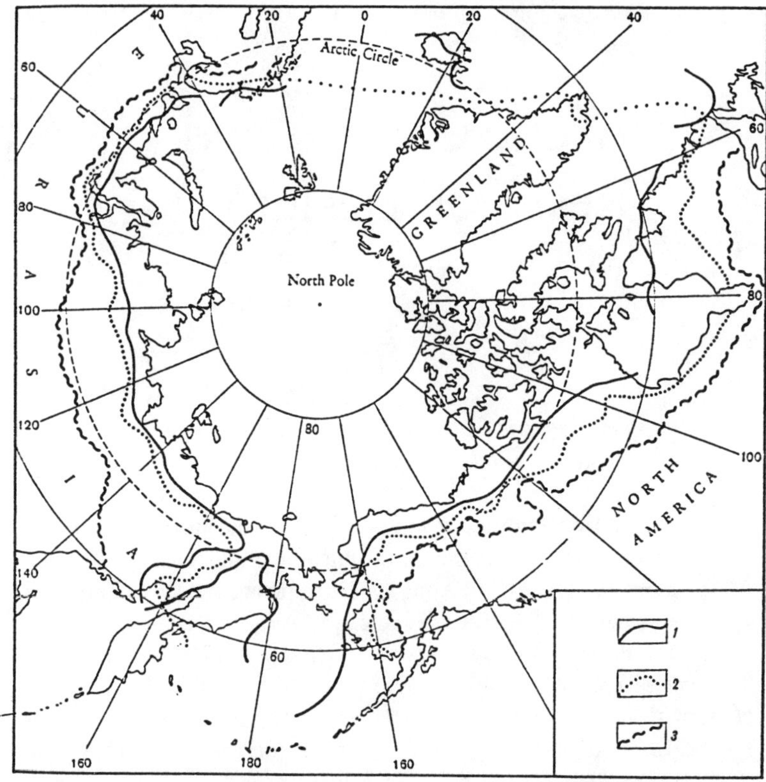

Fig. 1. Geographical and ecological boundaries of the Arctic. 1: July 10°C isotherm; 2: Arctic tree line (southern boundary of tundra zone—Aleksandrova 1977); 3: southern boundary of forest-tundra and shrub zone (Gardner 1981, Parmuzin 1967).

rion describes the North American Arctic neatly, where permafrost, the 10° C summer isotherm, and tree line all coincide closely. Permafrost runs askew of the Eurasian Arctic however, where it plunges deep into the continental forest zone in East Siberia and Yakutia, then veers northward off to sea on the Yamal Peninsula, leaving the Eurasian coast from Scandinavia to the Urals outside this Arctic boundary.

The most contradictory borders are the so-called "political" or "commonly accepted" boundaries, where either territorial boundaries of the northernmost administrative subdivisions of the circumpolar states, certain parallels of latitude (usually 60, 62, or 66° N), or some combination of the two are taken to represent the limits of the Arctic. Such combination boundaries are used, for example, in the multivolume serial *Arctic Bibliography* (Tremaine 1953: 5–6), the United States Arctic Research and Policy Act of 1984, which regulates American scientific activities in the Arctic (*An Arctic Obligation* 1992), and a number of international agreements.

Lastly, certain "cultural" or "anthropological" boundaries clearly distinguish the Arctic from neighboring regions. Names such as "Arctic nations," "Arctic-type economies," "Arctic societies," and so forth are frequently used in both scholarly and popular literature. Once again, these are more easily defined in North America than in Eurasia.

The Arctic as a distinct area among other cultural areas of pre-Columbian North America was first defined by Otis Mason (Mason 1896:646, 1907:427). Ever since, almost without exception, all classical cultural divisions recognize the Arctic as a separate cultural, natural, and anthropological sphere, determined, perhaps tautologically, by the standard interpretation of its limits as defined by the southernmost settlement of Eskimos and Aleuts. This "cultural" definition of the Arctic is accepted in all contemporary North American reference books, bibliographies, and anthropological maps (Damas 1984, Driver 1969, Driver and Massey 1957, Indians 1979, Kroeber 1939, Murdock and O'Leary 1975, Waldman 1985, etc.).

But, as often as American anthropologists reproduced this definition from one textbook to another, it seems never to have occurred to them that its usefulness is limited to North America: among the dozens of nations occupying the enormous landmass of the Siberian Arctic, Eskimos and Aleuts never constituted more than a few tiny enclaves on the Bering Sea coast. To consider the Arctic as truly circumpolar, we will need to find some other anthropological criteria for "the Arctic" that include Eurasia.

I know of only one attempt to map Arctic nations on a truly circumpolar, Eurasian-American scale, by American anthropologist Ernest Burch (1983). The first to deviate from the classical American anthropological definition, Burch put together an entirely workable comparative map of circumpolar native peoples, including all aboriginal populations of Eurasia and North America who live north of, and in some cases *south* of, Arctic tree line, in the forest-tundra, but who move into the tundra for part of the year. In this manner, about two dozen native peoples of northern Eurasian fall under Burch's "Arctic" rubric, and some northern Athapaskan and Algonkian (Naskapi)

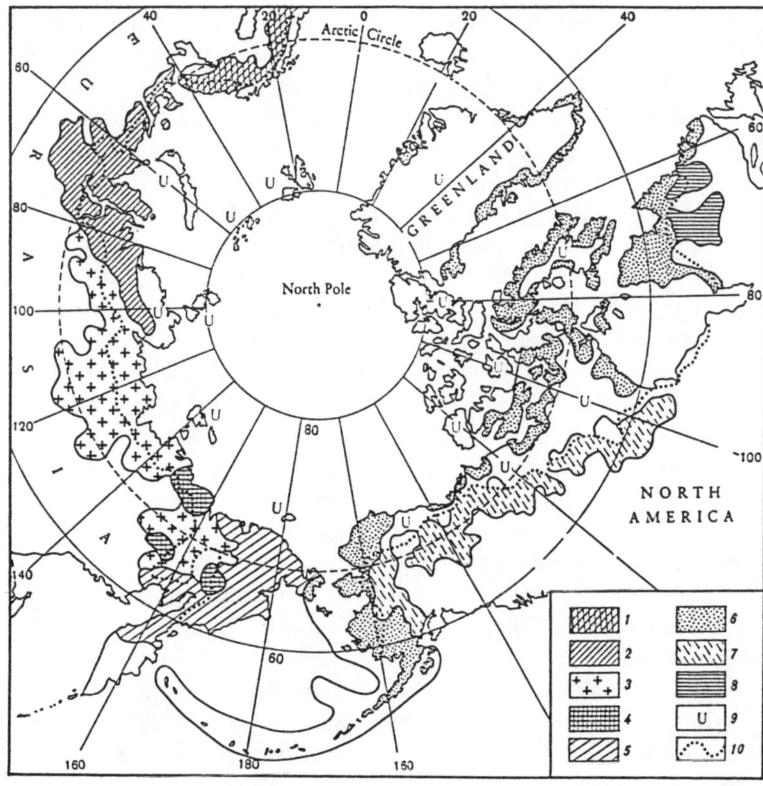

Fig. 2. Arctic indigenous nations around 1825. (Adapted from Burch 1983.) 1: Lapp (Saami); 2: Samoyed (Nenets, Enets, Nganasan); 3: Altaic (Evenk, Even, Yakut); 4: Yukagir; 5: Chukchi and Koryak; 6: Eskimo and Aleut; 7: Athapaskan (G'wichin, Koyukon, Hare, Chipewyan, etc.); 8: Algonkian (Naskapi); 9: Unoccuppied; 10: Arctic tree line.

groups joined the "Arctic" ranks along with Eskimos and Aleuts in North America (fig. 2).

This approach to Arctic anthropological boundaries makes the most sense to me. Hence, in this book we will consider as "Arctic" all those indigenous nations or their subgroups inhabiting tundra or forest-tundra areas north of the boreal coniferous forest in the early twentieth century. In Eurasia these were the northern groups of Norwegian and Kola Peninsula Saami (Lapp), the European and Siberian Nenets (including the "forest" Nenets), northern Izhma Komi, Khanty, Taz Sel'kup; the Enets, Nganasan, and Dolgan; north-

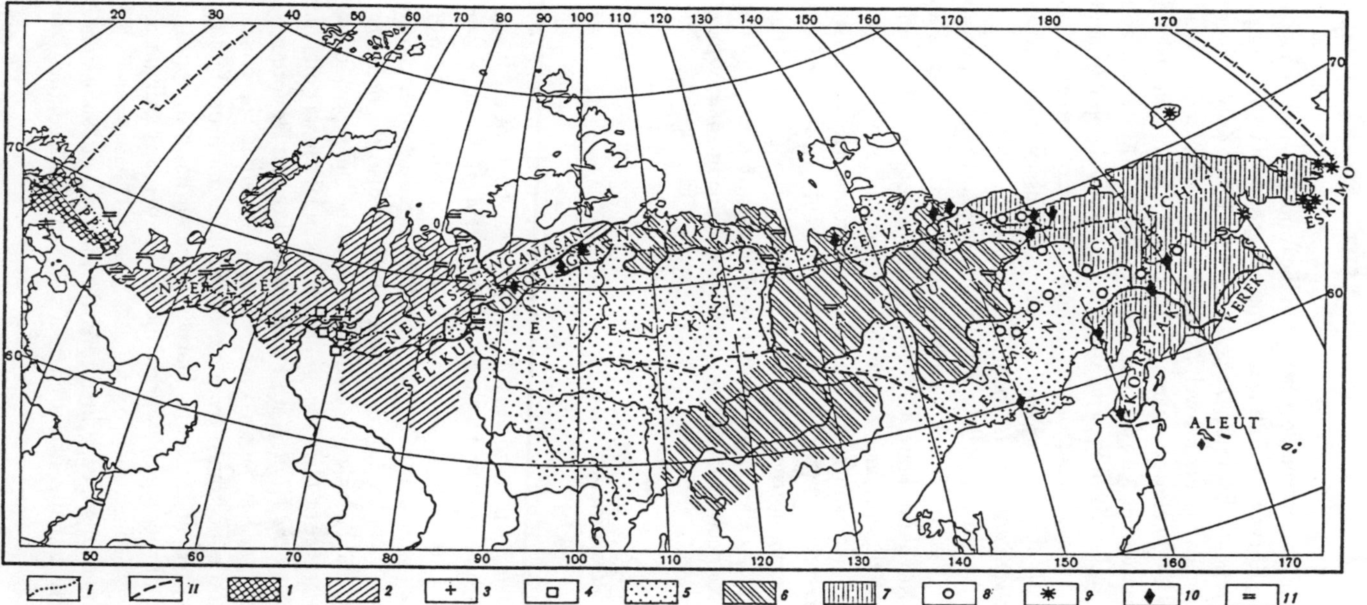

Fig. 3. Arctic nations of northern Eurasia in the 1920s. (According to the Polar Census of the USSR, 1926–27.) I: southern boundary of tundra zone; II: southern boundary of forest-tundra and shrub zone. 1: Lapp (Saami); 2: Samoyed (Nenets, Enets, Nganasan, Sel'kup); 3: Komi; 4: Khanty; 5: Tungus (Evenk, Even) 6: Dolgan and Yakut; 7: Chukchi, Koryak, and Kerek; 8: Yukagir and Chuvants; 9: Eskimo; 10:Mixed populations (e.g., "tundra peasants," Kolyma, Markovo, Gizhiga); 11: Russian (Pomors and Old Settlers).

ern Evenk and Yakut (reindeer herders); the tundra branch of Yukagir; Chukchi; Koryak (excluding the southern groups of Uka, Karaga, and Palana); Asiatic Eskimo; Kerek; Even of the lower Kolyma, Penzhina, and Anadyr rivers; as well as métis groups of mixed-Russian origin—tundra-dwelling peasants, the Chuvants, Commander Island Aleut, and settlers in Russkoe Ust'e, lower Kolyma, Markovo, and Gizhiga (fig. 3).[1] According to the 1926 census, the total population of the Russian Arctic was 69,500, of whom 62,000 were natives, 2,200 were ethnically mixed, and about 3,000 were Russian Old Settlers (*Pokhoziaistvennaia Perepis'* 1929).

In North America we will follow Burch in adding to the traditionally "Arctic" Eskimo and Aleut groups some northern Athapaskan (Gwich'in, Koyukon, Hare, Chipewyan) and Algonkian (Naskapi). Nearly all of these names appear at one point or another in this book. People living south of the ethnographic boundaries of the Arctic will correspondingly be referred to as "boreal," (from the Latin *borealis*, meaning northern, and the usual term in geographical parlance designating the taiga, or coniferous forest), thus emphasizing their close connection to the forest zone (Steegmann 1983, Winterhalder 1981, etc.).

Subsistence

Two terms recur more frequently than any other in the pages to follow: *subsistence* and *adaptation*. They lie at the heart of the book's theoretical framework and form the basis for several secondary concepts derived from them. To the best of my knowledge, the word "subsistence" was first used or at least legitimized in American anthropology by Robert Lowie (Lowie 1938; see also Bennett 1948, Hatch 1973) and became especially popular in the late 1960s, following the appearance of *The Ethnographic Atlas* and the first conference volume of *Man the Hunter* (see Damas 1969, Lee and DeVore 1968, Murdock 1967a, Rappaport 1967, Vayda 1969, etc.). The concept of adaptation is borrowed from general ecology and from biology, where it existed since Charles Darwin's time. It has also appeared widely in anthropological works since the mid-1960s (Alland and McCay 1973, Bennett 1969, etc.).

In the English-language literature, the meaning of "subsistence" varies widely. Usually, it is used as a synonym for "economy," for "means (or mode) of production," such as hunting, fishing, or foraging, or in an even narrower sense referring to a way of obtaining food or any other good for consumption within the community (Leeds 1976:139, Smith 1991:394). In the 1970s, with the boom in research programs on the economy and cultural heritage of Arctic residents, the term came to be used primarily for *traditional economies* and, subsequently, for contemporary hunting and fishing done by native people for their own use. The creation in 1978 of a special Division of Subsistence within the Alaska Department of Fish and Game officially cemented this new meaning into common use. Since then, tens if not hundreds of books and articles bearing the word "subsistence" in the title have been published, creating the need for specialized bibliographies on the subject (Anderson 1982, O'Brien McMillan 1982, etc.).[2]

In this book, I use "subsistence" in its most common meaning, that is, in the general sense of any human activity directed toward satisfying survival needs. But, much more frequently, I use three derivative terms: subsistence mode, subsistence pattern, and subsistence model.

Of these, *subsistence mode* has the broadest meaning. A mode of subsistence consists of the chief complexes of activities through which human societies provide for their food and overall survival. The number of subsistence modes ranges from five or six (gathering, hunting, fishing, animal husbandry, and agriculture; Murdock 1967a:154–55, Ellen 1982:128) to a few dozen in a detailed breakdown of mixed, transitional, and regional variations (Driver and Massey 1957:177, Murdock and White 1969:353, Krupnik 1988b:183, etc.). In this sense, synonyms in English-language literature would be subsistence economies (in plural), subsistence sources, economic patterns, procurement strategies, etc. "Economic-cultural type" (*khoziaistvenno-kul'turnyi tip*) would be the closest Russian analogue (see below).

A subsistence mode is a highly abstract category, or, more precisely, a continuum comprised of numerous local, ethnic, and temporal variations. Each variation can be examined in its own right as a "*subsistence pattern*" obtaining among a given population. This pattern can be defined as the complex of economic activities, demographic structure and settlement, economic cooperation, consumption and distribution traditions, that is, ecologically contingent forms of social behavior that assure collective survival using the resources in a given environment.

Both modes and patterns of subsistence are more meaningful for purposes of literary description and typologies than for field observation. The concrete manifestation of both is *resource management*, that is, the human action of harvesting resources from the surrounding environment. In contrast to subsistence, resource management can be an analytical concept. Ecologists differentiate between "rational" resource management, which considers the rate of reproduction of the exploited resources in providing for human needs, and "nonrational" resource management, which disrupts equilibrium in the affected ecosystems (Reimers and Yablokov 1982:61, 97). The concept of resource management comes close to the usual anthropological understanding of "economy" in traditional societies. But resource management lays much greater emphasis on the environmental side of economic activity—that is, the resources and ecosystem as a whole—and inevitably includes an intellectual component in the relationship of humans to their environment: knowledge systems, habits of apprehending and representing what one observes, methods of acquiring and transmitting knowledge and beliefs, etc.

It remains to define what I mean by *subsistence models*. A model is a simplified form of a local pattern of subsistence or resource management as practiced within defined temporal and spatial boundaries. We build or describe models for concrete research purposes—for example, for quantitative analysis or historical reconstruction. A model permits us to estimate population growth and density, to compare what a community produces with what it consumes, to trace energy flows in an ecosystem, or to assess human impact on game resources. Such a model can express only *some* of the actual relationships active in a subsistence system, but presents them in clearly quantified terms.

Classification Systems for Arctic Subsistence

Having defined the boundaries of the Arctic, and the meaning of subsistence, we can move on to establishing a classification for traditional modes of subsistence in the Eurasian Arctic zone. Several systematizations exist that concur well with each other and are suitable for this task (Bogoras 1929:599–600, 1941, Sergeev 1955:12, etc.). They all define *four* basic types of economy among the native Siberian population according to the main subsistence activity: fishing, land-game hunting, maritime hunting, and reindeer breeding.

At present, the most common Russian classification is one devised by Maksim Levin (Levin 1947:84–86) and reproduced in many subsequent publications (Levin 1958/1963:3–5, 1960:49, Levin and Cheboksarov 1955:4–7, 1957:44–46, Levin and Potapov 1956/1964, Chesnov 1970:16–17, Gurvich et al. 1970:39–43, etc.) Levin identified *five* indigenous economic modes in northern Siberia, which he called "economic-cultural types": (1) taiga/boreal forest "foot" hunting and fishing, (2) Arctic maritime hunting, (3) sedentary fishing in large rivers, (4) taiga hunting and reindeer breeding, (5) tundra reindeer herding.

Subsequent authors supplemented this list with a few additional modes without changing its overall format (Andrianov and Cheboksarov 1972, Chesnov 1970:16, Krupnik 1976b:60). In theory, these classifications are easily joined, especially where a specific period of time is concerned. For example, in the late nineteenth century almost no "foot" hunters or fishermen remained in the Siberian taiga or caribou hunters in the tundra, because most native hunters in Arctic Eurasia owned domestic reindeer by then (Bogoras 1930:403–404, map). Large areas were inhabited by a métis population, as well as Russian Old Settlers with their mixed economy combining fishing, hunting, fur trapping, gardening, and even farming in the southernmost regions.

In a similar way, while retaining a total of five modes of postcontact Siberian subsistence as per Levin, we can rename them slightly: (1) settled maritime hunting, (2) seminomadic hunting and herding, (3) intensive fishing, (4) intensive reindeer herding, and (5) métis and Old Settler mixed economies (Krupnik 1988b:183). The first three modes are very old, with origins going back to Neolithic cultures of northern Eurasia. In contrast, the other two—intensive reindeer herding and Old Settler subsistence—are very recent. Both arose no earlier than the seventeenth or eighteenth centuries and subsequently spread rapidly throughout the Eurasian Arctic zone.

In practice, each primary mode was represented by a large number of local, intermediate, or ethnic subdivisions. This fact is well known, but no unified classification exists of local variations throughout the Eurasian Arctic, while regional typologies fit together poorly (Charnolusski 1930, Golovnev 1986a, Orlovskii 1928a, etc.).

The situation with anything approaching a joint American and Siberian classification is even worse. In the first place, nothing like an accepted subsistence classification exists for the American Arctic.

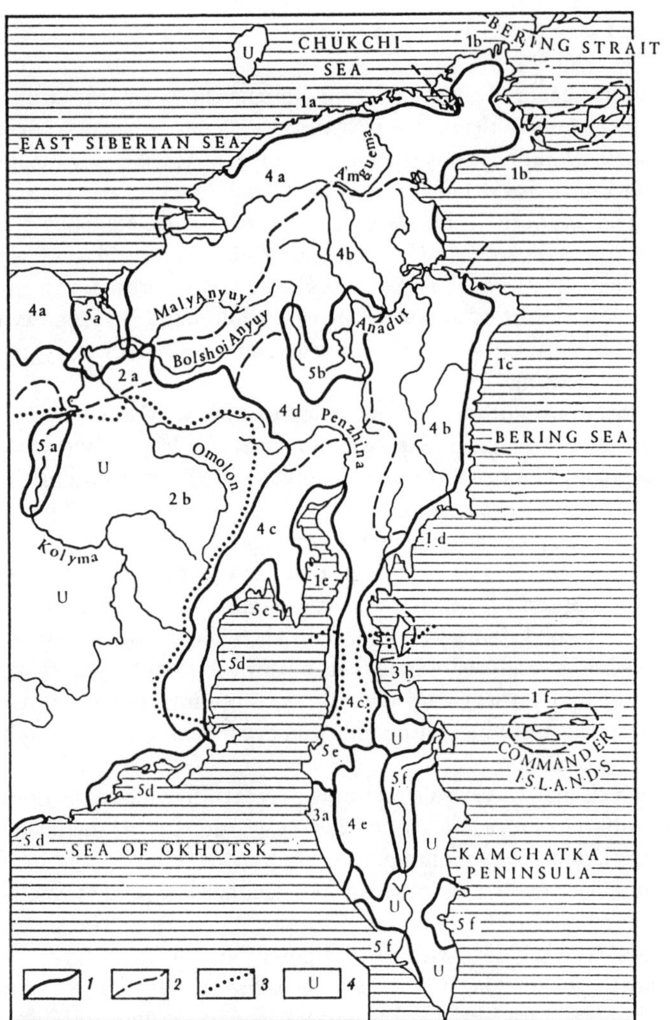

Fig. 4. Indigenous subsistence patterns in northeast Siberia around 1900. 1: boundaries of major subsistence modes; 2: boundaries of local subsistence patterns; 3: "anthropological" boundary of the Arctic; 4: Unoccupied or sparsely populated areas.

Settled Maritime Hunting: (1a) Arctic Chikchi, (1b) Bering Strait, (1c) Kerek, (1d) Eastern Koryak, (1e) Western Koryak, (1f) Commander Island, *Seminomadic Hunting and Herding:* (2a) Arctic tundra Even, (2b) Subarctic interior Even, *Intensive Fishing:* (3a) Itel'men, (3b) South Koryak, *Intensive Reindeer Herding:* (4a) Northern Chukchi, (4b) Interior Chukchi, (4c) Koyrak, (4d) Chuvants, (4e) Kamchatka Interior, *Metis and Creole Economies:* (5a) Kolyma, (5b) Anadyr River (Markovo), (5c) Gizhiga (northern Okhotsk), (5d) Ola and Okhotsk Kamchadal, (5e) Tigil' Kamchadal, (5f) Kamchatka Old Settlers.

The common view is that this enormous cultural area is united in general by a single subsistence mode—hunting, and maritime hunting in particular (Wissler 1917:7–8, Driver and Massey 1957:176–77, Driver 1969:24–25, Waldman 1985:43). In exactly the same way, the common subsistence type for the entire North American Subarctic is considered to be caribou and moose hunting, and, in some areas, fishing (Driver and Massey 1957:177). Russian sources usually adopt this extremely simplified classification with minimal additions (Andrianov and Chekobsarov 1972: map). Unfortunately Kroeber's pioneer research, which established twenty-five regional variations of Eskimo economic culture in the American Arctic alone, has never been continued (Kroeber 1939:23–24).

For the volume published in connection with Smithsonian Institution's "Crossroads of Continents" exhibit, the first steps were taken to break a trail in the direction of a circumpolar classification, which others may choose to develop. I prepared an article and map classifying regional subsistence patterns in northeast Siberia in greater detail (Krupnik 1988b:183), which Bill Fitzhugh further expanded to include northwestern North America, and then fit both into a complete map of the entire North Pacific region (Fitzhugh 1988:191–93) (fig. 4). Through this experience, it appears that we can connect the Siberian and American areas fairly easily, although the variety of subsistence modes is much greater in the Eurasian Arctic than in the American Arctic.

Studies of Arctic Subsistence: North America

The particular case of disjuncture between subsistence classifications in the Siberian and American Arctic demonstrates how the Russian and North American traditions of Arctic social science have developed in deep isolation from each other. In reality, this chasm was even wider. After contacts with western anthropologists were severed in the 1930s, Siberian ethnography turned into a self-contained and self-serving realm of science, abiding by rules of its own invention. By the time regular contacts were renewed in the 1960s and 1970s, two Arctic anthropologies had come into being, each with its own almost completely separate sphere of observation. Only in the last decade can we begin to see the first indications of convergence in the study of native subsistence.

To understand this process better, I will first attempt to summarize the basic stages in the history of ecological and subsistence studies in the American Arctic. Such studies are considered fairly new. As late as 1955, Margaret Lantis remarked bitterly in this regard, "Although nearly everyone who has written about Eskimo culture has admired its specialized adaptation to the arctic environment, almost no one in recent years has studied in detail any ecological problem connected with the Eskimo. . . . [A] survey of ecological research on Eskimo . . . culture in the American Arctic could be made very quickly" (Lantis 1955:195).

Of course, Lantis overstates the case somewhat. Since the early 1900s, many authors not only "admired" Eskimo culture, they also eloquently described principles of Arctic resource use, traditional and modified subsistence modes, environmental influences on settlement patterns, and the formation of ancient cultures (Birket-Smith 1936, Forde 1934, Larsen and Rainey 1948, Mikkelsen 1944, Steensby 1917, Sullivan 1942, Rainey 1947, Weyer 1932, etc.). Indeed, bona fide ecological studies began in the American Arctic in the early to mid-1950s.[3] Since that time, study on Arctic subsistence can be regarded as an independent sphere of research.

In less than forty years certain stimuli have triggered several distinct growth spurts in the subsistence studies field (see summaries in: Burch 1979, Krupnik 1988d, Usher and Wenzel 1987). The first was connected with the Project "Chariot" of the United States Atomic Energy Commission (Wilimovsky and Wolfe 1966) and, in particular, with the name of Don Foote and his "human geography of the Arctic."[4] Foote (1931–1969), a Canadian geographer, was a committed proponent of systems analysis of human activity in the Arctic. His research focused on traditional and contemporary subsistence systems of American Eskimos, and the method he used was directed toward modeling energy flows in complex ecosystems, from the environment to game populations all the way up to humans (Foote 1970b:263–64).

Foote's work contributed greatly to this research methodology (Foote 1960, 1961, 1965, 1970a, 1970b, Foote and Greer-Wootten 1966, Foote and Williamson 1966) and had an important influence on the next generation of Arctic anthropologists (Burgess 1974, Burch 1981, 1985, Hall 1971, Kemp 1971, etc.). Foote was the first to demonstrate the possibility of reconstructing an early-contact subsistence system using documentary and archival sources, contemporary observations, and local oral traditions. He is also to be credited with the first calculations of food values and caloric weights of the main Eskimo game species (Foote 1965:350–63, 1967:139–52).

Another motivating factor for subsistence studies came from Arctic archeology. Since the early 1960s, archeologists engaged in piecing together Eskimo prehistory in the American Arctic made active use of ecological data such as evidence of past climate changes, vegetation, and levels of human resource use (Campbell 1962, Giddings 1961, Laughlin 1963, Taylor 1963, 1966, etc.). By the early 1970s, the so-called "ecological school" came to predominate Arctic archeology (see chapter 6 for further detail).

In attempting to make use of ecological and environmental data, archeologists employed some preexisting terms such as "adaptation" and "subsistence," sometimes giving them a creative interpretation or different slant (Anderson 1983, Dumond 1980, Fitzhugh 1972, 1975, Hickey 1976, Laughlin and Aigner 1975, McCartney 1975, McGhee 1972, Sabo 1991, Yesner 1980b, etc.). Moreover, many showed great interest in reconstructing the traditional resource management practices of Arctic native peoples (Amsden 1977, 1979, Anderson et al. 1977, Binford 1978, Campbell 1968, 1978, Janes 1983, McCartney 1980).

The third surge in Arctic subsistence research derived from the multiyear Area Economic Surveys program conducted from 1958 to 1969 by the Industrial Division of the (then) Canadian Department of Northern Affairs and National Resources. The fifteen reports published under the auspices of this program formed the first groundwork of experience with regional synopses of contemporary native economies in the Canadian Arctic, including detailed data on local resources, game-catch statistics and land-use maps (Lotz 1976:23, Usher and Wenzel 1987: 149–50).

The ensuing formation of native regional corporations put the concept of subsistence at center stage in economic and political debates. Interest in native traditions of resource utilization grew sharply. In the mid-1970s, local corporations and government agencies began funding dedicated interdisciplinary research on the traditional ecological heritage by professional ethnographers, archeologists, and geographers (Braund et al. 1991, Brice-Bennett 1977, Burch 1981, Freeman 1976, Hall 1986, *Native Livelihood* 1979, etc.; see summaries in Burch 1979:87–91, Usher and Wenzel 1987:150).

The surge of interest in native land-use traditions attracted the attention of various state, national, and international governmental bodies engaged in natural resource conservation, including, among others, the Alaska Department of Fish and Game, Canadian Department of Renewable Resources, U.S. National Park Service, U.S. Fish and Wildlife Service, National Marine Fisheries Service, and the International Whaling Commission. These organizations actively sponsor studies of aboriginal subsistence and resource management traditions. Practically speaking, surveys of renewable resources and wildlife management represent yet another branch of subsistence studies in the American Arctic since the late 1970s (Anderson et al. 1977, Braund et al. 1988, Burch 1985, Durham 1979, Ellana 1983, Ellana and Sherrod 1986, Freeman 1974–75, Marquette and Braham 1982, Qiniqtuagaksrat 1980, *Report* 1979, Riewe 1977, Wenzel 1986, Worl 1982).

Thus, these three elements—an ethnohistorical orientation, an applied bent, and emphasis on preserving native cultural values—left their imprint on the profile of Arctic subsistence studies in North America in the 1960s–1980s. They were characteristic of the majority of both purely academic and contract research carried out by anthropologists and geographers. Both types of research were geared to analysis of aboriginal traditions of resource use, as well as such specialized topics as infanticide, social organization among Arctic hunting crews, and local variations in adaptive strategies in the Arctic (Balikci 1967, 1968, Damas 1969, Freeman 1967, 1971, Nelson 1969, 1973, 1980, Smith 1978, Van Stone 1974, etc.; for extensive references to such works, see Burch 1979, Usher and Wenzel 1987:149).

Studies of Arctic Subsistence: Siberia

Although studies of Arctic subsistence in Siberia similarly reflect contemporary social and political trends, the context in which they arose differed sharply from prevailing concerns in North America. Siberian subsistence surveys began many decades earlier than the North American studies and had already reached their peak by the 1920s and 1930s. At that time, they almost completely ceased, and the flame of interest in traditional economies and human-environment interactions among Siberian peoples was extinguished. Something of a revival has occurred over the past two decades, primarily due to the dual external influences of the natural sciences and the "ecology boom" in Western anthropology.

Even at the dawn of the twentieth century, many first-class regional economic surveys of Siberia had already been published in Russia, with rich description of native subsistence patterns including statistics on local fishing, hunting, and reindeer breeding (Buturlin 1907, Jochelson 1898, Mamadyshskii 1910, Olsuf'iev 1896, Prozorov 1902, Sliunin 1900, Suvorov 1912, etc.). These studies made full use of the well-developed mass of government economic data, older documentation from the eighteenth and nineteenth centuries such as native population and fur-tax registers, and administrative reports on the status and welfare of the native people. Such sources were invaluable for reconstructing early-contact subsistence and resource utilization among Siberian peoples.

With the arrival of Soviet power in Siberia and the Arctic, a State Committee on the North was formed in 1924 and mandated to develop and conduct Soviet policy concerning Siberian minorities. Quite quickly, the amount of information available increased. A number of national and regional northern journals appeared during the 1920s and 1930s, often presenting high-quality articles and subsistence-related reports, fully reminiscent of latter-day publications from the Alaska Department of Fish and Game Subsistence Division or the Canadian Area Economic Surveys (Andreev 1933, Andreev et al. 1935, Babushkin 1926, Druri 1936, Nechiporenko 1927, Orlovskii 1928a, b, Razumovskii 1931, Rozanov 1931, Sokolov 1935, Suslov 1930, Zenkovich 1938, etc.). Siberian subsistence studies received an enormous boost from publication of the Soviet Arctic Economic Census conducted by the Committee on the North in 1926–27 that covered Russian Arctic and northern Siberia from the Kola Peninsula in the west and up to the Pacific coast (*Pokhoziaistvennaia Perepis'* 1929, *Itogi Perepisi* 1929, *Materialy Pripoliarnoi* 1929, Bogoras 1932, Terletskii 1932a, b, etc.).

Local economic inventories, budget studies, and medical surveys of the native population were conducted in many areas of the Soviet Arctic in the 1920s and 1930s (Babushkin 1930, Kopylov 1928, *Krainii Sever* 1935, Maslov 1934, Mitusova 1925, Plettsov 1925, Saprykin and Sinel'nikov 1926, Shreiber 1931, *Tuzemnoe Khoziaistvo* 1929, etc.). In connection with the advent of state collectivization policy, dozens of expeditions were dispatched to conduct local land, game, botanical, and livestock surveys and to assess the state of the native economies.

An Academy of Sciences Arctic Commission, an Institute of Arctic Agriculture, Husbandry, and Hunting, and an All-Union Arctic Institute were all especially created, and published a plethora of reports concerning the status of indigenous reindeer and dog breeding, hunting, and fur trapping (Bunakov 1936, Gassovski 1939, Koviazin 1936, Krylov 1936, Mikhel' 1938, Podekrat 1936, Portenko 1941, Romanov 1941, Semerikov 1933, Vasil'ev 1936, etc.).

Hundreds of these reports remain in existence. Taken as a whole, they represent a unique information resource on native Siberian traditional and contact-era subsistence. There was nothing comparable for the American Arctic until the 1970s. A huge number of surveys languished as unpublished manuscripts and reports, and still can be found in any regional or local Siberian archive, as well as in central archives in Moscow, St. Petersburg, and Tomsk. Few found their way into bibliographic compendia (Sergeev 1955, Vasil'ev and Tugolukov 1987) or eventually to publication (e.g., Arkhincheev 1957).

For years, this rich tradition was virtually unknown to western Arctic anthropologists. Moreover, it was interrupted for a long time in Siberian ethnography itself. Closure of the Committee on the North (in 1935) and of several local agencies, strict censorship, and political repression of most specialists led to the complete extinction of this tradition of detailed statistical surveys of native subsistence by the early 1940s. For many decades the Russian literature with any relevance to native Siberian subsistence primarily consisted of reviews of traditional economies and material culture in the descriptive ethnographic vein, or apologetics for Soviet modernization.[5]

Certain works in the economic-cultural type tradition mentioned above were the only exception (Levin 1947, 1960, Levin and Cheboksarov 1955, 1956, 1957, Levin and Potapov 1956/1964, etc.). To these we owe the first rudimentary typology of native Siberian subsistence modes and experimental efforts at subsistence mapping. But the typology school of research was discontinued and made meagre further contribution to Siberian studies proper.

Only in the last twenty years have studies of native Siberian subsistence come to life again. Although classical ethnographic descriptions of economies and material culture continue to dominate the literature, the spectrum of Siberian anthropologists' interests has broadened noticeably. The field now includes such avenues of research as native environmental knowledge systems (Alexeenko 1974, 1976, Kulemzin 1984, Menovshchikov 1982, Smoliak 1982, Taksami 1976,

1984, Vdovin 1976), reconstructions of prehistoric subsistence modes (Golovnev 1988, Simchenko 1976, Vasil'ev 1979a), analyses of factors influencing transformation of native Siberian subsistence (Konakov 1987, Koz'min 1981, Krupnik 1975, 1976b, Lebedev 1978, Pika 1981, 1988), and comprehensive studies of local variations in hunting and reindeer-breeding economies (e.g., Konakov 1983, Krupnik 1976a, Lebedev 1980, Sirina 1992, Turov 1990).

Energy-flow studies in the spirit of Foote's "human geography" or "new ecology" remain marginal in Siberian subsistence research.[6] At present Siberian anthropology is graced by not one publication akin to hunter-gatherer studies, optimimal-foraging theory, diet- and game-breadth models, or studies of "bad-year" economics so popular in the West. Although ecological interpretations (primarily data on paleoclimatic and paleoenvironmental change) are increasingly seeping into Siberian archeology (Arutiunov 1975, 1982a, Arutiunov et al. 1982, Dikov 1979, Khlobystin 1973, 1982, Khlobystin and Gracheva 1974, Khlobystin and Levkovskaia 1974, Kosarev 1983), these works make but a modest contribution to reconstructing prehistoric subsistence patterns on a fully detailed level.

At the same time the popularity of resource biology as a field of investigation is growing rapidly, including analysis of the role of native subsistence in past and present human use of the Arctic. Until recently such works were few in number (Kirikov 1960, Krupnik 1987a, c, d, Pavlov 1972, Pika 1988, Syroechkovskii 1974, Vol'fson 1986). The absence of dedicated native organizations among Siberian peoples until fairly recently and the weakness of government agencies responsible for development of the native population limited funding for such research.

However, since the mid-1980s, with the development of ecological movements and new conservation programs throughout the former USSR, the idea of protecting aboriginal modes of subsistence has gathered broader support. Its proponents include biologists seeking to establish new protected areas in Siberia, such as the Beringia Heritage International Park and a biosphere reserve on the Commander Islands (Bogoslovskaia et al. 1988, Zimenko 1987). A few regional-level reports in the spirit of historical subsistence surveys conducted in the American Arctic have already appeared under the auspices of these programs.

Adaptation

If the term *subsistence* typically evokes a *structure* of interaction between a human population and its environment and resources, *adaptation*, implying as it does adjustment or accommodation, refers to a *process* of human culture. Like subsistence, adaptation is used to mean a wide variety of things (Alland and McCay 1973). Frequently, the speaker uses the word to define concrete modifications or features favored in a particular environment, or as a synonym for *adaptive process*, that is, the many everyday acts that cumulatively comprise cultural modification and development in a human society (Kirch 1980:103, Stern 1970:40–42). In any case, the adaptation concept was central to the study of cultural evolution in the 1960s and 1970s appearing in the titles of dozens if not hundreds of books and articles during that time.

The term gradually acquired a specific connotation in the anthropological field. Adaptation has come to be understood as the *process of development* by which a community chooses to embrace a particular culture, subsistence system, pattern of resource use, etc. as one of several possible paths to be taken in its particular environment. Both the process and product of this choice are denoted by the term *adaptive strategy*, which we can define as a specific cultural pattern formed by the many constituent adjustments people devise to obtain and use resources and thus to solve the problems of existence confronting them (Bennett 1969:14, Kirch 1980:129–30, Orlove 1980:251). Of course, any adaptive strategy is shaped, not only by the nature of the environment, but also by social values, cultural traditions, technological development, external influences, and a plethora of other factors.

A huge amount of anthropological research is devoted to analyzing the conditions under which this choice is made in various regions: the degree to which it is conscious or deliberate, the way in which active transformation of the environment is balanced against concession to environmental limitations, etc. In one way or another, most writers emphasize the role of *stress* as the most important catalyst for modulation and transformation in human societies, and I have taken it as the central theme in this book. Drawing from a variety of cases I will attempt to show how aboriginal peoples of Siberia and the Russian Arctic developed their subsistence and resource utilization systems under the influence of environmental and social stress, or, more precisely, the locally specific series of stress factors that constituted the conditions of their existence.

The "Equilibrium Societies"

Several other terms besides subsistence and adaptation were milestones in twentieth-century anthropology, as scholars made successive attempts to produce an adequate account of the interaction between human societies and the environment. One of these, "optimal population density," was first introduced by a British demographer, Alexander Carr-Saunders (1922:200). He defined this as the level of population density that favors maximum production per member of the community. This level is believed to depend upon the means of subsistence and the resource potential of the local habitat, and is regulated by certain biological and cultural mechanisms in a given society.[7]

Another term, *carrying capacity*, signifies the *maximum* population that can be maintained in a given type of economy without causing environmental degradation and disequilibrium. Adopted from population ecology, this concept was very popular in a number of the social sciences during the 1940s to 1960s as a way to explain mechanisms of regulating human communities and their impact on the environment (Alland 1975:64, Brush 1975:799–802, Hardesty 1977:195–211, Maserang 1977:474, Weeden 1985:116, etc.).

It is immediately obvious that both terms implicitly assume the existence of rigidly fixed linkages between human population levels and available resources. This view has its origins in pioneering studies in the field called "human ecology," and in early attempts to evaluate the role of human societies in relatively simple or closed ecosystems such as islands and tropical deserts (Adams 1935, Birdsell 1953, Thompson 1949). At the same time, it was based on the presumption that prehistoric and traditional societies were incapable of modifying their environments, and could only adjust to them in order to remain in equilibrium with available resources (Helm 1962:634–35). Furthermore, asserted the equilibrium theorists, human groups, like all animal and plant populations in the ecosystem, strive to maintain their numbers at twenty to thirty percent of carrying capacity (Birdsell 1968:230, Castell 1972:19, Divale 1972:233). The inevitable population increase had perforce to be regulated via infanticide, abortion, "voluntary death," intertribal warfare, or was mitigated naturally by periodic famines and epidemics.

In the 1950s and 1960s notions of strictly regulated, "equilibrium" societies commanded great popularity in research on prehistoric demography, archeology, and ecology of small-scale hunter-gatherer and early agricultural societies. This popularity was reflected in some Soviet publications as well (Averbukh 1967:18–24, Grigor'ev 1974:66, Vishnevskii 1976:24–27).

One refraction of the concept of equilibrium societies was the hypothesis that prehistoric and traditional societies exhibited a special mode of ecological behavior, centered upon a conservationist attitude toward and rational use of natural resources. This interpretation appeared in the 1970s and rode the wave of heightened social awareness of problems of global ecological equilibrium and environmental protection. In contrast to the rampant consumerism of modern industrial civilization, early hunters, pastoralists, and cultivators were depicted as "naive" or "intuitive" ecologists living in close natural harmony with their environment, intimately familiar with its rules and observing them religiously in their everyday lives (Hughes 1983, Vecsey 1980, White 1983, Williams and Hunn 1982; for an earlier review, see Martin 1978:157–62).

A particularly rarefied version of the equilibrium concept appeared in the so-called "new ecology," or neofunctionalism, which attempted to apply the methods and language of population ecology to the study of human cultures (Vayda and Rappaport 1968, Rappaport 1967, 1971; see reviews in Alland 1975:63–65, Anderson 1973:199–200, Ellen 1978:298–99, 1982:73–78, Hardesty 1977:15–16, Moran 1982:53–58, Orlove 1980:241–44, Vayda 1976:645, Vayda and McCay 1975:293–98). The key concept in new ecology was that of the ecosystem, an integrated association of living organisms, including humans, knit together by dynamic cycles of energy, matter, and information. *Homeostasis* was seen as a means of preserving the ecosystem intact, that is, the capacity of elements in the ecosystem for self-regulation and the tendency to return to a baseline state after any disruption or change. The concept of *self-regulation* replaced that of a passive, stable equilibrium: in new ecology, each element in the system, humans included, played an active role in its fate.

The popularity of the homeostasis concept was short-lived. Its many limitations elicited a storm of criticism (Allan 1975:64, Ellen 1982:186–91, Salisbury 1975:128–34, Smith 1984:69–70, Vayda and

McCay 1975:298–302), followed by a decline of interest in ecosystem research, and in ecological anthropology. Environmentally oriented anthropologists became absorbed in new lines of inquiry in the 1980s, and such words as homeostasis, ecosystem, and equilibrium societies practically disappeared from new publications.

So, whence the inspiration to revisit the terrain of "equilibrium societies" and human ecosystems, and even to postulate them as the central theme of this book? There are several reasons. The idea of homeostasis was never tested in the context of Siberian peoples and in recent years has attracted growing interest among Russian anthropologists (Pika 1986, Lebedev and Oborotova 1991). Research on other circumpolar social reconstructions such as patterns of indigenous gender ratios, infanticide practices, postcontact population decline, etc. has shown how classical stereotypes in Arctic anthropology often take on a completely different meaning and hue when examined in light of materials on Siberia (Krupnik 1985, 1990).

My chief desire, however, was to determine, if mechanisms of self-regulation even existed, how they operated in these traditional Arctic societies that were so characterized by frequent, profound, and well-documented transformation and environmental change. Siberia and the Eurasian Arctic in general represent an exceptionally rich field for this type of reconstructive research. Over the course of the past several centuries, the majority of Siberian peoples made a fundamental transition, from various forms of hunter-gatherer subsistence to a food-producing economy in the form of reindeer pastoralism. The emergence of reindeer breeding in Siberia was a spontaneous internal development and led to the proliferation of much greater cultural and economic diversity in the Eurasian Arctic than anywhere else in the North American Arctic or boreal zones.

The catalysts of this revolution, and its ecological, demographic, and cultural consequences, have yet to appear as the subject of a sustained and focused inquiry. It seemed to me that the concepts of ecosystem homeostasis and an equilibrium society might provide a thoroughly intriguing theoretical framework for such an investigation.

Research Methodology

The preceding served to guide my selection of a systems analysis and model building as the modes by which I would attempt to describe traditional subsistence forms. In the 1960s, ecological anthropology pioneered the method of joining these two approaches in case studies of small residential subsistence communities with a population of a few hundred people. The annual economic cycle and volume of production and consumption of such a community could be recorded in detail on the basis of field observation or of data culled from documentary sources.

Roy Rappaport (1967) and Don Foote (1965) first demonstrated the possibility of applying each of these methods to constructing quantitative subsistence models and evaluating their impact on the ecosystem. Since then, the number of documented contemporary, early-contact, and even prehistoric subsistence patterns has increased sharply, ranging from hunting, fishing, foraging, herding, to hoe-and-plough agriculture communities on four continents (see Ellen 1982:126–27).[8]

In the Russian ethnographic tradition the first and fairly rapid response to the ecosystem approach to subsistence studies was the idea of "anthropogeocenosis," first formulated by Valerii Alekseev (Alekseev 1975). By analogy with biogeocenosis, Alekseev defined this as a spatial system comprised of components, such as territory, human groups, and their food-producing activities, all interconnected by a network of functional linkages such as energy needs, food sources, information flows, and so forth (Alekseev 1975:19–20).

Any subsistence reconstruction—whether in the form of the small-scale human ecosystem of classical ecological anthropology or Alekseev's anthropogeocenosis model—presupposes generalization and consolidation of the units that make up the system into several main components. I believe there are four such basic building blocks in resource use and subsistence models of aboriginal Arctic societies.

1. The *exploited territory* is the sum total of all land by a community, utilized including significant natural resources for the given mode of subsistence. Exploited territory usually includes several terrestrial biotopes and marine areas where residents pursue maritime hunting, fishing, and shoreline foraging. It rests on the principle of human territorialism, the desire of any social unit for its own fixed habitat with preferential rights over resource exploitation there. In this sense, territoriality appears to be the most widespread strategy of traditional resource management and control over local biological resources (Cashdan 1983:46–47).

2. The *subsistence community*, in most human societies, coincides with the *residential community*, in the usual anthropological sense

of this term (cf. Murdock 1967b:79–82). The residential community is the most dynamic economic and social unit in a traditional society capable of demographic reproduction and relatively independent existence (Kabo 1986:4–6). It is usually a stable group of individuals who use a common territory and resources and thus work, live, and think of themselves as a connected group bound by consanguineal, affinal, and affiliative ties.

The heroic task of identifying and mapping native Siberian traditional residence communities was accomplished by Boris Dolgikh, who is probably the greatest twentieth-century Siberian anthropologist Russia has had (Dolgikh 1946, 1949, Dolgikh and Levin 1951/1962, Dolgikh and Gurvich 1970: map; see also Gurvich 1970, Vasil'ev et al. 1987). Dolgikh called the Siberian residence communities "territorial groups." He found the average population of these groups to be one to three hundred, and four to five hundred at the maximum.

To evaluate how effectively a community utilizes its resources we need to know its population, age-sex ratios, and the number of able-bodied people. Dynamic factors are also very important, including the birth rate, mortality and natural increase, the prevalence of various forms of population control, and the capacity for population growth in favorable conditions.

3. The *domestic animal population* is the only component of the human ecosystem that is completely determined and regulated by human economic activity. In native Siberian subsistence systems it consisted of domestic reindeer and dogs. The most important quantitative characteristics of this component include the number of animals, their age-sex structure, both natural and in captivity, how much food they required, and the amount of resources and human labor required to maintain them.

4. *Subsistence implements* are a category that represents all articles made by the community for its livelihood, including housing, storage, and other structures, tools, hunting equipment, transportation, clothing, and all manner of household items. In our case, we are concerned with the following characteristics of this component: the number and size of separate constitutive elements, their use life, the labor required to produce or annually replace them, and their use value in natural equivalents.

In any relatively closed subsistence system these main elements are connected by functional links that ensure the stable survival of the community through production, consumption, exchange, and utilization of local resources. The traditional method ecological anthropologists use to describe these relations is a detailed flowchart of the ecosystem that measures the energy (or other) flows through the basic components (see Ellen 1982:106–10, also Burgess 1974, Kemp 1971, Odum 1967, 1971, Parrack 1969, Rappaport 1971, Thomas 1973, etc.).

For my analysis of Siberian native subsistence models I employed a different approach, known in geography as the balance method. Essentially, it involves establishing income-expenditure equations for any form of matter or energy in the system and then identifying the actual net difference between them (Armand 1947:629–37). In any subsistence community we can calculate a *subsistence balance*, that is, the proportional relation between a community's needs for food, fuel, raw materials, and exchange, and the actual supply of these goods that is generated by all economic activities.

The most elegant way to do these calculations is through an annual subsistence balance, adding together all elements in the system for a complete economic cycle. Ideally, analysis of a subsistence system should be based on a series of several annual balances, preferably over different periods of time. The ratio of needs to actual supply shows how effectively a community used the resources it controlled, and to what degree its needs and population really were in "equilibrium" with the environment.

Since the 1960s, the standard practice is to measure internal linkages in complex human ecosystems in energy units, or kilocalories. Interestingly, using energy units to analyze native Arctic economies was first suggested by the Russian zoologist Sergei Buturlin in 1928. Long before the emergence of ecological anthropology, he identified the methodological advantages of this approach: it is universally applicable, easy to calculate, and permits comparison of subsistence and market production (Buturlin 1928:50–52). However, Buturlin's ideas were greeted unenthusiastically in Russia, and remained absolutely unknown in the west. Thirty years later they resurfaced completely independently in Don Foote's work, and were subsequently taken up by other researchers in Alaska and Canada.

Focus of the Present Study

The method by which I propose to analyze native Siberian traditional subsistence systems consists of the following: (1) selection of several model communities representing different economic types;

(2) quantitative analysis of relationships among the most important components in the ecosystem; and (3) computation of balances between needs and actual production for certain sequences of years to determine whether net consumption was positive or negative. The reader will find this reconstruction with requisite explanations and details in chapters 2 and 3.

Having established this methodology, I immediately want to be clear about its limitations. In general, any energetics approach, and a balance analysis in particular, emphasizes production and consumption. Thus, while it entails consideration of a broad range of human activities in the overlapping fields of economics, demography, natural resource use, and ecological behavior in general, it does not encompass the entire range of human adaptation. In the more traditional understanding, a system of cultural adaptations includes such things as housing, settlement, and various social institutions, as well as purely physiological mechanisms of human-environment interaction, such as diet, metabolism, and energy expenditures in work activities. These linkages are only indirectly relevant in the methodology I employ.

Reconstruction of traditional subsistence balances, as the reader will see, requires such voluminous quantitative data that constructing one of equal detail for the entire Siberian Arctic is hard to imagine. This natural condition forced me to focus on a few selected areas.

Geographically, the reconstruction is focused on the tundra zone of the Eurasian continent. By the early twentieth century, a wide spectrum of traditional and modernized subsistence patterns replete with multiple local and ethnic variations was represented in this zone, which extends almost eight thousand kilometers from the Kola Peninsula to Bering Strait.

Economically, the focus of our interest lies in the two main forms of subsistence in this zone, sea-mammal hunting and intensive reindeer pastoralism. Together they formed the basis of survival for more than forty thousand people, or approximately two-thirds of the native population of the European and Siberian Arctic. Over thirty thousand of these were reindeer herders conducting a highly productive economy, including the reindeer Chukchi, Chuvants, and Koryak, European and Siberian tundra Nenets, and Izhma Komi. Another ten thousand indigenous residents of the Eurasian Arctic were settled maritime hunters, namely Asiatic Eskimo, coastal Chukchi and Koryak, Kerek, and certain groups of Nenets and Saami.

Of all the subsistence patterns found in the Siberian Arctic, intensive reindeer breeding and maritime hunting stand out as the most stable and economically productive. As stable and productive forms of subsistence, they represent ideal models for analyzing mechanisms of supposed equilibrium between traditional societies and the natural resources they used.

Ethnically, reconstruction of subsistence balances is limited to three groups, among whom reindeer breeding and maritime hunting achieved the apogee of their specialized development. For reindeer breeding, these are the tundra Nenets and reindeer Chukchi, and for sea-mammal hunting, the Asiatic Eskimo. The ethnographic data on these three ethnicities constitute an abundant empirical basis for our task. In subsequent chapters, these are amplified with data on other peoples of the Eurasian Arctic zone, and of North America.

Finally, *chronologically*, the balance analysis is limited to the time period that gives us the most complete assemblage of sources. As I noted above, the most detailed statistical reports on native Siberian subsistence date from the 1920s and 1930s. These embrace census materials; inventories of local households, reindeer economy, and pasture use; records of game harvests; community population lists and vital statistics, etc. Thus, this time period appears the most promising for reconstructing traditional subsistence systems, albeit ones slightly transformed by contact with a market economy. Moreover, this period is still sufficiently recent that we can supplement written records with oral history, elders' recollections of their youth and childhood, and stories their parents passed down to them about life "in the old days." In the early 1970s, when I was beginning my ethnographic fieldwork in the Siberian Arctic, it was entirely possible to find people to tell these stories, since every village had more than a few elders born in the early 1900s, who remembered that period clearly.

All the reconstructions of traditional subsistence models of the Asiatic Eskimo, Nenets, and Chukchi in the early twentieth century were based on case studies of specific local hunting and reindeer-herding communities. These communities and the reasons for selecting them are discussed in the two chapters that follow.

But the method I use in this book does not consist simply of reducing a few subsistence systems, or, more precisely, their time-focused historical models, to a set of numbers and calculations. Like all elements of culture, subsistence systems have their own history. They evolve out of other forms that preceded them, and then, having reached a certain level of development, are replaced by others in the course of a logical transposition or as the result of ecological and/or social collapse.

This means that we should also regard each and every subsistence system as an *adaptive strategy*, that is, a defined mode of cultural adaptation embraced by a human community in response to specific ecological or social conditions—conditions that are themselves changing as a result of multifaceted ecological processes, contact with other cultures, technological development, and population growth. Only on the basis of a wide range of sources is it possible to trace these two interconnected but relatively independent dynamic processes. Paleoecology, archeology, and oral and documentary history allow us to peer more deeply into the past than does field ethnography, and to glimpse new relationships and interactions that previously have been obscured from view. This is the position from which I examine the evolution of Siberian reindeer pastoralism and maritime hunting in chapters 4, 5, and 6.

Shifting our lens through the course of the book from diachronic to synchronic views thus substantially strengthens the depth of field of the present analysis. In the pages that follow I make frequent use of this "zoom" technique to open up new perspectives on peoples and places that until now have rarely been explored, and even less explained. The degree to which I have succeeded, and thus bring us closer to answering the questions raised here, remains for the reader to judge.

CHAPTER TWO

Sea-Mammal Hunters of the Arctic Coast

Historical Setting

As one sails along the Chukotka coast in summer, even from some distance out at sea one can make out numerous irregular hillocks richly velveted with vegetation, bright green against the dark cliffs and gray cobble beaches of the Arctic shore. Here and there they are pierced by fragments of white whale bone, or the vertical turret of a whale's bleached jawbone standing in sharp relief against the dark humus of the coastal precipice. The strip of beach down below is littered with chunks of marine mammal bones, bits of driftwood, and giant whale skulls half-buried in the beach pebble or sand. These are the ruins of ancient villages of sea-mammal hunters, who abandoned them decades or sometimes centuries before, but left behind this clearly visible reminder of their presence there.

For several thousand years, the steep-cliffed, apparently inhospitable Asiatic side of Bering Strait has been the center of one of the most highly developed aboriginal marine hunting cultures in history. People were able to survive on these Arctic shores because they hunted marine mammals—whales, walruses, and seals—and used the other resources of the sea and the adjacent tundra. Now, when almost all the coastal population of the Chukchi Peninsula has been consolidated into several large villages deep in its bays and sounds, only two or three settlements, a few weather stations, and scattered seasonal hunting cabins attest to a human presence for hundreds of miles along the sea coast. However, not so long ago this whole coast was densely settled. As recently as the turn of the century several dozen aboriginal villages and camps existed here, until their inhabitants were subsequently relocated into centralized settlements.

The locations and names of the majority of aboriginal villages on the Siberian side of Bering Strait could be found on maps dating from as early as the mid-eighteenth century (*Atlas* 1964, Krupnik 1983:85–89). However, the first relatively complete data on the total coastal population of Chukotka and the size of their villages appeared only in 1895, in the coastal census conducted by N. L. Gondatti (Gondatti 1898, Patkanov 1912:892). This survey confirmed prior observations that this population was effectively divided into two groups of people, the coastal Chukchi and the Asiatic, or Siberian, Eskimos (Gondatti 1897b, Miller 1897, Vdovin 1954), who had been referred to in earlier Russian sources of the eighteenth and nineteenth centuries by the general name of "settled Chukchi." This division has been preserved and reinforced in both anthropological literature and local administrative practice ever since. Although the environment in which these two peoples lived and the resources they used shared many elements in common, making them closely related in their material culture, they represent two independent ethnogenetic traditions. The focus of our present study is the subsistence system of the Asiatic Eskimos, or, more exactly, a reconstruction of this system based on sources from the first decades of this century and oral histories preserved by local elders.

By the late 1800s the Asiatic Eskimos numbered approximately 1,300, or roughly one-fourth of the coastal population of the Chukchi Peninsula. Notwithstanding enduring and intensive contacts with emissaries of the external world—Russian and American traders, travelers, and whalers—they preserved a high degree of cultural continuity in their traditional modes of subsistence, social organization, and settlement patterns. The social structure of their everyday life was organized around five to six territorially based residential communities, which roughly corresponded to preexisting kinship-based tribes dating from the eighteenth and nineteenth centuries and presumably earlier (see Chlenov 1973:6–14, Krupnik and Chlenov 1979:20–24). Those communities typically included people living in one or more closely related villages or camps (see fig. 5). Each community and even each large sedentary village of 100 to 150 people or more constituted a relatively autonomous economic, social, and reproductive unit. A community had its own hunting territory whose boundaries were well known. It served as a breeding pool for the overwhelming

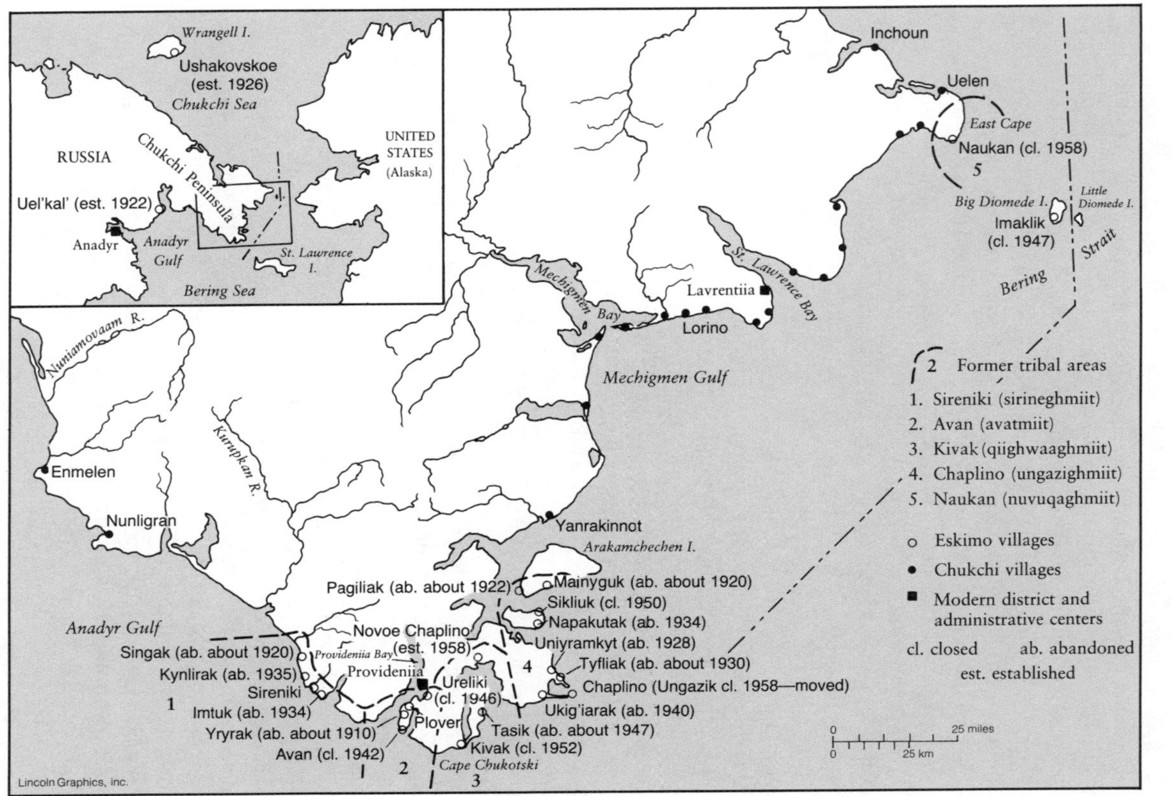
Wrangell I.
Ushakovskoe
(est. 1926)
Chukchi Sea
RUSSIA
Chukchi Peninsula
UNITED
STATES
(Alaska)
Uel'kal' (est. 1922)
Anadyr
Anadyr
Gulf
St. Lawrence
I.
Bering Sea
Inchoun
Uelen
East Cape
Naukan (cl. 1958)
5
Big Diomede I.
Little
Diomede I.
Imaklik
(cl. 1947)
Bering
Strait
St. Lawrence Bay
Lavrentiia
Lorino
Mechigmen Bay
Mechigmen Gulf
Nuniamovaam R.
Kurupkan R.
Enmelen
Nunligran
Yanrakinnot
Arakamchechen I.
Pagiliak (ab. about 1922)
Mainyguk (ab. about 1920)
Sikliuk (cl. 1950)
Napakutak (ab. 1934)
Uniyramkyt (ab. 1928)
Tyfliak (ab. about 1930)
Chaplino (Ungazik cl. 1958—moved)
Ukig'iarak (ab. 1940)
Tasik (ab. about 1947)
Kivak (cl. 1952)
Cape Chukotski
Anadyr Gulf
Novoe Chaplino
(est. 1958)
Provideniia Bay
Provideniia
Ureliki
(cl. 1946)
Plover
Singak (ab. about 1920)
Kynlirak (ab. 1935)
Sireniki
Imtuk (ab. 1934)
Yryrak (ab. about 1910)
Avan (cl. 1942)
1
2
3
4
2 Former tribal areas
1. Sireniki (sirineghmiit)
2. Avan (avatmiit)
3. Kivak (qiighwaaghmiit)
4. Chaplino (ungazighmiit)
5. Naukan (nuvuqaghmiit)
Eskimo villages
Chukchi villages
Modern district and
administrative centers
cl. closed ab. abandoned
est. established
0 25 miles
0 25 km
Lincoln Graphics, inc.

Fig. 5. Asiatic Eskimo tribal communities in the early 1900s. (Adapted from Hughes 1984:248.)

majority of marriage partners and as a laborpool for the formation of hunting boat crews whose cooperation in the harvest of large marine mammals was essential to the community's survival. The community regulated the distribution of meat, the celebration of annual rituals, and the fulfillment of general cycles of social life.

The overall population numbers and the size of individual Siberian Eskimo communities and their corresponding settlements are presented in table 1 for a period of more than forty years, beginning in the late 1800s. The majority of these settlements can be found on the earliest Russian maps dating from the mid-eighteenth century. Archeological evidence indicates that many of the settlements were fully established in the precontact time, while some, like Kivak and Sireniki, are at least 1,500 to 2,000 years old. Such continuity in what archeologists term the subsistence-settlement system in this area indicates the high degree of adaptation the aboriginal population had achieved to the environment it used and occupied. It is this close interrelationship between the Eskimo community and its environmental or ecological context that allows us to focus clearly on it as an independent ethnoecosystem, and to identify it as a highly appropriate model for balance analysis of the traditional resource utilization system.

In their size, their high degree of territoriality, and in certain general principles of social structure, the Asiatic Eskimo communities of the late 1800s were very similar to the kinship-based territorial groups, or "societies," that ethnohistorians have described among Eskimos of northern and northwestern Alaska, Seward Peninsula, and the Yukon-Kuskokwim Delta from this period and earlier (Burch 1975:10–13, 1980, Ray 1975:105, Shinkwin and Pete 1984). This similarity of social structure eases comparison between the subsistence models of peoples from both sides of Bering Strait. For purposes of reconstructing such models, we chose to focus mainly on five main communities of Asiatic Eskimos for which we have the fullest collection of narratives, archival records, and ethnographic field materials pertaining to the period from the 1880s to the 1930s.[1] Henceforth, we will refer to them by the names of their main settlements: Sireniki (Sighinek), Naukan (Nyvuqaq), Chaplino (Ungazik), Avan, and Kivak, and will employ the orthography current in Russian documentary sources of the 1920s–1930s.[2] Some data indicating the chief demographic and economic characteristics of these communities are shown in table 2. More detailed information on the history and social

TABLE I

Asiatic Eskimo Population by Villages, 1895–1937

Villages	1895	1901	1913	1923	1926	1932	1937
Sireniki	77	58	49	57	49	108	192
Imtuk	43	65	93	110	124	51	0
Kynlirak	0	0	0	0	0	39	0
Naukan	299	NA	NA	318	349	351	343
Chaplino (Ungaziq)	500	442	334	190	254	298	246
Ukig'iarak	0	0	?	0	0	13	?
Tyfliak	0	0	15	110	49	0	0
Uniyramkyt	0	0	45	NA	0	0	0
Napakutak	52	37	46	NA	41	26	0
Sikliuq	0	?	31	55	45	64	55
Pagiiliak	0	0	14	?	0	0	0
Avan	101	98	110	92	77	56	46
Ureliki (Ugrilyk)	0	0	?	52	32	43	63
Yryrak	24	9	15	0	0	0	0
Plover	0	0	0	0	0	17	21
Kivak	?	?	23	74	66	80	80
Tasik (Chechen)	140	94	54	52	32	NA	16
Subtotal	1,236	NA	NA	1,110	1,118	1,129	1,041
Other							
Wrangell Island	0	0	0	0	51	45	ca.50
Big Diomede Island	97	NA	NA	42	27	27	ca.20
Uel'kal'	0	0	0	52	105	ca.130	ca.180
Total	1,333	NA	NA	ca.1,300	1,301	ca.1,350	ca.1,310

SOURCES FOR SURVEY YEARS: 1895: Patkanov 1912:892; 1901: Bogoras 1904:29–30; 1913: Revizskie skazki 1913:584; 1923: Materialy po statistike 1925:xxvii–xxix; 1932: Orlova 1936:34; 1937: Materialy Chukotskoi zemekspeditsii 1938:29–33.

Major villages of the respective communities are shown in italics. NA: No data available. ?: Occupation uncertain.

TABLE 2

Asiatic Eskimo Communities

Communities	Survey years	Number of villages	Populations	Households	Boat crews *	Community members			Sled dogs
						Men	Women & aged	Children	
Sireniki	1923	4	167	31	9	44	58	65	158
	1933	3	215	35	10	54	76	85	176
	1937	1	193	36	8	53	67	73	234
Naukan	1923	1	318	55	14	75	91	152	280
	1933	1	332	62	15	86	101	145	295
	1937	1	337	64	12	85	98	154	286
Chaplino	1923	7	365	63	16	87	118	160	340
	1933	3	346	53	16	92	102	152	315
	1937	2	304	58	12	91	104	109	316
Avan	1923	3	144	27	6	35	56	53	89
	1933	2	112	18	6	34	42	36	116
	1937	2	105	19	4	28	38	39	132
Kivak	1923	2	126	23	5	27	38	61	138
	1933	2	113	17	5	25	35	53	120
	1937	2	96	17	4	30	32	34	180
Total for five communities	1923	17	1,120	199	50	268	361	491	1,005
	1933	11	1,118	197	52	291	356	471	1,022
	1937	8	1,035	194	40	287	339	409	1,148

SOURCES FOR SURVEY YEARS: 1923: Materialy po statistike 1925; 1933: Orlova 1936; 1937: Materialy Chukotskoi zemekspeditsii 1938. A version of this table was first published in *Arctic Anthropology* 25(1), 1988.

* Number of boat crews estimated according to local elders' memories.

structure of specific Siberian Eskimo tribes and villages was compiled by Mikhail Chlenov and the present author from 1971 to 1987 and has been presented extensively in various publications, to which the reader is referred (Arutiunov, Krupnik, and Chlenov 1982, Chlenov 1973, Chlenov and Krupnik 1983, 1984, Krupnik 1983, Krupnik and Chlenov 1979, etc.).

Traditional Resource Use

At this point, however, one question immediately arises that must addressed before we proceed further: to what degree did Asiatic Eskimo society of the early twentieth century retain the characteristics of an original subsistence system that predated widespread European contact, and, therefore, to what extent can we regard it as a valid basis for a retrospective analysis? By the beginning of the twentieth century Asiatic Eskimo society had already moved far beyond any kind of "prehistoric" state. It had been exposed to long-standing contact with the outside world, including widespread proliferation of firearms and other manufactured goods, and thoroughly penetrated by well-established commercial trade. Eskimo hunting resources had been heavily exploited by commercial whalers for two or three generations already. Often adult male hunters spoke English, and some spoke Russian, too. Many had worked on the American whaling ships and trading vessels, and had visited Nome or the Russian trading post of Novo-Mariinsk in Anadyr estuary several times. And, after planting a flag in the Chukchi Peninsula in the early 1920s, Soviet administrative power was increasingly brought to bear on native society, with its own agenda and plans for the communist transformation of life among the indigenous population.

At the same time, although these developments indeed had a substantial cumulative effect, traditional subsistence was altered much less by such changes in Siberia than in many other areas where Eskimo people lived. Sea-mammal hunting remained the primary source of food and subsistence. All the Eskimo communities were tenaciously located in the traditional resource territories that they had used as far back as anyone remembered. Until the 1930s no aboriginal settlements sprang up around missionary posts, trading centers, or whaling and fishing stations; that is, none of the communities shifted to and embraced life within an imported or radically transformed subsistence system. Except for one settlement, the villages still had no permanent European residents who might have destroyed or somehow regulated the annual economic cycle. Therefore, although the data from the 1920s and 1930s might be inadequate for an exact quantitative evaluation of the precontact subsistence system, they appear to represent the earliest well-documented synchronic section upon which it is possible to make a set of reconstructions of precontact and early-contact society that reach backward in time with varying degrees of completeness and reliability (Krupnik 1981b: 4–5). They thus present a unique opening to the upstream historical reconstruction of a reality otherwise closed to us.

The traditional and early-contact economy and culture, and specific aspects of hunting activities and social life among the Asiatic Eskimos, have been adequately treated in numerous works in the historical ethnographic literature, to which the reader is referred (Bogoras 1904/1975, Hooper 1856/1976, Hughes 1984, Krupnik 1980, Menovshchikov 1956, 1959, 1964, Orlova 1941, Shnakenburg 1939). Therefore, I wish here only to summarize those aspects of Siberian Eskimo resource utilization that bear directly on our further reconstruction of ecological balances, or that merit more attention than they have received to date.

Virtually all contemporary writers have observed that the outstanding feature in the way any Eskimo group utilized its environment was the high degree of both complexity and variability in its subsistence. The Eskimo resource utilization system is one in which inhabitants show great flexibility in using a whole range of resources available in the environment where they live. Over and above noticeable regional and structural variations, "seen everywhere in the Eskimo world, is an economy that is omnivorous or tending to be so by which the band exploits a wide range of faunal resources, . . . from whales to shellfish and caribou to lemmings" (Taylor 1966:118–19.)

Narratives and ethnographic records of the nineteenth and early twentieth centuries demonstrate that the Asiatic Eskimos were no exception to this general Eskimo pattern. Their primary subsistence base consisted of a wide array of marine mammal species, both pinnipeds—walrus, bearded seal, smaller seals, and sometimes sea lions—and cetaceans, including bowhead, gray, humpback, and beluga whales. In addition, it was substantially complemented by fishing, land-game and bird hunting, egg collecting at bird colonies, beachcombing for various sea products, and gathering edible plants from the inland tundra. Humans exploited virtually all available links in the food chain, such that the Eskimo community figured as a consumer on four or five trophic levels simultaneously, from the simplest forms of vegetation to large predators such as polar bears and carnivorous seals.[3]

The complexity of the traditional Asiatic Eskimo resource system shows up most clearly in the intimate relationship between where people chose to live and how they made use of the surrounding environment. Roughly twenty Eskimo settlements dotted the Chukotka coast in the late 1800s, and all but one had been abandoned by their residents or closed by order of the local authorities by the 1950s (Krupnik 1977, 1983, Krupnik and Chlenov 1979). If we look for a pattern in their locations, we find almost all of them nestled precisely at points of very high natural resource productivity. Typically, these were places where no fewer than three sorts of coastal-zone biological resources were found in peak concentrations.

The traditional pattern of village location also indicates that, in the past, Asiatic Eskimos employed at least two very different and location-specific forms of resource utilization, which required different harvesting niches and settlement strategies. The first was based upon the pursuit of large marine mammals, mainly whales and walrus. Eskimos exploited this very productive link in the food chain for relatively brief times during the course of the year when these animals migrated first north, then south, along the Chukchi Peninsula to and from their summer feeding grounds. Villages based on this procurement strategy were invariably located on the open coast with direct access to the sea, as close as possible to the routes taken by the animals during spring and fall migrations. All the largest villages fell within this category, that is, those that constituted the primary settlements of the initially tribal, and subsequently residential, communities. These included Chaplino, Naukan, Avan, Sireniki, Kivak, Imtuk, and others.

The second resource utilization system was based upon intensive, year-round seal hunting (ringed seal, bearded seal, and harbor seal). These are animals who live more or less permanently within a given territory and are therefore a more consistent and less mobile resource. Communities based on this resource strategy tended to be settled in more enclosed gulfs, straits, and bays, where there were also high concentrations of fish and marine life, as well as favorable conditions for aquatic fishing in the summer and for ice fishing and sealing in winter. Typically these settlements—Ugrilyk (Ureliki), Sikliuk, Pagiliak, Tasik, and so forth (see table 1)—were much smaller than those based on hunting walrus and whales, and were basically little more than permanent hunting camps, with twenty to fifty inhabitants.

Fishing, hunting, and gathering played an important role in both forms of subsistence strategies, and fish, birds, bird eggs, edible plants, and sea products were an essential part of the diet in all settlements, regardless of their location. However, not coincidentally, the majority of the old villages were in fact located in places with favorable conditions for fishing—on or near estuaries, lakes, and lagoons with reliable supplies of freshwater or anadromous fish. This largely reflected a risk management strategy—in the event that the marine-mammal hunt was unsuccessful, fish remained the single alternative source of food for humans and dogs, particularly in the winter months, when other resources were inaccessible.

Judging by the archeological evidence and the distribution of abandoned prehistoric settlement sites, the subsistence strategy of the Asiatic Eskimos remained practically unchanged throughout most of their history (see chapter 6). It was based on intensive exploitation of highly productive, spatially concentrated, and technologically harvestable resources of sea and land simultaneously. The seasonal hunting of migrating marine-mammal stocks formed the core of the economy. It provided a means for the sea-mammal hunters to exploit a biomass that was in fact the product of distant feeding grounds, and that migrated beyond their reach for most of the year. In addition, this was supplemented by exploitation of various locally available secondary resources. As a result, over the course of centuries the location and dimensions of the Asiatic Eskimo ethnoecosystem were determined by a cultural calculus of three main factors: complexity, or breadth of the available resource base, convenience for sea-mammal hunting, and minimizing distances between the various resources harvested.

Exploited Territory

The northern and southeastern edges of the Chukchi Peninsula just opposite Cape Prince of Wales, Alaska, and St. Lawrence Island was the historical territory of the Asiatic Eskimo from the eighteenth century through the first half of the twentieth. It is a mountainous region of moderately high elevation. Throughout most of its extent, rocky massifs plunge straight down to the sea, forming a highly irregular coast consisting of numerous uplifted mountain systems gouged by deep valleys. As late Ice Age glaciers melted and sea level rose, water advanced into most of these valleys, forming fjord-like bays such as at Provideniia, Tkachen, and Romulet, or lakes and lagoons barely separated from the sea by a narrow sandspit, such as at Kivak, Estikhet, and Imtuk lakes (Ionin 1959). Seen from the sea, this region looks like a crenulated series of small, half-moon bays divided by horns of high-cliffed capes. In the past each one of these curving bays was home to an individual Eskimo settlement, and the high rocky promontories in between served as natural boundaries demarcating its hunting territory.

Along this section of the coast there are relatively few places with sufficiently large, flat spaces to build a good-sized village. Therefore, Eskimo settlements were usually set up on a series of low terraces rising up from a sandspit or beach-rock shoal, or on a cliff overlooking the water. Accordingly, there came into being a recognizable stereotype for a "typically Eskimo" settlement site. Generally speaking, if you see a high cliff protruding into the sea, and beyond it a lake or lagoon separated from the sea by a narrow beach-rock spit, then at the base of that spit you are more than likely to find the remains of an old settlement. Above the dwellings, on a steep talus slope spilling down from the mountains above, you could expect to find a cemetery, and occasionally a small fortress-like structure of large boulders in the shape of a wall or a circle. Knowing, then, what to look for, it is often possible to predict quite accurately the locations of many ancient Eskimo settlements just by examining a good large-scale map of the coast (Chlenov and Krupnik 1984:8).

This stereotype of Eskimo settlements derives from several ecological conditions. The narrow spit dividing the lagoon from the sea served as a barrier between two aquatic environments, the saltwater world of the sea, and that of a freshwater lake, or brackish lagoon. As is always the case, at the natural intersection between two ecosystems one finds a higher concentration of living organisms, including harvestable fish, birds, and marine mammals. The rocky cliffs provide a niche for bird colonies and a good lookout over the surrounding territory. Below the ocean's surface, they inevitably drop off suddenly to great depths, and therefore give ready access to yet a third, near-shore ecosystem, which is also distinguished by its high biological productivity. The flat surface of the spit made an ideal space for launching and hauling out boats, for dragging ashore the catch and butchering it, and for erecting boat racks to hang and dry the walrus-hide-covered boats, as well as other household possessions. Relatively soft, sandy soils at the base of the slope permitted convenient digging for foundations of semisubterranean dwellings and for underground pits, where meat was stored.

In addition, in many Eskimo settlements, when summer came, it was customary to move the skin-covered frame tents that served as year-round dwellings down from the high terraces and slopes and set them up on the rocky shoal at the water's edge. These two areas, then, became the village's summer and winter grounds, as it were. According to the stories, this was the practice among the residents of several villages, such as Sireniki, Imtuk, Avan, Kivak, Tasik, Pagiliak, and Napakutak.

The total productive area accessible to the settlement, including meat-storage pits, boat racks, and the strip of beach used for processing and dividing the meat, could thus be as high as three to five, or even ten to fifteen, hectares for a large community of 150 to 200 residents or more. The degree to which human use transformed the natural landscape here was very high. Virtually all components of the local ecosystem were radically altered, including surface structure, upper soil layer, and vegetation. Therefore, these patches of the coast where traditional hunters lived should with all justification be considered anthropogenic landscapes of the Arctic, formed through centuries of constant human activity.

The territory used by a single Eskimo settlement or a community of a few settlements usually encompassed a narrow near-shore fringe no more than one to two kilometers wide. Further into the tundra the Eskimo territory gave way to the "land of the Chukchi," used by nomadic reindeer herders. The upper reaches of the deep bays and fiords, such as at Provideniia, Tkachen, and Romulet, were considered to belong to these Chukchi reindeer herders, as well as the interior of Arakamchechen Island, the south coast of which was used by Eskimos. However, no restrictions existed for coastal peoples venturing into or traveling through the tundra, and in particular no fixed boundaries were necessary between areas used by inland and coastal peoples, as they were so different in their subsistence focus.

Eskimos frequently visited the nearest reindeer herders' camp to exchange goods with them, traveling upstream by skinboat when the rivers were free of ice, and by dogsled in winter.

In addition, permanent rendezvous places for meetings between coastal hunters and reindeer herders existed until the early to mid-twentieth century. Such places were numerous and included, for example, sites in the middle course and in the estuary of the Kurupka River, along the edge of Penkignei Bay and at the head of Mechigmen Bay, to name but a few.

While no precise boundaries existed in the inland tundra between territories that Eskimos and Chukchi exploited, the seashore and the near-shore waters were fairly strictly divided between neighboring coastal communities and villages, whether Eskimo or Chukchi, by boundaries that were relatively unchanging and well known to all. For the time recorded we have no information about any violations and/or conflicts between neighboring coastal settlements over marine hunting areas. In the past the boundaries of a community's territory were strictly observed and to hunt on another's grounds without permission was considered improper behavior. Members of different communities sometimes used economic resources such as walrus rookeries or bird colonies cooperatively, but this was always regulated in some way on the basis of reciprocal agreement, famine relief, kinship affiliation, or consociation between neighbors.

Since the extent of the resource territory of an Eskimo community was usually determined by some natural markers, it did not always correspond neatly to the actual number of people in each community. Thanks to an intensive economy based on spatially concentrated marine resources, population density among the coastal Eskimos of the Chukchi Peninsula ranged from 1.2 to 1.4 per square kilometer, and, in places, as much as 5 to 7 per square kilometer, that is, fifty to sixty times higher than the average for the whole Chukchi Peninsula (e.g., 0.025 per square kilometer) and a hundred times higher than that of the reindeer herders in the continental interior (0.013 per square kilometer). In the eighteenth and nineteenth centuries, when the number of Eskimo settlements on the Siberian coast was much higher—thirty or forty on the southwest edge of the Chukchi Peninsula alone—the distance between them never exceeded eight to twelve kilometers, and the entire Asiatic side of the Bering Strait was both densely populated and actively utilized.

In addition to the residence area proper, an Eskimo community's territory included several types of exploited grounds. As shown in figs. 6 and 7, these included the marine hunting zone, highly productive fishing areas, places for hunting birds, for gathering seaweed and other edible plants. On the average, the territory used by a community included 40 to 60 square kilometers of coastal land (20 to 30 kilometers of shoreline) and 90 to 150 square kilometers of adjacent waters. The main hunt for marine mammals usually took place directly in front of the village. Until the use of outboard motors became widespread at the beginning of the 1930s, hunters relied upon either paddles or a sail while tracking an animal, so that killing their prey near the village significantly economized on the labor required to transport it to the place of butchering and consumption. Places where marine mammal stocks would regularly pass close to shore during their seasonal migrations were especially highly valued. Thus, residents of Sireniki and Imtuk recall stories of times when migrating bowheads used to pass within 100 or 200 meters from the shore there. This made the hunting significantly easier. In summer, the gray whale calves used to linger by the old settlement of Masik (Mechigmen) in Mechigmen Bay, swimming practically right up to the beach shoal, within easy reach for the hunters. On a visit to the Masik site in the summer of 1981, we saw for ourselves how the young gray whales swam in the sea right in front of the village, barely 100 meters from the ruins of the old dwellings (Bogoslovskaia and Votrogov 1982:37, Chlenov and Krupnik 1984:9–10, Krupnik 1984:109–10).

As the older informants frequently emphasize, numerous other food-producing activities were organized in the same way whenever possible. In the past, people could trap for Arctic fox, gather edible plants, and hunt for birds or seals sometimes right on the edges of the village, no farther than three or four hundred meters out their door. As a result, the more remote sections of the hunting territory were not used very intensively, or only when it was absolutely necessary. If the fishing sites, bird cliffs, or walrus rookeries were at a distance from the village, special expeditions to reach them by whaleboat or skinboat were periodically organized, from once to several times a year.

Old, abandoned village sites formed yet another important element in the hunting territory of an Eskimo community. When people abandoned one site and relocated to another not far away, the old territory nominally was transferred to the new community, and for a period of time was partially used by its former residents and their

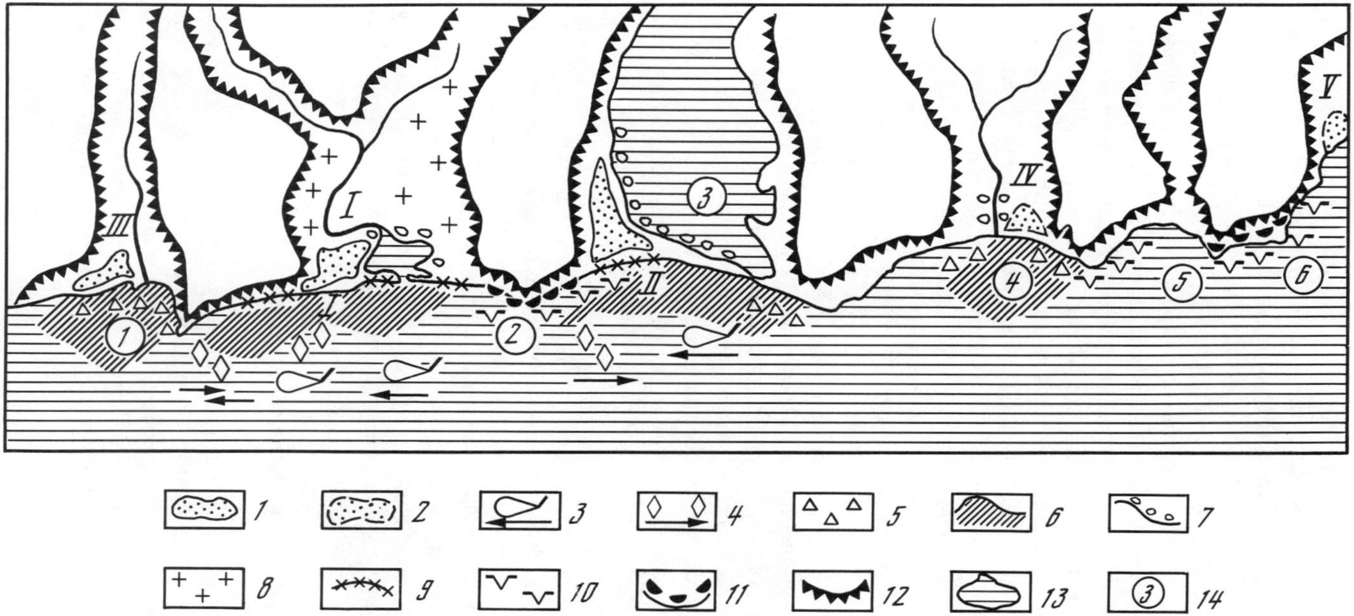

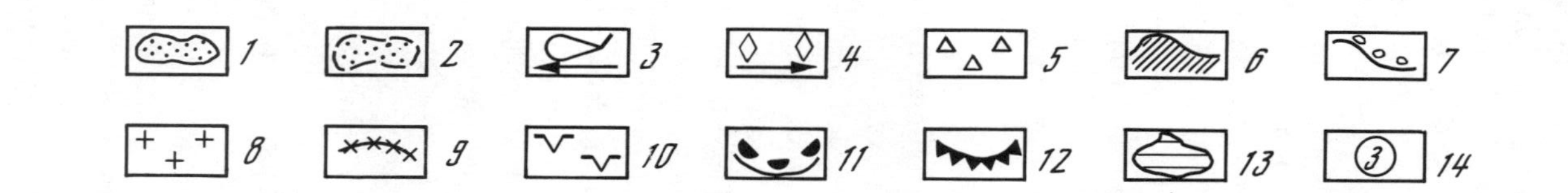

Fig. 6. Environmental use by Sirenik Eskimo community in the early 1900s. 1: occupied villages; 2: abandoned settlements; 3: major whaling areas and whale migration routes; 4: walrus hunting grounds; 5: areas for net-sealing; 6: main marine hunting zone; 7: fishing areas; 8: plant gathering area; 9: beach combing zone; 10: bird-hunting area; 11: sea bird colonies; 12: cliffs, rock debris, and hills; 13: lakes and lagoons; 14: local place-names (to be put on the map). (1): Kynlirak Bay; (2): Cape Ivraq; (3): Imtuk Lake; (4): Angytyquq Bay; (5): Cape Stoletiia; (6): Cape Aghnyq. *Village names*—I: Sireniki; II: Imtuk; III: Kynlirak; IV: Angytyquq; V: Atqallghhaq.

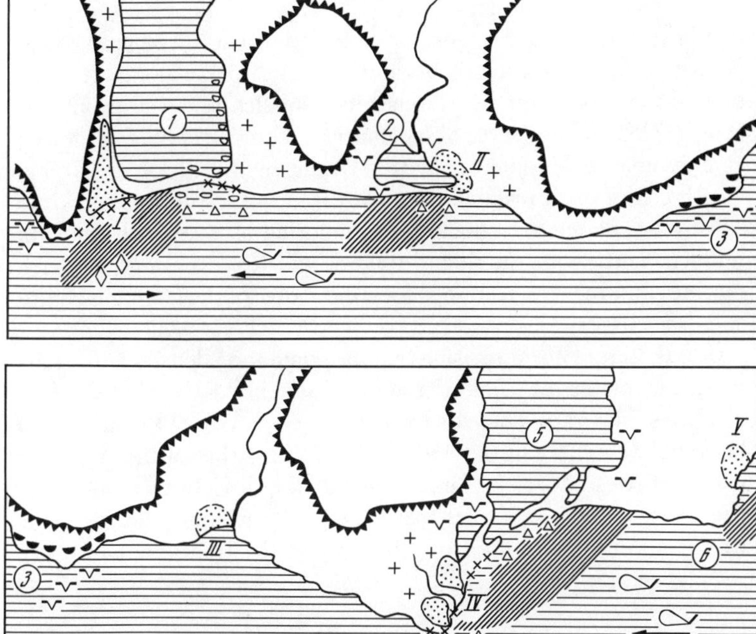

Fig. 7. Environmental use by the communities of Avan and Kivak. All symbols are the same as in Fig. 6. Numbers are place-names to be put on the maps. ①: Naivaq Lake; ②: Naivaqaq Lake; ③: Yuwaghyt Cliffs (Cape Chukotskii); ④: Cape Nizmennyi; ⑤: Kivak Lake (Lagoon); ⑥: Cape Nuvuq. *Village names*—I: Avan; II: Assiak; III: Kurupkyrak; IV: Kivak; V: Nuvuq.

descendants. In this way, the old settlements became seasonal hunting camps or short-term stations for subsistence activities, or backup hunting grounds if the hunt failed in the primary territory. If a community died out or migrated, its hunting areas might lie unused for a very long time, but anyone belonging to that community apparently continued to maintain an unwritten prerogative over their reuse or reoccupation.

If we compare the Asiatic Eskimo traditional system of resource utilization with published accounts of other Eskimo groups in Alaska, Canada, and Greenland, we find it adheres to many common principles of Eskimo subsistence practices. In all probability, however, the

Asiatic Eskimo would immediately stand out as the most sedentary of all the northern maritime hunting societies. They lived year-round in large, permanent settlements and did not disperse along the coast or into the tundra for the summer into smaller, seasonal groups or camps. This higher degree of sedentarism should probably be viewed as a comparatively late adaptation of the eighteenth or even nineteenth centuries. It resulted from increased specialization in Eskimo subsistence patterns, from close and enduring contacts with Chukchi reindeer herders of the inland tundra, and from the uniquely rich marine resource base teeming along the shores of the Chukchi Peninsula (see chapter 6).

It is therefore not surprising that the population density among the maritime hunters of Chukotka in the nineteenth and early twentieth centuries, one to two per square kilometer, was one of the highest to be found anywhere in the Arctic, approaching that of the Aleuts or the Northwest Coast Indians in North America (Testart 1982: 530, Weyer 1932: 109–10, Yesner 1980b:731). All this indisputably points to the exceptionally high productivity of the traditional resource management system.

The Hunting Community

In much of the ethnographic literature, the existence among aboriginal Arctic peoples of certain fixed type of age and sex structure and of special mechanisms for controlling population levels and growth is regarded as established historical fact. This view applies first and foremost to the Eskimos (Bogoras 1925: 29, Harrison et al. 1968: 411–15, Malaurie 1973: 48–50, Weyer 1932: 126, 132, etc.). Their demographic behavior is frequently taken as a model for all Arctic indigenous peoples, and the marriage norms prevailing among the Eskimo in the past, the practice of "voluntary death" among older people (senilicide) or killing children (infanticide) are cited in a broad range of cross-cultural analogies and theorization of demographic processes in primitive societies (Balikci 1967, Birdsell 1968, Carr-Saunders 1922, Kjellström 1974–75, Weyer 1932; cf. Krupnik 1985).

It is true that to this day we can only guess to what degree such occurrences were characteristic of Asiatic Eskimo society in general, and in the period under our consideration in particular. The available sources have only recently begun to receive scholarly attention. They include data from about twenty different population inventories of the Chukchi Peninsula between 1895 and 1939 (see table 1 above), genealogies assembled for Eskimo villages and communities by the author and Mikhail Chlenov, as well as copies of fairly complete local registries of births, deaths, and marriages beginning in the 1920s.

Taken together, these sources show that the Asiatic Eskimo population was, above all, highly dynamic. Both tribes and settlements fluctuated rapidly in size as a result of natural increase and migration. As genealogies and oral histories attest, frequent moves, relocations, and absorption into the community of families and even entire kin groups from other tribes were common occurrences in Eskimo life in the early twentieth century, as well as from the eighteenth century on.

The same sources permit us to reconstruct the demographic structure of the Asiatic Eskimo communities in the early twentieth century and to review its main characteristics, including the ratio of men to women, the proportions of adults of working age, children, and elderly people, and of people in their child-bearing years (table 3). For three communities—Sireniki, Chaplino, and Avan—it proved possible to piece together the entire family composition of all community members in the early twentieth century and to trace its dynamics longitudinally through four to five decades.

Based on table 3, the average demographic structure of an Eskimo community can be computed as follows: 25 to 27 percent men and 29 percent women of working age (16 to 59 years old), 2 to 4 percent elderly people (older than 60), and more than 40 percent children and teenagers divided between males and females more or less equally. The number of adult men determined the number of boat crews—groups of men hunting together that formed the basic work unit in the Eskimo community. The crew usually included four to six men and a few teenagers related by blood or adoption, each of whom had an assigned role and status in the hunt, the butchering, and the division of the meat. Three to four crews, that is, fifteen to twenty grown men, formed the minimum required to insure the necessary cooperation of efforts needed to kill, transport, and butcher a whale or to make a productive walrus hunt. In turn, this would be sufficient to provide a stable subsistence for not less than sixty to eighty people of various ages. Therefore, in the traditional Asiatic Eskimo subsistence system, six to eight hunting crews appear to be optimal for a village community with a total population of 130 to 160.

Compared to certain traditional Eskimo populations of Alaska,

TABLE 3
Demographic Parameters of Asiatic Eskimo Communities, 1895–1937

	1895	1901	1920	1926	1937
1. Total sample population	1,097	436	335	1,274	1,071
2. Average household size	7.26	7.14	5.23	6.04	5.35
3. % Males	48.4	48.6	46.9	48.6	50.7
4. % Females	51.6	51.4	53.1	51.4	49.3
5. Number of women per 100 males	106.8	105.7	112.0	105.8	97.2
6. % population in working age, 16–59	58.3	61.7	53.4	56.9	53.6
7. % population in active reproductive age*	44.6	45.9	39.4	38.3	38.6
8. % children under age of 10	31.2	NA	30.1	27.0	28.7
9. % elders over age of 60	1.5	5.0	2.1	3.5	4.6
10. % active hunters	27.4	29.3	27.5	26.4	27.3
11. Mouths to feed per hunter	3.6	3.4	3.6	3.8	3.7
12. Number of girls per 100 boys under age of 10	98.3	97.6	119.6	108.7	89.7

SOURCES: 1895: Asiatic Eskimo total, Materialy po statistike 1925; 1901: village of Ungaziq (Chaplino), Bogoras 1901; 1920: villages of Imtuk, Sireniki, Avan, and Urelik, based on author's reconstruction from genealogies; 1926: Asiatic Eskimo total, Poselennye itogi 1928; 1937: villages of Naukan, Sireniki, Chaplino, Avan, Kivak, and Ureliki, Knopfmiller 1940b.

* Male 20–49; Female 20–44.

Canada, and Greenland, the demographic structure of the Asiatic Eskimos at the beginning of the twentieth century stands out as fairly balanced. The even numbers of men and women, the high proportion of able-bodied adults and especially adult male hunters, and the high percentage of children under 16 years old all suggest both a fairly high degree of welfare among the population and a healthy ability in the community to reproduce itself demographically. This significantly weakens the hypothesis of depopulation, or "extinction," that was a recurring theme in some publications in the early decades of this century, according to which it was maintained that the Asiatic Eskimo as well as several other Siberian natives were gradually dying out (Krasil'nikov 1928, Patkanov 1911:129–30).

Based on the genealogies and data on births and deaths from local registries, it is possible to compile a fairly clear picture of demographic processes in Eskimo communities in the 1920s and 1930s. During this period, in the absence of any special means to control the population growth, the Asiatic Eskimo exhibited a very high birth rate of 50 to 60 births per 1,000. Over the course of her reproductive years, each woman bore an average of 6 to 8 children, and cases of

10 or 12 births were not at all uncommon. In two communities, Avan and Sireniki (for which the most complete records of vital statistics are available), 48 women of reproductive age gave birth to 144 children in the decade of the 1930s. Out of these, 22 women registered 4 or more births during this period, up to a maximum of 6 births in 10 years. Such figures show how high both total and age-specific fertility rates were in all cohorts from age 20 to 44, with each woman bearing an average of 7.4 children during her lifetime (Krupnik 1987b:100). Very similar data were collected among the Eskimos of St. Lawrence Island, where women who entered their reproductive years in the 1920s and 1930s had an average of 7.1 to 8.8 children. One-third of these women had 10 children or more, with a recorded maximum of 15 births (Byard 1981:70–75, Ellana 1983:144–47, 163–65).

If the birth rate in Eskimo communities remained stable and fairly high, the indicators for the death rates, in contrast, fluctuated noticeably. The average mortality rate among the Eskimos was also very high, not less than 45 to 50 per 1,000. In Sireniki in the 1930s 78 people died, an annual rate of 40 per 1,000. In Naukan, 146 died within a decade, or 44 per 1,000, on top of which an unknown number of deaths of newborns and children less than a year old were not registered. In Avan and Ureliki together, from 1931 to 1944, 72 people died, or 47 per 1,000.

A significant portion of these deaths occurred among children under the age of ten (table 4), and 40 percent of those were infants under a year old. The first health-care services appeared in the Eskimo settlements of Chukotka only at the very end of the 1930s or after 1940. Before that, the infant mortality rate was 25 to 35 percent of all newborns, and in certain years could be 35 to 40 percent or more. The age peak for mortality occurred among the working adult population from 35 to 45 years old in connection with the higher death rate among middle-aged hunters and women in their late childbearing years. This age group suffered greatly from the ravages of imported diseases and, in the past, apparently from famine, as countless folklore materials and stories from elderly informants attest. In adverse years, when disease or famine struck, the death rate could be as high as 90 to 100 per 1,000, and significantly exceeded the birth rate.

A complicating factor, unfortunately, is that the ages of elderly people who died in the 1930s are approximate at best. The Eskimos never had a tradition of counting one's calendar age, and during the first censuses the census-takers simply made an estimate based on

TABLE 4
Age-Grade Structure of Eskimo Mortality
(as a percentage of all recorded cases)

	Age at death, in years							
Community	0–1	1–9	10–19	20–29	30–39	40–49	50–59	60
Sireniki, 1930–44	39.9	27.6	8.1	4.9	2.4	4.9	4.1	8.1
Avan, 1931–44	31.6	13.2	6.6	7.9	14.5	7.9	11.8	6.6
Asiatic Eskimo total, 1939	47.1	17.1	7.1	7.1	4.3	2.9	5.7	8.6

SOURCES: The table has been calculated based upon local death records preserved at the District Archive for Vital Statistics (ZAGS) in Provideniia and the similar Archive in Anadyr'.

their own impressions. Therefore, it is more reliable to speak about a person's "genealogical age," that is, the order of reproductive generations according to the genealogies. Thus, among mature and middle-aged male Eskimos in the 1920s and 1930s (that is, people born from 1850 to 1890), only about 40 percent had grandchildren before they themselves died. According to reconstructed household lists for 1920 to 1923, for four villages with a total population of 350 (Sireniki, Imtuk, Avan, and Ureliki), only 9 out of 63 families spanned three generations, and only one woman lived to see her great-grandchildren. According to a household survey conducted by Waldemar Bogoras in Ungazik in 1901, there were 14 three-generation families within a population of about 450 people, that is, 18 percent of the 77 families in all, and not one family in which the lives of individuals from four generations had overlapped (Bogoras 1901).

According to Eskimo conceptions, most men and women were already considered "elders" by the time they were 45 or 50, that is, even before their reproductive years were ended. Although the existence of people 75 or 80 years old is accurately noted in the genealogies and documentary sources, it was entirely common for men to die from "old age" at 50 to 55, and women from 55 to 60, in addition to the "voluntary deaths" of invalids and disabled people of middle age.

Of course, on a circumpolar scale, the Asiatic Eskimo population would appear to be quite long-lived. It has been estimated that the Siberian maritime hunters showed a higher life expectancy than the Eskimo societies of the American Arctic, one that approximately equaled that of the Mesolithic population of Western Europe, but fell short of that of the Aleuts in the eighteenth and nineteenth centuries (Harper 1980:56–57, Laughlin and Harper 1979:9, Yesner

1980:731). This is significant because life expectancy is also considered to be one of the primary indicators of stability, welfare, and high social development in a traditional population (Laughlin 1966:485–87).

The total natural increase in Asiatic Eskimo communities was highly unstable and fluctuated drastically. In good years, when the hunt went well and no epidemics struck, the population showed substantial growth. For example, in Sireniki natural increase added eight individuals to a base population of two hundred in 1931, and twelve individuals in 1936, that is, 6 percent in one year. But "good" years alternated with those in which famines, epidemics, or accidents caused the deaths of entire groups of people, when the population would suddenly plunge down again to its previous level or even drop below it. It is precisely this model of reproduction that the old Ungazik Eskimo man, Kuvar, so eloquently described to Bogoras in 1901.[4]

I want to emphasize that when the Eskimo population decreased in adverse years it was primarily due to a sudden rise in the death rate among adults. Throughout the 1920s and especially the 1930s, the difference between the numbers of children who were born and who died at infancy, that is, the "pure" annual increase, remained high and constant, hovering around 20 to 25 per 1,000. In the early years of life, high mortality could gradually reduce the originally large age groups, but this tendency practically disappeared by adulthood. Barely more than a third of the population survived to be adults and have children of their own. Each child born had a 6 to 10 percent chance of living to be sixty or seventy years old. In the presence of such demographic features the Eskimo population possessed an exceptionally high *potential capacity* for rapid growth if socioecological conditions remained conducive, especially in periods when the death rate remained low among the adult population.

This conclusion is substantiated by yet another index—the average number of children per married couple who survived to adult age and produced their own offspring. According to the genealogies, for 172 Asiatic Eskimo couples who married between 1880 and 1920, this indicator was 2.47. When each couple produces 2 children who live to adulthood a population remains stable; if this indicator increases to 2.5, the population will triple in a hundred years, and if each couple has 3 children who survive to adult age, in a hundred years the total population will increase by eight times (Carr-Saunders 1922:105).

Therefore, Asiatic Eskimo society had the theoretical capability to double or triple its population every century. But this demographic potential could be realized only if auspicious socioecological conditions permitted.

All these figures sketch for us a picture of a particular type of demographic behavior in an early-contact Arctic population whose members practiced traditional forms of livelihood. They do not confirm the widespread representation of Eskimo societies as static and unchanging, with rigidly imposed limits on growth, a low birth rate repressed by artificial methods, a relative absence of women, and zero population growth. On the contrary, great fluidity in the size and composition of the population was highly typical for the Asiatic Eskimos, with a high birth rate and capacity for rapid growth. And, although adjusted natural increase was in fact low, the reasons for this lie elsewhere: the high mortality of the adult population, the truncated life expectancy of younger and middle-aged adults, and the huge demographic rifts resulting from death from exogenous causes, including epidemics, famines, and mass deaths from accidents and disasters.

The Material Basis of Subsistence

For centuries, a settled form of life and a complex, highly specialized marine hunting economy encouraged the development of a diverse array of hunting equipment and elaborate household utensils among the Asiatic Eskimos. Their traditional material culture was seemingly very rich in comparison to that of other indigenous peoples of the Eurasian Arctic. However, by the end of the nineteenth century Eskimo livelihood was already based to a significant degree upon manufactured, imported implements. Guns, wood-hulled hunting boats with sails, iron harpoon points and spear heads, hand-held grenades for killing whales, and various other metal implements and articles entered the Eskimos' lives to stay. All this equipment was imported by American and occasionally Russian traders and whaling ships, and traded in exchange for locally produced goods.

Some traditional subsistence technologies were preserved in the array of hunting-related articles, such as sealskin floats, straps made from sea-mammal skin, bone or ivory heads for harpoons, and nets for catching seals. Even here materials that had been widely used in the past but had a high trade value, such as walrus tusks and baleen, began where possible to be replaced with less remunerative products, including bone, wood, or reindeer antler. To a lesser degree these changes pertained to traditional means of marine and terrestrial transportation, such as skinboats, wooden dogsleds, sledges with ivory runners, as well as clothing and housing. On the whole, the material culture of the Eskimos of the late nineteenth and early twentieth centuries on the Asian as well as the American shores of Bering Strait appears to have achieved a remarkable blending of archaic aboriginal elements and ready-made manufactured items of European origin, as well as articles that were traditional in appearance but were actually invented or modernized under the influence of imported goods.

This conglomerate culture is clearly visible in the archeological remains and "garbage dumps" of Eskimo settlements from the period. To our eyes they now look like chaotic jumbles of marine-mammal bone remains, fragments of articles made from skin, wood, and metal, broken bits of glass or pottery from cups and dishes, empty gun cartridges, enamel pots and tea kettles, and pieces of wooden plates and clay oil lamps used in traditional life. This mix of local and imported articles can also be observed in burials of this period, allowing us to date many settlements and cemeteries with great accuracy (Arutiunov, Krupnik, and Chlenov 1982:54; for Alaskan Eskimos, see Kilmarx 1986).

The first accurate data on quantities of crucial hunting equipment in the Eskimo settlements of Chukotka, such as boats, guns, traps, and nets, were obtained during the Soviet Economic Census of the Far North of 1926–27. These data can be fleshed out with information from subsequent local inventories and from household surveys conducted from 1920 to 1930. For earlier years we have available partial lists of goods purchased by Eskimos, the accounts of travelers, and the recollections of contemporary informants from the older generation (Belikov 1927:120, Kirillov 1908:1776, Starokadomskii 1946:115, Suvorov 1914:193, Vdovin 1965:258–69).[5] Judging from all these sources, by the beginning of the twentieth century the Asiatic Eskimos obtained most of their hunting equipment, raw materials for clothing and housing, and main household items through trade, whether with Chukchi reindeer herders, American or Russian traders, or Eskimos from Alaska and Saint Lawrence Island. This not only placed their livelihood in deep dependence upon commercial and barter trade, it also demanded an enormous annual surplus of their own labor production to support such a substantial volume of trade.

Needs of the Eskimo Community

For our purposes, all the items of consumptoin required to sustain an adequate life cycle in the Eskimo community can be divided into five main categories: (1) food, (2) fuel for cooking, heat, and light, (3) dog food, (4) raw materials for making the many objects of everyday life, primarily skins for boat and house covers and for clothing, and (5) hunting surpluses for barter trade with Chukchi reindeer herders and with nonnative traders for manufactured hunting implements and food.

Information about the diet structure and daily or annual needs for food consumption of the Asiatic Eskimo of the early twentieth century are sketchy and not very reliable. Estimates in the literature of the ilk such as "one kilogram of meat per person per day" or "around two tons of meat per family per year" (Ekonomicheskii Ocherk 1939:90, Dokumenty 1946:9) are not much use for precise calculations, while materials from modern nutritional surveys apply to a much later period (Astrinskii and Navasardov 1970, Zaitsev 1970, etc.). Therefore, to estimate the traditional food requirements of the Asiatic Eskimo, I made use of comparable data on the food budget of various Eskimo groups in the American Arctic (Draper 1977, Harrison et al. 1968:345, Kemp 1971:107–108, Rodahl 1954:24, etc.) and reconstructions of consumption patterns assembled by Don Foote for the Eskimos of northwest Alaska in the mid-nineteenth century.

Foote determined the daily food-calorie norm to be 3,000 kilocalories per adult male, 2,500 kilocalories per woman and elderly person, and 2,000 kilocalories per child and subadult under sixteen years of age. Based on the average demographic structure (discussed above) of 25 percent men, 35 percent women, elders, and teenagers, and 40 percent children, the average rate of calories consumed on a community-wide basis can therefore be computed as 2,425 kilocalories per person per day, or 885,100 kilocalories per year, which we can safely round off to a working figure of 900,000 kilocalories per year, especially since Foote's norms in general appear slightly lower than the estimates of other authors. However, this should be considered as the *minimum level of consumption* necessary for the community's survival, since it does not reflect additional amounts of food for guests and sharing, or for increased consumption during festivals and times when food supplies were relatively abundant.

It is more complicated to estimate the relative proportions of basic components within the Eskimo diet—marine-mammal meat and blubber, fish, birds, plant products, and imported food items—which fluctuated radically during the course of the year and from one year to the next, depending on how successful the hunt was. They can only be estimated very roughly since reliable information in the references for the time studied is lacking altogether. When he compared data among various groups of American Eskimos, Foote concluded that 65 percent of the caloric content of the aboriginal diet came from protein and carbohydrates, and 35 percent from animal fats (Foote 1965:275). As a portion of the 2,425 kilocalories per day norm I have taken, this works out to consumption of 106 grams of fat (which has 8,000 kilocalories per kilogram) and 0.5–1.1 kilograms of marine-mammal meat, depending upon the actual proportions of other food sources in the diet.

According to Foote and other estimates in the literature, a traditional diet for the adult male Eskimo included not less than 1.8 to 2.2 kilograms of marine-mammal meat per day. In my calculations I took my average norms as 1.8 kilograms for male hunters, 1.2 kilograms for women, teenagers, and the elderly, and 0.8 kilograms for children under fifteen. This gives an average of 1.2 kilograms per day for all members of the community. Marine-mammal meat has an unusually high fat content—1.8 to 4.6 percent in seal meat, and up to 8 percent for walrus—so a daily ration of 1.2 kilograms of meat would yield 40 to 100 grams of fat. The addition of yet another 60 grams of blubber fully met all consumption needs and guaranteed a total of 2,165 kilocalories daily, or 89 percent of caloric intake. This level was considered to meet fully the consumption needs for marine-mammal products in accordance with traditional eating habits. The remaining 265 kilocalories, or 11 percent of the average consumption, came from reindeer meat, fish, birds, and purchased food. Of course, the actual amounts of each of these could well have exceeded this norm.

Unfortunately, there are no statistical data assessing inequalities of food intake between wealthier and poorer families in postcontact Eskimo society. That such inequality existed is clearly documented in Eskimo folklore sources and in the oral histories of elderly informants. It is known that, at that time, economic inequalities were expressed chiefly in the degree to which a household used imported food and was able to trade with the Chukchi reindeer herders. For the main food items—marine-mammal meat and blubber, fish, and birds—such inequalities were offset to a significant degree by prevailing norms of mutual assistance and sharing of food with relatives and neighbors. This would support our extrapolation of an "average" norm to obtain for all residents of the Eskimo community.

Like the majority of Eskimo societies throughout the American Arctic, the Asiatic Eskimos used marine-mammal oil for heat, light, and cooking, burning it in special stone or clay oil lamps. The available estimates of fuel oil consumption per family, or household, for both Asiatic and a wide range of other Eskimo groups from Canada and Greenland range from 670 to 2,700 kilograms per year; but on the average they fall between 800 and 1,200 kilograms per year. Some authentic estimates ran as "blubber from one hundred seals" or "three kilograms per day."[6] Based on my informants' estimates, average fuel oil use per family worked out to 1,125 kilogram per year, but considering the wide range of variability, I took for calculation purposes a slightly lower round figure of 1,000 kilograms per year per household. This is based on calculations that in winter, 4.5 kilograms of oil were burned each day (two oil lamps kept burning twenty-four hours a day), and 2.3 kilograms were used daily in spring and fall (one lamp, twenty-four hours a day), while in summer, 1.2 kilograms sufficed.

Dogs played a central role in traditional Asiatic Eskimo subsistence. Dogsleds were the sole means of transportation in the winter months. Without them, communication between villages along the coast, trade with the Chukchi reindeer herders, and fox hunting would have been impossible. Since a substantial portion of the hunting and fishing catch went toward dog food, the size of the dog team was usually a direct indicator of a family's well-being, and of how good a hunter its main provider was.

The typical fraction of the Asiatic food supply that went to dog food can be derived from local sources of the 1930s through 1950s, or borrowed from analogous estimates for American Eskimos. According to the available sources, a figure of 1,000 kilocalories per day, or 365,000 kilocalories per year appears to be a safe average (Bezumov 1960:40, Ekonomicheskie Obzory 1939:90, Materialy Anadyrskoi ekspeditsii 1950 for the Siberian side; and Burgess 1974:154, Foote 1970a:310, Freeman 1969/70:168, Kemp 1971:108 for the American

Arctic). This would be equivalent to average annual daily consumption of 0.7 kilograms of marine mammal meat: 1.0 kilogram per day in the winter, when the dogs are working, and 0.5 kilograms in spring, summer, and fall, that is, from late May to November. Alternatively, the same amount of calories could have been derived from 1.0 kilgram of sea-mammal intestines or waste parts, 2.0 kilograms of fish, 1 to 1.5 kilograms of dried salmon, or 150 grams of animal fat.

Information on the use of skins for various household and productive purposes can be eked out of various local sources of the 1920s and 1930s and supplemented by recollections of present-day elderly informants (Krupnik 1976c:26, Morzveroboinyi Promysel 1934:52, Rozanov 1931:54, Zenkovich 1938:61). According to these estimates, the average family of five needed four walrus skins, two bearded seal skins and twenty ringed or harbor seal skins annually, in addition to twelve reindeer skins (which were obtained solely through trade with the herders) for replacing dwelling covers, hunting equipment, clothing, footwear, and household items.

In this way, it proved possible to estimate annual basic consumption needs for food, fuel, and the most important raw materials in the Eskimo subsistence system, with some allowance for the margin of error resulting from rounding off all numbers to a value that facilitiates handling large sums. Using these norms, and knowing the number of people who lived there, the number of households, or dwellings, and the number of dogs, it was possible to calculate the annual consumption demands of the Eskimo communities, and to reconstruct the subsistence balance for each settlement. Thus, the annual needs for food, fuel, dog food, reindeer skins, and marine-mammal hides were calculated for five Eskimo communities in three standardized years: 1920, 1933, and 1937, as shown in table 5.

Given our present state of knowledge, however, it is impossible to enumerate exactly what amounts of other primary materials such as bone, ivory, wood, or baleen may have been used to make tools and household items before the arrival of European trade goods. As ready-made goods came into popular use, many of these materials, especially ivory and baleen, along with fur, reindeer skin, and marine-mammal hides, began to be drained off from the Eskimo subsistence system in exchange for imported goods. Baleen commanded a particularly high exchange value from the traders, which was used to make corsets and hoops for the long women's skirts then in fashion in Europe and America from the mid-1850s until as late as 1907. It is

TABLE 5

Estimated Annual Consumption Needs of Five Siberian Eskimo Communities

	Human food (10^3 kcal), including sea mammals				Blubber for heating and cooking	Skins			
Community/year	Total supply	Meat	Blubber	Dog food (10^3 kcal)	(10^3 kcal)	Walrus	Bearded seal	Small seals	Reindeer
Sireniki									
1920	150,300	102,404	29,258	57,667	248,000	155	62	620	372
1933	193,500	130,838	37,668	64,240	280,000	175	70	700	420
1937	173,700	118,347	33,814	85,410	288,000	180	72	720	432
Naukan									
1920	286,200	194,998	55,714	102,200	440,000	275	110	1,100	660
1933	298,800	203,582	58,166	107,675	496,000	310	124	1,240	744
1937	303,300	206,648	59,042	104,390	512,000	320	128	1,280	768
Chaplino									
1920	328,500	223,818	63,948	124,100	504,000	315	126	1,260	756
1933	311,400	212,167	60,619	114,975	424,000	265	106	1,060	636
1937	273,600	186,412	53,260	115,340	464,000	280	116	1,160	696
Avan									
1920	129,600	88,300	25,229	32,485	216,000	135	54	540	324
1933	100,800	68,678	19,622	42,340	144,000	90	36	360	216
1937	94,500	64,386	18,396	48,180	152,000	95	38	380	228
Kivak									
1920	113,400	77,263	22,075	50,370	184,000	115	46	460	276
1933	101,700	69,291	19,797	43,800	136,000	85	34	340	204
1937	86,400	58,867	16,819	65,700	136,000	85	34	340	204
Total									
1920	1,008,000	686,783	196,224	366,825	1,592,000	995	398	3,980	2,388
1933	1,006,200	684,556	195,872	373,030	1,480,000	925	370	3,700	2,220
1937	931,500	634,660	181,331	419,020	1,552,000	970	388	3,880	2,328

SOURCE: author's calculations.

extremely difficult to determine the volume of baleen thus exported, because it would have fluctuated greatly depending upon the prices of both imported and local trade goods. For example, at the turn of the century, bowhead whale baleen was sold for $1.50 to $4.00 a pound, so that the trade value from a single whale would have been from $2,000 to $6,000.

Judging by the records of exchange with whalers and traders, some of the goods the Eskimos traded were raw materials that, until that time, had held for them only a limited utilitarian value, and thus their exit from the subsistence system did not represent a particular drain upon it. This was true primarily of baleen, walrus ivory, and various types of fur. For example, in 1895, the residents of Avan negotiated with American ships for 4.5 tons of flour, 880 kilograms of biscuits, 800 kilograms of sugar, and other goods, in exchange for one-third of the baleen of a bowhead whale, 43 pairs of walrus tusks (approximately half their estimated annual walrus catch), 5 polar bear skins, 22 fox skins, 36 seal skins, and 140 reindeer skins, in addition to 14 sets of men's fur clothing for use by the Yankee whalers (Gondatti 1898:xxiii–xxiv). In the other case noted above, in 1908 the residents of Imtuk and Sireniki traded away 2,023 pounds of baleen (the yield from two small whales), 80 kilograms of walrus tusk (a third of the annual harvest), 288 fox furs, 58 reindeer skins, and 2 polar bear hides in exchange for 268 sacks of flour, 60 rifles with ammunition, one ton of dried bread and biscuits and other goods for a total worth of $5,400 (SS *Herman*, 1909). However, because of the continual price fluctuations and general instability of the volume of trade, I must reiterate that, for now, assigning a specific value to this outflow of goods and raw materials remains impossible.

Production in the Eskimo Economy

Yet another piece of the subsistence balance puzzle remains to be filled in, which is the actual amount of resources produced by the community in a given unit of time, such as the calendar year. To calculate this, we need to turn to statistics on production in the traditional economy of the Asiatic Eskimos.

Records of Asiatic Eskimo hunting yields by village were first kept beginning in the late 1920s, and by the early 1930s were kept regularly and reliably. There are some records for the early period, from

1920 to 1925, but they are patchy, or lump sums for the entire sea-mammal harvest for the area not by villages (Krupnik 1980:66–68, 1984a:212–22). These data, together with oral histories from old hunters from these villages concerning catch sizes in the 1920s, permit us to reconstruct approximate game statistics for five selected communities with a baseline year of 1920. Apparently, this is the earliest period for which it is possible now to evaluate the volume of the Eskimo harvest, relying on any statistical data and certain indirect calculations.

In all, there are data on thirty-seven annual harvests of most species of marine mammals in several Eskimo communities and villages between 1920 and 1937 (table 6). For four communities, these data simultaneously cover an entire six-year period from 1932 to 1937 (Sireniki, Naukan, Chaplino, and Kivak), and, in the case of Sireniki, an uninterrupted nine-year stretch from 1929 to 1937. These data are sufficient to estimate the productivity of the Eskimo subsistence system, and to examine its trends over time, comparing "good" and "bad" years, and even to compare the overall situation in the late 1920s with that in the mid-1930s. In calculating the balances, all hunting statistics for the 1920s were compared for plausibility with the estimated levels of consumption needs in 1920; those for 1930 to 1936 were compared with requirement estimates for the standardized year of 1933; and for 1937 we have both the estimated and recorded amounts of game harvested.

Unfortunately, local statistics did not include other elements of subsistence in the Eskimo economy such as fishing, bird hunting, or gathering edible plants. Nor did they include information on how much imported food Eskimos bought, or their trade with Chukchi reindeer herders. Only one source addresses this lacuna: the 1937 household inventory of the Chukchi Peninsula (Materialy Chukotskoi zemekspeditsii 1938:113–19). It contains catch statistics for marine mammals, birds, fur-bearing animals, and fish for all villages in the area, as well as partial data on imported food items obtained by Eskimo families from several villages, and specific instances of barter trade with reindeer herders (Knopfmiller 1940b). We used these materials to calculate complete subsistence balances for 1937, and for purposes of comparison with consumption needs throughout the 1930s.

For an even earlier period, it was possible to estimate harvests for all species based on recollections of about two dozen contemporary elderly informants from various Eskimo villages and taking 1920 as

TABLE 6

Sea Mammal Catch Returns by Eskimo Communities, 1920–1937

Community/year	Whale	Walrus	Beard. seal	Other seals	White whale
Sireniki					
1920[a]	3	135	180	450	2
1928	2	318	NA	NA	NA
1929	1	161	268	470	0
1930	1	114	116	460	3
1931	0	188	158	893	2
1932	5	232	162	487	2
1933	6	320	181	480	3
1934	3	640	322	667	1
1935	2	342	185	225	NA
1936	0	322	214	335	NA
1937	2	513	88	315	NA
Naukan					
1920[a]	1	300	84	2,520	15
1926	1[a]	209	125	1,318	NA
1927	1	NA	NA	NA	NA
1928	0	608	NA	NA	NA
1929	1	315	69	6,387	9
1930	0	345	NA	NA	42
1931	0	667	170	3,965	NA
1932	2	85	108	3,837	0
1933	2[b]	470	101	1,740	51
1934	2	114	97	1,329	12
1935	0	347	120	929	8
1936	3	163	197	2,063	22
1937	0	759	121	3,128	12
Chaplino					
1920[a]	1	400	212	1,990	0
1922	NA	501	NA	NA	NA
1928	NA[c]	118	NA	NA	NA
1932	1	225	82	2,895	NA
1933	1	310	147	1,100	NA
1934	0	618	214	1,384	NA
1935	0	584	150	2,182	NA
1936	0	586	116	2,654	NA
1937	1	609	173	3,092	NA
Avan					
1920[a]	1	90	56	520	5
1922	1[c]	80	NA	NA	NA
1933	1	NA	NA	NA	3
1934	0	NA	36	344	NA
1935	0	129	36	281	1
1936	0	72	27	249	NA
1937	0	227	52	667	3
Kivak					
1920[a]	1[c]	60	68	420	0
1932	1	84	49	311	NA

TABLE 6
Continued

Community/year	Whale	Walrus	Beard. seal	Other seals	White whale
Kivak					
1933	0	148	73	303	NA
1934	1	210	96	295	NA
1935	0	142	75	501	NA
1936	1	84	40	329	NA
1937	0	162	102	664	NA

SOURCES: Knopfmiller 1940; Menovshchikov 1959; Krupnik 1980.
[a] Estimate.
[b] Including one gray whale.
[c] According to elders' recollections, 6 or 7 bowhead whales were harvested in Chaplino between 1920 and 1932, 5 in Avan, and 3 in Kivak.

a baseline year.[7] Field research in Sireniki in 1975 yielded a fully reliable reconstruction of all aspects of subsistence activities for this community in the 1920s, including sea hunting, fishing, gathering, trade with reindeer herders, and purchase of food goods. Based on these data, I did a differential estimation for four remaining Asiatic Eskimo communities, which I then adjusted somewhat according to the fragmentary data of the Arctic Census of 1926–27 (which turned out to be not very accurate for the Chukchi Peninsula) or to analogous estimates of subsistence harvests for Alaskan or St. Lawrence Island Eskimos.

The final step in our reconstruction was to recalculate our raw hunting-yield figures per unit of consumption: kilocalories of food, dog food, or fuel oil, and number of skins for domestic use and trade. For this it was necessary to calculate a figure for the "average (energy) productivity" of a typical whale, walrus, seal, or bird carcass, of various kinds of salmon and other fish, or of an average reindeer carcass received in trade. Initially, I had my own set of these figures, based upon Russian sources and local documentation from the 1920s to 1950s, which I correlated with informants' accounts (Krupnik 1976c, 1978). However, in order to facilitate comparability of the Asiatic Eskimo subsistence data with similar calculations for other regions of the Arctic, it is highly desirable to use a single reconstruction methodology. Since Foote's estimates have already been used in subsistence reconstructions among Eskimos of Baffin Island, St. Lawrence Island, and the northern Alaska interior (see Burgess 1974, Foote 1965, 1967, Hall 1971, Kemp 1971, etc.), and since a systematic comparison between my figures and his revealed few discrepancies (table 7), most

TABLE 7
Average Weights and Caloric Values of Eskimo Game Species[a]

Game species	Kg live weight	Usable portion, 10^3 kcal: Meat	Dog food	Blubber
Bowhead whale	20,000	12,000	15,200	50,000
Gray whale (calf)	7,000	—3,540—		16,000
Walrus	820	200	40	1,500
White whale	700	360	66	1,800
Bearded seal	200	50	8	612
Seal (average)[a]	48	12	2	160
Polar bear	350	250	?	—
Brown bear	250	—200—		—
Elk (Siberian moose)	400	300	?	—
Fall caribou	120	132	30	—
Spring caribou	100	54	35	—
Domestic reindeer (clean carcass)	40	30	2	—
Dall sheep	80	80	?	—
Arctic hare	4	2.12	?	—
Geese[b]	2.5	2.18	0.5	—
Ducks[c]	1.0	1.1	0.2	
Ptarmigan	0.6	0.5	—	—
Salmon (various species)	per 1 kg	0.88	0.2	—
White fish	per 1 kg	0.72	0.2	—
Polar cod	per 1 kg	0.42	0.2	—
Other fish	per 1 kg	0.50	0.25	—
Duck eggs	per 1 kg	(1.5)	—	—

SOURCE: Author's calculation (Krupnik 1976c, 1978). See also Budagyan 1961; Foote 1965: 350–64; Smith 1991: 181.

[a] With 90% of ringed seal, 5% of harbor seal, and 5% of spotted seal in the harvest.
[b] Large waterfowl species—Eider duck, cormorant, Canada goose, etc.
[c] Smaller seabirds—guillemot, loon, auk, etc.

of the necessary figures for this study were taken from Foote's dissertation of 1965. Only after these very extensive recalculations could the volume of raw hunting yields be compared to consumption demand levels in five Eskimo communities and expressed in the form of annual subsistence balances.

Analysis of the Food Balances

The essence of a balance analysis of a subsistence system is to determine the difference, or balance, between the actual harvest and calculated consumption demand within a given community. The data we have allow us to construct such balances for 1920 and 1937 for five separate communities, for the Asiatic Eskimos as an entire group,

TABLE 8
Calculated Caloric Shares (percentage) of Various Food Items in Asiatic Eskimo Consumption

Communities	Sea-mammal meat and blubber	Fish	Seabirds	Bird eggs	Tundra plants	Beach products	Reindeer meat	Purchased products
1920								
Sireniki	87.2[a]	3.7	1.8	0.3	1.1	0.3	1.9	3.7
Naukan	90.8[b]	1.4	1.3	0.1	0.7	0.3	1.8	3.6
Chaplino	90.9[b]	1.9	1.3	0.2	0.7	0.3	1.1	3.6
Kivak	88.4[c]	4.2	1.0	0.2	1.1	0.3	0.7	4.1
Avan	85.5[c]	5.1	1.8	0.4	0.9	0.3	0.8	5.2
1937								
Sireniki	79.0[a]	5.2	0.7	0.3	1.0	0.3	1.1	12.4
Naukan	81.5[a]	1.5	0.9	0.1	0.7	0.3	1.5	13.5
Chaplino	70.2[a]	4.3	0.7	0.2	0.4	0.2	0.9	23.1
Kivak	83.6[b]	5.5	0.7	0.1	0.9	0.3	0.7	8.2
Avan	59.8[a]	9.1	0.8	0.3	0.6	0.2	0.7	28.5

SOURCE: Author's calculations. A version of this table was first published in *Arctic Anthropology* 25 (1), 1988.

[a] A total of 100% of the calculated supply according to estimated requirements (1.2 kg of meat and 0.06 kg of blubber per person per day), with general surplus.

[b] A total of 100% of the calculated supply for human needs, with a shortage in dog food.

[c] Available returns with a shortage in human food and/or dog food.

and according to the two types of their economy—that based upon large marine-mammal hunting from villages on the open coast, and that based upon seal hunting from smaller villages in bays and inlets.

These balances make it possible for the first time to determine the role of foods from the different types of subsistence activity—sea hunting, fishing, and gathering—in the Eskimo diet (table 8). In addition, we can conduct a year-by-year evaluation of the marine hunt, which was the source of 90 to 95 percent of subsistence production in the Asiatic Eskimo community. For this we have available data on subsistence needs and actual hunting yields of marine mammals for five communities—enough for a total of thirty-seven year-round community balances between the years 1920 and 1937 (table 9). These can be compiled for an evaluation of the overall productivity of Eskimo maritime hunting and to compare various aspects of its two main strategies (table 10).

In all we had at our disposal several dozen annual balances of the Eskimo sea-mammal-hunting economy from the first decades of this century. I will emphasize that within the limits of the entire North

TABLE 9
Calculated Supply of Sea Mammal Products (percentage) by Eskimo Communities, 1920–1937

Community	Year	Total supply[a]	Meat[b]	Blubber[c]	Skins: Walrus	Skins: Bearded seal	Skins: Small seals
Sireniki	1920	157.3	94.0	193.8	87.0	290.3	72.6
	1929	134.3	92.3	158.5	103.9	432.3	75.8
	1930	81.1	53.8	97.9	65.1	165.7	65.7
	1931	99.9	76.6	114.2	107.4	225.7	127.6
	1932	200.4	120.8	249.3	132.6	231.4	69.6
	1933	247.9	155.9	304.4	182.9	258.6	68.6
	1934	304.2	263.3	424.7	365.7	460.0	95.3
	1935	168.2	131.2	190.9	195.4	264.3	32.1
	1936	130.2	113.8	140.1	184.0	305.7	47.9
	1937	201.7	172.2	220.4	285.0	122.2	43.8
	Average	172.9	127.4	209.4	170.9	275.6	69.9
Naukan	1920	122.4	88.8	142.6	109.1	76.4	229.1
	1926	81.4	57.4	96.1	73.3	109.6	115.6
	1929	181.9	113.3	223.9	110.5	60.5	560.3
	1931	191.0	163.1	206.7	215.2	137.1	319.8
	1932	108.3	57.0	137.1	27.4	87.1	309.4
	1933	137.0	116.6	148.4	151.6	81.5	140.3
	1934	73.4	44.7	89.5	36.8	78.2	107.2
	1935	84.6	78.2	88.3	111.9	96.8	74.9
	1936	114.7	68.1	140.8	52.6	158.9	166.4
	1937	187.3	174.2	194.4	237.2	94.5	244.4
	Average	128.2	96.1	146.8	112.6	98.1	198.0
Chaplino	1920	121.6	92.0	139.8	127.0	168.3	157.9
	1932	110.1	68.2	138.3	84.9	77.3	273.1
	1933	100.0	73.1	118.1	117.0	138.7	103.8
	1934	154.0	129.4	170.6	233.2	201.9	130.6
	1935	156.2	126.8	176.0	220.4	141.5	205.8
	1936	161.8	129.5	183.6	221.1	109.4	250.4
	1937	189.1	154.7	209.1	210.0	149.1	266.6
	Average	141.8	110.5	162.2	173.3	140.9	198.3
Kivak	1920	88.3	51.8	110.9	52.2	141.7	91.3
	1932	112.2	67.2	144.8	98.8	144.1	91.5
	1933	115.4	90.9	133.1	174.1	214.7	89.1
	1934	192.3	137.8	231.8	247.0	282.4	86.8
	1935	122.9	92.0	145.4	167.1	220.6	147.4
	1936	110.8	66.8	142.7	98.8	117.6	96.8
	1937	144.6	98.3	182.4	190.6	300.0	195.3
	Average	126.6	86.4	155.9	146.9	203.0	114.0
Avan	1920	96.8	71.6	109.4	66.6	103.7	96.3
	1935	92.4	78.6	101.8	143.3	100.0	78.1
	1936	58.0	46.4	65.9	80.0	75.0	69.2

(*continued*)

TABLE 9
Continued

Community	Year	Total supply[a]	Meat[b]	Blubber[c]	Skins: Walrus	Skins: Bearded seal	Skins: Small seals
Avan	1937	164.9	139.7	181.6	238.9	136.8	175.5
	Average	103.0	84.1	114.7	132.2	103.9	104.8

SOURCE: Author's calculations. A version of this table was first published in *Arctic Anthropology* 25(1), 1988.
[a] Kcal of sea-mammal products obtained compared to overall demands.
[b] Human food and dog food consumption according to estimated caloric requirements.
[c] Human consumption, dwelling heating, etc.

American Arctic occupied by Eskimos, the only other places where it would be possible to conduct such an extensive analysis are in West Greenland, where statistics on local hunting—or, more accurately, on hunting products purchased at each trading station—have been kept since the 1800s. Nothing approaching such a full set of data exists throughout most of the Eurasian Arctic. All this increases the value of the Asiatic Eskimo materials for analyzing forms of adaptation among Siberian indigenous peoples to their harsh and challenging environment.

At the same time, a cautionary reminder: data from the 1920s and 1930s, like the recollections of elderly informants, reflects only the *latest phase* in the history of a traditional and already heavily transformed Eskimo subsistence system. This was a society with deeply disrupted resources, with a new, more effective harvest technology (firearms, American whale harpoons, etc.), and a strong orientation to a commercial market to sell at least a portion of its traditional products.

Nonetheless, in many ways life in this society remained immutable, adjusting its work activities to the traditional rhythms of hunting and distribution of the harvest. This rhythm did not change radically in either the early years of Soviet power, nor even with the onset of collectivization in the 1930s. In its early stages, collectivization in this coastal area primarily took the form of very simple forms of cooperation, such as associations or *artels* for cooperative sea-mammal hunting, and various consumers' cooperatives. Throughout the 1930s the efforts of Soviet officials on the Chukchi Peninsula were focused

TABLE 10

General Asiatic Eskimo Supply of Sea Mammal Products

(percentage of estimated requirements)

Year	Total supply[a]	Meat[b]	Blubber[c]	Skins: Walrus	Skins: Bearded seal	Skins: Small seals
Asiatic Eskimo, total						
1920	120.2	84.2	141.5	99.0	150.8	148.2
1932[d]	128.5	75.2	161.8	75.0	120.1	225.4
1933[d]	145.5	106.6	169.9	149.5	150.3	108.5
1934[d]	161.1	130.1	200.6	189.5	218.3	110.0
1935	126.1	104.5	139.7	166.9	153.0	112.3
1936	125.2	93.1	145.9	132.6	160.5	152.0
1937	184.0	155.6	201.3	234.0	138.1	202.7
Villages on the open seacoast						
1920	127.3	88.0	150.9	105.3	150.3	150.6
1937	189.2	170.4	200.2	256.6	103.8	165.6
Villages in bays						
1920	78.2	59.8	88.1	63.3	153.3	135.0
1937	121.7	59.2	170.5	56.4	259.1	415.9

SOURCE: Author's calculations. A version of this table was first published in *Arctic Anthropology* 25 (1), 1988.

[a] Kcal obtained, compared to overall requirements.

[b] Human food and dog food consumption according to estimated requirements.

[c] Human consumption, dwelling heating, etc.

[d] Excluding Avan community (no game returns available).

more or less on supporting and strengthening the traditional economic base of the indigenous population. The first artel-kolkhozes adhered to autochthonous customs for sharing all benefits of the hunt; they had no planning targets or indicators, and only weakly pursued collectivization of the means of production. Socioeconomic transformation did not lead to significant modernization of the prevailing ways of life until the 1940s and especially the 1950s. This means that the data from the 1920s and early 1930s characterize the final stage in a *transformed* traditional subsistence system, those from the 1950s depict the first stages of a *modernized* economic pattern, and the model from the mid-1930s to the late 1940s is to some degree reflective of an interstitial *transitional* situation.

Our balance calculations and informants' recollections confirm that, for the Asiatic Eskimo, this transition occurred under rather favorable socioeconomic circumstances. On the whole, the total hunting yields in the 1930s significantly exceeded the communities' consumption needs. In the good hunting years of 1931, 1933, 1934, 1935, and 1937, the marine-mammal yield more than met consumption needs for food, fuel, and dog food by a factor of 1.5 to 2.5, and clearly was so abundant it could not be fully utilized.

However, in spite of *surplus production* in individual years, Eskimo subsistence was characterized by unstable consumption, sharp interannual fluctuations in the hunting yield, and periodic shortages of food. The Eskimo economy appears to have been particularly precarious in the 1920s. Assuming a human consumption norm of 1.2 kilograms of meat per day and a full daily food ration for dogs, the catch did not fully meet consumption needs for marine-mammal meat in a single community (see table 9). This shortfall had to be bridged by increased consumption by humans of animal fat, or lower-quality food for the sled dogs. The role of alternative local resources such as fish, bird eggs, or edible plants, and, even more so, purchased or traded food products, was too insignificant to compensate for the failure of a hunting season. This means that the recollections of elderly informants, as well as the numerous references to the precarious situation of the natives in the 1920s are fully confirmed by our balance calculations (Arsen'ev 1927:36, Karaev 1926:139–42, Morzveroboinyi Promysel 1934:39, Vdovin 1965:303–305, etc.).

Estimating whether the supply of marine-mammal skins sufficiently met the Eskimos' needs for domestic use, trade, and barter is a more complicated matter. On balance, it would seem that in the 1920s the marine hunting economy fulfilled the overall demand for skins and hides, but each community experienced a shortage of certain types of skins (table 9). The only reliable and significant surpluses were of bearded seal in Sireniki and of the ringed seal in Naukan. But, in the 1920s, selling marine-mammal skins at the trading posts represented virtually the sole way that Eskimos could obtain trade items they needed, including food, guns, and ammunition. Thus, we find such striking figures as those for 1925, when hunters from seven Eskimo villages (Chaplino, Sikliuk, Avan, Ureliki, Kivak, Imtuk, and Sireniki) brought 3,116 sealskins for trade to the post in Provideniia Bay, and for 1927, when this increased to 3,665 at a time when the entire recorded harvest was only 3,000 to 4,000 seals a year (*Itogi Perepisi* 1929:281, Rozanov 1931:56). Such a trade volume was a matter of necessity precipitated by the absence of other products that could have been substituted for trading purposes. Not surprisingly, our older informants frequently referred to a severe shortage in the

1920s of sealskins for skin clothing and footwear in Imtuk and Sireniki, or walrus skins to cover houses and boats in Ureliki, Avan, and Kivak.

In the 1930s, in spite of significant expansion in the Eskimo hunting industry, in all but two communities, Chaplino and Kivak, the population experienced shortages of one species or another of marine-mammal skins. Such disproportions could be rectified by intercommunity trade, especially in the form of "presents" or reciprocity between relatives living in different villages. But, to support their normal way of life, the Eskimos needed even more skins than reported to trade with the reindeer herders.

The main trade between the coastal hunters and the Chukchi reindeer herders took place at the end of August and the beginning of September. The Chukchi assembled their herds in agreed-upon locations along the coast or in the larger river valleys and estuaries, where the Eskimos would come to meet them by large skinboats. In winter, people from the coast traveled directly to the herders' camps by dogsled. Trade traditionally took place between established individual trading partners, who sometimes maintained this relation over as much as two or three generations. The herders exchanged reindeer skins, meat, and fat, while the hunters brought marine-mammal products and some goods obtained from European traders, such as tea, tobacco, matches, tin dishes, and ammunition.

Judging from the subsistence balances, in the 1920s the Eskimo economy produced a surplus of only a few items, namely sealskins (bearded and ringed seal), and seal oil, and of course there were never enough imported goods for the Eskimos themselves. Therefore, the main trade flow into the tundra consisted of semiprocessed and finished items, such as hide straps, uppers for footwear, sealskin boots, waterproof anoraks made from walrus intestine, as well as stretched bearded seal skins and, occasionally, walrus meat. In return they received reindeer carcasses, on the average two to three for every Eskimo who came to trade, and six to eight reindeer skins, which was never enough for the coastal people's usual needs, estimated earlier as a minimum of twelve skins for an average family of five. Therefore, at that time, the Eskimos were forced constantly to make very economic use of the skins they had. Typically, people in the coastal villages replaced their reindeer-skin winter clothing only every two to three years, in contrast to the reindeer herders in the tundra, who got new fur clothing every year, or even twice a year.

In the 1930s, as the surplus product of the maritime hunting industry increased, the Eskimos began to bring larger quantities of meat, blubber, skins, and imported goods to trade in the tundra, which sharply increased the intensity of trade with the reindeer herders. Consequently, fresh reindeer meat began to appear more frequently in the coastal villages, and the condition and quality of the Eskimos' fur clothing improved. Evidently, such cyclical oscillations were typical for trade relations between the coastal and tundra residents.

In contrasts, as is well known, the volume of trade at the posts and with the American trading vessels before the posts were established was influenced by market fluctuations over which the local population had no control. The items that Eskimos brought to this trade were high-value raw materials—baleen, walrus ivory, furs, seal and bear skins, and, only in exceptional cases, processed goods, such as boots, gloves, and warm clothing. The Eskimo economy had access to only a limited amount of fur, and when the trade value of baleen plummeted after 1910, then stocks of other resources dwindled in the 1920s, the volume of this trade fell to the bare minimum to obtain the necessary means to support subsistence activities, such as guns, ammunition, traps, and iron implements, and a few food items such as flour, tea, and tobacco.

Improvements in equipment and harvests in the local hunting industry in the 1930s contributed to a revival of local trade in Chukotka and a perceptible increase in the proportion of purchased food in the Eskimo diet. Purchased food accounted for 10 to 20 percent of the diet in most villages in 1937, reaching a calculated high of 50 to 60 percent in Ureliki, in Provideniia Bay (table 8). Once again we are looking here at a case of long-term fluctuations in consumption trends. In the last years of the nineteenth century and the first years of the twentieth, when Eskimo products in general and baleen in particular commanded a high market price, the amount of goods imported for trade with them was even higher than in the 1920s and 1930s, and a substantial part of this was food, reaching as much as 15 to 25 percent of the diet and caloric consumption.[8]

If the volume of food *entering* the Eskimo subsistence system at the turn of the century can be defined, albeit in approximate figures, estimating how much food *left* the system through trade is much more difficult. Suffice it to say that when the Eskimos traded food products with the reindeer herders, the caloric content of the Eskimo products far exceeded that of the reindeer meat they received in exchange, inasmuch as the energy content of marine-mammal meat and fat is two to three times higher than that of reindeer. In contrast, trade at the posts and with American ships did not lead to a substantial food-energy loss from the local subsistence system, because it did not involve Eskimo food products. However, this commercial trade did require an enormous expenditure of energy in the form of labor, time, and hunting effort either to obtain items such as furs that would have had little utility value in the traditional subsistence system, or to bring in surplus amounts of resources they did use, such as marine-mammal skins, ivory, and baleen.

Both of these means of obtaining trade goods were used by the Eskimos in the late nineteenth and early twentieth centuries, but the second was more accessible, and preferable for psychological reasons. In 1937 the hunters of five Eskimo communities caught a total of about 300 Arctic foxes, or about 1.5 pelts per family, and 75 red foxes. In the same year in four of the southern communities (excluding Naukan) the trading posts received 976 walrus skins, 183 bearded seal skins and 3,880 sealskins (Knopfmiller 1940b: file 3), which represented 65 percent, 44 percent, and 82 percent respectively of the entire recorded take of these game species. Therefore, expansion of the Eskimo hunting industry in the 1930s can be partially explained as an effort by the local hunters to increase the volume of native products they had available to trade in exchange for imported food.

The same approach had been adopted by the Eskimos in the second half of the nineteenth century, when the demand for baleen was high, and they dramatically increased their hunting effort for bowhead whales. In those days, it was typical to see three to five harvested whales a year in many of the coastal communities (Bogoslovskaia et al. 1982:202–206, Krupnik 1987a:21–23, Marquette and Bockstoce 1980:15). That left their inhabitants with a huge surplus of meat, blubber, and dog food unimaginable in the precontact subsistence system.

Many sources have proposed a view of traditional Eskimo resource utilization as effectively "omnivorous." While confirming this view in general, our balance analysis of Asiatic Eskimo subsistence provides a new basis upon which the actual level of such an "omnivorousness"—that is, the proportions of various marine species in the traditional consumption structure—can be calculated. Though they hunted efficiently for a wide spectrum of marine game animals, including walrus, several species of seals, and whales, the Asiatic

TABLE 11
Shares of Various Sea Mammals Hunted in Asiatic Eskimo Subsistence Harvesting
(as a percentage; mean shares for 1920–1937 returns)

Community	Year	Item	Baleen whales	Walruses	Bearded seals	Other seals	White whales
Sireniki		Meat	13.4	71.7	9.1	5.7	0.2
		Blubber	28.3	41.2	19.6	10.7	0.2
Naukan		Meat	7.6	63.9	4.7	22.5	1.3
		Blubber	14.1	36.8	9.6	37.9	1.6
Chaplino		Meat	2.7	78.0	4.5	14.8	—
		Blubber	6.8	50.3	11.6	31.4	—
Avan		Meat	3.9	80.3	4.8	10.5	0.5
		Blubber	8.2	55.0	12.4	23.7	0.7
Kivak		Meat	9.4	73.6	7.2	9.8	—
		Blubber	20.0	43.8	16.8	19.3	—
Total	1920	Meat	10.8	66.5	6.7	15.3	0.7
		Blubber	24.1	34.0	13.9	27.3	0.7
	1937	Meat	2.5	83.0	3.2	11.0	0.3
		Blubber	7.6	56.8	9.0	26.4	0.4
Open seacost village							
	1920	Meat	12.0	66.6	6.3	14.6	0.5
		Blubber	26.6	33.9	13.0	25.9	0.6
	1937	Meat	2.8	86.2	2.3	8.5	0.2
		Blubber	8.5	62.7	6.8	21.7	0.3
Villages in bays							
	1920	Meat	0.0	66.1	10.6	21.7	1.6
		Blubber	0.0	35.1	22.8	40.2	1.9
	1937	Meat	0.0	40.6	12.4	46.1	0.9
		Blubber	0.0	16.0	19.8	63.4	0.8

SOURCE: Author's calculations. A version of this table was first published in *Arctic Anthropology* 25 (1), 1988.

Eskimo were indeed a "walrus people" (see table 11). They probably depended upon this animal more than any other Eskimo society, except perhaps neighboring populations of the Bering Strait area, such as the residents of St. Lawrence and King Islands, the Diomede Islands, and the village of Wales on the American side of the Bering Strait, with whom they shared very closely related patterns of resource utilization (Ellana 1983, 1988). The core of their existence was the walrus hunt, which provided 60 to 80 percent of the caloric intake for most villages, depending on how well the harvest went.

It was in fact the walrus hunt that served as the vehicle for maintaining an equilibrium among the population, its consumption needs, and its resources. Meeting their resource needs with any other species required a completely unimaginable use of time, labor, and energy. This is clearly indicated by the following calculations. The five communities studied (with their combined population of 1,100 in the 1920s to 1930s) had a total annual demand for meat and dog food of approximately one billion kilocalories. That volume of food could be supplied by an annual harvest of 1,670 "staple" walruses (the actual game statistics were 1,400 to 2,200, with an average of 1,500 for the 1920s and 1930s), or 75 whales (the actual figure was 4 to 8), 10,100 bearded seals (the actual catch was 550 to 600), or 43,500 small seals (the actual yield was 4,000 to 8,000). Living on fish alone would have been even harder, requiring an annual catch of a thousand tons, as opposed to the actual catch of 50,000 to 90,000 kilograms, not to mention anything so labor-intensive as hunting birds. Thus, in spite of its qualitative "omnivorousness," the quantitative role played by each of these species in the Eskimo diet was largely determined by how much human effort was required to catch it.

In addition, the actual relative weights of these species as components of the subsistence norm varied across space and time. Fig. 8 gives some sense of how each village tended to have its own distinct hunting profile and pattern of marine resource utilization. One can only be amazed at how, within one tiny ethnic population of 1,300 people with a highly homogeneous ecological and cultural system, each local community created its own unique management strategies for exploiting its environment and built its own relationship to the ecosystem. This spatial mosaic can be read as a geographical expression of the central mechanism driving the main adaptive strategy of the aboriginal maritime hunting culture: the great flexibility, and the sensitivity with which hunters shifted their emphasis from one harvested species to another in response to subtle changes and differences in the hunting environment.

A similar conclusion is suggested by a temporal analysis of food-budget inputs and outflows. It is well known that for all groups of Eskimos, production was characterized by a high degree of seasonality; that is, sharp oscillations occurred in economic activities depending on the time of year. Correspondingly, the size and composition of the hunting catches and, thus, the foods people ate, varied from one season to another and from month to month.

The Asiatic Eskimos' annual subsistence cycle was divided into four seasons, but these seasons were understood to refer primarily to the main species that was hunted during those periods, rather than to calendar months to which these activities typically corresponded. In

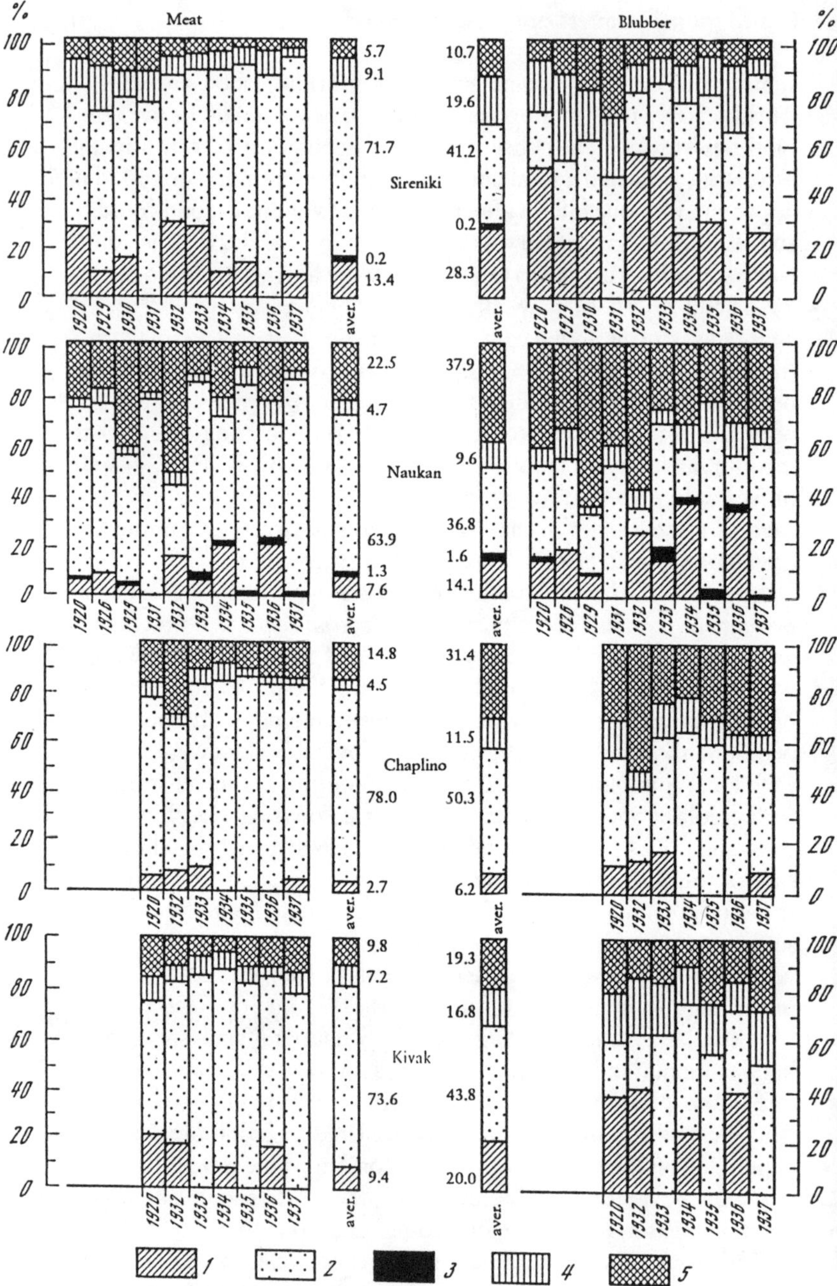

Fig. 8. Shares of various sea mammals hunted in the Eskimo harvest, 1920–1937, as a percentage of total caloric output. 1: baleen whales; 2: walruses; 3: white whales (beluga); 4: bearded seals; 5: other seals.

the winter, the main activity of the men was hunting for small seals through their breathing holes and along the edge of the shorefast ice, and this lasted from December to early April. Bearded seals migrated northward along the coast in April and May, and walrus and bowhead whales from April to June, so in the villages located on the open coast, the main communal skinboat hunt occurred in spring, which was considered to last from mid-April to June. Spring also heralded the arrival of the season for hunting migratory game birds. The short summer, from July to August, was dominated by fishing, bird hunting, collecting eggs in the bird colonies, and gathering edible plants and berries, with episodic skinboat forays to hunt walrus, bearded seals, and sea lions in open water, and to catch seals with nets in the bays, inlets, and estuaries. Regular large-scale cooperative skinboat hunting resumed in the fall as the large marine mammals began their migration south to winter feeding grounds. From September to October boat crews hunted mainly for walrus, and, in October and November, for bowhead whales. Although this was by no means always the case, the walrus migration often yielded a better harvest in spring, while to a certain extent the bowhead harvest tended to be more reliable in the fall.

According to the elders' accounts, game returns in a normal year greatly surpassed community needs during the spring and fall months, as the migrating herds of walrus and bowhead whales funneled through Bering Strait from south to north and back again. But in early and late summer the catch roughly equaled community needs, and during the winter fell far short. Thus, every year, prosperity and even survival of an Eskimo community were critically linked to two brief periods of hunting activity that corresponded to the seasonal peaks of walrus and whale migrations (fig. 9). During those two periods alone, as much as ten times as much meat was brought in as during the rest of the year put together. Thus, monthly game statistics show how, in 1933 in Naukan, more than 60 percent of the marine-mammal harvest for the entire year was caught in two months in the spring, from May to June, while February, April, and December accounted for 1.5 percent each, and November for only 0.5 percent (see Orlova 1936:49). A similarly oscillating pattern in intakes and outflows of energy was characteristic among many other Eskimo groups from Alaska to Greenland who depended for their subsistence upon seasonally fluctuating hunting resources (Burch 1985:114–16, Foote 1970b:265–66, Hertz and Kapel 1986:148, Kemp 1971:100).

To even out such seasonal variations, the Asiatic Eskimo laid in

1. Village of Novoe Chaplino, Chukchi Peninsula. (Author's photograph, 1977.)

2. Village of Sireniki, Chukchi Peninsula. Storage racks of whale jawbones. (Photograph by Sergei Bogoslovskii, 1980.)

3. Nenets reindeer camp, Ust' Kara area. (Author's photograph, 1974.)

4. Walrus hauling ground, Arakamchechen Island. (Photograph by Nikolai Perov, 1978.)

5. Local elders who assisted me during my fieldwork in Siberia, in photographs taken between 1974 and 1977.

(a) Kooi (ca. 1910–1985) and

(b) Utykhtykak (1914–1976), both in Sireniki;

(c) Nutal'ngaun (1914–1984) and

(d) Arengaun (ca. 1900–1985), both in Novoe Chaplino;

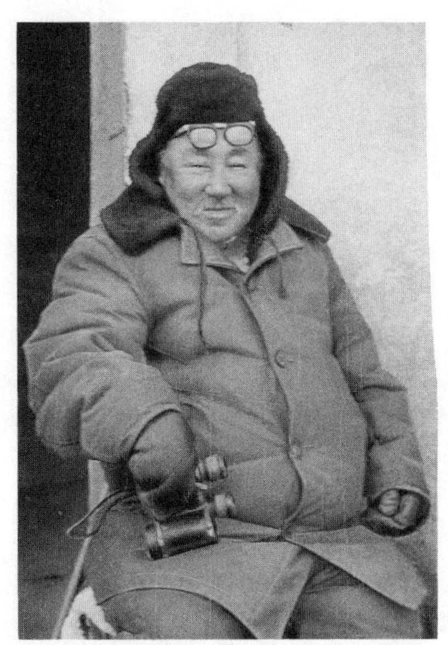

(e) Alexandr Ratkhugwi (1905–1977), in Sireniki;

(f) Egor Laptander (1911–?), Ust' Kara;

(g) Saiwak (1907–1979), in Sireniki.

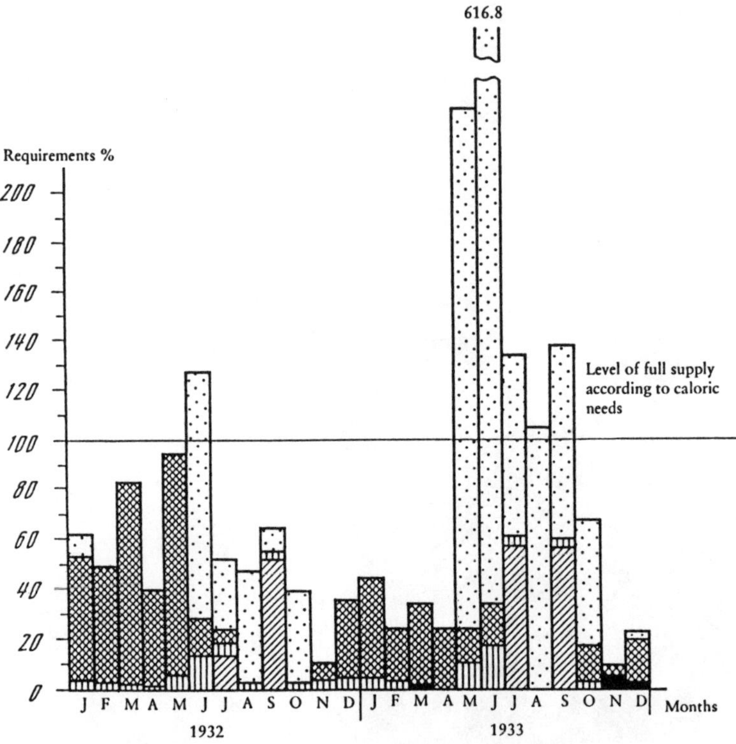

Fig. 9. Monthly supply of sea-mammal meat in the community of Naukan, 1932–1933. (Calculated according to catch records in Orlova 1936.)

large stores of food several times during the course of the year. During the spring and fall, slices of seal and walrus meat were dried for winter consumption. After the autumn hunt for whales and walrus, each family laid in 350 to 400 kilograms of fermented walrus meat and 150 to 200 kilograms of whale meat and blubber. Reserves of dog food and heating oil were prepared twice a year. In the summer, conserves of edible plants, berries, seaweed, and other sea products were prepared for the winter by mixing them in seal oil and blood. This follows the common view of food preservation and storage as one of the most effective human-environment adaptive strategies, because it permits societies based on the harvest of highly fluid natural resources to achieve more stability in their livelihood and their place of residence and, consequently, a higher population density (Testart 1982:527–30).

In this respect, the Asiatic Eskimos may be viewed as exemplifying a broader cultural-economic pattern of sedentary coastal inhabitants of the North Pacific area, whose livelihood as hunters and fishermen was based on seasonally variable marine resources. However, they remain distinctive in three main respects: (1) they exhibited an even higher degree of sedentarism, coupled with an unusually high population density, especially compared to North Alaskan coastal Eskimos, (2) they showed extreme reliance on maritime hunting with surprisingly weak emphasis on fishing and land-game subsistence, and (3) the ecosystem they exploited, or, more exactly, the pattern of exploitation they chose to apply to it, severely limited the availability of resources that could be harvested by less physically active members of the community, such as women, elders, and children, or even individual adult male hunters who did not happen to be members of boat crews at any particular moment in time.

Ecological Pressures of Native Subsistence

Thus far, we have examined traditional maritime hunting subsistence from an unabashedly anthropocentric view, as the unilateral human exploitation of available resources. In order to achieve a more accurate, two-way account of how the traditional maritime hunting system worked, we should consider one last component of the equation: what "ecological cost" did the positive subsistence balance of the Eskimo economy exact on the ecosystem of which it was a part? Our approach to answering this question was to determine estimated hunting pressure—that is, to calculte the impact of the Eskimo catch, both strikes and kills, as a percentage of total annual recruitment rate among the marine-mammal stocks the Eskimos hunted.

In the early twentieth century it appears there were approximately two to three thousand *bowhead whales* in the north Pacific Ocean and adjacent Arctic waters, the remains of the once-mighty Bering Sea, or Western Arctic stock devastated by the American commercial whaling in the late nineteenth century (Breiwick et al. 1984:491, Woodby Botkin 1993). Judging by estimates of the current population, the annual stock recruitment rate probably rarely exceeded 5 to 6 percent (various contemporary estimates range from 4 to 8 percent; see Braham 1984:51, Clarke et al. 1987:292, Fraker 1984:26–28). Only one, smaller portion of this stock follows a westward migratory gyre along the Siberian side of Bering Strait, perhaps several hundred in all, and Siberian native whalers' hunting efforts were limited to these animals (Bogoslovskaia et al. 1982). In the first decades of the twentieth century, the annual catch averaged eight to twelve whales per year, with an equal number of animals struck but not recovered (Krupnik 1980:68–69, Krupnik 1987a:23–24). In a "good" year, then, native hunting pressure might easily equal or surpass local stock recruitment. Although they represented only one-fourth of the population along the Chukotka coast, the Asiatic Eskimos were responsible for two-thirds of the bowhead whale harvest there, typically two to three whales in Sireniki and Imtuk, one to two in Naukan, one in Chaplino, while Avan and Kivak would take one whale, though not every year (Krupnik 1987a:23). Thus, the total pressure from local hunters of the Chukchi Peninsula and Alaska at this time amounted to thirty-five to fifty whales a year, including those animals that were wounded or drowned (Sonntag and Broadhead 1989:115). This was evidently the main factor in what appears to have been the very slow growth rate of this population right up until the aboriginal hunt was markedly reduced and ceased completely on the Chukchi Peninsula in the 1940s and 1950s.

Gray whale hunting in Chukotka was done mainly by the coastal Chukchi, and only occasionally by Eskimos, whose Alaskan kinsmen did not hunt for gray whales at all. The mean annual harvest for all native villages on the Asiatic side in the 1920s and 1930s was estimated at ten to twelve animals, mostly calves and yearlings. Such a level of hunting appears to have had little effect on this whale population, which at that time numberd from 3,000 to 6,000 and showed a consistently high recruitment rate throughout the following decades. This is confirmed by the rapid stock growth in the following decades, right up until the present maximum of about 16,000 to 20,000 animals, which is considered to be approximately the original precontact size of the population (Burns 1984:82, Reeves and Mitchell 1988:378). This contrast with the fate of the much more heavily exploited bowhead whale stock here is striking.

The *Pacific walrus* stock along the Chukotka shore is estimated to have been 50,000 to 60,000 in the 1930s (Knopfmiller 1940a:138, Zenkovich, 1938:60). Based on recent assessments of contemporary walrus stocks, annual recruitment to this population probably did not exceed 5,000 to 8,000 (see Fay 1982:256–61, Kibal'chich 1984:19). The native walrus catch in Chukotka in the 1920s was 1,500 to 2,500 animals, that meant a total population loss of 2,000 to 3,000, including wounded and unrecovered animals. By the mid-1930s it had more than doubled to 4,500 to 5,500, or 6,000 to 7,000 including losses and rapacious killing of animals that arose to support the then-growing market for ivory and ivory carvings. The Eskimos took 40 to 50 percent of the total native catch, again, as opposed to their 25 to 27 percent share of the population (Krupnik 1980:67, 69–70). In certain years, when a walrus industry was conducted from state-owned schooners as well, hunting pressure easily exceeded stock recruitment. As a result, native walrus hunting dropped off sharply in the following decade to a level at most half that of the 1935 to 1937 harvest (Dokumenty 1946:76, Materialy Anadyrskoi ekspeditsii 1950). The Bering Sea walrus population remained at a steady low level until the 1960s and only then began to grow, thanks to a rapid decrease in the hunting pressure and very strict conservation measures on both the American and Asian sides of the Bering Strait.

Hunting pressure on seal populations can be calculated but indirectly. The *bearded seal* catches, for instance, remained fairly constant at an apparently sustainable yield of 2,000 per year from 1910 until 1950. Evidently, this level of native hunting had no observable negative impacts on the bearded seal stock recruitment. Inasmuch as the bearded seal was never the focus of a commercial hunting industry, the current population in the Bering and Chukchi seas of 300,000 animals can be considered close to what it was in the early twentieth century (Burns 1984:84). In contrast, the *ringed seal* catch grew steadily throughout the 1920s and 1930s to an annual average of 30,000 to 35,000, 25 percent of which were caught by the Eskimos. In addition, an equal number are estimated to have been injured or killed but were lost before they could be recovered by the hunters. Although the total population of ringed seals in the Bering and Chukchi seas is very high, it is represented here as the composite of smaller, local herds or subpopulations, any of which is individually highly susceptible to overhunting. Therefore, the rapid decrease in the total Chukchi Peninsula ringed seal catch in the 1940s and 1950s, to 10,000 to 15,000, or only half of its level in the 1920s and 1930s, is most likely explained as the direct consequence of stock depletion among these smaller local herds over the previous two decades (Fedoseev 1965:210, 1984:143, Krupnik 1984a:217).

This increase in seal hunting, it would appear, originated around 1900 and resulted from the desire of local hunters to compensate for the gradual loss of resources and trade items that ensued from a decrease in whale and walrus stocks and a slowed demand for baleen. In the mid-nineteenth century, until the widespread appearance of firearms and the development of trade, the native hunt netted less than half as many seals—3,000 to 5,000 for all Asiatic Eskimos, according to my estimate (Krupnik 1980:77–78)—and could not have had any measurable effect on stock size and recruitment.

Asiatic Eskimo use of other marine animals—*beluga* (or white) *whales*, *narwhals*, *sea lions*, as well as *polar bears*—tended to be rather low, and probably had little effect on the population size. However, this effect was more significant at the margins of these animals' ranges, where their recruitment tended to be unstable even without human interference. Thus, native hunting may have strictly limited expansion of the polar bears' range southward. As it was, only a few dozen polar bears a year were killed on the Chukchi Peninsula, because they rarely strayed as far south as Bering Strait, but hunters tended to track and kill all those who did.

Eskimo exploitation of local *fish resources* and *fur-bearing land animals*, such as Arctic fox and red fox appears to have been too low to have any perceptible impact on those stocks. In contrast, however, Eskimo elders can identify a number of *seabird colonies* that were actively used for bird hunting and egg collecting in the early decades of the century, but that are now severely depleted.[9] It is also possible that this is the result of human overexploitation in the 1920s through the 1940s, since the territory occupied by the Asiatic Eskimos included only two bird colonies that were large enough to sustain substantial exploitation over an extended period—the cliffs on Cape Stoletiia, which were used by the Avan community, and the small islet of Nunanirak, in the hunting area of the Chaplino.[10]

The conclusions of this short overview are obvious. In the first decades of this century the Asiatic Eskimos and the native people of the Chukotka coast in general had a heavy impact on the resources they exploited. Through their hunting pressure, they regulated the main marine-mammal stocks they harvested. Modern studies maintain that to sustain a stable population level of large game mammals, human predation should not constitute more than 30 to 40 percent of its gross annual reproduction rate (Budyko 1967:32–33, Martin 1973:971, Watt 1971:133–35). This figure undoubtedly is too high for any marine-mammal stocks, which have a relatively slow rate of increase. Thus, the majority of seal species can sustain a total hunting pressure (that is, catch plus losses) of not more than 5 to 7 percent of their total population. This norm drops even lower for walruses and especially for whales, to 2 to 3.5 percent (Braham 1984:51–52, Fedoseev 1974:102–103, Kibal'chich 1984:24, Report 1988:112, Welch et al. 1992:351, etc.).

In addition, native hunting, especially of large marine mammals, tended to single out lighter and more accessible prey, such as yearlings, juveniles, or even females with nursing calves. The abundance of skulls of immature gray whales in abandoned village sites on the shore of Mechigmen Bay—Masik, Nykhsirak, Raupelian—bears witness to this. The native bowhead whale hunt was similarly slanted toward calves and juveniles until the rise of commercial demand for baleen, that is, until the mid-nineteenth century, and then again after demand fell off in the 1920s and 1930s. This is well confirmed by ethnographic, archeological, and osteological materials from both the Siberian and Alaskan sides of Bering Strait (see Arutiunov, Krupnik, and Chlenov 1982:84, 165–66, Krupnik 1980:78, Maher and Wilimovsky 1963:19; see also chapter 7). Until motor-powered boats came into use, the local hunters hunted only pregnant beluga whales, which float when killed and therefore could be shot from shore and then safely retrieved. In the native walrus hunt as well, the percent of calves, pregnant females, and nursing cows was very high, because these animals moved slowly and were easier to catch. All this significantly increased the impact of local hunting on the sustainability of the marine-mammal populations.

In the 1920s, the natural resource use of the hunters of Chukotka had seemingly reached a critical level, and it surged even higher in the 1930s. Obvious overhunting was observed in the "good" hunting years: 1931, 1933, 1935, 1937, and so forth. In short, the high productivity of Asiatic Eskimo subsistence in the first decades of this century had reached the point, and at times surpassed it, of *excessive natural resource exploitation*. Therefore, it is hardly possible to agree with the widely held view that the traditional Arctic maritime hunters did not cause perceptible disturbance to the resources they used and were incapable of destroying the ecological balance of their environments (Foote 1965:299–303, Laughlin 1972:382, Laughlin and Harper 1979:2–4, etc.).

Eskimo Adaptations

Let us now take stock of the picture presented by our reconstructed model of Asiatic Eskimo subsistence thus far. It hardly fits the usual textbook image of Eskimo communities as timeless ecological societies living in harmony with nature by means of strict regulation of their numbers and their consumption of resources. Quite to the contrary, the Asiatic Eskimos of the early twentieth century constituted a strikingly dynamic population, both spatially and demographically, and they maintained a highly effective hunting economy, which produced well-defined and, at times, clearly destructive, effects on the wildlife resources upon which they depended. On the whole, the economic base of Eskimo society was fully sufficient to maintain stability in everyday subsistence and steady population growth. But this positive subsistence balance was achieved on a basis of ecologically excessive exploitation of its primary resources, that is, by overhunting.

It is tempting to explain this situation as the ecological inheritance of decades of Euro-American commercial whaling and walrus hunting during the late nineteenth century, which catastrophically depleted the North Pacific marine-mammal stocks to a level from which they could never fully recover. According to the latest estimates, commercial whaling ships slaughtered more than 18,000 bowhead whales and 150,000 walruses in the Bering Strait area and adjacent waters of the Arctic coast between 1849 and 1914 (Bockstoce and Botkin 1980, 1983). According to recent estimates, the populations of bowhead and gray whales were reduced to 15 to 20 percent, and walrus to 30 percent of their original, precontact level (Braham 1984: 50, Burns 1984: 82). But, although commercial hunting did have a huge historical impact on the bowhead whale and walrus populations traditionally exploited by Asiatic Eskimos, by 1910 it fell to an economically insignificant level and has had no economic significance on the Chukchi Peninsula since 1910, or has been focused on other offshore marine species. Thus, it is safe to say that, for the first half of this century, the population dynamics of marine-mammal stocks off the Chukchi Peninsula were determined predominantly by the pressure of native hunting.

In the 1930s, Eskimo hunting catches increased, I have argued, largely as a function of the widespread penetration of commercial Soviet state policies, which took the form of improved hunting equipment, and increased Eskimo consumption of imported goods, which in turn required increased procurement of Eskimo trade items with which to purchase them. During this time, native pressure on certain marine wildlife stocks—walrus, whales, and small seals—swelled by 150 to 200 percent. Older hunters recall how excited they were when, with the introduction of outboard motors in the early 1930s, it was suddenly possible to pursue walrus, beluga, and gray whales on the open water, which had rarely, if ever, been done before, and led to dramatically increased catches. Other sources from that period note, for example, that hunting increased at walrus rookeries, and that many previous regulative norms of traditional hunting behavior were abandoned (Gapanovich 1923:324, Liprandi 1933:58, Nikulin 1941:42, Petrukhin 1926:56, Shnakenburg 1939:56).

The Asiatic Eskimo were indisputably the chief actors in this ecological shift. While constituting only 25 percent of the coastal population, they pulled in 30 to 45 percent of the marine-mammal catch, and thus maintained a hunting industry nearly twice as effective as that of the maritime Chukchi. In all the larger Eskimo villages, as a rule, sea-mammal production exceeded consumption of both human and dog food. Not infrequently, it happened that large amounts of meat and blubber could not be fully utilized and simply rotted and went to waste. Our informants tell us that each year, after the start of the spring hunting season when fresh supplies became available, people cleaned out their meat storage pits, throwing out the remains of the last season and laying in fresh supplies from the new. Old meat was not used, even for dog food, because as long as the hunt was successful, there would always be more than enough fresh supply. This attitude and practice also appears to account for the extraordinary humus buildup found in the top layer of soil in all the ancient villages along the coast, which excavations have shown to be up to several meters thick. The ruined pits of abandoned underground dwellings, ravines, and ditches became *ad hoc* garbage pits for vast quantities of discarded marine-mammal meat, blubber, and bones.

Does this give any grounds to speak of Eskimo hunters as engaged in "conscientious regulation" of their hunting activities and their impact on the wildlife resources upon which one's community's livelihood depended? After all, the aboriginal Arctic hunter never engaged with his ecosystem as a self-conscious game manager, but as an active resource consumer, who had the right and physical capability to kill as much game as seemed necessary to satisfy his consumption needs. Within this framework, it is not surprising that Eskimo hunters did not restrict their harvests to the bare minimum amount of food essential for their survival, but took as much from their environment as it would yield. This orientation, combined with the uncertainty engendered by seasonal and annual instability in weather and game conditions, could lead to 200 to 300 percent surplus harvests in good hunting years. But this surplus inevitably alternated with food shortages in the lean winter months, or in bad hunting years.

On the other hand, I do not mean to suggest a view of Asiatic Eskimo hunting as "irrational" or rapacious, or entirely transformed by Euro-American contacts and commercialization. Eskimos living on the American side of the Bering Sea, and especially on St. Lawrence Island, King Island, and the Diomedes, settled along the chief marine mammal migration routes, and used their resources in a way one might view as similarly "irrational," with harvests far exceeding population demands (see Collins 1940, Ellana 1983, Perri 1976:84–86, Vinogradov 1949:188–89). It is probably fair to say that even before the nineteenth century and the advent of American whaling ships and the proliferation of firearms, the hunting practices of native peoples did have a significant impact on the marine-mammal population off the Chukchi Peninsula. One can refer to some 1,500-plus gray whale skulls stored at the Masik site alone, virtually all of them from nursing calves and yearlings (Chlenov and Krupnik 1984:11–12). North of Masik, in the abandoned village of Raupelian, we unearthed a ceremonial field pinioned by almost fifty polar bear skulls. Similar ritual accumulations of skulls and bones of other hunting species—bowhead whales, walrus, and even seals—dot the Siberian coast (see Arutiunov, Krupnik, and Chlenov 1982:114–22). As a very conservative estimate, even in conditions of precontact aboriginal subsistence, native hunters could annually wipe out a third to a half of the natural recruitment of a large marine-mammal population in its annual migration along the Chukchi Peninsula.

The importance of the cited figures on population growth and reproduction in Eskimo communities for our reconstructed subsistence model should also not be ignored. Genealogies compiled for individual families and for communities as a whole permit us to apply the established model of reproduction with a high birth rate, high death rate, and a variable, but positive natural growth at least up to the mid-nineteenth century. The abundance of old, abandoned villages on the Chukotka coast also attests, if not to direct leaps of population, then definitely to the high mobility of Eskimo communities, and to sharp spatial fluctuations in the territories they utilized.

All these facts clearly reflect a certain set of established economic and demographic mechanisms, or adaptations of the Arctic sea-mammal hunters, which it is possible to consider as the underlying principles of this model of resource exploitation. Some of these have been thoroughly addressed in the literature and need not be reconsidered in great detail here: the flexible and complex (or omnivorous) nature of the resource base, optimization of labor expenditure in resource exploitation, and storage of large amounts of food, among others (see Fitzhugh 1972, Foote 1970b, Sabo 1991, Taylor 1966, Testart 1982, Yesner 1980b). To this list now let us add the following adaptations that emerge from our reconstruction of the Asiatic Eskimo subsistence system of the 1920s and 1930s:

1. Although highly sedentary and closely tied to relatively small and strictly limited areas of intensive resource exploitation, the Asiatic Eskimo communities preserved an outstanding degree of flexibility in both their size and their structure. This held true for smaller socioeconomic subsets of the community as well, be it village, hunting camp, or boat crew. Such "openness" of social norms governing population density and group formation can be seen as a highly efficient adaptation to environmental conditions of endemic instability and rapidly fluctuating variability in the marine resource base.

2. Even in the most densely populated areas of the subarctic coastal region some unoccupied territories were reserved as buffer zones between neighboring communities. The hunting grounds of village communities that had died out or dispersed were not vigorously exploited for a long time afterward, or were used only as "emergency" hunting grounds in times of necessity by members of adjacent communities.

3. Population dynamics in Eskimo societies were determined, not through deliberate methods of population control (such as infanticide, abortion, or wars), or by a low birth rate, but through the constant mobility of the population and a very high death rate, especially among the able-bodied adult population, who were most vulnerable to famine, epidemics, and hunting accidents.[11]

4. As people advanced in years, they aged quickly and died early. This led to very rapid turnover between generations of a family, and between one food-producing or reproductive cohort and the next. In a nonliterate society this increased the amount and flow of information in the process of socializing children and teenagers, who had to be included in productive activities as early as possible. Simultaneously, the fragility of integenerational transmission of cultural traditions increased. On the one hand, this facilitated rapid incorporation of socioeconomic adjustments and change; on the other, it

meant that old and venerable cultural traditions could be lost almost overnight as a result of epidemics or famine.

5. In conditions of continuous cooperation and mutual assistance, the actual economic units within the communities were the aggregations of the smaller, constant groups of adult male hunters—the boat crews—whose primary task was the hunting of particular areas or resources. The well-being of the entire community, therefore, could be measured not so much by its size and territory as by how many main hunting crews it had to support it, and how cooperatively they worked together.

6. In a normal year, subsistence harvests were intended to exceed the consumption needs of the population by a fair margin. Such overproduction was necessary to create *surplus food reserves,* which served as a kind of insurance in case the hunt failed in the following season or year (Testart 1982: 527). However, this creation of surplus reserves should probably be viewed primarily as a psychosocial strategy of risk management, since it constituted a central motivating force in the social, spiritual, and reproductive life of the hunting community, but did not prove to be a reliable guarantee against starvation during the famines that periodically swept through the area.

7. Traditional maritime hunting primarily targeted the easiest and most accessible prey: calves and juveniles, pregnant and nursing cows, and animals whose mobility was diminished as they lay on ice floes, on hauling-out grounds, or at rookeries. By focusing on this segment of the stock, even more threatened by indigenous hunting through higher losses of wounded or scared animals, the real ecological cost of such predation was far greater than any plain estimation based on the size of aboriginal population or on its technological capabilities would suggest. Therefore, it is entirely possible that depletion of marine resources on a local scale was an entirely common phenomenon in the traditional subsistence system.

This final conclusion is particularly significant. Based on the principle of human-environment stability (ecosystem homeostasis), this kind of human behavior based on regular overexploitation of its resource base inevitably should lead to ecological crisis and collapse of the subsistence system. However, as our reconstructed model shows, this particular ecological-economic relation supported stable reproduction in the Eskimo communities. And, considered in a broader historical context, it maintained a cultural continuum in the Bering Strait area for two thousand years or more.

This, however, returns us to our initial question: to what degree did the contact society in the early twentieth century retain the characteristics of the indigenous subsistence model that existed up until widespread European influence? Obviously, the data from the 1920s and 1930s do not provide quantitative assessments of the precontact subsistence mechanisms because they represent qualitatively different economic and demographic phenomena. But they do establish a basis for our analysis—like a snapshot or a synchronic cross-section of the flow of human activities across space and time, from which one can venture to make "upstream" reconstructions reaching further back into the past with varying degrees of completeness and reliability.

When, however, one relies heavily on indirect data and extrapolation from estimates, and examines resource utilization from the retrospective distance of historical hindsight, actual subsistence trends inevitably become generalized to smooth curves. These create the illusion of stability and "equilibrium" and suggest conscious resource management. As the Eskimo example shows, this apparent stability obscures the dynamic aspect of settlement patterns and the highly spasmodic nature of game supplies and demographic reproduction. In that case, our further task becomes one of making use of archeological or documentary sources to discern what principles of adaptation may have lain beneath the behavior of prehistoric Arctic sea-mammal hunters, and how they resemble or, on the contrary, contrast with those of their postcontact descendants, who hunted in the same waters centuries later. We will embark on this in chapters 6 and 7.

But we have yet another possibility at our disposal: to compare different synchronic models of Arctic resource utilization, that is, to compare the ecological-economic patterns of the sea-mammal hunters of the Chukchi Peninsula with some other contemporary native societies that organize their subsistence along quite different lines. Here, the most insightful comparison would be with the nomadic reindeer herders of northern Siberia, who represent a fundamentally different model of cultural adaptation to the same general Arctic environment.

CHAPTER THREE

Reindeer Pastoralists of the Inland Tundra

Introduction

Numerous ethnographies from the past three centuries have left us a wealth of vivid images of the traditional nomadic reindeer pastoralists of the Eurasian Arctic. Observers deemed them "the healthiest" and the "most prosperous" tribe of Siberian aboriginal peoples, and made much of their apparent economic and social well-being as compared to other native groups (Bogoras 1931:93–94, 1932:33, 1934:19, Gapanovich 1925:51–52, Mel'nikov 1925:161, Patkanov 1911:127, etc.). These tundra nomads were least accessible to the tentacles of Russian administrative power, and demonstrated great determination and resilience in preserving their everyday life and social structure unchanged. The reindeer Chukchi showed themselves both favorably inclined to and well organized for successful military resistance, and, along with the coastal Chukchi and the Eskimos, were the only native peoples of Siberia to rebuff the Cossack troops who swept into the area during the 1700s. Through that they preserved for a century semiautonomous status for themselves within the Russian empire. In spite of diligent efforts by Russian Orthodox missionaries, many groups of reindeer pastoralists—the West Siberian Nenets, the tundra Enets, Nganasan, Chukchi, Koryak, and nomadic Chuvants—staunchly maintained their own spiritual beliefs and rituals and successfully resisted conversion to Christianity throughout the 1800s and early 1900s.

The reindeer herders themselves emphasized the belief that they occupied a special position among the native peoples of Siberia. Some of their folk sayings, such as "Our food walks around us on its own four feet" and "Our food grows even while we sleep" (Bogoras 1931:93, Sergeev 1955:56), reflected how reindeer pastoralism was perceived to be endowed with greater economic stability than other forms of Arctic subsistence, such as land-game hunting and trapping, fishing, or marine-mammal hunting. Reindeer herders never experienced the ravages of famine that visited the coastal communities regularly, and more than once they actually saved the sedentary hunters and fishers from starving to death.

Local household and economic surveys conducted in the 1920s and 1930s, and the Soviet Arctic Economic Census of 1926–27, confirm this traditional image of the reindeer pastoralists as enjoying a relatively high standard of living compared to most sedentary native populations in Siberia. However, with the onset and expansion of collectivization among the tundra population in the mid-1930s, attitudes toward traditional reindeer pastoralism changed. Commentators instead found it expedient to depict the nomadic economy as "archaic" and "backward." They emphasized how thoroughly it was imbued with a spirit of exploitation and "class conflict," and the abject poverty of the great majority of the tundra population. Statistical material on the traditional reindeer-herding economy practically disappeared by the late 1930s and began to filter in again only after the mid-1970s (Golovnev 1986a, b, Konakov 1985, Krupnik 1976a, Lebedev 1978, 1980, Turov 1990, Vasil'ev 1976, etc.). There is thus some highly contemporary and critical value to piecing together subsistence balances for the traditional tundra reindeer economy, in that it allows us to reevaluate this question of its efficiency, and to compare it with other types of native resource use in the Siberian Arctic.

To conduct a quantitative analysis of northern Eurasian reindeer pastoralism throughout its entire extent, however, would be an overly ambitious—and perhaps scientifically injudicious—undertaking for our present purposes. Across the huge spaces of the northern Eurasian tundra, reindeer-breeding societies displayed a remarkable diversity of locally varying ecological and ethnic forms. In reality, northern Eurasian "reindeer nomadism" is more accurately defined as an ecological-economic continuum of human activities in which the reindeer plays a part. At one end of this continuum, we find the large-scale commercial herding of the Izhma Komi with primarily commodity-oriented production for established external markets. At the other would be a variety of complex, relatively diversified systems of multiple-resource use, in which small-herd, free-ranging herding is combined with other subsistence activities. For example, some Chukchi, Nenets, and Saami who pastured their herds closer to littoral areas on the Chukchi Peninsula, Barents Sea and Yamal Peninsula, and Kola Peninsula, respectively, actively engaged in sea-mammal hunting. Most of the Nganasan, the tundra Enets, the northern Sel'kup, Evenk, Yakut, and the tundra Yukagir hunted regularly for wild reindeer (caribou) in addition to breeding domestic herds.

In the former Soviet ethnographic literature, this entire continuum is typically subsumed under the accepted epithet of the "tundra reindeer herding cultural-economic type" (Levin 1947:85, Levin and Cheboksarov 1955:5–6, Levin and Potapov 1956:14, Chesnov 1970:16, Andrianov and Cheboksarov 1972:8). Attempts to analyze it regionally—to identify and sift out local or typological variations—were initiated in the 1920s and 1930s, then abandoned for many years, and have been renewed only recently (Lebedev 1978, 1980, Krupnik 1976a, Golovnev 1986, et al.). However, the labor intensity required for such a task indicates the need for a separate ecological investigation of the variations of traditional Arctic reindeer pastoralism throughout Eurasia, or even a series of such endeavors. V. Charnolusskii, for example, identified roughly twenty variations and degrees of mobility in the annual economic cycle among 1,700 Kola Peninsula Saami in the 1920s, depending upon the pasture area, the herd size, and the availability of other resources (Charnolusskii 1930). Even among the comparatively homogenous group of Yamal Nenets reindeer pastoralists, a minimum of four different local variations of subsistence were observed: "tundra," "Arctic," "southern tundra," and "forest-tundra" (Golovnev 1986:181–85). Countless such maps and richly descriptive classifications of traditional subsistence activities, pasture use, and migration routes in tundra reindeer herding compiled in the 1920s and 1930s have survived to the present intact, and await contemporary ecological interpretation and analysis. Our ultimate goal at present thus should be to piece together an evocative and sensitively detailed map of the variegated local subsistence forms that prevailed within a general loose framework that might be designated most tentatively under the rubric "aboriginal Arctic reindeer pastoralism." This goal is, of course, a long-term one, and, although it provides a well-defined sense of direction for the pages that follow, by no means do I aspire to achieve it immediately.

We can, however, begin to fit together the first pieces of this mas-

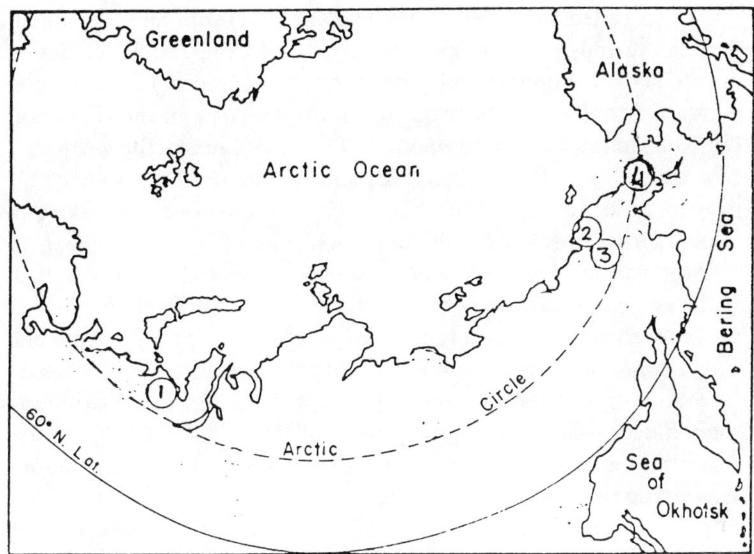

Fig. 10. Location of the Arctic herding populations considered in chapter 3. 1: Ust' Kara Nenets; 2: Kuvet Chukchi; 3: Ichun' Chukchi; 4: Kychaun Chukchi.

sive puzzle, and, as with complex jigsaws, it is usually easiest and most rewarding to start with pieces that form relatively defined corners and borders. Indeed, at opposite ends of the Eurasian North, we find two peoples who illustrate the most highly specialized model of reindeer economy widely practiced in the west and far east of northern Eurasia: the European and West Siberian Nenets, and the Chukchi.[1] This model was characterized by large-scale extensive reindeer herding and a continuously nomadic way of life. The sweeping plains landscape in these particular regions lent itself to large pasture ranges and elongated nomadic routes, and shaped the emergence of the extensive herding model there.

From the full extent of these combined territories, where a total nomadic population of ten to twelve thousand people pursued this type of natural resource exploitation, we will select four smaller areas to examine in greater detail (fig. 10). These include one Nenets territory, the extreme eastern portion of the Bol'shaia Zemlia (Great Land) tundra, the two Chukchi territories of the eastern Chaun lowlands and one on the southeastern Chukchi Peninsula.

The first of these was used in the early 1900s by a mixed community of so-called Kara Nenets, made up of kin groups and individual families variously of Bol'shaia Zemlia, trans-Ural, and Kolva River origin. Most members of this group and their descendents, about six hundred people, now live close to the Arctic coast in the village of Ust'Kara in the Nenets Autonomous Okrug, located at the northeast edge of European Russia. I reconstructed the traditional resource utilization model of these Kara Nenets based on interviews conducted with elderly informants in the summer of 1974.

Archival and literary materials of the 1920s and 1930s, coupled with my field data of 1975 and 1977, formed my primary sources on the latter three subareas of reindeer Chukchi. For the Chaun Chukchi I also made use of a parish household record made by the Russian Orthodox missionary Andrei Argentov in 1850. For information on the reindeer pastoralists of the Chukchi Peninsula, I used oral histories from the older generation of reindeer herders and coastal hunters now living in the villages of Sireniki, New Chaplino, and Yanrakynnot. This last group is especially interesting because it maintained direct and regular contact with the residents of the Eskimo villages that were the subject of the preceding chapter. Thus, it affords us a fascinating opportunity to examine from the perspectives of both the sedentary and nomadic populations what role interactions between the tundra reindeer herding and coastal marine-mammal-hunting economies played in the native subsistence system.

Reindeer Nomadism and Its Resource Strategies

Thanks to the early reports of ethnographers and travelers, and the later statistical records of the 1920s and 1930s, traditional tundra reindeer herding has been described more fully and in more detail than any other type of aboriginal economy in the Eurasian Arctic.[2] We will summarize here only those aspects that pertain directly to reconstructing the traditional subsistence balances that follow.

In contrast to the sea-mammal-hunting communities, where cooperative hunting and butchering of the catch contributed to a relatively even distribution of the primary food items—marine-animal meat, blubber, and oil—the nomadic community did not function as an integrated social and economic unit. Domestic reindeer were owned as private property by the individual household, usually headed by the oldest able-bodied male. Thus, the welfare of each family—that is, its economic strength and prosperity—depended directly on the size of the owner's herd. Statistical records from the 1920s and 1930s clearly show how even the amount of food people ate varied greatly between wealthy and poor households. Among the European Nenets, poor families consumed about ninety kilograms of reindeer meat a year, which was equal to only 43 percent of what wealthy families ate (Ekonomika Bol'shezemel'skoi tundry 1934:180). Converted into calories, this constituted less than one-eighth of a family's annual energy consumption needs. This disparity was even larger among other nomadic groups. Among the reindeer Chukchi, wealthy families ate 2.5 times more reindeer meat than poor ones, and wealthy Koryak herd owners ate 3 times as much as poor ones (Bilibin 1933:39, Garusov 1967:55).

Accordingly, subsistence balances for the traditional herding economy must be reconstructed based on differential levels of production and consumption for each basic economic stratum. Directly prior to collectivization, 5 to 10 percent of the richest families owned the largest portion of the reindeer stock—from 30 to 40 percent among the Bol'shaia Zemlia Nenets, and 50 to 70 percent among the Chaun tundra and Chukchi Peninsula Chukchi (see Anadyrskii krai 1935:36, Arkhincheev 1957:74, Babushkin 1930:159, Plettsov 1925:12, Shmit 1939:6). Two-thirds of the remaining pastoralist households owned too few reindeer to make it economically feasible or worthwhile to herd them independently. For most of these people, the only way to survive was to enter into an inequitable partnership with a wealthy family to pasture their herds cooperatively. In return for their labor, the members of the poorer family received a share of the yield from the richer herder's stock.[3] The other alternative was to engage actively in hunting, trapping, and/or fishing, in order to maximize the amount of food or trade products obtained from the family's exploited territory.

The first of these methods was much more prevalent among the reindeer Chukchi, while the European Nenets leaned heavily toward the second. In either case, the nomadic community functioned as a loosely connected alliance of relatively independent camp units. Each family and herding camp moved within its own microcosmic environment, and had its own microvariations of subsistence practices depending upon the size of the herd, the number of its members fit for herding, the nature and level of their herding skills, and even particular family habits or traditions. In sum, the main characteristics to be kept in mind for the traditional subsistence system of Arctic herdsmen are the *disparity* in how local environmental resources were used and the striking *inequality* with which the products of those resources were consumed.

However, one general tendency held quite strictly and constantly true: the more reindeer a family owned, the more focused it was on herding, and the less importantly hunting, fishing, gathering, and marine-mammal hunting figured in its subsistence. And, inversely, the fewer reindeer a household owned, the more fully its members tried to extract the maximum value of all the resources of their own territory: fish, fowl, fur-bearing and game animals, marine mammals, edible plants and berries. In contrast, owners of large herds tended not to engage in any significant hunting or fishing for themselves, preferring instead to trade reindeer meat, skins, or live reindeer for any food items they needed (*Krainii Sever* 1935 : 56–64, Krupnik 1976a:75–76, Lebedev 1978 : 24–25, Sergeev 1955 : 20).

Within the parameters of this general rule, there were specific local cultural and historical differences between the subsistence systems of the Nenets and Chukchi. Among the Nenets herders, for instance, fishing was the next most important form of livelihood, supporting the existence of poor families throughout most of the year. Fishing held no such importance for the Chukchi herders, especially among their northern and northwestern branches, located closer to the Arctic Ocean. In their diet its role was filled by marine-mammal meat and blubber, which the herders usually obtained from the coastal hunters in exchange for reindeer products. In addition, many poor Chukchi pastoralist families hunted for marine mammals for their own personal consumption. On the other hand, marine hunting was weakly developed among the reindeer Nenets, with the exception of the few semisedentary residents of the Barents and Kara Sea coasts, (see chapter 6), and even there it was conducted for purposes of trade only, not for personal food consumption (Golovnev 1988, Krupnik 1976a).

There were also considerable differences in the role plant gathering played among the two nomad groups. Edible plants constituted a very important part of the Chukchi diet, and almost every family put away up to 100 to 150 kilograms of berries, leaves, and stems of tundra plants. On the other hand, edible plants played a minimal role in the diet of the Nenets herders (Krupnik 1976a:71–72). However, the Nenets used a large quantity of purchased foods, such as flour, bread, crackers, sugar, and butter. Imported food goods were introduced to the European and West Siberian Nenets beginning in the sixteenth and seventeenth centuries. In the late 1700s it was estimated that the annual consumption of flour among the European Nenets per capita was already up to 80 to 160 kilograms, which leveled off at about 130 kilograms per capita in the mid-1800s (Bakhrushin 1956:87, Islavin 1848:33, Lepekhin 1805:227, Voprosy i otvety 1787:33). By the early 1900s the average Yamal Nenets family of six bought 1,000 kilograms of flour to bake bread, 80 kilograms of butter, and 30 kilograms of sugar a year (Evladov 1927:8). These and other characteristics of the subsistence of the reindeer herders are well-reflected in the statistical sources of the 1920s and 1930s.

Land Use and Pasture Rotation

According to several early references, traditional Arctic reindeer herding abided by a relatively stable land-use system with fixed or long-term active pasture sites and nomadic routes.[4] As among the sedentary marine hunters, the basic functional unit of land use was the *community*. In this case, the community was a local nomadic group, based either on coresidence and herding cooperation, as was the practice among the European Nenets and Chukchi, or, less often, on patrilineal clan ties, as among the Yamal Nenets. In certain regions, however, such as Kolguev Island and Yamal Peninsula, pastures within a local group's territory were explicitly assigned to individual households (Brodnev 1959:71, Podekrat 1936:73–74, Zhilinkskii 1923:47, Zhitkov 1913:206–207). In any case, within the boundaries of the group's territory each herding camp or individual herder had its "own" pastures and base camping place for summer grazing, and for the annual roundup, slaughter, and festival in the fall. By customary right, the same people might hold tenure to these places for a very long time.

The traditional land-use system among the tundra pastoralists was based upon the common law of nomadic peoples, however, it was also reasonably flexible.[5] There are reports that the migration routes and all possible changes in pasture use were determined by the herders on the basis of reciprocal arrangements, usually for one or two seasons and as much as a year ahead (Popov 1952:4, Shmit 1939:92, Zhilinskii 1923:46). Infractions of long-established boundaries were encountered extremely rarely and presupposed certain punishments.

However, these were not always enforced. Attaching particular territories to pastoralist communities, herding groups, and even especially powerful individual herders was also actively supported by the Russian tsarist administrators prior to 1917, who saw it as an opportunity to govern and collect taxes more efficiently from the nomadic population.

Thus, the smallest human unit in the traditional land-use system was sometimes an individual family, but more usually the herding group, or camp. The herding camp was a temporary or long-term aggregation of 2 to 5 families, or roughly 10 to 25 people, usually related to each other by blood, marriage, or by established partnership. A group of 8 to 12 camps from the same general vicinity (100 to 250 people) formed the next larger social unit of subsistence. Waldemar Bogoras, who named this amalgamation of herding groups literally a "neighborhood," reported that the families that went into one were almost always constellations of relatives, "branching off from one common root" and connected through marriage and traditions of mutual aid (Bogoras 1931:97, 1941:192). Families and camps of herders pasturing their herds in one river basin or in reference to a single central point, such as a trading post (usually from 200 to 600 people), formed a higher-level social grouping, which normally had its own name and local consciousness. These groups formed the base of regional subethnic stratification of the nomadic indigenous nations. Boris Dolgikh was the first to dub such entities "territorial groups" and to map their territories in Central Siberia as of 1926–27 (Dolgikh 1946:57–59, 1949:74, Dolgikh and Levin 1951:105–106). Continuing in this vein, Burch subsequently accomplished the same task for the entire Arctic area (Burch 1983), while Vasil'ev, Sokolova, and Tugolukov (1983) recently produced a summary list of such "ethnoterritorial groupings" among all the indigenous peoples of the Russian Arctic and Siberia.

The primary social unit of traditional subsistence used in this study should probably be considered to be the *group of neighboring herding camps*, which for the time studied was in effect a communality of neighbors related by blood and marriage. It was this relatively stable economic and demographic collective that implemented and regulated tenure over its territory, including the annual herding routes and grazing pastures allotted to individual camps and families. These latter experienced more rapid turnover in their internal composition, and formed the most flexible and subordinate element of the community. Significantly, similarly to the village communities of settled sea-mammal hunters, in the 1920s and 1930s it was these groupings of adjacent camps that came to serve as the basic link in local administration and Soviet economic reorganization of the nomadic population, such as the "native," then nomadic soviets, or executive committees, and cooperatives. Their average population was about 120 to 180 people (with an actual range of 60 to 300) grouped into some 5 to 12 more or less permanent camp aggregations. In sum, the total number of such units of traditional nomadic subsistence was about 50 to 70 for the entire population of reindeer Chukchi, about 40 to 50 among the Bol'shaia Zemlia Nenets and Komi from the Pechora to the Kara River, and roughly the same number for the Nenets nomads of the adjacent part of northwestern Siberia, including Yamal Peninsula.

The data from local inventories conducted in the 1920s and 1930s contain rich descriptions of the physical geography of the tundra herders' territories.[6] These inventories were the first to document in detail the traditional land-use systems of reindeer pastoralism, which continued unchanged right up until the enactment of Soviet collectivization policy in the late 1930s and 1940s. The essence of this system lay in the regular, sequential alternation of seasonally used pastures during the winter, early and late spring, summer, and so forth. Within the boundaries of their resource territories, the herders completed annually repeating migration circuits. In the plains area of the Arctic tundra these migrations were typically meridional; that is, in the lengthening days of spring the herders set out northward from tree line to spend the summer near or on the Arctic Sea coast, and then retraced their journey south again in the fall.

The length of the annual migration of different pastoralist groups seems to have been determined primarily by the width of the tundra zone where they lived, that is, by the distance between the northern edge of the forest and the Arctic Sea coast. For the European Nenets, tree line fell further south and this distance increased as one progressed from west to east: from 150 to 200 kilometers in the westernmost Kanin-Timan tundra, to 450 to 600 kilometers in the eastern regions of the Bol'shaia Zemlia tundra in the northern trans-Urals (Semerikov 1933:6–8, Terletskii 1934:43). In contrast, the length of the Chukchi reindeer herders' annual migration increased in the same manner from east to west, as one moves deeper into the heart of continental Siberia. On the Chukchi Peninsula, it was only 50 to 100 kilometers; it increased to 100 to 150 kilometers in the upper Anadyr'

River basin, and reached a maximum of 200 to 400 kilometers in the western Chaun tundra (Anadyrskii krai 1935:40, Shmit 1939:56, Vdovin 1965:159, author's field data 1975). However, within every herding neighborhood there was another, highly noticeable disparity in pastoral migration, which was that wealthier families usually migrated much farther than did poorer ones.

If the migration route was longer than 150 or 200 kilometers, the nomads usually spent four to five months in the winter pastures, where they moved the herd only a short way once or twice a month, depending on the size of the herd. They spent two to three months in the summer and early-spring pastures with approximately the same mobility, and three to four months on the migration routes, in transit from one seasonal pasture area to another.[7] During the latter months of the year, with the exception of brief breaks for calving, slaughter days or festivals, the herds might progress along their route as much as fifteen kilometers or more a day. With such extended nomadic tracks, only the staple summer and winter pastures were fixed, and sometimes also the calving and slaughter grounds. On the other hand, the migration paths from one pasturing area to another were used simultaneously by several herding groups and various north-south routes could be chosen alternately from year to year depending upon the weather or grazing conditions in a given year.

The tenure system of winter and summer pastures was abandoned only in extremely hard years, when herding families in flight from heavy snowfalls, winter thaws, lack of fodder, or epizootics gathered in the well-known pastoral "refugia" for each region (see Babushkin 1930:65, Shmit 1939:22) or left the area completely to use the lands of groups to whom they were related. Thus, stable tenure over pasture lands in the traditional land-use system hinged upon making allowance for short-term shifts in the right to use those lands during emergency situations. This also was regulated by pastoralist common law and by prevailing social norms of intra- and inter-community mutual aid and reciprocity (Brodnev 1959:71, author's field data 1974, 1975).

The choice and quality of the winter pastures were evaluated by the herders according to ease of grazing, the nutritional quality of the deer fodder, and the distance to the winter fairs and trading posts. Additional requirements for summer pastures were considered to include proximity to sources of firewood and water, the abundance of mosquitoes, and the risk of epizootics. Since the summer fishing, hunting, and marine hunting season played an important role in the annual subsistence cycle of most herding families, summer pasture sites near "fishing" rivers and lakes were key landmarks in the permanent system of group and family territories. Not surprisingly, if herders found a place that met all their criteria for summer pastures, they showed a strong preference for using the same sites from year to year (Semerikov 1933:5, Shmit 1939:54). As one of the best experts on Nenets lifestyle commented, "Each reindeer herder takes up his own particular places on the fishing lakes, from which one owner or another catches fish from year to year" (Evladov 1929:55). Elderly Nenets herders I interviewed in Ust' Kara in 1974 could almost always name where specific families grazed their summer herds in the 1920s and 1930s, and described topographic features of these places, even after they had lived continuously in the village and not seen those places for as much as twenty-five years.

We can estimate the density of the nomadic population and its impact on the environment based on data from the 1920s' and 1930s' inventories of large administrative districts and individual herding groups (that is, the "native" or "nomadic" soviets). Among the European Nenets, population density was 0.025 to 0.038 per square kilometer, while the Chukchi showed a much lower density of 0.008 to 0.013.[8] This means that the average size of a territory used by a pastoralist community of some one hundred to two hundred people was 3,000 to 8,000 square kilometers for the Nenets and 8,000 to 15,000 square kilometers in the Chukchi tundra area.

The calculated stock density was also 1.5 to 2 times lower among the Chukchi than among the European Nenets or Komi, who maintained 30 to 90 reindeer and 80 to 120 reindeer per one hundred square kilometers of forage land, respectively (see *Anadyrskii krai* 1935:33, Gassovskii 1939:26, Ioffe 1937:13–17, Shmit 1939:5–6, Vasil'ev 1936:10–14). The herd density is considered to be determined by the biological productivity of the tundra pastures, and usually corresponds to the maximum carrying capacity of the *limiting* element in the pasture rotation cycle, that is, those seasonal-profile types of pasture that were in the shortest supply (Andreev et al. 1935:352–53, Iudin 1969:8). Exceeding this carrying capacity inevitably led to overgrazing, deterioration of the fodder, and subsequent malnutrition and losses of reindeer from starvation in the next hard year to come. Thus, after an initial jump in recruitment, the herd size fell back to or even below its former level.

There were three salient differences, then, between these two ethnic groups of Arctic reindeer herders chosen here for subsistence analysis. Among the European Nenets the population density was three times higher, herd density was twice as high, and the size of a herding community's territory was substantially smaller than among the reindeer Chukchi. These are proxy indicators of apparently different adaptive strategies by two reindeer-herding peoples, both equally representative of a single cultural-economic type and an outwardly similar system of subsistence traditions.

Demography of the Nomadic Community

Unfortunately, we have access to far fewer statistical records pertaining to the demographic structure and dynamics of the tundra pastoralists than for the sedentary peoples of the Russian Arctic. Household lists for the nineteenth and early twentieth centuries exist for isolated groups only, as up until the early twentieth century they are represented primarily by tax registers focused on able-bodied males, or by parish records. Civil registration of births and deaths in the nomadic Arctic population started in most Siberian districts only in the 1930s and 1940s, and remained highly erratic and sketchy right up until the 1950s. As a result, the basic demographic characteristics of the traditional Arctic pastoralists often can be gleaned only indirectly by computation and interpolation.

In tables 12 and 13, age-sex structure data drawn from various lists and censuses of sometimes-overlapping and/or partial samples are shown for the European Nenets from 1883 to 1932, and for the reindeer Chukchi from 1850 to 1937. As shown, both pastoralist populations display a relatively high percentage of children (40 to 45 percent), and an inflated percentage of elderly people (6 to 10 percent), especially in comparison to the sedentary coastal hunters, but a correspondingly lower share of adults of working and reproductive age. In effect, this means that, within the traditional reindeer-herding subsistence system, every adult working male bore a greater burden for supporting a larger number of nonproductive members of the community than was the case among the coastal hunters.

The contrast in proportion of men to women between the Nenets and Chukchi is even more striking, especially among adults. Among Nenets adults (ages 16 to 59), there were from 110 to 115 men for every 100 women. For the reindeer Chukchi (and Koryaks, too) the figures

TABLE 12
Demographic Parameters of Nenets Herding Population, 1883–1932

	1883	1897	1920	1926	1932
1. Total sample population	421	2759	1612	1325	1022
2. Average household size	NA	NA	NA	6.6	5.9
3. % males	51.8	52.7	53.3	52.9	52.0
4. % females	48.2	47.3	46.7	47.1	48.0
5. % population of working age, 16–59	57.2	59.0	53.5	50.9	47.2
6. Number of women per 100 males, age 16–59	91.2	86.3	93.0	87.3	92.3
7. % children under age of 16	32.3	32.6	44.5	43.3	45.5
8. % elders over age of 60	10.5	8.4	4.4	5.8	10.3
9. % adult males	29.9	31.7	27.7	27.2	26.3
10. Mouths to feed per adult male	3.3	3.2	3.6	3.7	3.8
11. Number of girls per 100 boys under age of 9	87.5	93.2	72.9	104.2	95.7

SOURCES OF DATA FOR CALCULATIONS: 1883: Kanin Tundra (Yakobii 1893); 1897: Bol'shaia Zemlia Tundra (Babushkin 1930); 1920: Pechora Nenets District (Babushkin 1930); 1926: Bol'shaia Zemlia Tundra (Babushkin 1930); 1932: Bol'shaia Zemlia Tundra (Nenets and Komi, Ekonomika Bol'shezemel'skoi tundry (1934).

are exactly reversed—88 to 90 men per 100 women. Comparison of this indicator among a larger number of North Eurasian indigenous peoples argues against considering this to be a function or artifice of reindeer pastoralism: the sex ratio among the reindeer Chukchi resembled that of their marine-mammal-hunting Chukchi and Eskimo neighbors, while the ratio found among the Nenets approximated the sex ratio among the Sel'kup and Nganasan, who lived near them but were engaged in caribou hunting and small-scale herding. Therefore, it would seem that the differences between Nenets and Chukchi sex ratios were probably more a function of culture and genetics than a reflection of particular human-environmental adaptations of an economic nature.

Based on this demographic structure, we can proceed to reconstruct the average age-sex composition of the pastoralist community. A median Nenets herding group of about 150 people would have included 33 to 35 adult working men, 3 to 5 adolescents, 30 adult women, 8 to 12 elders, and 65 to 70 children under 16 years old. Roughly the same picture would hold true for the Chukchi nomadic neighborhood, but with the ratio between adult men and women reversed.

As we recall, however, the herding community did not form a compact group and was divided into eight to twelve independent

TABLE 13
Demographic Parameters of Chukchi Herding Population, 1850–1937

	1850	1926	1926	1933	1937
1. Total sample population	1385	2081	268	138	1411
2. Average household size	4.1	NA	5.8	NA	4.6
3. % males	51.2	48.0	46.0	44.8	47.2
4. % females	48.8	52.0	54.0	55.2	52.8
5. % population of working age, 16–59	51.8	50.8	38.4	51.3	55.3
6. Number of women per 100 males, age 16–59	102.0	109.9	123.9	122.2	122.7
7. % children under age 16	44.6	40.8	NA	42.3	38.3
8. % elders	3.5	8.4	NA	6.5	6.7
9. % adult male	25.7	24.2	17.2	23.1	23.7
10. Mouths to feed per adult male	3.9	4.1	5.8	4.3	4.2
11. Number of girls per 100 boys under age of 10	92.5	106.2	NA	110.0	131.6

SOURCES OF DATA FOR CALCULATIONS: 1850: Chaun Chukchi (Argentov 1850); 1926: Chukotski District (*Poselennye itogi* 1928); 1926: Chaun Native Council (*Itogi perepisi* 1929); 1933: Ichun' community (Arkhincheev 1957); 1937: Chaun District (Shmit 1939).

microunits or camps. Census data from the 1920s and 1930s show that the average Chukchi camp numbered 20.7 people and consisted of 4 families or households (3.8 to be exact), while the Nenets herders' camp comprised only 2.5 family units, or 13.6 individuals (cf. *Itogi Perepisi* 1929:74–85, *Krainii Sever* 1935:114–21). This means that, for pastoral life and work, the Chukchi nomadic group usually was divided into fewer but larger units than a Nenets community of the same size. In addition, the Nenets also showed a higher number of small camps consisting of members of only one family (40 percent in 1933). That the Chukchi camps were larger and more permanent than the Nenets' appears to be explained in two ways. First, each Chukchi camp had larger reindeer herds, roughly one thousand animals per camp as opposed to four hundred to five hundred among the Nenets; and second, the Chukchi had a lower proportion of adult working males in their population, which engendered a shortage of herders.

The high percentage of children in the tundra pastoralist communities, combined with a striking differential between young age cohorts, attests to a high birth rate, very high infant mortality, and rapid intergenerational turnover in the population. This conclusion is confirmed by fragments of information available about reproduction in the nomadic population. According to data from a series of inventories in the 1920s and 1930s, the cumulative birth rate among the Nenets herders was fifty to sixty-five per thousand. Taking into account the low relative proportion of women of childbearing age (18 to 20 percent), this rate was close to the physiological maximum. It was associated with a very high rate of mortality of forty to sixty per thousand, especially among newborns and infants, 30 to 50 percent of whom never survived their first year (*Krainii Sever* 1935:9–15, Plettsov 1925:14, *Pokhoziaistvennaia Perepis'* 1929:226–27). According to genealogies compiled for the Ust' Kara Nenets in the 1920s and 1930s, each woman gave birth to an average of eight to nine children, but as in the coastal hunting villages, only two to three of them survived to maturity. All the same, in relatively favorable years when epidemics or natural hazards did not strike, the nomads could achieve an annual growth rate on the level of 0.5 to 1.0 percent.

Owing to the absence of similar demographic data, indicators of natural increase among the reindeer Chukchi can be determined only indirectly. Thus, according to censuses of the Chaun Chukchi in 1850 and 1937, the calculated average size of a one-year cohort of children under eight years old consisted of 30 to 35 individuals per 1,000 of total population (see Argentov 1850, Shmit 1939:148). Given that not less than 30 to 35 percent of Chukchi infants died before they were a year old,[9] the actual birth rate was probably closer to 50 or 55 percent. That places the Chukchi birth rate at a level similar to or slightly under that observed among the European Nenets. Based on Argentov's family register, of 53 newborn infants and children less than one year old who were recorded in 1850 for a group of 1,350 Chaun reindeer Chukchi, 23 percent were the firstborn child in their families, 21 percent a second child, 46 percent were third or fourth, and 10 percent were the fifth or more, up to a seventh child in one family, who was born to a 47-year-old mother. These figures support the highly authoritative opinion of Waldemar Bogoras that the reindeer Chukchi's fertility and overall stamina were the highest compared to all other neighboring peoples (Bogoras 1904:35, 1932:33).

Early ethnographies and records registered no trace that the tundra pastoralists limited population growth by any artificial means. Here Bogoras made a special point of emphasizing that the practice of infanticide was absent among the Chukchi (Bogoras 1904:48, 1907:513); Jochelson also found no evidence of it among the reindeer Koryaks (Jochelson 1908). There are no reports of widespread infanticide among other traditional reindeer pastoralists of Arctic Siberia, such as the Dolgan, Nganasan, Enets, etc. (Afanas'eva 1980, Dolgikh 1954, Popov 1946). Instead, names of twins, including both boys and girls among the Enets (Dolgikh 1954:39), or recorded instances, among the Dolgan, for example, where babies born prematurely at seven or eight months were nurtured and kept (Popov 1946:53) seem more to argue against the existence of infanticide among the native peoples of northern Siberia, or, at any rate, against its practice in those situations in which it was typically encountered among Eskimos of the American Arctic.

Judging by the household lists, demographic pyramids, and genealogical charts, the main mortality peaks in the Chukchi population occurred at three points: during the first years of life, from forty to forty-five, and from fifty-five to sixty-five. Bogoras explicitly noted the large number of old people in the herders' camps and their extreme old age in comparison to the coastal villages (Bogoras 1931:99–100, 1934:21). The lower proportion of adult men should probably be interpreted as an idiosyncrasy of Chukchi herding practices and of the extremely rigorous conditions for the herders there. As is well known, the Chukchi did not have herd dogs, nor did they use reindeer to pull sleds in the summer months. For one-third of the year, men guided the herds across the tundra by foot, and carried their possessions with them on their backs. All this drastically increased the physical burden on a herder's life, and led to increased mortality among them. Nonetheless, as with the Nenets, in good years free from epidemics and natural catastrophes to disrupt or destroy the annual life cycle or customary pasture routes, the high birth rate could easily lead to rapid natural increase among the reindeer Chukchi.

This reproductive model baldly contradicts long-standing widespread assertions that reindeer peoples were "dying out" or their populations leveling off because they had lower fertility or were incapable of rapid population growth (*Itogi Perepisi* 1929:ii–iv, Krasil'nikov 1928:97–100, Patkanov 1911:130, Sergeev 1934:32, Terletskii 1932a:48, 51). It is true that, according to the early censuses and surveys, both the European Nenets and reindeer Chukchi populations were relatively stable (see chapter 5). But this only means that the main factor in population growth among the Arctic nomads was not low birth rates but the sharp surges in mortality in individual adverse years. Therefore, we have here the same type of traditional demographic dynamics as in the communities of the settled maritime hunters described in the previous chapter.

Domestic Animal Stocks

The entire welfare of the Arctic pastoralists and their sole means of mobility and survival in the harsh tundra environment lay in their *domestic reindeer*. Each Nenets and Chukchi household maintained on the average from 180 to 250 of them, while a mid-sized pastoralist community of eight to twelve neighboring camps might account for a cumulative herd stock of 5,000 to 10,000 reindeer. Exact figures for certain districts, ethnic groups, and/or local communities are to be derived from various Russian sources of the 1920s and 1930s (Babushkin 1926, Gassovskii 1939, Druri 1933, *Itogi Perepisi* 1929, *Naselennye punkty* 1928, Plettsov 1925, Shmit 1939, etc.).

The domestic reindeer stocks experienced annual cyclical fluctuations in both numbers and biomass, which were controlled by human intervention in natural reproductive processes. The herders regulated both the age-sex structure of the grazing herds and their size, which reached a maximum in the summer months and a minimum in spring during the calving period. After the spring calving the number of deer usually increased sharply (e.g., by 50 percent); by the following spring, after a full annual cycle was completed, it dropped back down to its original level (see Terletskii 1932b). This fluctuation was more pronounced among the large-herd owners, with a greater initial surge in the spring, followed by sharper drops occasioned by the summer and autumn slaughters for reindeer skins and meat for trade. To a significant degree all these elements of domestic reindeer population dynamics were inherited from the ecology of wild northern reindeer, which was only partially altered by humans through the process of domestication and controlled grazing. And, of course, natural factors—epizootics, spring thaws and crust ice, freeze periods or snowfalls during the spring calving—could all sharply decrease the stock in a very short time and drastically change its subsequent annual dynamics for several years to come.

Sources from the 1920s and 1930s provide data clearly illustrating how the age-sex composition and total productivity of reindeer herds characteristically differed between wealthier and poorer herders, and these differences were typical for all Arctic nomads.[10] In the herds of less well-to-do families, not less than one-fourth of the herd, and sometimes from 30 to 40 percent, were adult male harness deer, and annual recruitment was relatively low, not more than 35 to 40 percent of the original herd size. Prosperous households, on the other hand, could maintain more breeding does and as a result achieve a higher calving rate of 50 to 55 percent.

During a typical year, a tundra reindeer herd might increase on the average by 10 to 15 percent of its initial size. Theoretically, this should have led to a large productive surplus for the herders. However, according to some estimates, traditional subsistence herding was at best only two-thirds as productive as what was considered theoretically possible within a system of rational, commercially oriented management (Preobrazhenskii 1953, Rochev 1969).

Dogs were incomparably less significant than reindeer in the subsistence system of the tundra herders. Statistically speaking, dogs played an approximately equal role in Nenets and Chukchi life—3.47 per family among the Bol'shaia Zemlia Nenets, and 3.68 among the western reindeer Chukchi (*Pokhoziaistvennaia Perepis'* 1929:129, 134). But the basic purposes to which the use of dogs was oriented were different and produced contrasting patterns in how dogs were distributed among the families or herders' camps. The Nenets primarily raised dogs to herd the deer. Therefore, almost every household had herd dogs, and the larger the reindeer stock grew, the more dogs were needed. In contrast, the Chukchi used dogs for transportation, not herding, so they primarily had sled dogs, and in fact the number of dogs in a given camp was more likely to inversely reflect the size of the herd—the fewer reindeer, the more sled dogs a camp normally kept. In principle, each Chukchi herders' camp needed one full dogsled team, or eight to ten animals, but the actual distribution by families and camps was highly uneven.

Food for the dogs came from the scraps and waste products of cleaning fish and butchering reindeer. The majority of herders, whether Nenets or Chukchi, did not prepare any special winter supplies of dog food. For our purposes this means that, in contrast to the model of the coastal hunting villages, we cannot identify dogs as a separate line item in building the subsistence balances of the reindeer-herding community.

Subsistence Implements and Their Recycling

The ceaselessly mobile way of life of the tundra pastoralists left a heavy imprint on the development of their material culture, encouraging a significant simplification of the procurement equipment they used in their work and daily life. The only essential tools in a reindeer herder's kit were his thong lasso, and, if he were Chukchi, a special herder's staff. It was considered that the best lassos were made from bearded seal skin, which the reindeer herders obtained through trade with the coastal sea hunters. If bearded seal skin was not available, then lassos were made from strips of reindeer hide.

By the late 1800s all tundra reindeer herders had obtained firearms. The Nenets obtained theirs from Russians, and the Chukchi primarily from Americans. However, they possessed far fewer guns than the marine-mammal hunters of the coastal villages had. In 1926, there was roughly 1 gun for every whole herding family—the Bol'shaia Zemlia Nenets had 1.2 and the Chaun Chukchi 1.1 (*Itogi perepisi* 1929:74–81, *Pokhoziaistvennaia Perepis'* 1929:33–37). Because of the weak development of hunting, the role of firearms in pastoralist subsistence was minimal and the demand for ammunition was not great.

The reindeer pastoralists used a very limited range of manufactured iron tools and implements, even into the early twentieth century (see Bogoras 1904:209–14, Khomich 1966:82–84). Traps, axes, and other items were obtained directly from traveling traders or indirectly through sedentary communities. The herders usually manufactured their own sleds, boats, and other wooden items, however the Nenets sometimes bought finished wooden boats from the Russians, Khanty, or Komi. Since the late 1800s, the Nenets made fishing nets and seines from Russian-made horsehair twine. Chukchi herders used handmade thong nets for catching small seals, and nets made from reindeer sinew or thin strips of reindeer hide for fishing, as well as weirs and hooks.

The main mode of transportation available to the herders was, of course, reindeer-drawn sleds, and each household had a fairly large number of them. The Bol'shaia Zemlia Nenets had on the average twenty-five per family, and the Chaun Chukchi seventeen to twenty (*Itogi Perepisi* 1929:74–81, *Pokhoziaistvennaia Perepis'* 1929:33–37). In addition, each Chukchi camp maintained one or two dogsleds. The herders themselves used primitive tools to make all their own sleds, which did not have any iron parts. Larch, fir, or birch was used for making sleds, boats, and skinboats (as well as the frame poles for the portable tent dwellings). This wood was gathered during the winter pasturing along the northern edge of the forest or during special long-distance trips once every two or three years. Dogsled harnesses were made from reindeer hide and thongs of bearded seal skin. The bone parts were crafted from reindeer antler or bone, or, in rare instances, from the tusks of walrus or woolly mammoth.

The pastoralists made clothing, footwear, tent coverings, and bedding from domestic reindeer skins. Every family usually had two sets of coverings for the portable, wooden-framed dwelling, which the Nenets called a *chum*, and the Chukchi, *yaranga*. One was for winter and the other for summer, although the summer ones were usually simply winter ones that had begun to show the signs of wear and tear. Nenets families whose annual migrations brought them closer to the forest, usually made summer coverings for the *chum* by sewing large panels of boiled birchbark together with reindeer sinew. The birchbark was gathered during the winter grazing period or obtained through trade with the more southerly located Khanty. According to interviews with elders, such coverings lasted at least ten to fifteen years; being light, durable, and waterproof, they were considered far superior to summer covers of reindeer skin, which had to be changed every two or three years.

Every year, all herders tried to sew a full suit of new fur clothing for winter, and footwear for every member of the family from the skins of young deer killed in the autumn. Rich Chukchi herders might even have two new suits each winter, and then, after wearing one a bit, exchange it in the coastal villages or Russian settlements (Bogoras 1941:178–79). Beginning in the late 1800s, the Nenets, and slightly later the Chukchi, began to fashion their outer summer garments from manufactured fabrics such as cotton or worsted broadcloth bought from Russian traders. Izhma Komi and Kolva Nenets pastoralists, who were probably the most acculturated among the northern nomads, sewed almost all their summer clothing from manufactured cloth. Chukchi herders made their own sealskin boots from the skins of animals they caught themselves during the summer, or obtained the materials, ready-made uppers, or finished boots through trade with marine-mammal hunters.

We see from this brief summary that, by the time studied, numerous imported trade goods and items formed a regular part of life in the subsistence activities of tundra nomads, as well as certain raw materials obtained from the settled communities. Nonetheless, the traditional economy of the Nenets and especially of the Chukchi maintained a distinctive degree of autonomy and almost completely sufficed to meet all the community's consumption needs based on indigenous production alone.

Consumption Needs of the Pastoralist Community

To calculate the herders consumption needs for all the basic elements of life, I proceeded to establish estimates of community demands for food, skins, fuel, and trade goods. In order to arrive ultimately at balance results that could be compared, I used the same methodology that I used in chapter 2 above to construct subsistence balances for the Eskimo sea-mammal hunters.

Food. Several estimates can be found in the literature of the actual caloric content of the diet of various northern herders, including the Nenets, Chukchi, Saami, and others (Alekseeva et al. 1972:24–25, Astrinskii and Navasardov 1970:205–207, Danishevskii 1968:102–105, Dobronravova and Kuindzhi 1962:112–14, Zaitsev 1970:200, Øgrim 1970:50, etc.). However, to achieve the best comparability of results, I concluded it would be better to employ the same norms as were accepted for Eskimo maritime subsistence. Thus, the norms adopted were 3,000 kilocalories per day for adult males, 2,500 for women and elderly people, and 2,000 for children. Based upon the age-sex community structure outlined above,[11] the average daily norm for reindeer pastoralists worked out to 2425 kilocalories per day for the Nenets and 2,400 for the Chukchi, or 885,125 and 876,000 kilocalories per year respectively. As with the Eskimo case, we will make things easier on ourselves and proceed to work with a round figure of 900,000 kilocalories per year.

The food of choice among all tundra herders was indisputably domestic reindeer meat, followed by the internal organs and blood of a freshly killed deer. The total caloric content from the carcass of one adult deer, including forty kilograms of meat and twenty-five kilograms of other edible parts, can be estimated at 52,100 kilocalories. One calf represents 47,100 kilocalories, including thirty kilograms of meat and fifteen kilograms of internal organs.[12] Taking into account that in the past the reindeer herders tried to kill primarily younger deer for meat, or older or weak animals, we can take 49,000 kilocalories as an average figure for one deer. This means that if all food consumption needs were satisfied by the products of reindeer husbandry, it would require killing 18.5 deer a year for every member of the family, be it 17 adults or 19 calves, or, assuming an average family of 5.5, 95 to 100 reindeer per household per year.

We cross-checked this calculation against some of the established estimates of the *actual slaughter rate* of reindeer for private consumption among various groups of tundra pastoralists in the 1920s and 1930s. These were available from local statistical sources and ethnographies of the period, and are shown in table 14. Then, taking it one step further, we were able to compile a corresponding breakdown of this estimate according to three main socioeconomic groups for both the Nenets and Chukchi pastoralists, making additional use of interviews with elderly informants. It turns out that the statistically average family of five to six killed thirty-five to seventy reindeer a year for personal consumption, excluding festivals, hospitality for guests, and related uses. The actual figure depended heavily upon that family's resources and location on the socioeconomic scale. For comparison, among Alaskan Eskimo caribou hunters, a family of six to seven required annually sixty-five to seventy-five reindeer or caribou, although these were larger, heavier animals, and thus of greater food value per carcass (Campbell 1978:191, Foote 1965:296–97).

If our figures are justified, then reindeer husbandry sufficed to meet only 40 to 70 percent of the nomads' annual food consumption norm. In that case, food products from hunting, fishing, gathering, and trading became a vital necessity. Only in the wealthier households did consumption of reindeer meat come close to meeting or fully satisfying the family's energy needs. In those families, other foods simply added variety to the diet, or conveyed social prestige.

Clothing. We determined the herders' annual demand for reindeer skins for clothing, footwear, making, and repairing *chum* and *yaranga* covers, and for other items of daily use based upon various documented estimates and informant data. The figure we accepted for a family of five was 40 skins per year, which should, however, be considered the *minimum requisite norm*. Well-off families who could afford to, or larger-than-average families, actually would have used far more.[13] This annual minimum norm corresponds well with similar estimates for other reindeer-herding groups, e.g., 25 skins of forest reindeer or 50 skins of tundra reindeer per family among the Taz River Sel'kup (Lebedev 1978:17), and 36.5 per family among the neighboring Turukhan River nomads (Suslov 1930:33). Among the Alaskan Eskimos, for example, the Noatagmiut, a minimum of 57 to 65.5 caribou skins were used per family (Foote 1965:297–98).

Fuel. To heat and light their homes, the reindeer herders used fire-

TABLE 14
Estimated Reindeer Slaughter for Domestic Consumption by Native Herders

Population/time	Source	Reported estimate	Annual equivalent	
			Per person	Per household
Anadyr Chukchi, early 1930s	1	4 reindeer per family per month, or 48 a year	10–12	48
Chukchi and Koryak, 1920s	2	1 reindeer per family a week	10	54
Chaun Chukchi, 1930s	3	50 reindeer per family a year	8–10	50
Anadyr Chukchi, 1930s	4	1 reindeer per family every 4 or 5 days	12–15	70–90
Anadyr Chukchi, 1930	5	70–80 reindeer per family a year	13–15	70–80
Penzhina Koryak, 1930s	6	10 reindeer per person annually	10	50–60
Nomad Koryak, early 1930s	7	1 reindeer per family weekly (poor herders)	9	54
Nomad Koryak, early 1930s	7	1 reindeer every three days (rich herders)	20	122
Nomad Koryak, 1920s	8	5 reindeer per person annually	5	25–30
Dolgan, 1930s	9	Not less than 40 reindeer per family a year	7–8	40+
Taz Sel'kup, 1920s–1930s	10	4 reindeer per family a month	10	48
Scandinavian Saami, 1950s	11	10 reindeer per person annually	10	50–60

SOURCES: 1: Druri 1933:75; 2: Bogoras 1932:47; 3: Arkhincheev 1957:57; 4: Vasil'ev 1936:99; 5: Anadyrskii krai 1935:44; 6: Krylov 1936:53; 7: Bilibin 1933:39; 8: Sergeev 1934:116; 9: Popov 1935:201; 10: Lebedev 1978:17; 11: Foote 1965:297.

wood, which they gathered from their resource territories, as well as driftwood, dried moss, and bone. In the inland tundra, the inner chamber of the Chukchi *yaranga* was heated with a small lamp fueled by the tallow rendered from reindeer bones. Nearer the seacoast, where they could either hunt marine mammals during the summer or have regular contact with the sedentary maritime hunters who did, the reindeer Chukchi used seal and whale oil to heat their tents. Lacking any kind of estimates for fuel consumption, we settled on the reasonable estimate that the reindeer herders used half the marine-mammal oil they procured for food, and half for fuel.

Trade needs. The herders obtained all their manufactured trade goods, including firearms, ammunition, iron implements, fabric, and flour, as well as most of their marine-mammal products (hides and straps, footwear soles and uppers, meat and oil) in exchange for the reindeer meat and skins of their domestic reindeer, or furs from animals they hunted. Many Bol'shaia Zemlia Nenets families also processed fish to sell to Russian traders, or used the harvest from their occasional sea-mammal hunting forays for trade.

We can get a rough estimate of the quantity of native resources that wound up at the trading posts because this would have been reflected in how much the herders bought there, which is documented in the Arctic Census of 1926–27. The average Bol'shaia Zemlia Nenets family bought 478 rubles worth of goods each year, which was equivalent in local prices of the time to the total of six Arctic fox pelts, twenty reindeer skins, three hundred kilograms of reindeer meat (six to eight carcasses) and one hundred kilograms of fish. For all the Chukchi of the Kolyma area, the average sum of purchases per family was 172 rubles per year, which in local prices was equivalent to the value of three Arctic fox furs and ten reindeer hides (*Pokhoziaistvennaia Perepis'* 1929: 54, 106, 234–37).

Calculated in this way, the volume of domestic reindeer meat and skins used for trade purposes (seven carcasses and twenty skins per family for the Nenets, and ten reindeer skins for the Chukchi) appears somewhat low compared to actual figures. In 1924, for example, according to the data of a local survey, the Bol'shaia Zemlia Nenets sold an average of four hundred kilograms of reindeer meat per family (equivalent to nine to ten carcasses), and thirty-nine reindeer skins (Plettsov 1925 : 17). Also, the Chukchi herders expended an additional portion of meat and skins in exchange with the coastal population. The available estimates range from 0.4 percent of the standing stock (Chaun Chukchi, 1937) to 4 percent (for all the Chukchi herders of the Kamchatka Province in 1926) and even 11 percent (Chukchi Peninsula, 1931) (Arkhincheev 1957: 58, Olenevodstvo 16, Orlovskii 1928a:47, *Pokhoziaistvennaia Perepis'* 1929:148–49). As an average norm, we will take five carcasses and ten skins per family as the expenditure of meat and skin for barter and sale among the Chaun Chukchi, and for the nomads of the Chukchi Peninsula, fifteen carcasses and fifteen skins. Therefore, the total trade and sale norms were roughly similar for both reindeer peoples, and henceforth these were the averages we used in the subsistence balances.

Productivity of the Herding Economy

An exact estimate of the reindeer yields for any actual calendar year is a pivotal piece in the subsistence balance. All balances were calculated on the basis of four communities of tundra pastoralists—the Ust' Kara group of Bol'shaia Zemlia Nenets (30 families of 144 people in 1926), the Kuvet group of the Chaun Chukchi (46 families of 221 people in 1926), the Ichun' group, also from the Chaun Chukchi (47 families of 226 people in 1937), and the Kychaun group of the reindeer Chukchi of the interior Chukchi Peninsula (30 families of 139 people in 1937). All of these statistical groups conformed to actual bands of the nomadic population—the "native" or "nomadic" soviets at the time of the 1926 census or the household survey of 1937.

Unfortunately, the data available for reconstructing subsistence balances of the selected communities are extremely limited. Figures comparable to the detailed annual catch statistics by village that I located for Eskimo economy, which would track reindeer stock trends or actual annual yields for local groups throughout the 1920s and 1930s, are available only for scattered years and do not appear very reliable. Consequently, most indicators of reindeer production could only be defined by interpolating between more general figures for larger administrative districts. Naturally, this leads to a certain austerity in the eventual reconstruction of pastoralist subsistence, especially compared to the more richly detailed Eskimo model.

First of all, it was necessary to take account of the socioeconomic stratification of the communities selected and to divide their constituent families into three categories: small herders with private stock of 150 reindeer or less, mid-size with herds of 150 to 500, and large herders with 500 or more reindeer. For the Ust' Kara Nenets this was extrapolated from the average stratification rates that prevailed among the Bol'shaia Zemlia tundra Nenets as a whole in 1924 (Plettsov 1925:10). I borrowed figures for the Kuvet and Ichun' Chukchi from analogous data for the Chaun region in 1937 (Shmit 1939:6),

TABLE 15
Reindeer Economy of the Siberian Native Herders

	Ust' Kara Nenets, 1926	Kuvet Chukchi, 1926	Kychaun Chukchi, 1931	Ichun' Chukchi, 1937
Number of households	30	46	30	47
Herd size (beginning of the year)	6,300	12,270	7,896	12,290
Herd increase through calving	3,045	5,443	3,995	6,305
Herd spending through year	1,526	4,038	3,198	4,626
Including:				
Food consumption		1,371	1,160	3,146
Payment for labor	1,056	NA	NA	80
Trade and exchange		812	838	60*
Losses through calving	269	1,544	639	504
Other casualties			561	836
Animals lost	201	241	NA	NA
Herd size (end of the year)	7,839	13,781	8,693	14,049
Food output (10^3 kcal)				
Slaughtered animals	45,444	67,179	56,840	154,154
Perished reindeers	NA	37,829	15,288	21,707
Traded and exchanged carcasses	NA	39,788	41,062	6,860*

* Low estimates (insufficient data).

while for the Kychaun group I located actual figures for all households and camps in 1937 (Materialy Chukotskoi zemekspeditsii 1938).

The stock dynamics and approximate volume of pastoral production were figured initially by these property categories, then were added together to calculate community totals. I constructed a preliminary age-sex chart for the herd and all indicators for its annual dynamics: reproduction, loss to disease and predations, harvesting for personal consumption and for sale or exchange. The Ust' Kara case was reconstructed on the basis of 1926, using averages taken from the 1926–27 Arctic Census for Nenets households in the Bol'shaia Zemlia tundra. Figures from the same source, but for all the reindeer Chukchi of Kamchatka Province, formed the basis for my Kuvet model. Information on the Ichun' group was gathered in the Chaun regional inventory of 1937, while for the Kychaun Chukchi I used data from the eastern part of Chukotka District collected in 1931 (see table 15) (Babushkin 1930:100, Ekonomika Bol'shezemel'skoi tundry 1934, *Itogi Perepisi* 1929:208–10, Olenevodstvo:16, *Pokhoziaistvennaia Perepis'* 1929:148–49, Shmit 1939:12).

Taking into account that the reindeer Chukchi considered it dishonorable to leave a carcass to rot in the tundra and tried to salvage the meat of deer that had been lost by natural causes or killed by wolves, I increased the amount of actual consumption for the Chukchi by adding one-half of the number of animals who died by natural causes, including newborn calves, to the reported domestic slaughter, having assigned to newborn calves one-tenth the caloric value of an adult deer. The Nenets herders did not eat the meat of dead animals, with the exception of calves that died at birth.

I reconstructed food-yield figures from hunting, fishing, and gathering, based on a variety of sources. Information provided by elderly herders, including their estimates of food budgets in the 1920s and 1930s, was used for the Ust' Kara Nenets and Kychaun Chukchi. Data from the Arctic Census of 1926–27 were applied for the Kuvet Chukchi, and from the local inventory for 1937 for the Ichun' Chukchi. Production from each activity was calculated for each of our three classes of herders, and then for the community overall (table 16). To determine the caloric value of the hunting and fishing catch, I used the same estimates from Don Foote's work as were used for the Asiatic Eskimo subsistence model in chapter 2, with a few additions as needed (table 7). Thus, all pastoralist subsistence production was set up to facilitate direct comparison with the sedentary maritime hunting economy.

The last step was to compute the share and caloric value of imported food goods. I selected flour, breads (including hardtack and crackers), sugar, and butter as the four most important items.[14] For the Ust' Kara, Ichun', and Kychaun communities, I based my estimates of how much people bought or used of these items on information from Nenets and Chukchi elders. For the Ust' Kara group these numbers were adjusted to reflect actual data from the 1924 local household survey (Plettsov 1925:19–20; also see Evladov 1927, Mitusova 1925, Saprykin and Sinel'nikov 1926).

The total amount of reindeer skins is fairly easy to establish based on an estimate of total reindeer killed for food, whether for personal consumption or to sell. In addition, it is possible to estimate that the reindeer herders managed to utilize roughly another half of skins of reindeer that had died naturally or been injured or killed by predators, plus three-fourths of a skin from calves that died in birth (stillborn hide), which was considered to be a trade good of high value.

It is more challenging to come up with some figure for the marine-mammal food products the herders obtained from hunters living on

TABLE 16
Estimated Subsistence Harvests of Herding Communities

	Ust' Kara Nenets 1926	Kuvet Chukchi 1926	Kychaun Chukchi 1931	Ichun' Chukchi 1937
Land game species				
Caribou	23	NA	NA	NA
Elk	7	NA	NA	NA
Dall sheep	NA	27*	NA	NA
Black bear	NA	2*	1	NA
Arctic hare	455	114	242	97
"Geese"	1,050	400	245	58
"Ducks"	1,045	114	253	119
Ptarmigan	3,550	1,460	980	245
Sea mammals				
Walrus	NA	28*	NA	3
Bearded seal	NA	23*	NA	7
Small seals	NA	274*	NA	315
Fish (kg)	29,605	3,900	3,950	3,538
Edible plants (kg)	2,480	6,900	4,500	6,700
Bird eggs (kg)	223	?	?	?
Total harvest (10^3 kcal)	36,109	74,761	8,169	38,807
% estimated food requirements	27.8	37.6	6.6	19.1

SOURCE: Author's calculations.
* Actual catches, according to 1926 Census.

the coast. This amount depended precariously upon how the hunt fared in the coastal communities from year to year, and could dwindle considerably for multiyear periods, as discussed in chapter 2. Unfortunately, there are only isolated references to this in the documentary sources (Knopfmiller 1940b, Terletskii 1967), and the estimates of my Chukchi and Eskimo informants varied widely. It was possible to make an average estimate only for the Kychaun reindeer Chukchi in 1931, assuming that each family of herders received not less than fifty kilograms of marine mammal meat and fifty kilograms of blubber through trade, which provided 5 percent of their annual energy requirements.

Analysis of Subsistence Balances

We calculated the subsistence balances for the tundra herders in the same way as for the sea-mammal-hunting communities in chapter 2. However, there was one difference: the balances were calculated ini-

TABLE 17
Annual Subsistence Balances of the Herding Communities

	Ust' Kara Nenets, 1926	Kuvet Chukchi, 1926	Kychaun Chukchi, 1931	Ichun' Chukchi, 1937
Estimated food requirements, (10^3 kcal)	129,600	198,900	125,100	203,400
Estimated expenses for trade and exchange (10^3 kcal)	6,300	11,270	22,050	11,515
% food requirements	4.9	5.7	17.6	5.7
Total food output (10^3 kcal)	157,103	222,252	135,162	222,698
% estimated requirements	121.2	111.7	91.9	103.6
Shares (%) in subsistence economy[a]				
Herding	35.1	62.5	57.7	80.8
Land hunting	10.3	3.8	2.1	0.4
Sea hunting	—	30.4	—	15.5
Fishing	16.4	1.4	2.3	1.3
Plant gathering	1.1	2.1	2.2	2.0
Purchased food	53.4	1.3	4.4	3.9
Exchanged food	—	—	(6.5)[b]	—
% total annual subsistence balance	+16.3	+1.4	−24.8	+3.8

SOURCE: Author's calculations.
[a] Including all food obtained through hunting, fishing, and gathering but excluding reindeer meat that has been bartered and traded.
[b] Low estimates (insufficient data).

tially for the three categories of herders (small, mid-size, and large), and only then were added together to compile a total for the whole pastoralist community, as shown in tables 17 and 18. In this way, we could evaluate the difference in pastoralist subsistence as a function of herders' econoomic status.

According to the reconstruction, three of our four nomadic communities showed a positive net balance between subsistence production and consumption needs during the reference years, which were 1926, 1931, and 1937 for the Ust' Kara Nenets, the Kuvet Chukchi, and the Ichun' Chukchi, respectively. This means that production was greater than total needs, including nonessential expenditures for trade or exchange. At first glance, this would appear to prove that the aboriginal reindeer economy was indeed highly efficient, and the well-being of the pastoralist population high.

The Ust' Kara Nenets appear to have achieved an especially high degree of stability. As table 18 shows, all three categories of herders had a positive or nearly even net subsistence balance. However, in

TABLE 18

Annual Subsistence Balances of Herding Communities

(according to herd size)

	Ust' Kara Nenets, 1926	Kuvet Chukchi, 1926	Kychaun Chukchi, 1931	Ichun' Chukchi, 1937
a: Small herders (up to 150 reindeer)				
Number of households	17	34	23	35
Population	71	163	99	168
Total herd size	1,203	2,098	621	2,118
% Total food supply compared to requirements	100.2	59.4	26.6[a]	46.6
Shares of various activities (%)				
Herding	12.4	21.8[b]	6.4	20.0
Land hunting	15.9	4.5	3.0	0.5
Sea hunting	*d*	28.6	NA	18.4
Fishing	23.2	1.7	3.9	1.9
Plant gathering	1.6	2.1	2.3	2.1
Exchange	*d*	NA	7.0[a]	NA
Purchased food	47.1	0.7	4.1	3.7
% subsistence balance[b]	+1.5	−44.8	−74.6[a]	−55.6
b: Mid-size herders (151 to 500 reindeer)				
Number of households	10	5	3	5
Population	52	24	18	24
Total herd size	2,659	1,632	1,070	1,632
% total food supply compared to requirements	120.9	170.7	74.8[a]	133.4
Shares of various activities (%)				
Herding	39.7	78.9	60.2	108.2
Land hunting	6.1	2.6	0.7	0.2
Sea hunting	NA	84.8	NA	16.8
Fishing	12.5	0.8	1.3	1.9
Plant gathering	0.8	2.1	1.7	2.1
Exchange	*d*	NA	5.0[a]	NA
Purchased food	61.8	1.8	5.9	4.2
% Subsistence balance[b]	+20.0	+76.6	−3.8[a]	+28.4
c: Large herders (500 reindeer and more)				
Number of households	3	7	4	7
Population	21	34	22	34
Total herd size	2,438	8,540	6,205	8,540
% total food supply compared to requirements	159.5	227.0	298.6	406.5
Shares of various activities (%)				
Herding	100.1	218.7	286.3	399.3
Land hunting	1.3	1.7	0.2	0.1
Sea hunting	*d*	*d*	*d*	*d*
Fishing	3.4	0.8	0.7	1.1

TABLE 18
Continued

	Ust' Kara Nenets, 1926	Kuvet Chukchi, 1926	Kychaun Chukchi, 1931	Ichun' Chukchi, 1937
a: Small herders (up to 150 reindeer)				
Shares of various activities (%)				
Plant gathering	0.6	2.1	1.8	1.4
Exchange	*d*	NA	5.5[a]	NA
Purchased food	54.1	3.7	4.1	4.6
% subsistence balance[c]	+54.4	+162.8	+301.8	+391.0

SOURCE: Author's calculations.
[a] Insufficient data (low estimates).
[b] Including payment for labor.
[c] Including reindeer meat that has been bartered and traded.
[d] No data; insignificant for food balance.

this case, first impressions are misleading. Small and mid-size herders could only maintain a positive subsistence balance if they relied heavily on purchased food items or received additional reindeer products from wealthier households. In total, purchased foods accounted for over half the Ust' Kara Nenets's total caloric intake, actually outweighing the total procurement from reindeer, hunting, fishing, and gathering all together. This bears witness to the very strong dependency of Nenets subsistence upon supplementary "external" sources of food, from which one can infer that their own resource utilization system had already become insufficient to meet their needs.

These balances confirm the above-mentioned thesis that the share of reindeer products in the diet of the tundra population had waned by the opening decades of the twentieth century. If we consider that actual consumption among the Ust' Kara Nenets was 100 to 110 percent of their estimated caloric requirements (allowing for some surplus), and the herders themselves consumed all food items they acquired through trade, the share of calories from reindeer meat in their diet did not exceed 15 percent among the small herders, 20 to 25 percent among mid-size herders, and 40 to 50 percent among large herders. Even allowing for some forms of redistribution via mutual assistance, frequent food-sharing, hospitality, and visiting, these figures indicate that in poor and mid-size households supplies fell short of demand for reindeer meat, which was by far the preferred and most prestigious of all traditional foods. In addition, this shortage of fresh meat was experienced most acutely during the summer months, when poor and even well-off herders shifted to eating fish to avoid killing any more of their reindeer than necessary in order to conserve their herds.

The relative scarcity of reindeer meat supply to demand is supported by the recollections of elderly Ust' Kara Nenets herders and reconstructions of their family food budgets during the 1920s and 1930s (Krupnik 1976a). A more important point, however, is that the Ust' Kara Nenets found themselves in a position where, in order to receive more energy-efficient manufactured food goods through trade, they began to sacrifice not only commodity items from their indigenous economy (furs, marine mammal oil, high-value fish) but also reindeer products they needed themselves. At the time, the market prices could be quite similar for items with differing caloric values. Thus, for example, in 1926, a hundred-kilogram sack of flour cost 17.5 rubles as opposed to one hundred kilograms of reindeer meat at 14.6 rubles, but the flour provided 350,000 kilocalories, while the same volume of venison yielded only one-third to one-half that amount, roughly 100,000 to 180,000 kilocalories.

The reconstructed balance also shows how many reindeer skins the Ust' Kara Nenets used, purchased, and sold in each of the three property groups. Even assuming that half, or 135, of the skins of reindeer that died from natural causes were used, the total estimated slaughter of 1,050 reindeer barely met the community's domestic need for 1,200 skins, and thus left no surplus for trade. Given the herd sizes that existed, this means that the Ust' Kara Nenets sold reindeer hides at the expense of their domestic consumption. Once again this confirms the stories of elderly herders I collected in 1974, who all recalled that life was very hard from 1900 to the 1920s. People did not have enough meat, or used it sparingly, along with purchased food items, and constantly lacked adequate reindeer skins to make clothing and repair house coverings.

In principle, a similar situation could be observed in the three Chukchi communities we examined. It is true that Chukchi depended upon purchased food items for their subsistence far less than the Ust' Kara Nenets did. In the Chukchi diet, these constituted only 1.5 to 4.5 percent of the caloric intake. This conveys a sense of the high degree to which traditional Chukchi subsistence was specialized in herding, as well as the degree to which they relied upon their own subsistence economy. However, even with maximum utilization of all the products of reindeer, including the meat and hides of deer that died from natural causes and predation, a positive or at least neutral subsistence balance was possible only if it was supplemented by intensive marine hunting or trade with the coastal population.

In all three Chukchi communities, the group of small herders constituted about three-fourths of the population. The production estimated for them provided less than half of their energy requirements (table 18a). Therefore, sustained existence for them was possible only through cooperation with the wealthier herd owners, whose stock sizes and slaughter rates were large enough to yield a substantial surplus of reindeer products each year. The calculated balances thoroughly support the references of the 1920s and 1930s indicating that it was an economic necessity for small-scale herdsmen to attach themselves to owners of larger herds. This is vividly illustrated by a budget analysis study of several Ichun' Chukchi families and camps conducted by Il'ia Arkhincheev in 1933 (Arkhincheev 1957).

Yet another conclusion was confirmed. As stratification deepened among the reindeer Chukchi and the bulk of the herds was increasingly concentrated in the hands of a small number of wealthy households, an enormous stream of poor pastoralists was released upon the tundra. In other words, a kind of "surplus labor" pool had accumulated in the nomadic population, whose needs substantially outweighed their personal resources for production. This situation closely resembles other traditional nomadic societies characterized by private or household property rights over animal stocks, where some individual families had too many animals and not enough people to pasture their herd without help. However, among the reindeer Chukchi socioeconomic differentiation reached such an extreme that it became a factor that threatened an already delicate equilibrium between the population's needs for survival and what they actually produced. In these conditions, any disruptive external influence or deterioration in their environmental circumstances could easily provoke a shortage of resources for most members of the nomadic community.

However surprising it may seem, one form that such external interference assumed was the presence of the populous coastal village communities so close by, whose residents maintained a keen and constant interest in reindeer products. My analysis of subsistence balances presents completely new insight into relations between the nomads of the tundra and the sedentary hunters of the coast, especially regarding the role that exchange with coastal people played in the subsistence economies of various herding groups. In areas where it was possible for pastoralists to have regular contacts with the settled population, trading reindeer meat for marine-mammal meat and blubber gradually became established as a crucial way to replace their own products with a higher-calorie "foreign" source of food.[15] That is, such trade played the same role for the Chukchi as purchasing Russian food goods did for the European Nenets.

For the most part, this dependency was exhibited in those areas where herders' pasturing and migration routes passed sufficiently close to the coastal settlements and where trading-partner relationships had been established with the sedentary hunters and maintained over the course of many years. In 1931, according to data from a local survey, the herders of the eastern Chukchi Peninsula slaughtered approximately 11 percent (sic!) of their domestic stock strictly for exchange with people on the coast. On the average, this represented twenty-five to thirty reindeer per herding household, and only one-fourth less than the number they killed for their own domestic consumption. This figure is almost double the trade level that I estimated for the Kychaun community, which was the group closest to the shore and most involved in the trade with coastal people. This works out to six to eight reindeer carcasses that each coastal family stood to receive in exchange for the marine products and commercial goods they brought to trade, at least for our benchmark year of 1931.

In 1937, trade with the coastal hunters on the Chukchi Peninsula absorbed more than 1,600 reindeer carcasses from 3 interior herding communities alone—Kychaun (139 people), Ioniveem (204 people) and Inemnei (110 people) (Terletskii 1967; fig. 5). In some smaller camps, which had fewer reindeer but were located nearer the coast, as much as 15 to 30 percent of the slaughter went to trade, undermining stock growth as well as numbers of reindeer killed for personal consumption.

In a very real sense, then, survival for these and other herding camps located close to the littoral was effectively "subsidized" by exchange relations with the coastal people, who provided a regular supply of marine-mammal meat and oil. Judging from the reconstructed balance structure, a positive net subsistence balance among the Kychaun Chukchi could be achieved only as a result of consumption of the imported meat and blubber, the proportion of which in the diet of the herders could reach as much as 30 to 35 percent. My informants, reindeer Chukchi from the peninsula's southeastern edge, recalled how in the 1920s and 1930s Eskimo hunters from the coastal villages visited their camps several times during the course of the winter with dogsleds piled high with marine-mammal meat and blubber to trade.

In their efforts to obtain the reindeer skins and highly valued reindeer meat they needed, the sea hunters tended to suck the near-coastal herding communities dry. Thus, a symbiotic relationship developed between the two subsistence systems where the herding and hunting models intersected, and the herders in particular appeared to live to a significant degree off the foodstuffs imported from the coastal population.

It is true that in each concrete case it appears that the immediate terms of trade clearly favored the reindeer people. According to unwritten equivalents operating during the winter of 1919–20, "in exchange for one whole reindeer carcass the expected trade is a sealskin bag filled with oil [approximately fifty kilograms of sea-mammal oil—*I.K.*], or else the skin of a large seal; in exchange for the skin of one old reindeer, they trade the skin of a small seal, but for the skin of a six-month-old calf [which was preferred for sewing winter garments—*I.K.*] they pay three to four seal skins, while for a white or striped calf-skin they pay six to seven seal skins" (Sverdrup 1930:266). But the ultimate ecological and economic cost of such trade to the small and middle-sized herd owners was burdensome indeed. After all, they were compelled to give up their own reindeer products, which they themselves acutely needed, in exchange for items that were a genuine surplus to the coastal hunters—straps, skins, and oil of the marine mammals. This means that in certain areas it was the herders who were in the position of greater dependency in relation to the hunters, and not the reverse as is commonly argued in the early literature. Only one author from the 1920s (actually a trade agent in the area since 1912), at least of those who were better informed on the subject, reached a conclusion similar to mine! He made a special point of emphasizing that "the herders are far worse off than the coastal dwellers, and are constantly in a position of insurmountable indebtedness to the latter" (Karaev 1926:149).

In places where regular contact with the coastal hunters was not possible, the herders were forced to engage in seasonal marine hunting themselves. The Chaun herding communities Chukchi, who left the coast and went deep into the tundra for the winter, achieved a positive subsistence balance largely by hunting for marine mammals in the summer—mainly small seals, but also bearded seal and walrus. In the Kuvet and Ichun' communities, for example, summer sea hunting provided from 15 to 30 percent of the annual caloric intake of the diet according to my calculations. Further south along the coast and deeper into the interior, where maritime hunting did not take place, this portion of small and mid-size reindeer-herding families' diet was filled by summer fishing.

Thus, in spite of numerous differences, the Nenets and Chukchi pastoralist subsistence shared highly similar features. These included: (1) the depressed proportion in their diet of the reindeer products they themselves produced, (2) the degree to which the welfare of the overwhelming majority of families depended upon the development of supplementary food-producing activities and the presence of purchased or bartered food products, and (3) the vital necessity of cooperation, mutual assistance, and complementary labor relations between wealthier and poorer households. In the absence of such adaptations, the number of domestic reindeer could not have met the needs of the pastoral population. By the beginning of the century, in the herding communities we examined, an equilibrium no longer existed between the size of the human population and the resources it used. In this respect, the circumstances in which pastoralist subsistence found itself prior to the coming of Soviet power in the 1920s were not so different from the situation of the hunting economy of the coastal people around the same time.

Conclusion

The subsistence balances that I calculated based upon data from the 1920s and 1930s reflected the status of a very highly developed, specialized form of a nomadic Arctic economy. Although the choice of four herding communities was more or less a random one, their production and consumption levels were in most cases interpolated from actual observed averages from much larger geographical or administration areas. This increases the representativeness of the results. They do confirm that, prior to Soviet modernization, the majority of nomadic people made their living only by entering into unequitable alliances with a few wealthier households, in which they effectively exchanged their labor for food, or by supplementing their herding with additional procurement strategies: trading for large amounts of purchased food (e.g., the Bol'shaia Zemlia Nenets, and Nenets in general), pursuing an active maritime-hunting industry (e.g., the Chaun Chukchi, and the Arctic Chukchi in general), trading with the sedentary people (Chukchi Peninsula herders), or fishing, as in the case of the nomads of the southern and interior regions.

Theoretically, the instability in pastoralist subsistence may be attributed to three possible variables. These include: (1) a temporary drop in the productivity of nomadic economy resulting, for example, from a sudden decrease in the size of the domestic stock, (2) the relatively limited numbers of domestic reindeer compared to the actual potential of the grazing areas, and (3) the growth of the nomadic population, which had exceeded the carrying capacity of resource utilization.

The first proposition can hardly be confirmed. By the late 1920s and early 1930s, the reindeer herders of the Russian Arctic had already survived the effects of a civil war, market destabilization, and the disruption of established relations of trade and exchange. Throughout most of Siberia, they had regrouped from those negative economic impacts to build up the reindeer stock to a very high level. For the next thirty years, until the early 1960s, the total reindeer stock in Arctic Russia never reached such a high level again, and, in the Nenets and Chukchi areas in particular, reindeer breeding never regained, except for a short period in the 1970s, the stock volume it had displayed prior to collectivization, (Dmitriev 1925:110–11, *Narodnoe khoziaistvo* 1972:810, Syroechkovskii 1982:69, Ustinov 1956:15). Nor were the ecological conditions that prevailed during the second and third decades of this century particularly inauspicious for traditional reindeer economy in Arctic Eurasia (see chapter 4 below). Thus, we can safely consider that the productivity of the indigenous subsistence as we have calculated it was sufficiently high, if not absolutely maximal.

The second hypothesis also does not hold up under critical scrutiny. Based on contemporary estimates of how many reindeer the available forage could support, by the end of the 1920s the domestic reindeer stock had already reached its maximum sustainable population, at least in the western and eastern Russian Arctic. The limits of extensive herd growth were evidently exhausted, and an increase in traditional herding productivity was possible only by transforming it into a market-oriented enterprise, which would have involved a fundamental reorganization in the land-use system. This inevitably would have required radical dislocations in the native subsistence system, including mass sedentarization—which in fact occurred in the course of Soviet policies in subsequent decades.

Obviously, the main reason for the disruption of equilibrium between the pastoralist and his resource base was the slow but unswerving natural increase in population among nomadic peoples. All the characteristic hallmarks of such an imbalance were already observed among the Nenets at the turn of the century: increased density of pastoralism per given unit of land, overgrazing of pastures, herders purchasing food on a mass scale. These phenomena were also evident among the Chukchi in a less acute form. But, given the lower density of the Chukchi nomadic population, the gravity of the situation here was exacerbated by the exaggerated socioeconomic inequality and greater disparity in consumption rates than was the case among the Nenets. In principle, the Nenets and Chukchi subsistence models can be viewed as two different evolutionary forms of "overcrowded" pastoralism responding to the gradually building pressure of population growth.

The subsistence balances prove that for the time studied there was no "harmony" between human communities and their environments either on the Arctic coast nor in the inner tundra of northern Eurasia, and there was no strict equilibrium between natural resources and population growth. Under these conditions, in my opinion, the coastal hunters actually were more advantageously situated. Although, practically speaking, their positive subsistence balance was sustained by excessive exploitation of their resource base, the coastal people were able to produce adequate supplies of all necessary items, plus a surplus for trade with the herders.

It is true that this situation came to pass as a result of the exceptionally fortuitous location of the coastal hunting villages directly in the seasonal migration paths of several stocks of large marine mammals. This placed them in an ideal position to reap the benefits of the rich biological productivity of the Pacific and Arctic oceans. Hence, with improvements in their hunting equipment and supply base, the marine hunters managed virtually to *double* the output of their subsistence economy. At the same time, the herders had already exhausted the possibilities for achieving such a sharp increase in production within the traditional resource utilization model.

The energy-equivalent estimates of foods derived from their territories by the reindeer-herding and marine hunting communities also disprove the hypothesis that the productivity of tundra pastoralism was higher than that of other types of indigenous Arctic economies (see Bogoras 1931:93, 1941, Sergeev 1955:42). In reality, in terms of productivity, Arctic pastoralism did not measure up in many respects either to sea hunting in the Bering Strait area or, obviously, to intensive fishing such as that which amply sustained the sedentary peoples of the Amur-Pacific region. The most effective way to compare the efficiency of two subsistence systems is through the lens of their respective indicators of energy use, that is, by calculating the energy value of all subsistence goods derived by the community from its environment, then estimating that value as a share of the total amount of solar radiation absorbed by that area in one year (Odum 1971:104–16).

This final ratio can be considered its own measure of success for the subsistence system. Among the Kuvet Chukchi, for example, in 1926, this indicator was only 0.0000014 percent (14×10^{-9}), and among the Ust' Kara Nenets it was 0.0000035 percent (35×10^{-9}), if their calculated production is correlated with the total pasture area used by each herding group, as shown in table 19. For the Eskimos of Sireniki, this indicator was 150 to 500 times higher! Specifically, the rates were 0.00048 percent ($4{,}800 \times 10^{-9}$) in a bad year (1930), and 0.00078 percent ($7{,}800 \times 10^{-9}$) in an exceptionally favorable year (1937)—again, if "their" ecosystem is considered to consist of the narrow coastal strip and the five-kilometer marine zone around the village that they used (see chapter 2).

We can put these figures together to paint a fully evocative picture of efficiency in both the nomadic and sedentary models of Arctic resource management compared to various types of traditional subsistence in other regions of the world.[16] As shown in table 19, in favorable years the productivity of the Arctic hunting economy was fully comparable to that of tropical horticulture, although it would not have been capable of sustaining as large or as densely settled a total population, and it was achieved by hunting *migratory* stocks of marine mammals, that is, by exploiting, as it were, the resources of an artificially expanded ecosystem. This result is consistent with the common assessment of the northern maritime subsistence economy as one of affluent foragers, rich enough to support the development of a sophisticated social organization and elaborative indigenous culture (Cohen 1981, Arutiunov et al. 1982, Suttles 1968, Testart 1982, Yesner 1980b, etc.).

TABLE 19
Energetic Productivity of Selected Traditional Subsistences

Population	Mode of subsistence	Subsistence efficiency %	Subsistence efficiency $\times 10^{-9}$	Population density (persons per sq km of usable area)
Kuvet Chukchi, Siberia	Reindeer herding	0.0000014	14	0.012
Ust' Kara Nenets, Arctic Russia	Reindeer herding and fishing	0.0000035	35	0.034
Sirenik Eskimo, Siberia	Arctic sea-mammal hunting	0.00048	4,800	2–4
Sirenik Eskimo (good hunting year)	Arctic sea-mammal hunting	0.00078	7,800	2–4
Amazon Indians,* Brazil	Tropical rain forest hunting & gathering	0.000026	260	0.4
Tsembaga Maring,* New Guinea	Slash-and-burn horticulture, pig husbandry	0.00117	11,700	23.8
Dodo Karimojong,* Uganda	Cattle herding and sorghum cultivation	0.0014	14,000	27.4
Quechua Indians,* Peruvian Andes	Intensive root cultivation and herding	0.00135	13,490	NA
Bengalis,* West Bengal	Intensive irrigated agriculture and milking husbandry	0.0163	163,000	191.6

SOURCE: Author's calculations.
* Author's estimates based on Odum 1967, Rappaport 1971, and Ellen 1982.

At the same time, differences in productivity and population density of the nomadic and sedentarized models of Arctic subsistence reinforce our conception of them as representing fundamentally different strategies of adaptation to the Arctic environment. Thus, the key organizing principle behind the coastal model was the choice of maximally productive small areas of land and sea where several of the migratory resources used were highly concentrated. In contrast, the nomadic strategy represented an attempt to use as large a territory as possible in order to reduce the human impact upon the highly fragile resources of the tundra ecosystem.

In that case, do the nomadic and sedentarized subtypes of aboriginal Arctic economies constitute essentially different forms of human survival in this environment, products of an evolutionary selection whose climax implies the death or degradation of other, less efficient, and unsustainable intermediate forms along the way? To answer this question, we need to take a more expansive historical perspective in which we identify how the development of these two models can be traced out in the wider context of long-term social and ecological processes in Arctic Eurasia. The following chapters are devoted to this task.

CHAPTER FOUR

The Challenge of Change in the Arctic Environment

Introduction

In the preceding chapters I examined subsistence systems of the indigenous peoples of Arctic Eurasia through a single synchronic lens trained upon the first decades of this century. In order to understand how and why these particular adaptations developed, and their past and present relationship to one another, I now propose to evaluate the evolution of these systems in a historical retrospective. Although a long-term historical approach obviously uses different sources and methods of analysis than a temporally focused balance analysis, they share a common purpose, that is, understanding the relationship between humans and the ecological niche they occupy. The very concept of a "subsistence system" reflects an assumption that the dynamics of the system are determined by the combined effects of two types of change: changes in the physical environment, and social change, especially ethnic or cultural shifts. Although maintaining a strict boundary between the two is not always easy, we clarify our analysis by attempting at least conceptually to do so, because the organizing principles underlying social structure and change differ substantially from those governing biophysical order in the natural world.

Ideally, this approach would involve the construction of two relatively autonomous time frames, one for human history and another for environmental change. We would then attempt to synchronize the two and to find interconnections between them. However, this is more complicated than it appears. The ethnic and economic history of the native peoples of the Eurasian Arctic can be recaptured with some degree of reliability only since the appearance of documentary sources, in effect, since 1600 or so. This time frame constitutes a serious information barrier, separating the realm of guesswork and reconstruction from a factual "ethnographic past" fully accessible to documented analysis and even direct field investigation.

For several decades, Russian ethnohistorians have devoted prodigious effort to recording the cultural dynamics of Siberia and Eurasian Arctic peoples throughout the last three or four hundred years. Beginning with fifteenth- to seventeenth- century Russian and West European narratives and chronicles, they have introduced a mass of documentary sources into the ethnohistorical literature, which appears impressive indeed. The detail, evocative descriptiveness, and sheer extent of these records far surpass the documentary base for any other native ethnic group of the circumpolar area, with the possible exception of the Eskimos of West Greenland and the Scandinavian Saami. Several thorough ethnohistorical monographs summarize the accessible written, ethnographic, archeological, and folklore sources for both the European Russian and the northeast Siberian Arctic areas discussed in chapters 2 and 3.[1] Thanks to these and many other publications, we can establish, with an entirely tolerable degree of unavoidable ellipses, the basic stages in the subsistence history of all three native peoples in our study—the Eskimo, Nenets, and Chukchi—since approximately 1600.

Proceeding further into the murky depths of the past, we enter the realm of what is called Arctic "prehistory." Here we are obliged to set the needle of our intellectual compass for fragmentary and sometimes highly debatable archeological data, or the still more ambiguous methods of paleolinguistic analysis. In the prehistoric period, our knowledge of ethnocultural evolution among Arctic peoples is rife with gaps and omissions. At some points our "blind spots" stretch for centuries, and our chronological scale becomes tentative indeed. But even here we can trace out stages in the development of aboriginal subsistence systems. I will attempt to reveal these stages for the reader in the chapters that follow.

Unfortunately, the environmental history of the Eurasian Arctic has been much more scantily studied for the same period of time. There are as yet neither regional studies nor general overviews that scrutinize this area with anything like the depth and breadth of Christian Vibe's well-known monograph on the climatic and biological history of Greenland (Vibe 1967). Such data as exist are for the most part poorly systematized, and show little or no correlation with stages in the ethnocultural history of the indigenous peoples of the Arctic.

Meanwhile, virtually all contemporary investigations indicate that it is precisely in the Arctic that the effects of environmental change are typically more pronounced, and occur on a greater magnitude than anywhere else on earth. Along with the overall extremeness of climate, this characteristic is now recognized as the primary distinguishing ecological feature of the Arctic environment (see Banfield 1975: 546–47, Dunbar 1973: 179, Kriuchkov 1976: 131–33, Roots 1985: 3–4, Tikhomirov 1971: 41–42, 1974: 241, Uspenskii 1970: 738, etc.). The Arctic and Subarctic ecosystems fringing the mid-latitude ecumene are remarkably sensitive to the slightest changes in natural conditions. The complexity of climatic cycles and the fragility of all biotic relationships found here contributed to continual and endemic instability in all biological communities, from genuine if short-term "explosions" to equally acute crises and "crashes" of subsistence resources on a mass scale.

Instability in the wildlife populations that form the foundation of human survival in the Arctic was especially typical of tundra ecosystems in the continental interior, with their relatively low species diversity and truncated food chains. However, at times this factor was no less important along the Arctic littoral, where ecological dynamics were determined by vagaries of annual migrations by marine mammals, anadromous fish, and flocks of waterfowl. By entering into this system of relationships, humans themselves became witnesses to and sometimes victims of these continual ebbs and flows in the environment.

"The history of Greenland," as the Danish zoologist Christian Vibe so evocatively wrote, "is a testimony of prosperity and poverty following each other in rapid succession. Oral as well as written records from the last centuries, and archeological finds from the last four to five thousand years unfold the same picture. The periods of prosperity, after a few scores or at most a few hundred years, were succeeded by correspondingly long periods of decline, when settlements, parts of the country, or all of Greenland were depopulated and lay uninhabited. . . . The climatic fluctuations forced the sea mammals and sea birds of Greenland to look for new foraging grounds . . . , leaving Man starving behind" (Vibe 1967: 13).

This picture holds equally true throughout the circumpolar Arctic, including the Arctic regions of Eurasia. Such an ecological background created completely unique conditions for the evolution of aboriginal subsistence systems. Therefore, the successful and stable human exploitation of the Eurasian Arctic, from the interior forest-tundra to the ice-covered islands and rocky coastlines proved possible because of certain specific forms of economic, cultural, and social adaptation.

But before we consider what these forms were we need to fill in the remaining gaps and reconstruct, however tentatively, basic components in the ecological dynamics of the Eurasian Arctic as far back in time as is within our reach. Since climate has long been acknowledged as the primary agent of ecological and environmental change in the Arctic (Govorukhin 1947:324), our first step will be to examine the history of Arctic *climatic change*. Using available sources we will then proceed to examine, respectively: the recurrence of extreme climatic and/or natural phenomena, fluctuations in Arctic game populations, and population cycles of domestic animals. In this way we can identify building blocks of ecology and environment from which we will subsequently reconstruct how and why Arctic peoples came to develop the particular strategies of resource use that they did.

Climatic Change in the Eurasian Arctic

By this time, a fair amount of evidence has accumulated attesting to multiple and distinctly documented changes in climate in the Eurasian Arctic zone, from Scandinavia to the Chukchi Peninsula, over the past two thousand years. Unfortunately, for the time being these data remain poorly systematized and have not been assembled into a unified schematic or system on a regional scale, as has been done for a number of other areas throughout the circumpolar Arctic. The Siberian Arctic has not received adequate paleogeographical study, and it is harder to apply some common methods of reconstructing recent climatic events in this area, such as using medieval documents and chronicles or multicomponent archeological records.

Neither are the large-scale paleoenvironmental models geographers use to study Holocene climate change in the Arctic of much help. The usual time-interval in these models consists of the entire Holocene period, that is, the last twelve thousand years, subdivided either into four large stages (transitional late glacial, postglacial, interglacial climatic optimum, and recent cooling), or seven to ten smaller stages rounded off to the millenium corresponding to the Blitt-Sernander chronology. These chronologies suffice for archeological reconstruction of ancient prehistory in the Arctic and surrounding boreal regions (Barry et al. 1977, Dekin 1972, Dikov 1979, Kosarev 1974, 1983, Khlobystin 1973, Khlobystin and Levkovskaia 1974, McGhee 1972, Powers and Jordan 1989). However, the large time-intervals upon which they are based do not yield the finer resolution we need to discuss the *ethnohistory* of indigenous peoples. Especially in the later stages, described in detail in Russian records of the past four or five centuries, a glaring lack of correspondence in scale is immediately obvious between the two chronologies, paleogeographical and ethnohistorical. Squaring this discrepancy requires a much more detailed chronological sequence based on smaller intervals of centuries or even decades.

One does not have to be a geographer to comprehend the difficulties of establishing such a detailed climatic history for the huge expanse of the Eurasian Arctic. The final word here will go to the paleoclimatologists, who face the formidable task of attempting to pull together contrasting and even contradictory evidence of various kinds and from many observation points throughout the Arctic into a single, more or less coherent model. For our investigation of the Eurasian Arctic, therefore, albeit conditionally, we will have to rely upon an approximate chronology compiled on the basis of what sources are currently available. The obvious lacunae may in part be glossed with data from elsewhere in the circumpolar north, or adjusted using more reliable data on climate changes in the temperate zones during the past thousand years. While using such an *ad hoc* synthesis is clearly a matter of necessity, in the absence of concrete data it is justified.

Figure 11 represents my attempt to compile a chronology of climatic change in the Eurasian Arctic for the past thousand years (fig. 11). From my analysis of the data I was able to identify no less than twenty comparatively short periods since around 1000 C.E., each lasting from thirty to eighty years and comprised of two alternating climatic states, warming and cooling. Curves within the main graph present selected information about related changes in other components in the environment. I relied on the following sources drawn from a wide spectrum of primarily Russian references to establish the time parameters of this periodization and the prevailing conditions of each period:

1. Historical evidence about navigation and ice conditions recorded for the European Arctic. Such data are available for the Barents and Kara seas since the sixteenth century, and for northern Europe, Iceland, and Greenland since the tenth century, but only since the eighteenth or nineteenth centuries for northeast Siberia (Berg 1956b, Itin and Sibirtsev 1936, Lamb 1977, Nazarov 1947, 1949, Zhilinskii 1919).

2. Tables of fluctuations in the rate of tree growth (dendrograms) along the northern tree line, in the forest-tundra zone and the northern taiga. Tree-ring data are available covering the period since the twelfth century for Western and Central Siberia and Norwegian Lapland, since the fourteenth century for the Kola Peninsula, and since the sixteenth and seventeenth centuries for most other regions of the Eurasian Arctic (e.g., Adamenko 1963, Briff et al. 1988, Lamb 1977, Lovelius 1979, Molchanov 1976, Polozova and Shiiatov 1976, Shiiatov 1975, Turmanina 1970).

3. Evidence of fluctuating rates of forest regeneration and of latitudinal and vertical fluctuations in Arctic tree line. Such data are available for Lapland and northwest Siberia on a broad scale since the twelfth century and since the fourteenth to eighteenth centuries for other areas of the Eurasian Arctic (Akimov and Bratsev 1957, Andreev 1956, Lovelius 1970, Norin et al. 1971, Riabtseva 1970, Shiiatov 1967, 1979).

4. Evidence of alpine, continental, and subsoil glaciation and radioisotope-geochemical data on the composition of glaciers. These are available for the seventeenth century and later from the northern Urals and Scandinavia, since the eleventh century onwards for glaciers on Spitsbergen and Severnaia Zemlia, and since the eighteenth to nineteenth centuries for other areas of the Eurasian Arctic (Adamenko 1963, Chizhov 1976, Denton and Karlen 1973, Kotliakov and Troitskii 1985, Vaikmiae et al. 1984). The Eurasian data are thus much younger than those obtained from Greenland and Ellesmere Island ice cores.

5. Reports from written records and the results of instrumental observations. These begin in the eighteenth and nineteenth centuries in the Eurasian Arctic, in the fifteenth and sixteenth centuries for adjacent territories (northern Russia and Scandinavia), compared to the late eighteenth century for Greenland and the Canadian Arctic (Berg 1938, Betin and Preobrazhenskii 1962, Borisenkov and Pasetskii 1983, Bradley 1973, Chizhov 1976, Karlen 1982, Shnitnikov 1969, Vibe 1967, Weidick 1982).

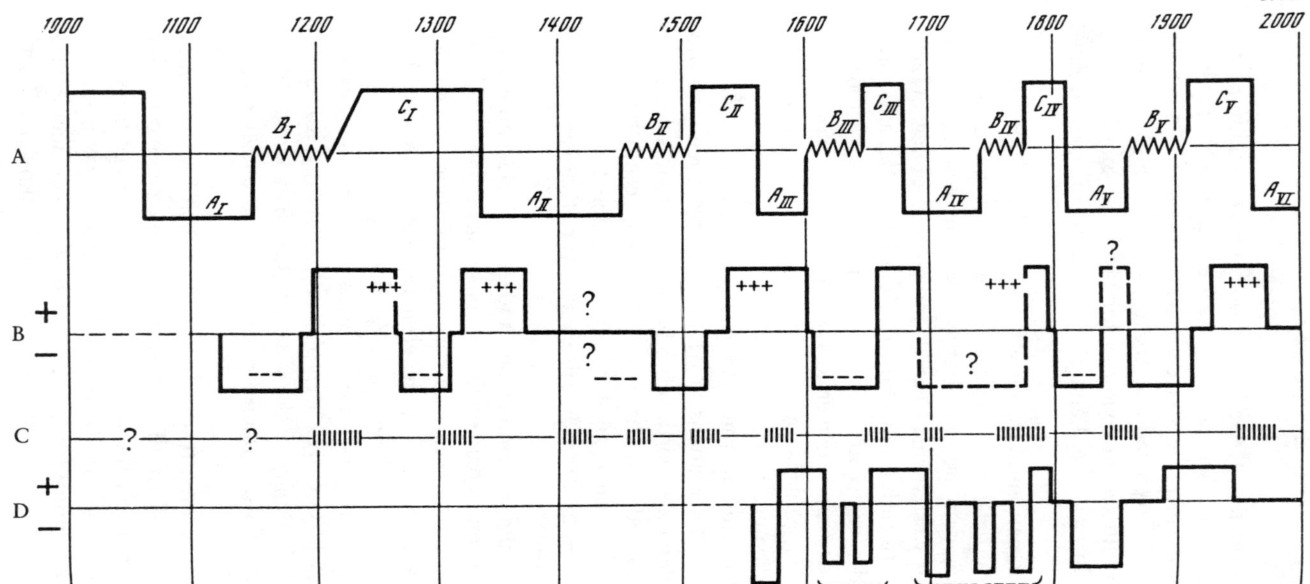

Fig. 11. Chronology of environmental change in the Eurasian Arctic during the past thousand years. A: Climate changes in Greenland (Vibe 1967). *A:* Phases of dry, cold, and stable climate; *B:* phases of humid and unstable climate; *C:* warming phases, with degradation of the polar ice.

B: Phases of Arctic tree-line expansion northward (+), and of retreat southward (−); and of increased (+++) versus suppressed (−−−) tree growth in northern Eurasia (according to Shiiatov 1975 and 1979).

C: Phases of forest regeneration along the southern borders of tundra zone in Lappland (Lamb 1977), marking warmer and more humide climate conditions.

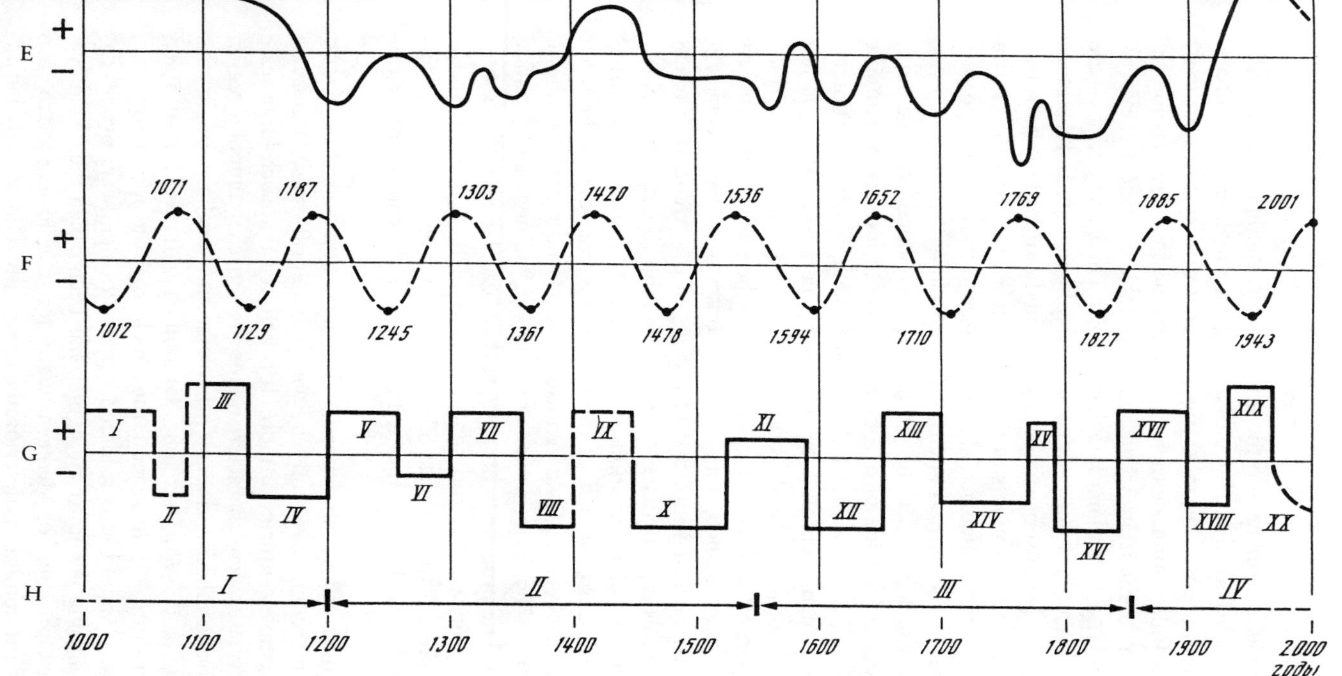

D: Phases of increased (+) and decreased (−) annual growth of northern coniferous species along the Arctic tree line in northern Eurasia (cumulative series, according to Lovelius 1979).

E: Temperature curve for Iceland (Bryson 1977:513).

F: Temperature and sea-ice trends in Greenland and northern Atlantic (adapted from Vibe 1981:211). (+): Phases with high summer temperatures and heavy ice; (−): phases with low summer temperatures and low summer ice.

G: Chronology of warming (+), and of cooling (−) phases in Arctic Eurasia (author's reconstruction).

H: Major climatic phases of the present millenium (according to Wendland and Bryson 1967). *I:* Neo-Atlantic; *II:* Pacific; *III:* Neo-Boreal; *IV:* Recent.

Of course, a number of difficulties arise in attempting to coordinate and adjust for discrepancies among such a variety of sources. But, for our purposes, the most important conclusion to draw is that, in the past millennium, neither the climate nor the overall ecological situation in the Eurasian Arctic remained stable or static, but experienced quite regular and marked fluctuations. These fluctuations were at times felt acutely in the realm of everyday human life and therefore became recorded in subsistence practices and oral traditions. In this way, the native inhabitants of the Eurasian Arctic, from the tundra to the seacoast, became actual eyewitnesses to the ceaseless process of changes in the natural environment unfolding before their eyes.

In general, I consider this chronology of climatic change sufficiently reliable for the past four to five centuries, that is, for the period which is reasonably well reflected in ethnohistorical sources. Of course, such a chronology, like any generalized model, is not capable of noting all local climatic blips throughout the great Eurasian expanse from the Kola Peninsula to the Bering Sea. Scholars have long since demonstrated that the onset of any particular climatic phase occurred in different regions of the Arctic at different times, and this is particularly true of short-term climatic change. According to several observations, the greatest asynchronicity occurred between the extreme ends of the Eurasian Arctic, that is, between the Scandinavian and Kola Peninsula region and northeast Siberia (Itin 1936:80–89, Khotinskii 1977:180–84, Vaikmiae and Punning 1982:33). The proposed chronology, therefore, largely reflects conditions in the western and central sectors of the Eurasian Arctic. Extrapolating it to northeast Siberia is contingent upon corrections indicated by local calibration with historical accounts or other evidence.

The climatic intervals defined within the period from 1000 to 1500 C.E. are more tentative, and here we are better off to use large-scale units of whole centuries or more. It is believed that such large-scale climatic phases were characteristic for the entire circumpolar region during the past thousand years (Adamenko and Lovelius 1976, Bryson and Wendland 1967, Diaz 1989, Graumlich 1991, Kelly et al. 1984, Zolotokrylin 1988). In general, the epoch from the 900 or 1000 C.E. to 1300 C.E. should be considered a period of significant overall climatic warming in the Arctic, which has been called the "Medieval Climatic Optimum" or Medieval Warm Episode. From 1300 to 1500 C.E. climatic conditions deteriorated drastically. This period of instability and rapid environmental change is considered transitional to the following phase of a long-term cooling trend, from 1550 to 1850 C.E., commonly known as the "Little Ice Age." The period of climatic warming that began in the mid-nineteenth century is generally called the "Contemporary Warming" phase in the Arctic.

When we compare this proposed Eurasian chronology with existing diagrams of historical climatic change in Greenland, Scandinavia, Baffin Island, Alaska, and other areas of the Arctic, both correlations and discrepancies emerge (see Andrews et al. 1981, Andrews and Miller 1979, Cropper 1982, Jacoby and Cook 1981, Minc and Smith 1989, Nichols 1975, Stanford 1976, Vibe 1967, 1981, Weidick 1982, etc). Such an examination, however, lays the best foundation for more broadly based pan-Arctic recontructions and comparative systematic analysis of basic stages in the economic history of indigenous communities throughout the Arctic area.

In analyzing local climatic change throughout the Arctic, many authors have emphasized the effects of more or less regular climatic cycles or general environmental rhythms that are closely connected to climate. First identified in the 1950s and 1960s, these cycles vary in duration, ranging from 5–6, 11, 22, 30–50, 50–60, 80–90, 160–180, to 250–300 years or more (Adamenko and Lovelius 1976, Lovelius 1970, Maksimov 1954, Prik 1968, Shiiatov 1967, 1975, etc.). Thus, they overlap and periodically coincide with each other, at frequencies dependent upon the amplitudes of the cycles involved. Similar cycles have been noted in adjacent boreal forest areas and in many other regions of the world. In this case, the proposed chronology shown in figure 11 primarily reflects mid-length climatic shifts of less than a century (from 30–50 and 50–60 years) or bridging at most two centuries (80–120 and 160–180 years). Climatic fluctuations shorter than thirty years do not register on this time scale. Environmental changes associated with them will be examined separately below.

It is very important to assess the degree of change in the ecological situation in the Arctic according to climatic cycles of various durations. Taken together with paleogeographical reconstructions, instrumental observations from the past two centuries indicate that average annual temperatures can fluctuate 2 to 3° C over long-term cycles such as 1800, 900, or as few as 250–300 years, and 1 to 2° during mid-length and short-term cycles such as 50–60 and 80–120 years (Andrews et al. 1981, Bradley 1973, Cropper 1982, Diaz et al., 1989, Gribbin and Lamb 1980, Minc 1986, etc.). Such fluctuations were sufficient to produce marked phenological effects on the timing and duration of the seasons, such as freezing and breakup of rivers and the amount of ice cover in Arctic waters, which are clearly documented in the paleoclimatic record. During long-term warming periods, Arctic tree line advanced 100 to 150 kilometers north, shrinking the total area of tundra. During cooling trends, tree line receded and the tundra area expanded accordingly (Nichols 1972, Norin 1974).

Such climatic shifts had an enormous influence on biological processes in northern ecosystems. In particular, they determined the abundance and tempo of population growth among game species used by the indigenous population. Ultimately climatic change led to profound changes in aboriginal subsistence activities and resource management systems.

Extreme Natural Phenomena

Since the nineteenth century, extreme environmental conditions—severe winters, drought, flooding, snowstorms, gales, and so forth—have been observed to occur on a periodic basis in many regions, including Eastern Europe and European Russia (Borisenkov and Pasetskii 1983:7–12, Chizhevskii 1973:38–39, 102–110). Using data from Russian and European chronicles of the eleventh to seventeenth centuries, the Russian climatologist Mikhail Bogolepov was the first to arrive at a complex system of five-, six-, eleven-, and thirty-three year cycles of climatic "disturbances" for mid-latitude Europe. He defined such "disturbances" as periods of increased instability in weather conditions. Unfortunately, comparable sources are not available for the Eurasian Arctic zone, or at any rate have not found their way into academic circulation. For most of the region we have only scattered materials dating from the late 1700s or early 1800s on, and these still need to be sorted and systematized.

Nonetheless, that there is a regularity and periodicity to extreme environmental phenomena in the Arctic is beyond doubt. In adjacent areas with much milder weather conditions, such as the Central Russian Plain, literally dozens of atypical natural phenomena were recorded in each of the past several centuries—drought, storms, fires, and extremely harsh winters (see Borisenkov and Pasetskii 1983). There is every reason to assume that the frequency of similar ecological "disturbances" would have been even greater in the Arctic. I will confine myself here to presenting a few of the clearest examples, referring primarily to the European Arctic and northeastern Siberia.

Severe winters and heavy snowfall

It has long been established that cold winters with heavy snow tend to occur every three to five years in the Russian Plain, and on a ten- to twelve-year cycle in the nether reaches of West Siberia and Kazakhstan (Nasimovich 1955:326, Formozov 1946:76–82). In the northwestern Russian boreal zone, the data show that the winters of 1916–17, 1928–29, 1939–40, 1940–41, 1941–42, and 1946–47 were extremely harsh ones (Formozov 1959:192). This works out to a similar cycle of a severe winter approximately every ten to twelve years.

For the regions of the Eurasian Arctic with which we are concerned, only a few scattered references indicate severe winters with heavy snowfall, such as 1894–95 in the Kolyma River basin, 1896 on the Kamchatka Peninsula, and 1909–10 in the Bol'shaia Zemlia tundra (Nasimovich 1955:326, 356). However, data documenting the duration of ice cover at the city of Arkhangelsk on the White Sea since the mid-eighteenth century do yield a clear ten-to-twelve-year pattern of cold winters. In the twentieth centuries these were the winters of 1903–05, 1915–18, 1929–32, 1943–45, 1958–60 (Shnitnikov 1969:22). Anomalously low January temperatures on the Kola Peninsula formed a nearly identical eleven-year cycle from 1880–1960 (Prik 1968:14). In West Greenland even a four- to six-year subcycle of colder-than-usual winters has been established (Vibe 1967:27).

Records on the extent of sea-ice cover and summer navigation conditions form a valuable if indirect source for reconstructing the frequency of unusually severe winters in the Arctic. In what is perhaps the first known case of international scientific cooperation in the Arctic, as early as 1595 Russian walrus hunters shared reports with Dutch navigators on the Barents expedition, explaining that the amount of ice in the straits around Novaia Zemlia varied from year to year and that the effects of a severe winter adversely affected navigation conditions in the following year (Zhilinskii 1919:39). If two severe winters occurred in a row, by the third year ice conditions rendered navigation in the Kara Sea extremely treacherous.

Historical records of ice conditions in the Kara Sea exist since the mid- to late 1500s. The period from 1860 to 1950 is the most fully documented, and reveals nine periods of increased multiyear ice cover. All correlate with sequences of severe winters occurring around 1862, 1871–73, 1882–86, 1891–92, 1902–03, in or around 1912, 1925–28, 1934–35, and 1944–46 (Nazarov 1947, Zhilinskii 1919). As we see, this series of cold winters once again yields a clear eight- to ten-year pattern. Analogous increases in ice cover have been observed in other Arctic waters: every fourteen years in the Chukchi Sea, at eleven-year intervals in the East Siberian Sea, and every nine years in the Laptev Sea, although the records in these areas are less regular and thorough (Itin and Sibirtsev 1936, Nazarov 1949).

Interestingly, local-level cycles of harsh winters appear to reinforce the effects of larger-scale Arctic cooling trends. Thus, when short- and long-term cycles coincide, the results appear to be cumulatively amplified. This may well be the origin of certain winters that became legendary for their severity (the winters of 1643, 1764–65, and 1847 qualify for this distinction in the European Arctic; Berg 1956b:172). If more than one cycle peaks simultaneously, climatic conditions may cross a threshold and enter into a protracted positive-feedback period, thus accounting for notably extended periods of enlarged icecover occurring at regular intervals, for example, about once a century in the Kara Sea (in the 1620s, the 1730s, the 1820s, and, most recently, from the late 1910s to the early 1920s) (Berg 1943:18, 1956b:172, Nazarov 1947:653).

Terrestrial crust ice

More detailed information exists on the incidence of crust ice on land, also indicating a pattern of periodic recurrence. It is well known that the survival of all Arctic animals is threatened far more by winter thaws and subsequent crust-ice formation than by extreme cold. This is why Arctic ungulates and species of birds that remain in the Arctic year-round suffer large-scale losses far more frequently during warmer, erratic winters than during colder but stabler ones.

The more maritime western and eastern extremes of the Eurasian Arctic are in general prone to crust ice, as well as the High Arctic islands and coastal regions. However, the most severe winter icing, that paralyzes the tundra on the magnitude of tens of thousands of square kilometers at once, occurs at regular intervals. Thus, crust ice gripped Kolguev Island in 1911–12, 1920–21, and 1931–33, the northeast Bol'shaia Zemlia tundra around Ust' Kara in 1947, 1960, and

1971, and the Novaia Zemlia Islands in 1899–1900 and 1917–18 (Formozov 1946:77–78, Geptner et al. 1961:354, Nasimovich 1955:325, Podekrat 1936:101–102, author's field records 1974), that is, either every ten to twelve years or, half as often, every twenty to twenty-five years. In all likelihood, acute winter land-icing corresponds to climatic cycles of similar duration.

When several climatic cycles coincide, winter icing can be catastrophic. Elder herders in the Bol'shaia Zemlia tundra recall three such periods, which occurred at twenty-year intervals, in the early 1930s, the 1950s, and the 1970s. Heavy icing was encountered on the Chukchi Peninsula in the early 1920s, the late 1940s, and the early 1970s, that is, approximately every twenty-five years.

Hot summers

Data on the recurrence of extremely hot summers in the Eurasian Arctic are highly fragmentary. We know, for example, that the temperature soared to 30 degrees Centigrade and higher in the lower Pechora River region in 1887, and in the Malaia Zemlia tundra in 1931. In the northeast Bol'shaia Zemlia tundra, the maximum July temperature reached 29 to 30° C in 1943, 1954, 1957, 1963, and 1974—once again fitting the ten- to twelve-year pattern (Ust' Kara weather station records). It appears that extremely high summer temperatures occur in shorter cycles as well: five to six years and even every three years. These short-term cycles are indirectly reflected by decreased ice cover in the Arctic seas. Thus, the Kara Sea was observed to be entirely ice-free in the summers of 1920, 1923, . . . 1929, 1932, 1935, 1938, 1941, and 1943 (Burke 1936:86, Itin 1936:89, Nazarov 1947:654).

Yet another indication of extraordinarily hot summers occurring on a cyclical basis comes from data on the frequency of wildfires arising in the tundra, forest-tundra, and the northern taiga in particularly dry years. Summer fires can ignite spontaneously, without any human interference. In the Canadian Arctic a soil horizon is described with traces of terrible fires dated to the middle of the second millenium B.C.E. (Nichols 1975:69). Tundra fires are recorded throughout the entire area from Alaska to Greenland and thus are connected with periods of rapid climatic warming.

Bogolepov was the first to determine that, according to medieval Russian chronicles, large fires occurred in the Central Russian Plain approximately every thirty-three years. A twenty-year pattern of big fires appears to have been more typical in the northern part of the taiga and forest-tundra zone. For example, a series from Alaska runs: 1871, 1891, 1910, . . . 1947, and 1969, and another, from the lower Ob' region in West Siberia: 1826, late 1840s, then 1867 (Kirikov 1960:23, Le Resche et al. 1974:149). An unusually complete series from Archangel'sk region shows the twenty-year-average pattern nicely: 1614, 1647, 1668, 1688–90, 1710, 1735, 1756, 1790, 1800, 1825, 1840, 1860, 1877, 1899, and 1920 (Vakurov 1975:5).

Over the past two or three centuries, several catastrophic fires have been recorded in the Eurasian Arctic. These sweep through hundreds of thousands of square kilometers, such as ones in the forest-tundra east of the Kolyma River in 1776, in the lower Yenisei basin, and east right up to the Lena-Indigirka watershed in 1859, and through the entire northern taiga zone in the mid-1730s, the mid-1930s, and the early 1970s (Kirikov 1960:23–24, Vakurov 1975:6–7).

Cold summers

Less information is available on the recurrence of extremely cold summers, characterized by extreme frosts and generally chilly weather, which usually affect navigation, summer maritime hunting, and also cause heavy losses to Arctic bird populations. Thus, in the Bol'shaia Zemlia tundra years, with consistently cool summer temperatures (July minimum less than −1.5° C) recurred in clusters every eight to ten years: in 1947, 1948, and 1949, in 1959 and 1960, and in 1968 and 1970 (Ust' Kara weather station records). Analogous clusters of cold summers were noted on the Chukchi Peninsula in the early 1920s and 1960s, when the summer months experienced large quantities of sea ice, cold winds, storms, and a marked deterioration in hunting conditions.

The native population has long been aware of short-term fluctuations in summer temperatures in connection with three-, four- and five-year cycles of Arctic sea-ice cover. "In the words of the Chukchi living near Cape Shelagskii, one can observe this well-known cycle in the condition of the ice here—every four years (by other reports, five) the ice piles up and presses hard upon the shore, and then a time comes when it goes away again" (Tolmachev 1911, cited in Itin 1936:78). And, although the frequency of summer arrival of the ice differs from one area of the Arctic to another, the existence of such a pattern, evidently, has been demonstrated in many regions (see Nazarov 1949:20–23, 27 for greater detail).

Thus, a preliminary review of the sources already reveals a definite periodicity in extreme natural phenomena, discernible even against a prevailing background of generally severe weather conditions in the Arctic. In individual years these rhythms of "climatic disturbances" could accumulate and then the frequency and intensity of disruptions in the usual weather regime would be sharply amplified. Such conflations of particularly dangerous weather phenomena were recorded in the medieval chronicles in the Central Russian Plain, the North Sea coast, and other areas of Western Europe. One would expect to find them in the Arctic as well.

To conclude with a particularly clear illustration, we can take the period from 1921 to 1926 on the Chukchi Peninsula. Both the interior and the coast were gripped by fierce crust-ice conditions. Entire herds of domestic reindeer perished. And, owing to the abundance of sea ice, strong winds, and storms on the surrounding seas, the sea-mammal hunt was unsuccessful in 1922, 1923, and 1925. Not long before that, around 1915, catastrophic autumn storms practically destroyed the village of Ungazik on Cape Chaplino. Village residents fled from their homes and scattered along the whole southeast coast of the peninsula from the Anadyr River to St. Lawrence Island (Aivangu 1985:53, Krupnik 1983:82–83).

Evidently, such periods were not at all rare in the history of the Arctic. One would expect them to figure in written records, folklore, and the oral traditions of the native people. In 1975, I recorded a folklore text in the village of Sireniki, which recounts how huge numbers of ancestral Sireniki people died as a result of a storm that swept all the adult male hunters out to sea on ice floes. Stories about natural disasters are sufficiently popular in Eskimo folklore that they undoubtedly reflect a true perception among Arctic residents of the environment they live in as a highly unstable one (see Minc 1986).

Fluctuations in Wildlife Populations

Periodicity in biological processes, that is, changes in animal populations and plant productivity that occur on a regular, cyclical basis, is a characteristic trait in the way the living world is organized. Arctic ecosystems display periodicity with exceptional clarity. A huge literature exists on population fluctuations in game animals of the Arctic and Subarctic, but presenting it all in these few pages would tax the reader excessively. Therefore, I will confine myself to commenting as succinctly as possible on the species of Eurasian Arctic game that played the greatest role in native subsistence systems.

The most important animal in Arctic subsistence has always been the *wild Eurasian reindeer-caribou* (*Rangifer tarandus*). Humans have hunted reindeer since the ancient past. However, the productivity of reindeer has always been affected by idiosyncratic population dynamics accented by rapid surges and sharp crashes, and fluctuating geographic distribution.

Although it is poorly systematized, there is a strong information base concerning wild reindeer-caribou population fluctuations in the Eurasian Arctic. The population has been known to experience mass-scale crashes on many occasions, for example, as a result of unusually severe winters with heavy snowfall, catastrophic crust-ice conditions, or epizootics (see Geptner et al. 1961: 353–54, Kishchinskii 1975: 161–65, Naumov 1933: 53). The Russian missionary Father Andrei Argentov described "entire fields" strewn with the bones of perished reindeer, victims of an epizootic that ravaged the Aniui River westward from the Chukchi Peninsula in the 1850s (Mikhel' 1938: 78).

Some Russian authors have defined fairly regular ten (actually, ten- to fifteen-) or twenty-year cycles in the ebbs and flows of the reindeer population. They attribute these, for example, to lichen recovery cycles or climatic fluctuations (Formozov 1935: 58–60, Geptner et al., 1961: 356, Semenov-Tian'-Shan'skii 1948a: 9–10).

Longer-term intracentury cycles of fifty to ninety years are even more clearly visible for North American caribou. Christian Vibe has described reindeer population peaks that occurred in West Greenland from 1720 to 1740, 1830 to 1840, 1910 to 1920, and in the 1960s, during dry, cold climatic phases. Corresponding minimums in the reindeer population occurred from 1760 to 1810, 1860 to 1900, and 1920 to 1950 (Vibe 1967: 163–79; see also Meldgaard 1986). Similar population fluctuations recurring at intervals of sixty to ninety years have also been noted for caribou herds in Alaska and the Canadian Arctic (Burch 1972, Haber and Walters 1980, Hemming 1975, Minc 1986, Yesner 1980a, etc.).

Based upon written and archeological evidence and Eskimo oral tradition, Meldgaard has constructed a model of the wild reindeer-caribou population cycle in Greenland (Meldgaard 1986, 1987). The duration of the cycle ranges from 65 to 115 years. It consists of a very short phase of sharp rise in the numbers of caribou (about ten years long), a relatively short phase when caribou are plentiful (10 to 25 years), and by far the longest phase, of *minimum* population (35 to 70 years). The abundance phases are normally accompanied in Greenland by a very rapid increase in the caribou range from the inland tundras to the seacoast. Large herds of caribou begin a regular migration pattern, and a native Greenlander hunt of these herds ensues. Conversely, during phases when stock is at a minimum, the caribou area shrinks and the herds congregate in a few refugia pastures in the interior regions. Large seasonal migrations cease, caribou hunting declines, and the total population falls precipitously—until the next such cycle begins.

We would expect to see a corresponding dynamic in the Eurasian Arctic as well, and, in fact, a similar population dynamic has been observed among wild reindeer-caribou in the tundra zone of northern Eurasia. In one of our areas of particular interest, northeast Siberia, Russian sources are available to reconstruct fully documented intracentury cycles in the caribou population, going back almost 350 years, that show amazing congruence with the Greenland cycles (see summaries in: Mikhel' 1938:67–77, Portenko 1941:77–84, Kirikov 1966:237–40, Kishchinskii 1967:146). When Russians first arrived in northeastern Siberia in the 1640s and 1650s, the caribou population was evidently not very large (the "minimum" phase). It swelled rapidly in the early to mid-eighteenth century and appears to have remained high right up until the beginning of the nineteenth century. One intermediate "minimum" phase around 1760–70 presumably went unrecorded when the Russian presence in the northeastern Siberian Arctic slackened sharply as a result of unsuccessful wars with the Chukchi. Reports of a new "minimum" appeared around 1810 through the 1820s. During these two decades, the wild reindeer herds failed to reach the Kolyma River on several occasions, disrupting the established migratory route and pitching the native population into severe famine (Vrangel' 1948:227, Gurvich 1966:136–37). But then the stock recovered, migration routes resumed, and native people resumed large-scale caribou hunting on a regular basis.

A new contraction in the Kolyma caribou population began in the 1840s. By the 1860s, the seasonal mass migrations of reindeer herds across the Kolyma River and its tributaries had completely ceased. Reindeer remained abundant in the Anadyr River basin, but, nonetheless, instances of "shortfalls" occurred here more than once, dooming the native population to famine, as in 1877, 1889, and 1894. The situation changed in the mid-1890s when the caribou stock in the northeast began climbing rapidly again. Regular hunting at river crossings resumed in the lower Kolyma and middle course of the Anadyr. It continued steadily until 1905–10, then once again was followed by an acute population plunge. Huge stocks numbering in the thousands vanished almost overnight, leaving behind scraggly groups of hundreds or even tens. These fragments of the former herds somehow survived until the 1950s–60s, then once again began to increase (Obukhov 1967:17, Zaitsev 1966:9).

Caribou populations show evidence of similar fluctuations in several other areas of the Eurasian tundra and forest-tundra zones, including northern Yakut-Sakha, Koryakiia, the Taimyr Peninsula, West Siberia, and the Kola Peninsula (Druri 1949, Geptner 1960, Kirikov 1960, 1966, Naumov 1933, Skrobov 1967, Vershinin 1972, etc.). These pulsations are very similar in their structure and effects. In the basic pattern common to all Arctic ecosystems, the wild reindeer-caribou population builds quickly, then crashes even more sharply. After the crash, the population experiences a prolonged minimum, during which the wild-reindeer-caribou range shrinks noticeably and migratory routes are disrupted.

Unfortunately, we currently lack sufficient data to establish a reliably synchronized chronology of population cycles throughout the Eurasian Arctic, let alone to postulate any single unifying model encompassing these fluctuations as they occur throughout the circumpolar realm. Like climatic cycles, the pan-Arctic pattern of medium-length wild reindeer-caribou cycles may well be an asynchronic one. Similarly to climatic cycles, however, the available data suggest that wild reindeer-caribou cycles do occur simultaneously in a broad range of places as widely separated as, for example, the West Siberian Arctic, northeast Siberia, Alaska, and Greenland, and that, in general terms, these cycles conform to the common pattern of a caribou "optimum" and "minimum," when both population and distribution shrink drastically. Given these observations, and the close relationship between climate and wildlife dynamics, it seems entirely plausible that these biological and climatological phases might indeed be closely related. Almost two decades ago, I presented data illustrating the close fit between wild reindeer cycles and climatic fluctuations, relating reindeer ups and downs to cooling and warming phases in the Siberian Arctic respectively (Krupnik 1975).[2] This issue will be covered in more detail in the following chapter.

I would particularly like to point out that in spite of a general reduction in the Arctic caribou stock over the past two to three hundred years, as a result of the development of reindeer husbandry and increased human harvesting, the *periodicity* of caribou population cycles in many regions seems unaffected by intensity of hunting pressure (Burch 1972:356, Nellemann 1969:150, Vibe 1967:166–74). The recent increase in the wild reindeer population in central Siberia illustrates this well. In spite of intensive industrial development activities in the area, a drastic increase in poaching, and intensified game harvests throughout the 1960s and 1970s, surveys show the Taimyr herd alone swelled from some 150,000 to 575,000 head (Syroechkovskii 1982:63–67, Zabrodin 1976:11–12).

Finally, the data attest to the existence of still longer-term, multiple-century population fluctuations among wild reindeer-caribou. We have indications of such long-term cycles occurring in Greenland, the Canadian Arctic archipelago, the West Siberian Arctic, and the Alaskan interior (Anderson 1981:75–76, Bockstoce 1979: 90, Khlobystin and Gracheva 1974:82–83, Meldgaard 1987:245). In all these cases the caribou herds dwindled markedly or completely disappeared around the end of the first millennium C.E. or the beginning of the second, during what is usually called the Little (or Medieval) Climatic Optimum circumpolar warming trend. Reconstructions by Minc and Smith show a long-term low in the northern Alaska caribou herd from 1100 C.E. to the early sixteenth century. Subsequently, the animals regained their former abundance north of the Brooks Range, remaining stable until the late nineteenth century (Minc and Smith 1989:26–35).

The historical dynamics and distribution of *elk* (*Alces alces*) are somewhat better known. Elk, like its "cousin," the North American moose, is another very important Arctic game species. Sixty- to ninety-year population cycles show up for elk even more clearly than for caribou. In the forest belt of European Russia, periods of high elk population were observed in the late 1700s, from 1850 to 1880, and from 1940 to 1960. These surges alternated with abrupt population decreases in the early 1800s and from 1890 until the 1920s, when elk completely disappeared throughout a large area (see summaries in Reimers 1972, Syroechkovskii and Rogacheva 1974).

In the Eurasian Arctic, elk population cycles have been recorded most fully, once again, in the far northeastern region. In the late 1700s elk were abundant throughout the entire tundra and forest-tundra zone up to the mouth of the Kolyma River, the Aniui and Chaun watershed, and the middle course of the Anadyr and the Penzhina rivers. Around 1810, the population began to decline, and during the 1820s and 1830s it was considered a rare event indeed to kill an elk anywhere in Kolyma Region. Elk reappeared in the lower Kolyma in the mid-1800s, but then experienced another sharp crash, and went completely extinct in the valleys of the Kolyma, Anadyr, Gizhiga, and Penzhina rivers by the end of the century. The herds began to regenerate in the early 1900s, and by the 1960s regained their former range up to the Arctic and Okhotsk Sea coasts, thus once again reaching the boundaries of their late eighteenth-century maximum (Kishchinskii 1967:144–45, Mikhel' 1938:83–88, Portenko 1941:87–89, Vershinin 1972:116–19).

This pendulum effect, by which elk moved back and forth between tundra and forest-tundra, was even more pronounced in other areas of northern Eurasia. In the 1880s–90s, hunters from northern Karelia and the Kola Peninsula almost never encountered elk; by the 1930s they were regularly sighted in the area further north on the Barents Sea coast. Until 1940 there were no elk in the Nenets Autonomous Area; by the 1950s and 1960s they reappeared throughout all of Arctic Russia up to the Arctic Ocean. During the same period, elk herds on the left bank of the Yenisei River pushed 450 to 500 kilometers northward, up to 67 to 68° N, and established themselves in pasture grounds devoid of elk since the mid-1800s (Makridin 1962:1090–91, Naumov 1934:64–65, Semenov-Tian'-Shan'skii 1948b:92), Syroechkovskii 1974:184–85).

From the 1920s to the 1940s, the population and range of elk and moose also expanded in Scandinavia and in Alaska, where they suddenly appeared on the Arctic coast (Chesmore 1968:528, Le Resche et al. 1974:147–52, Lebedeva 1972:302–303). Evidently, large-scale elk-moose population cycles develop fairly synchronically in various locations in the Arctic, and occur in geographically disconnected areas simultaneously.

Periods when the elk population increased in the Eurasian Arctic —the late 1600s, the late 1700s, the 1850s to the 1880s, and the 1930s to the 1960s—correspond closely with climatic warming phases. During these warming phases, elk moved in droves into the forest-tundra and even the tundra zone as far north as 72 to 73° N, spilling out in large swaths on the Arctic Ocean littoral.

With the presence of elk-moose this far north documented during recent warming trends, it seems probable that elk bones found on the Novosibirsk Islands, on Reindeer Island in the Kola Gulf, and in a prehistorical site at Cape Shmidt on the Chukchi Peninsula correspond to earlier such warming periods (Semenov-Tian'-Shan'skii 1948b:91, Vereshchagin 1967b:22). In this respect elk-moose and wild reindeer-caribou are "antagonistic" animal species, in that favorable ecological conditions for caribou are unfavorable for elk, and vice versa. In contrast to caribou, elk and moose fare very poorly during cold winters with heavy snowfall, while their numbers and range increase rapidly during warm years, and especially following summer fires (Bishop and Rausch 1974:569, Geptner et al. 1961:315, Le Resche et al. 1974:149, Reimers 1972:82).

A similar relationship exists between the two principal fur-bearing animals of the Arctic—the *Arctic fox* (*Alopex lagopus*) and the *red fox* (*Vulpes vulpes*). Periodic population fluctuations have been reported for both species since the early 1900s. Fox dynamics are traditionally identified with population cycles in their main prey species. For the Arctic fox, this is the lemming, while red fox prey mainly on tundra voles and white hares. The humble northern lemming is world-famous for its population peaks. In the tundra these occur every three to four years (Chitty 1950, Lack 1957, Severtsev 1941, Siivonen 1950). The Arctic fox population also peaks on a three- to four-year cycle, usually tagging behind the lemming peak by one year. In addition to three- to four-year and ten- to twelve-year cycles, both species of fox display long-term cycles of twenty to thirty years. These long-term cycles are evident on a broad geographical scale (Nazarov 1979:102–106, Smirnov 1967:88–89, Vibe 1967:108–10, 135–43).

During climatic warming trends in the Arctic, the red fox, like the elk and moose, rapidly shifts its range northward into the tundra. In so doing, it actively crowds the Arctic fox and will even take over Arctic foxholes (Chirkova 1967:111–12, Parovshchikov 1959:224–26). Conversely, the Arctic fox, similar to the caribou, thrives during climatic cooling phases.

Sharp population fluctuations have been observed among other species of Arctic fur-bearing animals as well. The *Arctic hare* (*Lepus arcticus*) experiences regular population explosions alternating so predictably with catastrophic epizootics that researchers speak in terms of monitoring ebbs and flows in the "hare tide." The Arctic hare cycle is between eight and twelve years long, leading many authors to correlate it either with eleven-year cycles of solar activity, or with extremely cold winters and wet summers, which occur on the same frequency and tend to foster epizootics (Elton 1934:55, Lack 1957:252–54, Naumov 1939:73–75).

Data on hunting harvests in northern Yakutia have been used to establish a three-year cycle of peaks in the *ermine* population (*Mustela erminea*). Northeast Siberia appears to experience a fairly regular "attack" of wolves (*Canis lupus*) on an average of every twenty years. In the Kolyma and Anadyr basins, for example, these wolf surges occurred in the 1820s, . . . 1860s, the 1880s, the very early 1900s, and in the mid-1930s (Mikhel' 1938:17–18, 44, Portenko 1941:14–15, Romanov 1941:11, etc.). Finally, a few data point in the direction of a population cycle among the Eurasian grizzly bear (*Ursus arctos*), which in certain years migrates far northward into the tundra right up to the shores of the Arctic Ocean. It is possible that these migrations coincide with the nine- to twelve-year peaks observed among grizzly bears in the boreal forest range further south (Mikhel' 1938:14–16, Romanov 1941:118–19).

Like the stocks of land mammals discussed so far, populations of Arctic *waterfowl* and *seabird* colonies also vary cyclically over time. In various regions of the Arctic, bird colonies have been observed to expand and decline sharply on an annual and multiyear basis, both along the coasts and in the inland tundra. Data from places as varied as the Kola Peninsula, the Asiatic side of Bering Strait, Koliuchin Island, and the Yamal Peninsula all show fluctuations in rookery populations and the size of the annual moulting flocks and shifts in habitual nesting territories (Bianki et al. 1967; Liudmila Bogoslovskaia 1985, personal communication, Krechmar et al. 1978, Rakhillin 1970, Tomkovich and Sorokin 1983, Uspenskii and Kishchinskii 1972, etc.). Observers have usually correlated these fluctuations with adverse weather conditions during the laying and hatching seasons—sudden drops in temperature or snowfalls, etc.—or with epizootics. Christian Vibe established a fairly regular twenty-five- to thirty-year cycle for the common eider (*Somateria mollissima*) in Greenland, based on a series of population increases in 1805, 1830, 1855, 1885, and 1925, divided by steep declines (Vibe 1967:43–44).

Inland tundra birds also display rather regular fluctuation patterns. Regular "harvests" have long been observed for the willow ptarmigan in the European Arctic, occurring, on the average, every ten or twelve years. These alternate with catastrophic crashes, and periods of massive mortality, which can take the dramatic form at times of entire flocks perishing in the sea, as occurred in the mid-

1880s, the late 1890s, from 1906 to 1907, and again in 1916 (Voronin 1978:147–48, Golitsyn 1881:78, Formozov 1935:97–98). In 1916 so many ptarmigan died in the ocean that "the bodies of drowned birds were cast up in such numbers on the shores of the Bol'shaia Zemlia tundra that in places they form a shoal a fathom deep" (Solov'ev 1927a:21). The willow ptarmigan population shows a more or less identical ten- to twelve-year frequency all across the Arctic, as recorded from northeastern Siberia, Canada, and Greenland (Braestrup 1941, Lack 1957, Portenko 1941, Vibe 1967, etc.).

Three- to four- and ten-year cycles have been described for *predatory tundra birds* such as the snowy owl, and have been associated with the population dynamics of their usual prey—lemmings, tundra voles, and hares. Six- to ten-year cycles are typical for several *game birds* of the forest-tundra and northern taiga, such as partridge, wood grouse, and black grouse. These species experience population crashes during extremely severe winters or in years with hazardous freezing conditions during the summer hatching season (Belykh and Konechnykh 1976:46–47, Semenov-Tian'-Shan'skii 1938:295–98).

The population dynamics of *sea-mammal* game species are clearly defined in the Arctic. It is believed that sea mammals' relatively slow reproduction rate and high longevity militate against such short cycles as five-to-six or ten-to-twelve years. But, for years, both native hunters' observations and game statistics have indicated a cyclical pattern to sea-mammal harvests over time, noting sharp fluctuations in the annual catch of bowhead whales, walrus, various seal species, and even of polar bears in many regions of the Arctic (Freeman 1969–70, Krupnik 1984a, Maher and Wilimovsky 1963, Mikhel' 1938, Minc 1986, Portenko 1941, Vibe 1967, etc.). These fluctuations are largely determined by weather conditions during the hunting season each year, especially the date when boats can first be launched and the hunt commences, and the abundance of animals in the offshore hunting areas. For example, in Chukotka, in years when the ice goes out late or there are frequent summer storms and high winds, the sea-mammal hunt is always unsuccessful. In northwest Alaska, in the ancient Eskimo whaling villages of Point Hope and Barrow, success of the spring whale hunt depended heavily on the time of formation, the direction,and the size of narrow cracks or leads of open water between the shorefast and sea ice. According to local whalers, the worst hunting years are ones with heavy winds, precipitation, fog, and sudden thaws during the spring months (Minc 1986:62–65).

For our purposes, however, it is more useful to trace relatively long-term shifts ("pulsations") in sea-mammal distribution and range in conjunction with mid-length and long-term (multicentury) climatic fluctuations. During Arctic warming phases sea-mammal migratory routes typically shift northward into colder waters, and, during cooling phases, the animals make a commensurate shift back to the south, into Subarctic latitudes. Many archeologists have successfully made use of this pattern in reconstructing the dynamics of prehistoric hunting conditions in various polar regions, including north and northwest Alaska, Labrador, Greenland, and the Canadian archipelago (see chapter 6).

Such changes are characteristic for the main Arctic *fish species* as well. During phases of climatic warming in the Arctic, the ranges of warmer-water fish shift far to the north. Thus, in the 1930s, herring suddenly showed up along the coast of Greenland, where it had never been seen before, while Atlantic cod, which had barely reached as far north as the southern tip of the island thirty years before, was found as far north as 72° N. A similar situation occurred in the Barents and White seas, and in the North Pacific Ocean. With the onset of the 1940s–50s cooling phase, warmer-water species such as salmon moved back south again, and large quantities of cold-water Arctic cod (*Boreogadus saida*) and capelin reappeared in their place (Berg 1958:147–49, Burke 1936:87, Vibe 1953:166–68).

Historical sources indicate analogous long-term fluctuations dating back to the eighteenth century at the least. They frame the shorter eight- to twelve-year cycles observed in the chief species of food fish in many regions of the Eurasian Arctic, such as the Kola Peninsula, northern Kamchatka, and the Kolyma and Anadyr' basins. In Kolyma, for example, catastrophic shortages of anadromous fish occurred in 1810–13, 1821–22, 1829–31, 1844–45, 1850–54, . . . 1905, and 1911–16. In Anadyr', shortages were noted in 1867, 1877, and 1888 (Gurvich 1966:136–41, 150, Olsuf'ev 1896:54–55). There is every reason to suppose that this biological "see-saw" has operated in the Arctic since as far back as we care to consider.

Similar examples of cycles in Arctic wildlife could fill many pages more. However, the facts presented, I believe, are sufficient to convey a sense of the ceaseless dynamism inherent in the Arctic biotic environment, a dynamism that results from a complex system of interconnected biological pulsations of various frequencies, the most important of which appear to be 3–5, 10–12, 20–25, and 50–80 years long. Inasmuch as population fluctuations of many animals are closely interdependent, when cycles of several species peak simultaneously it can lead to genuine "explosions" of game animals and plentiful hunting resources in the tundra world. But, in the same way, if several species reach an otherwise-normal nadir concurrently, it can have an equally inexorable, internally reinforcing effect, and can trigger periods of biological crises and massive mortality in a community's entire range of hunting species simultaneously.

Such devastating "crises of survival" are documented from time to time across the Eurasian Arctic. Nikolai Gondatti, for example, recorded the recollections of local native elders about a gigantic plague that accosted virtually all species of game in the Anadyr' basin in the early 1880s.[3] Usually, such game catastrophes occurred in years with extreme weather conditions as well, when the usual cycles of native subsistence were already badly disrupted. Such was the case around 1820 in the lower Kolyma River valley. For several years in a row, fish stocks practically vanished *and* the caribou and elk populations crashed. The period from 1821 to 1822 was especially terrible for the local population, when both bad weather and an epizootic among the sled dogs kept hunters cooped up in camp, unable to venture out in search of game (Gurvich 1966:136–37, Vrangel' 1948:227).

A number of similar overall game "catastrophes" can be cited from throughout the Arctic.[4] The main point I want to emphasize is that, while hunting pressure increased on several species of valuable game animals during the postcontact time, overhunting would not have produced a *simultaneous* population decrease in so many species at once. To native residents such disappearances of game represented utterly "natural disasters" which occurred without warning and could in a painfully short time completely wipe out the established system of resource utilization.

Epizootics in the Domestic Animal Population

Instability was as common among domestic animal populations as among wild ones. Accounts from the 1800s tell of devastating epizootics among both reindeer and dogs, which caused, according to eyewitnesses, indescribable terror among the local people. "During epizootics, reindeer die throughout the tundra in herds of thousands. Enormous graveyards appear, cavernous places infected with a terrible disease. The reindeer die, and rot where they fall. The herders are in a panic, and are changed overnight from wealthy people to beggars. They ride away from the dead herd on the few animals left standing on their feet, just to keep them alive. . . . No one buries the corpses in these graveyards. . . . [A]s a result the entire tundra is infested with the ghostly bones of dead reindeer" (Sosunov 1925:35).

Domestic Reindeer

The most detailed statistics on domestic reindeer stocks are preserved from the tundra zone of European Russia beginning in the early 1870s. Data are also available for this area on herd losses from epizootics since the 1870s. In normal years the Nentets and Komi herders experienced a natural mortality rate of from five to ten percent of their stock size. In years of epizootics and extreme weather conditions mortality could rise to thirty or forty, and even fifty percent. Crushing epizootics caused by anthrax and necrobacillus (hoof-and-mouth disease) had especially devastating effects on the local reindeer economy. In a period of only twenty-five years, from 1885 to 1910, these herders lost more than 500,000 reindeer, with an average herd size of 300,000 to 350,000 (Babushkin 1930:167, Krupnik 1975:29, Terletskii 1932b:14–15, 35).

Early accounts of epizootics among domestic reindeer in the Russian tundra zone date from the late 1700s, but reliable records of stock losses begin only around 1850. Massive reindeer mortality from epizootics was documented in the early 1830s, the mid-1840s, . . . , 1874–75, 1886–88, 1896–98, and in 1907. Losses occurred on a much smaller scale in 1915–16 and 1925 as well. The incidence of these epizootics form a highly regular series based on ten-year intervals, a pattern first identified by Russian veterinary surgeon Nikolai Ekkert based on his observations of catastrophic anthrax outbreaks in 1887, 1897, and 1907 (Mamadyshskii 1910:60–61). Reindeer stock dynamics during the period show its effects clearly (fig. 12).

Anthrax typically strikes the tundra in years with hot, humid summers. Therefore, the frequency of outbreaks can be correlated with eleven-year climatic cycles or with the internal rhythm of a bacterial catalyst closely related to them. Necrobacillus epizootics also almost always occur during hot years and in the past usually coincided with anthrax outbreaks (Kuratov 1925b, Naumov 1933, Sdobnikov 1933).

Anthrax does not occur in northeastern Siberia, where high rein-

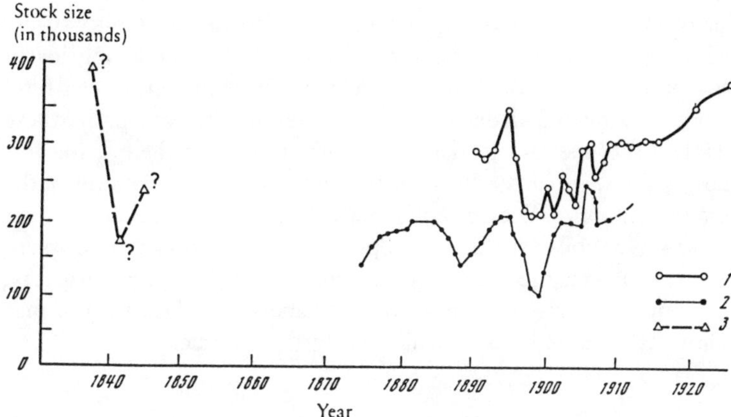

Fig. 12. The domestic reindeer population and its fluctuations, 1840–1925. 1: Bol'shaia Zemlia Tundra; 2: Mokhcha District; 3: Rough estimates for entire Arkhangel'sk Gubernia (Arctic Russia).

deer losses corresponded either to summer necrobacillus outbreaks, or, more commonly, to bad icing conditions in winter and spring. For example, in Chukotka, such losses were experienced in the late 1890s, from 1900–10, 1919–23, and in the late 1920s; that is, they also recurred approximately every ten to fifteen years (Karaev 1923:15, Vdovin 1965:167, 169; author's field data 1975).

The intensity of such epizootics and high mortality cycles among domestic reindeer was evidently subject to longer-term fluctuations as well, whether of decades or a century or more. Thus, in the Arctic zone of European Russia, severe outbreaks of anthrax occurred in 1886–87, 1896–97, and in 1907, resulting in reindeer losses of approximately 200,000, 190,000, and 150,000 respectively. But then, from 1910 through the 1920s, even before the advent of wide-scale vaccination programs for reindeer, the impact of epizootics subsided naturally. Overall, it appears that the previous peak of epizootic activity in Arctic Russia was during the 1830s and 1840s, while in the intervening years, especially from 1850 to 1880, as in the period from 1910 to 1930, the reindeer economy was free from devastating losses.

Dogs

Data compiled on mortality among local dog populations in West Greenland, Labrador, and northern Canada suggest a certain regularity and recurrence in dog epizootics (Braestrup 1941, Chitty 1950). Although there are several reports on extremely high dog losses among both the aboriginal and métis native communities of Arctic Siberia, to my knowledge no one has undertaken to systematize these data as they pertain to native dog breeding. Nonetheless, for certain regions, we can easily identify ten- to fifteen-year patterns of the major epizootics. For example, on the Chukchi Peninsula epidemics took severe tolls on the dog population in the early 1890s, 1901–1904, 1908–15, 1920, and 1933 (Gondatti 1898: viii, Shmit 1939: 115, Vdovin 1965: 188–89). A more detailed analysis of these records may allow us to extend this sequence out further in time.

Summary: The Arctic as a Human Econiche

The facts presented, I think, amply confirm my main conclusion, namely, that nowhere in the Arctic is there such a thing as a stable, normal, or "typical" environment. It is misleading even to conceptualize the Arctic in such terms. Any "normal," or, shall we say, "average," state is in reality at most a short-term transition from "bad" to "good" or back again, in a network of continuous fluctuations intimately interlinking all components of the Arctic ecosystem. As we have seen, nothing escapes this process of change. Game and birds, climate and ice, tundra and sea—all are in ceaseless motion.

A similar instability found its ecological expression in the arena of human subsistence in the Arctic. Therefore, by the time an Arctic person approached old age, he or she necessarily garnered memories of numerous events in an entire span of personal environmental "history," and from this derived a sense of short- and medium-term environmental shifts. However, a single individual human memory would not capture longer-term wildlife cycles of a century or more, and it was these that led people to pick up and migrate from one general area to another as the stocks of certain animal species they used for subsistence dwindled and others increased.

This all speaks to the complexity of ecological dynamics and the crucial importance of interrelationships within Arctic ecosystems. Ecosystems in the lower latitudes may have a strong tendency toward *homeostasis*, that is, to return to a baseline state in which all functions tend toward a condition of permanence, or entropy. Among living organisms of the Arctic, homeostasis would be hard to achieve at all. Relatively complex and stable ecosystems, in which a large number of predator species exploit many kinds of prey, are maintained here only in areas of exceptionally rich biological nodes along the coasts, mainly near the southern edges of the polar zone. Most of the vast expanses of Arctic tundra are dominated by younger and "poorer" ecosystems characterized by a simplified internal structure, low species diversity, and a dense, highly competitive network of links between predators and prey.

It is just such Arctic ecosystems that are most susceptible to continuous internal fluctuations. All natural cycles in the Arctic have far shorter time intervals and markedly greater amplitudes than we find in the more complex ecosystems of the temperate and tropical zones. The most important subsistence species of game and birds are usually drawn into the short cycles of their prey, such as lemmings, Arctic voles, and Arctic cod. Consequently, populations at both trophic levels fluctuate more or less synchronically throughout enormous areas. Moreover, this trend increases as we move progressively inland within the Arctic region from the Bering Sea and Scandinavia to Yakutia. As continentality and climatic extremeness intensify, so do the amplitudes of "disastrous" biological pulsations and the severity of subsistence catastrophes (Uspenskii 1970:738).

Therefore, it is clear that the Arctic environment privileges those species of animals and plants whose populations are capable, not only of enduring drastic environmental disruptions, but also of recovering quickly in more favorable years following such events. Ecologists say such species "live under the influence of *r*-selection," where *r* signifies the rate of growth in a population. This emphasizes how important rapid reproduction is to survival for these species.

Continual mobility and the use of large harvesting areas comprise the other pivotal adaptation of Arctic organisms. As Max Dunbar bluntly put it, in order to cope with adverse changes in their environment, Arctic species "desperately need space." Arctic ecosystems draw upon their large spatial dimensions as a source of strength, allowing areas that suffer the most from periodic ecological disruptions to recover quickly (Dunbar 1973:180, 185).

This spatial adaptation also provides a good explanation for the high mobility of almost all species of Arctic fauna, which typically have only weak attachment to specific habitats. All nonhibernating Arctic animals make seasonal or extended migrations to lower latitudes or within the polar zone itself. In addition, they might easily change their feeding, breeding, or calving grounds each season of the year. Therefore, expanding the harvesting area increases the cumulative stability of the Arctic population, and vice versa: any loss in territory becomes a real threat to existence for any Arctic wildlife species (Bergerud et al. 1984:19, Dunbar 1973:180).

Ecologists think that it is these two conditions—the capability to recover quickly and to shift habitats periodically—that render Arctic ecosystems relatively resilient to external disruption (Banfield 1975:549, Dunbar 1973:182). In this respect the Arctic environment is certainly more fluid than the tropical rainforest ecosystem, with its shocking abundance of living organisms, or the desert, which has an even lower species diversity and biological productivity than the Arctic, but no less fragile. In its natural state, an Arctic ecosystem pulsates in space and time, easily changing or even dissolving in a very short time in one area, but invariably reestablishing itself in another. When preexisting natural conditions resume, the ecosystem is capable of reconstructing its former spatial and species structure in its former habitat quickly, thanks to high mobility and growth rates among the chief players in its biological cast.

In my opinion, two vectors have overarching significance in shaping the geography of Arctic environmental change. One, which I propose to call the "north-south axis," is illustrated nicely by the elk-reindeer interaction described above.

In climatic warming phases in the Arctic, all wildlife species energetically shift northward, colonizing new habitats. On land, "warmer," boreal species—elk, red fox, bear, wolf, marten, otter, and arboreal birds—penetrate into the forest-tundra and tundra zones and even reach as far as the shores of the Arctic Ocean, pushing local tundra species northward before them (Formozov 1959, Parovshchikov 1959, Skrobov 1958). At sea, pagophilic cetaceans and pinnipeds—bowhead, walrus, narwhal, beluga, and ringed seals—expand their range into high-latitude, interior sectors of the polar basin, and warmer-water species move up into the southern frontiers of the Arctic to replace them. But, with the advent of subsequent climatic cooling, the biological "see-saw" tips in the other direction, and the "colder" species of Arctic fauna—polar bear, Arctic fox, narwhal, reindeer, beluga, and Arctic cod—begin the shift from the north back to the south again.

Such cycles are as invariable as they are ephemeral, and as inexorable as the reasons they occur, namely, the macrophysical forces that determine large-scale fluctuations in the Arctic environment. Therefore, in most polar regions one can identify "warm" ecological phases with one set of subsistence resources and "cold" phases with another set (or set of quantitative ratios) of primary game species. These phases may vary in their duration or intensity from one location to another as a result of how several natural cycles of differing frequencies coincide. In addition, in different areas of the Arctic, the regional profile of subsistence species during "warm" and "cold" phases may vary greatly. What is important here is not universality, which is highly unlikely in the enormous circumpolar area in any case, but, rather, the general principle.

We can call the other axis of ecological change in the Arctic that of the "land and sea." According to the data presented in this chapter, both the inland tundra and coastal zone experience alternating periods that are more or less favorable for different aboriginal resource use patterns, depending upon the abundance of game species, the ice cover, and weather regime, etc. I think that the contrasting organization of the coastal and interior aboriginal subsistence systems described in chapter 3 conveys a sense of how this quality is reflected in the rhythmic composition of life in the littoral and inland tundra biomes.

But what about the people behind these "systems?" Were the inhabitants of the Eurasian Arctic ruled by the same ecological exigencies that shaped their complex and ever-shifting daily world? Or, did accumulated experience and the wisdom of the centuries give them tools to work out special cultural and social mechanisms for taming or even transforming their environment, as some authors claim?

We are ready now to search for answers to such questions. In the chapters that follow we will do so by reexamining aboriginal maritime hunting and reindeer-herding subsistence adaptations in a new light, that of their ecological persistence and response to environmental change. By such explicitly mutual consideration of the history of humans and the history of nature in the Arctic we may hope to achieve a new synthesis of the relationships between the two.

CHAPTER FIVE

The Rise of Reindeer Pastoralism in the Arctic

Introduction

The moment at which reindeer breeding appeared in the Eurasian tundra and began a process of dispersal throughout its farthest reaches is the most important turning point in the cultural history of the native peoples of the Eurasian Arctic. It was this process that led tundra herders to develop their subsistence system, with its highly refined structure of production and distribution, as described in chapter 3. With all justification, Siberian reindeer herding can be considered one of the clearest—and also one of the best-documented—illustrations of the transition from a mode of subsistence primarily or substantially based on hunting or foraging to an economy based on intensive and highly specialized livestock pastoralism—in effect, a transition from appropriation and extraction of natural biological resources to genuine economic production.

This transition was fundamentally important in the economic and social development of the peoples of the Arctic. Unfortunately, owing to the paucity of available archeological data and substantive historical sources prior to the 1600s, the exact timing and circumstances of the rise of reindeer pastoralism in the Eurasian tundra remain an open question. We are certain only that the appearance of domesticated reindeer and the subsequent development of a large-scale intensive reindeer economy as a specialized form of subsistence were two highly disjunct events. These developments were separated in time by several hundred years, and possibly took place in different areas as well. The date of the former has not been established with any degree of certainty and remains the subject of speculation and heated debate (see Ingold 1980, Shnirelman 1980, Vainshtein 1972). We know only that it occurred some time before 892 C.E., since in that year the Norwegian chieftain Ottar sent a letter to King Alfred of Norway informing him that he owned six hundred domestic reindeer (Ingold 1980:103–104, Maksimov 1929:24). The latter event, as I will attempt to show, belongs to a much later time period and can be reconstructed in great detail based upon extant written sources.

The currently prevailing opinion was first set forth by the Russian anthropologists Glafira M. Vasilevich and Maksim G. Levin (1951). According to their view, reindeer breeding was first introduced to the western and central regions of northern Eurasia by ancient Samoyed cattle breeders from the mountainous regions of southern Siberia. This evidently occurred no later than the end of the first millennium C.E. (Vasilevich and Levin 1951:78–81; see also Vainshtein 1972:123, 1981:119–23, Vasil'ev 1979b:64–66, Maksimov 1929:22–24, Shnirel'man 1977:29–30). Initially, reindeer were kept in small herds and were used for milking and/or transportation, as both pack and saddle animals. It is true that the skills for using semitamed or domesticated reindeer as hunting decoys or even as pack animals may have already existed among indigenous peoples of the tundra, who hunted wild reindeer. Reindeer breeding, or, at any rate, the skills associated with it, is believed to have reached the Yukagir, Koryak, and Chukchi of northeastern Siberia only several centuries later, evidently via the ancient Tungus (Gurvich 1983, Shnirel'man 1980, Vasilevich and Levin 1951). One highly interesting perspective suggests the possibility of an autochthonous hearth of reindeer pastoralism among the Chukchi and Koryak in northeastern Siberia itself (Zolotarev and Levin 1940, Vdovin 1950, 1973, Simchenko 1976, 1978, Volfson 1984). Unfortunately, for the time being, it remains insufficiently supported by evidence from either the historical or the archeological record.

Ethnohistorical Records on Reindeer Pastoralism

One way or another, by the time of Russian contact in the 1600s, a complex subsistence system dominated by hunting and fishing, and supplemented by small-scale reindeer breeding prevailed among most of the inhabitants of the Eurasian tundra. These included the

Nenets, the ancestors of the tundra Enets, some Nganasan, Yukagir, northern Evenk and Even, the Kola peninsula Saami, and the nomadic portions of the Koryak and Chukchi (Gurvich et al. 1970, Simchenko 1978). Medieval Swedish sources indicate a similar pattern among the Scandinavian Saami of the 1500s and early 1600s (Mériot 1984, Wheelersburg 1991). At that time, domestic reindeer were used almost exclusively for transportation and the herds were kept very small. According to early records from the 1600s, individual herds never exceeded one hundred head. Meat and skins for food, household needs, raw materials, and trade came only from hunting wild reindeer, which at one time had been the basis of life for all nomadic peoples of the Arctic.

Only in the 1700s did the domestic reindeer stock begin to grow, and the onset of this growth occurred virtually simultaneously in the western and eastern ranges of the Eurasian Arctic. In one of my very first publications I attempted to trace this process among the European and West Siberian Nenets, for whom there is relatively more information contained in Russian records than for other indigenous peoples of the Eurasian Arctic (Krupnik 1976b). Archival documents, information from the Siberian chronicles, and reports from European travelers confirm that the Nenets's total stock of domestic reindeer remained extremely small throughout the 1600s. Any herder who owned as many as forty reindeer was considered "mighty"; reindeer were strictly conserved and were slaughtered for meat in emergencies only. Hunting and fishing played the main economic role in Nenets life, with game, and caribou meat in particular, serving as the staple food. The Nenets made clothing and shoes from the skins of wild reindeer and other fur-bearing animals, as well as coverings for their portable tent dwellings, and used them to pay tribute and taxes (Alekseev 1932:273, 296, 1936:201, 249, 272, Dolgikh 1970:25–26, Kolycheva 1956:78–80). A few available domestic reindeer—and not every family, seemingly, had them—were used solely as transport and sacrificial animals, or served as a means of exchange, for bride-price, for example. Since the entire population of European Nenets in the late 1600s was approximately 1400, or no more than 300 to 350 families (see records in Dolgikh 1970, Kolycheva 1956, Vasil'ev 1979), the total stock of domestic reindeer pastured between the White Sea and the Ural Mountains could not have exceeded more than 10–20,000.

Thus, the subsistence system of the early-contact Nenets differs not only qualitatively from that described in chapter 3, but also in its essential form. In the 1600s it is possible to speak only of some *elements of livestock breeding* that existed within the basic framework of a foraging economy, while in the more recent period we are concerned with a fairly developed pattern of nomadic pastoralism, based on regular slaughter of domesticated animals for household subsistence purposes (see chapter 3). This mode of subsistence has been aptly termed "carnivorous pastoralism" (Ingold 1980:176). Within this framework, it would be more accurate to identify the early-contact Nenets as "late hunters" rather than as reindeer herders and to locate them in a subsistence category of their own: "reindeer-moved hunters and fishermen of the tundra and forest-tundra." Their way of life then pulls into sharper focus if we view it as an intermediate form of subsistence between people who hunted on foot for wild reindeer, and those who might be called authentic nomadic pastoralists.

Nenets of the 1600s were far from the only people to engage in this transitional mode of subsistence. Various sources show that it also existed at the very same time among the Scandinavian Saami (Mériot 1984), the Enets (Dolgikh 1970), and the nomadic Chukchi (Vdovin 1948, 1965, 1975), as well as among the Nganasan until the mid- to late 1800s (Dolgikh 1952, Popov 1948), the northern Sel'kup until the mid-1800s (Lebedev 1980), and the tundra reindeer Yukagir until the early twentieth century (Gurvich 1975). None of these peoples had very large numbers of domestic reindeer, but this in itself did not influence their basic orientation to using local resources. Like the seventeenth-century Nenets, they all used reindeer almost exclusively for transportation, and obtained food, clothing, housing, and other everyday items through hunting and fishing.

However, in the mid- to late 1700s in the Eurasian Arctic zone occupied by Nenets, the population of domestic reindeer suddenly began to grow, and the herds increased surprisingly quickly. By the end of the century it is estimated that there were more than 160,000 domestic reindeer in the European Nenets area alone—a tenfold increase in some 100 years. Wealthy Nenets herders usually had a stock of 1,000 or more reindeer, mid-size herders had between 100 and 200, and the poorer ones at least 20 or 30 (Latkin 1853:106–107, Lepekhin 1805:229, Voprosy i otvety 1787:4–5). Even keeping in mind the inaccuracy and possible exaggeration of these estimates, they nonetheless indicate that something approaching a "reindeer revolution" took place over a hundred years, or during the course of only four to five generations in the human community.

Russian early-contact records paint a similar picture for a number of other native peoples throughout the Eurasian Arctic. Beginning in the mid-eighteenth century, the record indicates that large-scale reindeer breeding and its associated pastoralist subsistence system appeared progressively among the Chukchi (Vdovin 1948, 1965, 1975) and the Koryak (Gurvich 1983), then the Enets (Dolgikh 1970) and Khanty (Koz'min 1980). Another explosion occurred from the 1850s to the early 1900s, among the Dolgan (Popov 1948), northern Komi (Zherebtsov 1982), Nganasan (Dolgikh 1952, Gracheva 1983, Popov 1948), northern bands of Yakut (Gurvich 1977), Sel'kup (Lebedev 1978, 1980), and the Finnish and Kola Peninsula Saami (Konakov 1988, Luk'ianchenko 1971, Nikkul' 1975). As the domestic herds grew, the wild deer population fell, and hunting for wild reindeer, which until then had played the central role in the subsistence of all these peoples, gradually receded into the background. By the end of the nineteenth century, among many peoples—the European Nenets, Komi, Koryak, and most of the reindeer Chukchi—wild reindeer hunting had virtually disappeared.

Explanatory Models

This is the general historical layout of Eurasian reindeer herding currently accepted by a growing number of Russian Siberian researchers. However, there is no agreement as to what could have triggered such rapid growth among the domestic reindeer population in the 1700s and 1800s, or, conversely, what factors were responsible for repressing it before that time. Some scholars connect this surge with the contemporaneous strengthening of Russian state power in Siberia, which they associate with a reduction of intertribal wars, the establishment of the rule of law, and support of Russian officials for the "inclinations of wealthy reindeer herders toward private property and enterprise" (Gurvich 1983:115, Gurvich et al. 1970:54). Although this explanation has some merit, it cannot be considered a full and final one. In fact, many of the main loci of the boom in native reindeer breeding were found in the areas of intertribal wars of continuous feuds of one ethnicity against another: Chukchi against Koryak, Obdorsk against

Pustozersk Nenets, eastern Nenets against Enets, etc. These areas remained heavily beleaguered by bloody conflicts and raids, whether between native groups or with the Russians, well into the late 1600s even mid-1700s.

Therefore, it is probably safer here to say that the effects of Russian expansion constituted a *conducive social climate* rather than the main *agent provocateur* for the rise of reindeer pastoralism in Eurasia. In fact, in a few individual cases, Russian scholars tend to pick out local factors that explain why and when a particular group of Siberian people actually shifted to a reindeer economy. For example, the Chukchi stole their reindeer from the neighboring Koryak and Yukagir (Bogoras 1931:108–12, Vdovin 1948:69–70). The Nenets and the northern Sel'kup gradually wiped out their wild reindeer herds through overhunting, partly in response to the market demand from the growing fur trade (Lebedev 1980:86–87). The Enets shifted to spending the entire summer on the move throughout the tundra and thus were exposed to a more nomadic way of life (Dolgikh 1970:134), and so forth. Unfortunately, what little we can glean from the historical sources about the indigenous peoples of Siberia in the time of early contact does not immediately suggest any satisfactory general reasons why the numbers of domestic reindeer stock would have shot up so suddenly, nor why the tundra population in fact chose to make a transition from nomadic hunting to this newer, more time- and labor-consuming means of subsistence. At the same time, the speed with which extensive reindeer pastoralism took root and spread virtually simultaneously throughout remote and seemingly unconnected corners of the Eurasian tundra zone, from the Fenno-Scandian Peninsula to the West Siberian tundra and the Chukchi and Kamchatka peninsulas thousands of kilometers away, inevitably suggests that some kind of underlying general trends existed that strongly favored, and perhaps even dictated, this process and the transition to a reindeer economy throughout most of the area.

In search of such a set of general conditions governing this dramatic transformation, some scholars have tried to establish a connection between the rise of reindeer pastoralism and various ecological changes in Arctic Eurasia, especially climatic change (Khlobystin and Gracheva 1974:84–85, Khlobystin and Levkovskaia 1974:240, Leeds 1965:98, Dikov 1989). However, not one of these explanations rests on a comprehensive argument. In my opinion, the *ecological* aspect of the mechanism of transition to large-scale reindeer herding should have been fairly universal, while the *social* factors in this process probably varied among different peoples in their local environments and historically specific circumstances.

Ecological Model

Since the Arctic domestic reindeer were free-ranging year-round, the size and health of the herds fluctuated considerably. As in any form of pastoralism, the number of animals faltered under the influence of adverse external factors. Chief among these were unrelenting crust-ice conditions, harsh winters with heavy snowfall, and summer epizootics, as discussed in chapter 4. Any change in the environment had a direct impact upon the physiological condition of the reindeer and their reproduction rate, and, of course, on the quality of the pastures that nurtured them.

Indeed, the appearance of a reindeer economy in Arctic Eurasia is a classic case on which to test our thinking about the genesis and dispersal of a new form of subsistence. Unraveling the interaction between ecological and social factors by calculating their composite effect can shed greater light on our understanding of how such a process occurs. However, in order to use ecological data effectively in a reconstruction of the history of the Arctic reindeer economy, we need first to establish clear answers to two questions: (1) Exactly which environmental changes or conditions can we define as ecologically favorable (or adverse) for indigenous reindeer breeding? (2) What exactly has been the history of change in the natural environment of the Eurasian Arctic during the past several centuries?

At present we know a fair amount of information concerning ecological factors in traditional reindeer pastoralism. It is known that the domestic tundra reindeer is highly adapted to very low winter temperatures, and its physiological "comfort zone" goes as low as −25 to −30°C (Geptner et al. 1960:306, Panin 1930:60–64, Slonim 1966:46). However, it is true that especially severe winters take a toll on the reindeer and weaken their condition by spring.

Climatically, the short Arctic summer season is the true test for domestic as well as wild reindeer, for that is when they gain most of their fat to survive the long Arctic winter. It has long been established that the tundra reindeer is very poorly adapted to high summer temperatures. If the temperature rises to 10°C the reindeer are already noticeably uncomfortable, and if it climbs still further to 15° and higher the animals begin to suffer a variety of physiological malfunctions (Davydov 1960:71–74, Segal' 1960:239, Zhigunov 1961:81–84). On such warm days the reindeer lose their appetites and stop grazing. They suffer rapid weight loss, weaken, and become unfit to ride or to carry goods. Evidently, this is how the tradition arose among many Arctic pastoralists—the Chukchi, Koryak, and also the Dolgan and Nganasan up to the early 1900s—not to subject the reindeer to any transportation work during the summer.

In the warm days of summer, especially in clear, dry weather with little or no wind, biting insects greatly increase their activity, which exhausts the reindeer even more. After a hot, dry summer the rut goes poorly and the herd has little strength built up for the long journey to the winter pastures. As a result more reindeer perish during the winter and spring months, and the offspring are weak. This in turn means that fewer newborns survive the calving season to reach maturity by the next fall. In the end, as was shown in chapter 4, the summer weather conditions determine the character and degree of disease losses in the herd, which remain relatively low during a cold and rainy summer and increase sharply in a hot summer as a result of the generally exhausted and weakened state of the animals.

Weather conditions also have a direct bearing on the biological productivity of the pastures. In winter the frequency of crust ice, the thickness of the snow cover, and the formation of a solid snow crust too thick and tough for the reindeer to break through, all directly affect the animals ability to forage. In a warm, dry summer the lichens that form the reindeer's most nutritious food for the rest of the year grow much more slowly than when the summer is cool and wet. The lichens themselves are brittle and fragile, so that the pastures are much more susceptible to reindeer trampling. Lastly, in hot years the fire danger rises in the tundra (see chapter 4), and, in the tundra and forest-tundra, it takes several decades for reindeer moss pastures to regenerate themselves in burned-over areas (Gorodkov 1926:154–55, Sdobnikov 1933:217, Iudin 1969:9).

All these data definitely show that the health of aboriginal reindeer pastoralism depended heavily upon the overall ecological situation. Ecologically favorable years for domestic reindeer (and thus for the native reindeer economy) were characterized by moderate precipitation; damp, cool summers; and relatively cold winters free from drastic temperature fluctuations. Such conditions are generally associated with periods of climatic cooling in the Arctic. In contrast, ecologically adverse years for tundra reindeer herding are those with warm, erratic winters when frequent thawing leads to the formation of crust ice, coupled with hot, dry weather during the summer months. Conversely, these conditions are associated with climatic warming trends. Finally, years with erratic weather conditions, unexpected freeze-thaw cycles, and frequent precipitation take the worst toll on reindeer breeding. Such conditions are most commonly found during general periods of climatic transition from a warmer climate to a cooler one.[1]

Against this general background, we can now proceed to analyze the historical sequence of climatic events in the Eurasian tundra zone in the last thousand years, based on the climatic reconstruction outlined in chapter 4. For each of the twenty climatic phases defined during this millennium (see fig. 11) we can actually rate the environment based on how favorable or adverse it was for the development of reindeer pastoralism. Practically the entire first half of this millennium, with its protracted warming phases, followed by the abrupt onset of a cooling trend with highly erratic weather conditions, appears to have exhibited an overall negative effect on native reindeer herding. Then, more stable cooling phases clustered recurringly during the late 1500s to early 1600s, throughout most of the 1700s and the early 1800s, as well as the first decades of this century.

Since wild and domestic reindeer are physiologically very similar and would thus respond to climatic conditions in virtually identical ways, it will hardly come as a surprise that these periods of climatic cooling conducive to reindeer herding coincide with times when the wild reindeer population peaked in the Eurasian Arctic, as reconstructed in chapter 4. It is crucial to understand from this that such periods were doubly significant for the expansion of native pastoralism. On the one hand, ecologically favorable periods foster the natural preconditions for domestic reindeer breeding in that fewer reindeer die, their physical condition improves, and their reproduction rate increases. On the other hand, because the wild reindeer population would have shown strong growth during these periods as well, the presence of abundant hunting resources alleviated the need to slaughter domestic herds for consumption.

Social vs. Environmental Agents of Change

Thus, the environment appears to have provided certain natural conditions to make reindeer breeding possible. However, the human ability and decision to make good use of these possibilities ultimately depended upon whether and how particular triggering social conditions conjoined at any moment in time. And here, it would seem, we may find a plausible framework that ties together what little we know about the social history of the native peoples of Arctic Eurasia. In fact, the first known period of *ecologically* favorable conditions for indigenous pastoralism, the late sixteenth to the early seventeenth century, witnessed a drastic deterioration and destabilization in the social environment. It came as the result of the Russian invasion of Siberia, which brought military subjugation and internecine conflict to the indigenous population, along with epidemics and forceful relocations. Such social conditions were unarguably inhospitable to the development of a reindeer economy. On the other hand, in the next ecologically favorable period, which can be considered to have lasted from the beginning of the 1700s right through the middle of the 1800s, socioeconomic forces stimulating the growth of pastoralism were clearly emerging in connection with the entrenchment of government power, the development of trade throughout Siberia, and the attenuation of intertribal conflicts. Such conditions must have encouraged new economic relations, stabilized the domestic reindeer herds and property rights over them, and allowed a certain depth of new subsistence experience to accumulate.

Indigenous reindeer pastoralism burgeoned in the Eurasian Arctic throughout the 1700s as a result of two interwoven factors—socioeconomic transformation and environmental change. Together, they created the conditions in which remarkably similar subsistence practices spontaneously developed in distant, geographically disjunct areas throughout the extent of Eurasia.

What could the mechanisms have been that triggered such a rapid increase in the domestic reindeer population among the Nenets and the Chukchi in the 1700s, or among other peoples in the following centuries? Social factors in this process have been cited elsewhere by various Russian authors (Gurvich et al. 1970:54, Lebedev 1980:86–91, Vasil'ev 1976:325–36, Vdovin 1975:154–55). Therefore, I will only quickly name the chief ones among them: the beginning of social stratification on the basis of wealth and property among the native peoples, which was supported, and in places even stimulated by, the Russian administrators; the demise of previous norms of clan solidarity and support, and therefore a new-found possibility for individual owners to accumulate large private herds; an increased demand for reindeer for transportation in fur trapping and fur trade; and a growing demand for transportation services required by the Russian administration. Students of the Scandinavian Saami cite basically the same factors, and note that their significance also became widespread only in the 1600s and even 1700s. In the Saami case, however, still other factors played an influential role: hunting lands were expropriated by Swedish and Norwegian settlers, exorbitant taxation and consequent rapacious hunting decimated the wild reindeer stock, and the imposition of rents for pasture lands increasingly inhibited extensive grazing practices, and so forth (Beach 1981:66–70, Lundmark 1989:38–39, Vorren 1974–75:249–52, Wheelersburg 1991:343–44).

Purely biological factors affecting reindeer population growth were evidently no less important. Summer grazing conditions improved markedly, summer and winter mortality among domestic reindeer dropped, and the reproduction rate showed a direct increase. It has been noted that the fall rutting season goes much more easily after a favorable, that is, a relatively cool and wet, summer. Fewer cows are barren, and one-year-old females or even calves born that year become fertile and conceive (Sdobnikov 1933:209, Semerikov 1933:15–16, Solov'ev 1927b:26).

Lastly, it appears that by this time experience in selective breeding had accumulated to a threshold sufficient to manipulate the age-sex structure of the herd, and this factor certainly hastened the transition to reindeer husbandry. The pastoralist strategy *per se* is oriented toward maximizing the numerical size of the herd rather than its productivity. Surplus males are castrated, and females are never slaughtered unless and until they are barren (Ingold 1980:78). Accordingly, as soon as the number of domestic reindeer exceeds the minimum necessary for transportation purposes (as was the case in the hunting economy), a selective slaughter becomes possible, in which the most productive animals are spared. These consist primarily of females, and a special "transportation" contingent of male animals selected for castration out of the general herd.

In sum, various factors engendered faster growth and a general improvement in the physical condition of the reindeer. In turn these developments encouraged herders to build up their stock, to regard the reindeer increasingly as the main measure of wealth, prestige, and social status, and eventually to transform them into their most important source of income.

Transition to the Reindeer Economy: The Earliest Records

Narratives and Russian records permit us to trace exactly how the transition occurred from a primarily hunting economy with small-scale reindeer breeding for transportation to the model of pastoralism we examined in chapter 3. Elsewhere I have described this process as based upon data from the Nenets (Krupnik 1976b). Notwithstanding the inevitable variation in local environments and practices, the majority of tundra nomads passed through a succession of specific stages in making this transition to a pastoralist economy.

The first of these stages is readily identified as the *initial period* of aboriginal reindeer breeding. It began with the appearance of domesticated reindeer in the tundra zone and extended into the 1600s. In some regions it lasted even until the 1800s and early 1900s. As I have already mentioned, this first stage was characterized by a mixed-foraging form of subsistence in which hunting and fishing predominated. The tundra people obtained their staple food from wild reindeer meat, fish, and wildfowl. They made fur clothing and covered their tents with the skins of wild reindeer or other game animals. The few domestic reindeer they kept were used for transportation only, and perhaps for certain ritual purposes.

The next stage is the *triggering period* of reindeer pastoralism. It began with the rapid increase in reindeer stocks and the appearance of large herds numbering first in the hundreds, then in the thousands, which belonged to individual owners or herder groups. However, this process by no means meant that the former hunting subsistence was suddenly replaced by one of a livestock economy. Numerous records testify that at this stage (corresponding to the early to mid-1700s for the Nenets and Chukchi and the early 1900s among the Nganasan), wild reindeer (caribou) hunting and fishing continued to play the central role in subsistence—indeed, sometimes at the expense of reindeer breeding (Kolycheva 1956:77, Popov 1948:19, Vdovin 1965:12–15, Voprosy i otvety 1787:30, Zuev 1947:35). The annual economic cycle of the tundra people continued to be organized around the main food-getting activities pursued, and caribou hunting still served as the main resource base for food, housing, trade, and tax obligations, supplemented by land and sea hunting and fishing, just as before.

Vasilii Zuev provided a clear evaluation of the Siberian Nenets's subsistence in the mid-eighteenth century based upon his participation in the Russian Academy of Sciences expedition of 1768–74: "Their economy can be divided such that they regard fish as their food, and reindeer as their wealth. If the fish are not running, these reindeer-men, who don't even know how many reindeer are in their herds, complain about hunger just as much as poor men. And while these wealthy men suffer from the same hunger, they are loath to kill their own reindeer" (Zuev 1947:68).

It is interesting to see how similarly the records describe reindeer peoples' subsistence across a range of places and times, be it Nenets, Chukchi, and Koryak in the early to mid-1700s, Nganasan, Enets, and northern Sel'kup in the mid- to late 1800s, or the Scandinavian Saami until the late 1700s.[2] Throughout this period herd sizes among all these peoples numbered in the thousands, but they continued to use domestic reindeer only for drayage, and strenuously avoided killing them for food. In emergencies, when they did kill deer for food, this was done in a special manner so as to avoid spilling any of the reindeer's blood, which was considered sinful (Gracheva 1983:8, Kosven 1962:279, Popov 1948:55, Vdovin 1974:118). The meat of wild game, first and foremost that of caribou, was considered more desirable and more prestigious than that of domestic reindeer, to which the nomads were then relatively indifferent (Bogoras 1904:72, Dolgikh 1952:8, Simchenko 1976:84).

At first glance, these facts suggest a strange dissonance between the social and subsistence, or food-producing, roles of reindeer breeding. Such a "dissonance" appears coherent only in the transition to large-scale reindeer husbandry was not directly evoked by a crisis in the previous modes of activity or the exhaustion of traditional food resources, as many writers have suggested. This means that the development of livestock production, even in its unique, Arctic form, is not always connected with a crisis in hunting or preceded by the development of sedentary land cultivation. In this case, as we see, it arose in the context of a hunting economy during a comparatively favorable time that retained its old focus of livestock breeding for transportation.

Interactions Between Wild and Domestic Herds

The role that overhunting of wild reindeer played in the rise of Arctic pastoralism deserves separate treatment. It is often argued that wild reindeer stocks decreased in tandem with and proportionately to an increase in domestic ones. Alternatively, it has been suggested that a drop in the caribou population had already occurred even before the advent of a large-scale reindeer economy, and in some way served to trigger its growth (Gurvich 1977:52, Drury 1949:25, Ingold 1980:118, Khlobystin and Gracheva 1974:81–82, Vdovin 1965:10). This opinion is hard to support. Throughout the Eurasian tundra zone this process was actually rather recursive, gradually ebbing and flowing over time. As data presented in chapter 4 indicate, during some periods the wild reindeer population might grow in numbers parallel with the domestic herds. Records confirm this for various regions during the mid-1700s, the early and very late 1800s, and especially the mid-1900s, when a substantial increase in wild reindeer stock was observed in many areas of the Eurasian Arctic, including the Taimyr Peninsula, northern Yakutia, and the Kola Peninsula.

In fact, periodic increases in the caribou population evidently played an important role in supporting reindeer husbandry, especially in its initial period. Availability of hunting resources provided the indigenous people with the time necessary to accomplish the transition gradually: to transform a hunting society to a herding one, to develop a new annual cycle, and to acquire experience in handling, pasturing, and protecting large herds. After all, the reindeer herders would not have begun overnight to slaughter their own domestic stocks on a regular basis, having made a neat transition from hunting wild reindeer to "hunting" domestic ones, as Bogoras once believed (Bogoras 1933:243). Old stereotypes oriented toward accumulating and conserving as many domestic reindeer as possible must have been deeply embedded and it took time for these tendencies to recede. Without this transformation, it would not have been possible to establish a food-producing reindeer economy as the dominant form of subsistence.[3]

Such a *transitional period* for large-herd pastoralism may have lasted anywhere from 80 to 150 years. It appears to have taken at least 50 to 80 years among the Nenets and Chukchi, and about the same amount of time or slightly less among the Koryak, that is, from the late 1600s to the mid- to late 1700s. The transition lasted the longest among the tundra Enets and the Nenets of the lower Yenisei, covering about 150 years, from the late 1700s to early 1900s.[4] We can date the termination of this transition period from the first records of nomads regularly slaughtering their domestic reindeer and using their meat and skins for subsistence needs. Such reports first appear for the reindeer Koryak in the 1770s and for the Chukchi in 1790 (Kosven 1962:282, Titova 1978:113, 125).

At this *climax stage*, elements of a crisis situation apparently did catalyze a broad-scale shift to the new subsistence strategy. Among almost all the Arctic nomads who practiced reindeer breeding, sooner or later a moment came when hunting wild reindeer was no longer an adequate source of food and skins for themselves and for trade. Thus it became necessary to harvest their own domestic herd and to conduct a regular slaughter. It is the onset of this practice that chiefly heralds the transformation of aboriginal reindeer breeding into a genuinely productive economy, or, once again to borrow Ingold's phrase, "carnivorous pastoralism." Most commonly, this qualitative leap was in fact correlated with a direct reduction in the caribou population.

As noted in chapter 4, the population of wild reindeer/caribou is naturally prone to cyclical fluctuations that have little to do with excessive human hunting, the proliferation of firearms, or other human causes. In the broadest sense, the wild reindeer in Eurasia decreased in numbers at times when unfavorable ecological conditions predisposed aboriginal pastoralism to decline as well, that is, with phases of climatic warming or of unstable weather in the Arctic. Thus, even though the numbers of domestic reindeer herds were also diminishing simultaneously, the ecological pressure may have pushed both domestic and wild stocks into the same limited "refugia pastures," that is, those that remained usable even during climatic turmoil—the best, most secure areas, which were free from crust ice, heavy snowfalls, or blizzards, especially during the calving period. Moreover, during these periods of decline, the wild reindeer suffered more from human hunting, too—both in a relative sense, since the weakened stock's reproductivity was depressed and could not replenish itself with its former speed, and in absolute numbers, since the human population and its consumption needs would have swelled during the preceding era of favorable conditions.

According to data presented in chapter 4, there are at least four such periods of rapid caribou extinction that can be identified throughout the Eurasian tundra zone since the 1700s. By the late 1700s wild reindeer had become rare in at least five areas: the Scandinavian Lapland, the Kanin-Timan and Malaia Zemlia tundras, the Koryak uplands, and the eastern portions of the Chukchi Peninsula. The second "low" virtually eliminated wild reindeer from the Bol'shaia Zemlia tundra and the Amguema and Chaun River valleys by the mid-1800s. On the Kolyma River and its tributaries, and on the Anadyr' River, mass migrations of reindeer ceased by the late 1800s or very early 1900s. Around the same time, the reindeer population fell drastically in the Taz and Turukhan River basins, in northern Kamchatka, and throughout most of the Kola Peninsula. The latest crash in the caribou population of the Eurasian Arctic occurred as recently as the 1930s in the Urals, the Yamal and Gydan peninsulas, and in northern Yakutia. Again, what all these places and times have in common is that they were characterized by unfavorable conditions for native reindeer-breeding economies as well.

It is even more striking that the majority of the tundra nomads made the transition to food-producing reindeer pastoralism in remarkably similar cyclical waves. This can hardly have been coincidental. Two waves seem to have been set in motion almost synchronically from the western and eastern extremes of the Eurasian Arctic zone, eventually meeting in the middle. The new pastoralism seems to have appeared first among the Scandinavian Saami and the reindeer Koryak, evidently shortly before or after 1700, when sources noted that both these groups had already amassed huge reindeer herds that they actively used for food and skins (Mériot 1980:64–66, Shnirel'man 1980:114, Vdovin 1973:214–16, Wheelersburg 1991:344).

By the late 1700s reports began to surface of Kanino-Timan and Malaia Zemlia Nenets conducting a regular slaughter of their domestic reindeer for food. Again, these were counterpointed with similar reports from the Chukchi Peninsula in the east (Titova 1978:125, Voprosy i otvety 1787:4–5). A reindeer economy had supplanted hunting and fishing among most of the Bol'shaia Zemlia, the Yamal Nenets, and the reindeer Chukchi by the mid-1800s. The next counterpoint pair were the Saami of the Kola Peninsula and northeast Finland and the northern Sel'kup, by the late 1800s (Konakov 1986, Lebedev 1978, Luk'ianchenko 1971, Nikkul' 1975). The overwhelming majority of Dolgan, tundra Enets, Nganasan, and northern Yakut made the transition to a large-scale reindeer economy between 1900 and 1930 (Gurvich 1977, Popov 1935, 1948, 1952). Thus, it was only in the early twentieth century that nomadic pastoralism, advancing simultaneously from western and eastern cusps of the reindeer-breeding area over a period of two hundred years, ultimately converged in central Siberia, and established itself as the prevailing form of subsistence throughout the Eurasian tundra zone.

A shortage of food does not appear to have been the main catalyst that impelled herders to adopt the practice of a regularized slaughter of domestic stocks at the same time that the role of hunting was diminishing in their subsistence. Rather, it was the supply of reindeer skins, which increasing fell short of needs for clothing, shoes, housing covers, and other household items. If necessary, reindeer meat could be replaced by fish, fowl, or sea-mammal meat, or even flour purchased from Russian traders as was the case among the Nenets, as discussed above. But there was virtually no substitute for caribou skins for human survival this far north. No other material was readily at hand from which to make clothing and housing that would hold up to the demands of the polar environment.

The need for reindeer skins was even more acute because it did not consist simply of forty to fifty "statistical" skins a year for every household (see chapter 3). Each type of need required a minimum threshold quantity of a particular *kind* of skin, available only at certain rather fleeting times of year. As reindeer Chukchi have explained to me, only very short-haired skins are used for sewing the inside set of winter fur clothing, for which herders made a special slaughter at the end of July. Skins for the outer set of fur clothing came from the August slaughter, and had longer hair. The skins of deer killed at the beginning of September were thick and warm enough to make the fur cover of the *polog*, or the inner sleeping chamber inside the Chukchi *yaranga* dwelling. Furs from the very latest, October slaughter were usually reserved for trade with the coastal hunters. The latter needed the warmest clothing possible made from maximum-growth winter-coat reindeer skin, since sea hunting, whether on open water or in the sea ice, often involved long periods of sitting or standing in the cold with little or no movement. A dearth of any particular kind of these skins at any of these times jeopardized the process—as vital to survival in the Arctic as having sufficient food to eat and enough fuel to cook and heat one's home—of refurbishing warm winter clothing, the dwelling cover, and hunting equipment every year. At first, reindeer herders might respond to this shortage of skins by turning to poorer-quality and lower-status clothing made from smaller fur-bearing animals (Arctic foxes, Arctic hares, etc.); ultimately, they began killing their own domestic reindeer on a regular basis.

Other Factors in the Pastoralist Transition

In some areas, additional factors accelerated the transition to reindeer economy. In beginning to consume domestic reindeer meat on a daily basis, the Nenets and the Kola Saami may have been partially influenced by Komi reindeer herding, which was a full-blown and market-oriented activity since its inception in the early 1800s. The Komi are known to have killed large numbers of domestic reindeer on a regular basis in order to sell the meat and skins as early as the first decades of the nineteenth century (Islavin 1847:71–72, Latkin 1853:117, Konakov 1986:46). Komi practices of selling reindeer meat on a widespread basis and using it to pay wages for hired labor undermined the formerly conservative attitudes of Nenets and Saami to their herds and stimulated the latter to use their reindeer for consumption and trade.

A comparable external stimulus for the reindeer Chukchi and Koryak to shift to the new form of subsistence came not so much from wars and reindeer-rustling raids on other herders' camps, as some authors suggest, as from barter and trade with the coastal communities of Eskimos, Maritime Chukchi, and Koryak, as well as Russian métis from the Kolyma, Gizhiga, and Anadyr rivers. When the caribou population fell, the sedentary communities lost a significant source not only of food but, more importantly, of skins for winter fur clothing, which could now be obtained only from the pastoralists. For example, caribou had practially disappeared from the Chukchi Peninsula by 1800, by which time explicit documentation attests to well-established trade contacts between the coastal and tundra peoples (Titova 1978:98, Sarychev 1952:185, Vdovin 1965:52, 1975:154–55). It may be that this dense interface at the extreme western and eastern ends of the Eurasian Arctic contributed directly to establishing a large-scale reindeer economy here much earlier than in north-central and northeast Siberia, where mixed hunting-and-herding subsistence prevailed at least until 1850 and in places well into the early 1900s.

Pastoralism and Population Growth

The widespread and regular slaughter of domestic reindeer for food and other daily uses substantially changed tundra nomad subsistence. Most importantly, it served to even out consumption during the course of the year. Regularized slaughters reduced the sharp seasonal fluctuations in the type and abundance of food that are so characteristic of a hunting economy, and "lean seasons" disappeared from the regular annual cycle. We can expect that such increased stability in subsistence would be reflected in an increase in the reindeer herder population. Contrary to Ingold's statement that no significant demographic increase resulted from the shift from hunting to pastoralism (Ingold 1980:80–81), Russian records strongly suggest that such an increase indeed occurred in the Arctic.

Here again, pertinent data have been systematized for the European Nenets better than for any other nomadic group (Babushkin 1930:36, Dolgikh 1970:22, Kolycheva 1958:82–84, Krupnik 1976b: 67–69, Vasil'ev 1979b:75–85). During the 1600s, when the most common form of subsistence was foraging—that is, hunting and fishing, with small-scale reindeer breeding for transportation—the total population of European Nenets (calculated from the number of adult males who payed fur tax), was 1,300–1,400 people. We can accept this as some kind of "carrying capacity" for that subsistence model, extrapolated from fragmentary and in some cases unreliable records.

The European Nenets population appears to have increased slowly throughout the 1700s, to a tenuous total of 1,800–1,900 by the 1780s. But then it proceeded to increase threefold in a period of some eighty years (1780–1860). By 1860 it peaked at around 5,500–6,000, then stabilized at that level with some small-scale oscillations for the next hundred years (table 20). Interestingly, this "population explosion," that is, the period of maximum growth, coincided not with the appearance of large reindeer herds in the early 1700s but, fifty to eighty years later, with the transition to herding for food production. In the overall context of rapid population increase among all the Nenets during these years, this growth spurt hit the western groups from the Kanin and Timan tundras earlier than the eastern groups in the Bol'shaia Zemlia tundra—in the 1700s, as opposed to the first half of the 1800s, respectively. This fits well with the evidence that wild reindeer disappeared in the western tundra earlier than in the east-

TABLE 20
Population Growth of the European Nenets, Mid-1500s to 1933

Year	Number	Year	Number	Year	Number
Mid-1500s	1,360	1839	4,807 (2,374)*	1886	6,267
Late 1600s	1,400	1841	4,495 (2,390)*	1893	5,466
1781	1,940 (976)*	1844	5,540	1897	6,113 (3,070)*
1795	NA (1,512)*	1848	5,752	1902	5,430
1798	NA (1,627)*	1851	5,580	1906	6,093
1801	3,100	1858	4,907 (2,530)*	1913	6,217
1811	NA (1,955)*	1864	5,668	1926	5,235
1816	3,323 (1,935)*	1873	6,050	1933	5,302
1835	4,372 (2,390)*	1880	5,598		

SOURCE: Babushkin 1930, Dolgikh 1970, Krupnik 1976b, Vasil'ev 1979b.
* The number of males is shown in parenthesis.

ern, and that the Kanin and Timan Nenets had shifted to a diet based on meat from their own reindeer and flour purchased from Russia by the late 1700s.

Thus, according to Dolgikh's calculations, the European Nenets population increased approximately *400 percent*, from 1,400–1,500 to 5,500–6,000, in a period of 150 to 180 years, from slightly before 1700 to approximately 1850 (Dolgikh 1970:22). After the 1850s, population dynamics were influenced by periodic decreases when epidemics hit or massive losses occurred among the reindeer herds, triggering rising mortality and out-migration of herders to the Ural mountains during bad epizootic years, such the late 1860, the 1880s, and the early 1900s. Precisely this type of demographic behavior extended well into the first decades of the twentieth century (see chapter 3). This means that the figure of 5,500–6,000 would seem to have emerged as the new carrying capacity of the same physical area under the new, more productive system of resource utilization.

Unfortunately, estimates for other peoples of the Eurasian Arctic are less forthcoming, but similarly confirm that rapid population growth followed the transition to a large-scale reindeer economy. Thus, according to Dolgikh's rather speculative estimates, the nomadic Chukchi may have been about 2,000 in the 1600s, and by the late 1800s had swelled to 8,800, after which it more or less leveled off (Dolgikh 1960:554–55, Gurvich 1966:191, 1982:207–10). It would appear that here, too, the reindeer economy as a form of subsistence was approximately four times more productive than hunting for wild reindeer combined with fishing and sea-mammal hunting. The same picture was observed among the reindeer Koryak. In the mid-1700s they numbered 1,200 to 1,300. By the end of the eighteenth century this grew to 1,500, then increased two and a half times in the next fifty to eighty years. By around 1900, their population also stabilized around this new, higher level of 3,700 to 3,800 (Dolgikh 1960:563, Krupnik 1990:12, Vdovin 1973:217–23). Finally, the Saami population in Lule Lappmark in northern Sweden increased surprisingly at the same four-fold rate, in the course of its transition to pastoralism, from the early 1600s to the late 1700s (Lundmark 1989:39).

The Established Pastoralist Economy

Beginning around 1850, the population growth stopped and proceeded to stabilize during subsequent decades. This signaled that the reindeer economy had entered a new phase. I call this the period of *dominance* by large-scale reindeer herding in the Eurasian Arctic. This stage endured almost forty to fifty years, well into the twentieth century, that is, until the onset of widespread social modernization and the subsequent suppression of the native economy by the Soviet state. The subsistence system of this pre-Soviet, economic dominance stage is described in detail in chapter 3.

The rapid growth of the pastoralist population in the 1700s and 1800s was not due solely to a high rate of natural increase. Migration from the coastal villages also played an important role, as people were drawn by the economic opportunity offered by the new form of resource use (Gurvich 1982:206). But this flow could not be sustained for very long. Given the socioeconomic differentiation among the herders, and the accumulation of large stocks in the hands of individual wealthy owners, spare "niches" for additional population were rapidly filled. As early as the late 1700s, a new stratum of dislocated, impoverished herders emerged. These people were forced to give up herding of their own and to take up work as hired laborers, commercial fishermen, or sea-mammal hunters. Deepening economic stratification among the nomads once again led to some increase in the sedentary or semisedentary population, whose economy by this time consisted mainly of hunting that was heavily oriented to trade. Thus, yet another subsistence pattern arose in the Eurasian Arctic, based on fishing, commercial fur-trapping, and sea-mammal hunting with active consumption of purchased food and the use of small-scale herding for transportation. Some variations of this subsistence pattern will be examined in more detail in chapter 6.

This second round of sedentarization and increase in the coastal population was stimulated by the relative stabilization that had been achieved in the domestic reindeer herds. It is true that we can trace its trend only in very general terms in certain areas of northern Eurasia: the Scandinavian and East European Arctic (from the late eighteenth or even early to mid-nineteenth century), northern West Siberia (from the mid-nineteenth century), and Chukotka and Kamchatka (from the early twentieth century). This trend consisted of alternating periods when the domestic reindeer stocks plummeted catastrophically as a result of epizootics or adverse weather conditions then recovered relatively quickly to or near its former level (see chapter 4).

Consequently, the development of a large-scale reindeer economy in Eurasia resulted not only in displacement of wild by domestic reindeer throughout broad swaths of the territory. A particular type of population dynamic for domestic animals became the new pattern for tundra ecosystems. This pattern is typical of any nomadic livestock breeding and is characterized by high fertility, an increased ratio of animals to pasture area, and very sharp stock decreases during years of epizootics and large-scale natural losses, followed by rapid restoration to some level of "carrying capacity."

Summary and Conclusions

In this chapter, we have retraced the historical steps by which a pastoralist reindeer economy evolved in the Eurasian Arctic zone. Like any traveler of the tundra, we have constructed our path one stage at a time, with a keen eye to successive changes in both the physical and social environment. Now, in looking back over the total distance traveled, it seems fair to say that, in the course of the past few centuries, the cumulative effect of the changes involved was so great as to constitute a genuine subsistence revolution. This revolution signaled the transition of the indigenous population from an appropriative hunting economy with proto-elements of animal husbandry for transportation to a highly specialized productive economy based on carefully refined methods of livestock breeding. From our point in time it is difficult to evaluate precisely to what degree the absorption of Siberia into the Russian empire accelerated this process. Based on the historical record, however, the transition to intensive reindeer husbandry clearly emerges as a process that was an autochthonous achievement of the people of the Arctic and a natural outcome of evolution in their systems of resource utilization.

In the course of a very short time between the eighteenth and the nineteenth centuries, the entire structure of human relationships with the environment was radically transformed. Three fundamentally different subsistence systems superseded each other in succession: (1) mobile hunter-fishers with supplementary reindeer herding for transportation, (2) nomadic hunters with large-scale transportation-reindeer pastoralism, and (3) specialized nomadic reindeer herders. In some regions, in the second half of the nineteenth century, yet another, "secondary" subsistence form appeared, in which reindeer breeding was pursued along with commercial hunting or fishing and active consumption of purchased food. The resultant variation in ethnic and regional forms of aboriginal reindeer economies by the twentieth century was huge. One can only be amazed at the flexibility of this adaptive strategy, its capacity for rapid adjustment, and its malleability in unique sociohistorical or natural conditions.

Such a clear capacity for rapid growth, at least for certain periods of time, clearly overturns statements found in the literature declaiming the "decelerated historical evolution," or stagnation of traditional native economies in the Arctic (Gurvich and Dolgikh 1970:5, Vdovin 1973:216, 1975:143). Actually, quite the opposite appears to have been true. Perhaps as a function of the extremely rapid and acute nature of ecological and social change typical of the Arctic in general, the process of transition to a food-producing economy took only 150 to 200 years here. As is well known, this is a considerably shorter period than comparable transitions required in other areas of the world.

In exactly the same way, the history of the Eurasian Arctic shows us that the processes of local population growth can progress as quickly, if not more quickly, than in ecologically milder areas. It is hard to find another well-documented historical example when the transition to a productive economy brought about a fourfold increase in the nomadic population in the space of a few generations. The growth rates among the European Nenets and the reindeer Chukchi at the turn of the eighteenth to nineteenth centuries are all the more amazing in that they were achieved in traditional societies situated in extreme environments, frequently beleaguered by epidemics and intertribal conflicts, and totally devoid of any medical care.

The history of large-scale reindeer economies in Eurasia gives us the first facts for an analysis of patterns of evolution in Arctic societies. The economic immobility of these societies, as seen by some scholars in a long-term historical perspective, can evidently be explained, not as the result of inherent "stagnation" in extremely harsh environments, but by the specific way in which cultural process in the Arctic native societies was expressed. The speed of economic and social changes was determined each time by a precarious balance of ecological and sociohistorical factors. At any given moment, the *concrete direction* of each respective trend played an enormous role.

When both social and environmental trends move in similar directions simultaneously, they push the process of change along at a rapid pace. The eighteenth-century domestic reindeer boom in Eurasia exemplifies one such confluence of social and ecological forces, when a favorable ecological trend in the Arctic environment coincided with certain social stimuli. The same was equally true for the precipitous plunges in the Siberian wild reindeer population from the early 1700s to the early 1800s, when ecologically unfavorable conditions coincided with powerful hunting pressure induced by the introduction of firearms and a commercial market for reindeer hides. The dislocation of wild reindeer by domestic in the most vulnerable areas on the Arctic islands and coastlands accelerated the crash in the caribou population.

We will remind the reader that the fall in large-scale commercial reindeer husbandry in Alaska from 1930 to 1945, which occurred as the result of undeniably negative economic conditions (see Olson 1969), also took place during an ecologically unfavorable phase for the reindeer population.

What could possibly have happened in these cases when the vectors of social and economic forces were not congruent or even actually opposed each other? One could suppose that their influences could have combined and countermanded each other. One such period certainly was from about 1500 to 1650, when it appears that the ecological conditions in the Eurasian Arctic must have favored the growth rate of domestic reindeer, but the social situation was extremely tense owing to the Russian invasion, constant military conflicts, epidemics, and mass relocations of the native population.

I believe that with sufficient motivation we can find other examples of similar cases. But large-scale reindeer economies in the Eurasian Arctic are as yet too young, and the early stages of pastoralism are poorly documented in written records and even less in archeological remains. Therefore, to analyze the role of social and ecological factors in the development of Arctic subsistence societies it is more profitable to turn to the history of a far older and archeologically better-documented native economy, namely, sea-mammal hunting.

CHAPTER SIX

The Evolution of Maritime Hunting

Introduction

The history of maritime hunting in the Arctic is many millenia long. The oldest traces of sea-mammal hunting in the high latitudes were discovered on the north coast of Norway and the Kola Peninsula, and the eastern Aleutian archipelago (the Anangula site). Dating techniques show them to be about eight thousand years old (Fitzhugh 1975:343, 355, Gjessing 1975:88–89, Gurina 1990:9, Laughlin 1980:62–79, McCartney 1984:121–23, Workman 1988:35, etc.). In the more extreme environs of the Arctic Basin, sites belonging to interior hunters who conducted some seasonal coastal fisheries first appeared about 4,500 years ago. These evidently originated in northern Alaska (the Arctic small tool tradition), and subsequently spread rapidly eastward along the Canadian Arctic coast, throughout the Arctic archipelago, and into northern Greenland (Ackerman 1988:66, Aigner 1985:163–64, Anderson 1984:84–85, Giddings and Anderson 1986:290, Maxwell 1985:37–51, Workman 1988:35). Thus, as much as 4,000 years ago, maritime hunting permitted humans to occupy enormous uninhabited expanses on the shores of the Arctic Ocean and even to penetrate deeply into the central polar basin as far as 80 to 82° N.

In the Eurasian Arctic, studies of prehistoric and traditional maritime subsistence systems have focused primarily on ancient Eskimo cultures of the Chukchi Peninsula. With its amazing plenitude of marine resources, the Bering Strait region was one of the primary centers of sea hunting in the entire circumpolar region. A sedentary coastal economy has been able to develop uninterrupted here for the past 2,500 years. If we count the recent find of an aboriginal hunting camp on Wrangell Island, we might be tempted to extend this period yet another millennium back in time. But remains of such an ancient culture have yet to be discovered on the Siberian mainland (Ackerman 1984:106–108, Dikov 1977:210–12, 1979:165–68).

Excavations of ancient settlements and burial sites along the coast of the Chukchi Peninsula indicate that, for more than two thousand years, the ancestors of contemporary Asiatic Eskimo and maritime Chukchi based their subsistence upon sea-mammal harvesting. Two thousand years ago, ancient hunters were already harvesting the same species Eskimos hunted in the early twentieth century—whales, beluga, walrus, and seals. At the same time they actively utilized other resources in their environment, supplementing their maritime economy by hunting terrestrial game and fowl, fishing, and foraging for shellfish and tundra plants. Permanent villages with large, semi-subterranean dwellings appeared on the coasts of Bering Strait no less than two thousand years ago. Unique anthropogenic landscapes slowly formed around these villages, preserving remains of human habitation through the centuries up to the present day.

Based on such archeological remains, we can divide the history of maritime subsistence systems in Chukotka into several chronological stages. These stages correspond mainly to the well-known archeological sequence of ancient Eskimo cultures: Old Bering Sea, Okvik, Birnirk, Punuk, Thule, and so forth (see Ackerman 1984, Arutiunov 1982, Arutiunov and Sergeev 1975, Dikov 1979, 1989, Giddings 1960, Rudenko 1947, etc.). During the Old Bering Sea–Okvik time (roughly 500 B.C.E. to 500 C.E.), maritime subsistence focused on walrus hunting. A preponderance in the archeological record of small harpoons and tools made from reindeer antler indicates that the procurement system of the subsequent Birnirk period was based primarily on the hunting of seals and wild reindeer. The Punuk model (around 800 to 1300 C.E.) reflects a clear emphasis on cooperative hunting of large whales and an overall flourishing of an aboriginal whaling culture. The subsistence system of the Thule culture that followed (ca. 1500 C.E.) is strikingly reminiscent of that practiced and ethnographically documented among Asiatic Eskimos and coastal Chukchi in the eighteenth and nineteenth centuries. Although whaling retained its cultural and symbolic significance, seal hunting once again moved to the fore. Subsistence balances in Eskimo communities in the early 1900s closely echoed this pattern (see chapter 2).

In the past 2,500 years, the Eskimo coastal economy of the Chukchi Peninsula experienced several distinct periods of expansion. Such "high" periods were in turn clearly delimited by alternating periods of decline. Population decreases and even cultural regression probably accompanied the latter, "low" periods, which included the mid-Birnirk era (500–700 C.E.), the second half of the Thule era (1300–1500 C.E.), and the eighteenth to early nineteenth centuries. Archeologists have reconstructed a similar wavelike pattern of alternating phases of growth and decline for prehistoric Eskimo societies on St. Lawrence Island and the American side of Bering Strait (see Anderson 1981, Bandi 1969, Bockstoce 1973, Giddings 1960, Giddings and Anderson 1986, etc.).

Climatic Models of Eskimo Subsistence Trends

What explains this strikingly nonlinear development of Eskimo subsistence systems, that meanders across the panorama of Arctic history with the mathematical regularity of a tundra river? In the last fifteen to twenty years, researchers have mainly sifted through changes in the Arctic environment for clues, and, in particular, for evidence of climatic change. In the 1960s and especially the 1970s scholars considered this interpretive framework to be simultaneously more integrative and more sensitive than earlier theories that traced basic stages in Eskimo history to migration, diffusion of cultural values, or displacement by other peoples into new environments.

In brief, the "ecological interpretation" of Eskimo cultural evolution runs as follows. In the rigorous Arctic environment, the nature of subsistence was crucially dependent upon the slightest change in the natural resources people used. The abundance and species profile of the community's resources were not constant and varied in response to climate change. Warming trends drew larger numbers of large sea mammals into Arctic waters, and thus communal hunting for whales and walrus increased at these times. This supported increased population in the coastal communities, and a more sedentary maritime subsistence pattern consequently expanded northward to the higher latitudes.

Conversely, during climatic cooling trends the larger sea mammals tended to shift southward from the high latitudes, and Arctic maritime hunting was correspondingly individualized and weakened. In such periods the role of walrus and whale hunting waned noticeably in Eskimo subsistence, while the significance of caribou hunting, sealing, and fishing grew. The coastal population shrank, communities that had once been large and unified fractured apart, and the resulting bands became more mobile. Therefore, cooling periods favored the development of inland variations of Eskimo culture, or the interior Eskimo subsistence traditions, as they are commonly called (see further detail in Anderson 1981, Bockstoce 1973, 1979, Fitzhugh 1972, Fitzhugh and Lamb 1986, McGhee 1969, 1972, 1984, etc.).

Certain stages in the history of the coastal culture of Asiatic Eskimos on the Chukchi Peninsula in fact fit into this ecological interpretation neatly. Thus, the Birnirk subsistence system emphasized caribou hunting and active sealing in and along the edges of the ice, while the importance of open ocean walrus and whale hunting declined. Therefore, archeologists have long connected the appearance of the Birnirk culture on the Chukchi Peninsula, as in Alaska, with the onset of a climatic cooling trend in the Arctic around 300 to 500 C.E. (Anderson 1984:90–91, Bockstoce 1979:89, Dikov 1979:215, Stanford 1976:90).

The subsequent long-term climatic warming trend that spread through the Arctic later in the same millenium is just as unanimously invoked to explain the rise of the Punuk and closely related early Thule culture in Alaska around 800 to 900 C.E. Whales were both plentiful and easily accessible in Arctic waters during this period, and this supported the development both of a flourishing Eskimo whaling industry and the appearance of large, long-term settlements (Anderson 1981:74, Dikov 1979:218, 1989:56). Finally, Punuk culture receded and late Thule culture spread to the Chukchi Peninsula around 1400 C.E., coincident with a new cooling phase in the Arctic ushered in by the "Little Ice Age." Archeologists have relied upon that climatic cooling to explain the decline of aboriginal whaling, the resumption of sealing and caribou hunting, and the desertion of large coastal villages during this period throughout the entire Eskimo ecumene from Chukotka to Greenland (see Aigner 1985, Anderson 1981, Arutiunov 1982, Dikov 1989, McGhee 1972, 1984, Maxwell 1985).

The "Adaptation" Framework

Though fairly convincing, climatological explanations popular in the 1960s and 1970s have increasingly come under fire for being overly simplistic and displaying a pronounced tendency toward environmental determinism (see Anderson 1981:78–80, Fitzhugh and Lamb 1986:359–60, McGhee 1983:23, etc.). These theories treat oscillations in Arctic natural resources as simple binary alternations—game species seem either to be disappearing completely or to have miraculously recovered. The true dynamics of Arctic ecosystems, as we have seen above, were engaged in constant and multilateral equilibration, something in the manner of several gymnasts performing separate routines simultaneously on one trampoline. A falling population of some game species usually was matched by an increase in the others.

Secondly, ecological explanations generally neglect the role of such important mechanisms in cultural dynamics as the population growth, accumulation of hunting knowledge and skill, and intercommunity contact, including exchange of technology as well as environmental change stemming from aboriginal hunting itself. Clearly, these factors played a role throughout the course of human history in the Arctic.

Frustrated with these inadequacies, critics of the purely ecological perspective responded with more sophisticated conceptualizations (Anderson 1981, Bockstoce 1976, Dumond 1980, Fitzhugh 1972, 1975, McCartney and Savelle 1985, Vasil'evskii 1985, etc.). In varying ways, they presented the history of Arctic coastal cultures as an *adaptation*, that is, an active, deliberate adjustment to concrete ecological circumstances in which human beings draw upon and choose from among the technological skills and accomplishments available to them.

Most people now prefer to view the evolution of Arctic maritime hunting cultures as a *series of adaptations*, that is, as a process of sequentially accumulating cultural and social mechanisms that have enabled hunters to exploit the polar edges of the human ecumene for a very long time. We have already discussed some of these mechanisms in our review of Asiatic Eskimo society in the early 1900s (see chapter 2). Other adaptations, such as minimizing risk and uncertainty, optimizing flexibility of choice, maximizing energy extraction, and rotating among seasonal procurement strategies have been thoroughly described for other Eskimo groups in various regions of the Arctic (Minc 1986, Sabo 1991, Savelle and McCartney 1988, Smith 1981, 1984, 1991, etc.).

In this chapter, I want to demonstrate certain additional adaptive principles that are fundamental to understanding coastal subsistence systems in a long-term historical perspective. They are mainly based upon archeological and ethnohistorical illustrations from the Chukchi Peninsula, including data from some recent surveys conducted there in the late 1970s and 1980s.

Trends and Recurrent Cycles in Eskimo Resource Utilization

The well-known hypothesis suggesting the multifaceted, or "omnivorous" nature of the Eskimo economy was first advanced in the 1960s, and has maintained its central position in analysis of Arctic subsistence systems ever since (Taylor 1966:119). It applies no less persuasively to resource use among Paleoasiatic inhabitants of the Chukchi coast. For two thousand years, native peoples of the Chukchi Peninsula have drawn simultaneously upon all the available species of hunting resources in their marine and terrestrial food chains.

However, Eskimo subsistence, like most human economies, did not escape a general evolutionary tendency toward using ever more productive, stable, and, at the same time, more labor-intensive, resources in the environment. Hunting the largest sea mammals such as whales and walrus required more complex hunting technology and organization, but compared to other subsistence activities could yield a maximum harvest in the shortest period of time. Yet, without sufficient labor resources to store large amounts of meat quickly, the hard-won catch would rot. So, utilizing such "feast-or-famine" meat supplies also required considerable additional energy to create large food reserves.

Taken together, these two activities—cooperative, time-limited hunting, and rapid preservation of food resulting from sudden bursts in the supply—encouraged sedentarism and population consolidation. Settled, dense communities led to and reinforced a greater complexity in social organization and social life. In short, among the variations of Eskimo subsistence, we can view whale and walrus hunting as the means of harvesting available natural resources that most enhanced social complexity. We might even call it a kind of "climax stage" in Arctic maritime resource use.

This view provides the key to explaining inconsistencies in the historical development of indigenous whaling, which show up so clearly and, at first glance, so strangely, in the archeological data. At an absolute minimum, whale hunting arose on the Chukchi Peninsula no less than two thousand years ago (see summaries in Krupnik 1984, 1987a, Krupnik et al. 1983). Bones and baleen of the large bowhead whale (*Balaena mysticetus*) and large toggling harpoons have been excavated in Old Bering Sea and Okvik sites, interspersed only occasionally with bones of the smaller-sized gray whale (*Eschrichtius robustus*). Such archeological data indicate that whaling focused primarily on bowhead whales. But, then, larger bones are virtually absent from Birnirk hunting camps and storage pits (500 to 800 C.E.), while the number of bones from small whales (gray) noticeably increases. In Punuk sites (900 to 1200 C.E.) the picture once again reverses: remains of smaller whales disappear, while we find huge quantities of bone and baleen from large, bowhead whales, along with tools for hunting them, including toggling harpoons, heavy killing lances, and fragments of slate flensing knives.

In 1976, the discovery of a truly amazing archeological site shed new light on our interpretation of the Punuk subsistence model. This monumental construction is located on Ittygran Island, a small outcrop off the western coast of the Chukchi Peninsula. Working among its deliberate geometric lines, we soon felt a palpable reverence for this prehistoric whaling culture, and began to refer to the site as "Whale Alley." And this is the name by which it has come to be known ever since (Arutiunov et al., 1979, 1982, Chlenov and Krupnik 1984).

Two parallel rows of bowhead whale skulls form the primary lines of the monument, set at regular intervals in twos and fours in the ground. Ramparted by several whale mandibles propped firmly and vertically in the ground, and accompanied by more than a hundred stone-lined pits and other lithic structures, the skull formation stands sentry along a gravel spit on the shore for a distance of six hundred meters (fig. 13). In all, fifty to sixty whale skulls, almost thirty whale jaws, and hundreds of rocks and stones went into building the Whale Alley ritual complex. Construction required a tremendous and sustained investment of labor by several dozen people, drawn, it appears, from a number of villages in the region. Eerily suggestive of a polar Stonehenge, not least in the high degree of social organiza-

Fig. 13. "Whale Alley," Chukchi Peninsula. Groups of bowhead whale skulls and jawbones set in the ground. (Drawing by Sergei Bogoslovskii, 1981. Reproduced by permission of *The University Museum Magazine*, University of Pennsylvania.)

tion and surplus production such an engineering feat implies, this is the only monumental ritual center of this type on the Asiatic side of Bering Strait (Arutiunov et al. 1981, 1982:99–100.). Nothing similar is described in the literature anywhere else in the Arctic.

The onset of the cooling phase between 1500 and 1700 C.E. appears to have abruptly reduced the efficiency of indigenous whaling, leading to the disruption, then to the complete obliteration of the elaborate social scaffolding that must have been necessary to build Whale Alley. Whale hunting continued during this period only in a few well-located communities on either side of Bering Strait. The arrival of American whalers after 1850 engendered a short-term revival in indigenous whaling. The replacement of Eskimo hunting weapons with modern European ones, and a surging demand for bowhead whale baleen, quickly reintensified the hunting. Larger native villages on the Chukchi Peninsula, such as Ungazik, Imtuk, Avan, Naukan, and Uelen, frequently harvested three to four whales a year again (Marquette and Bockstoce 1980:14–16, Krupnik 1987a:21–25).

But this peak was not sustained for long. Overhunting by the

Yankee whaling ships so reduced the whale stocks that, by the late 1800s, indigenous harvests were once more on the decline. Only a few villages continued whale hunting, mostly as a subsidiary element in their subsistence system (see chapter 2).

The history of indigenous whaling on the American side of Bering Strait shows a similar pattern of troughs and crests. In addition, traces of yet another prehistoric culture have been found on Cape Krusenstern, reflecting still more archaic forms of hunting whales. This Old Whaling Culture, as it is called, has been dated at 1450 to 1250 B.C.E. and was thus separated in time from the subsequent Old Bering Sea subsistence pattern by an interval of almost a thousand years (Anderson 1984: 88–89, Giddings 1960: 127, Giddings and Anderson 1986: 317). This entr'acte was presumably characterized by cooler climates and thus by coastal hunters whose survival depended primarily on sealing and hunting wild reindeer-caribou.

Consequently, in the Bering Strait region we have a classic *spiral-shaped development* of the resource utilization system, with four phases of rebirth, or activization, during favorable conditions (the end of the second millennium B.C.E., the end of the first millennium B.C.E., the ninth and tenth centuries C.E. and the late nineteenth century C.E.), separated by fairly distinct epochs of decline or extinction. All growth periods in the aboriginal whaling industry were connected to one degree or another with climatic warming phases in the Arctic, and, in this case, the earlier "ecological interpretations" appear justified.

At no time during periods of Arctic cooling, however, did whales disappear completely from the polar basin and thus directly cause a decline in the native whaling industry in a simple linear effect. Rather, deteriorating ice conditions and shifts in whale migration routes gradually shortened the hunting seasons and increasingly disrupted the communities' and boat crews' annual subsistence cycles. "Bad years," when the hunt went poorly and famines occurred, gradually accumulated into "bad times." Decreasing efficiency of the old subsistence system became hard to ignore and no doubt became a cause for change.[1] Even so, occasional or even quite regular whale hunting could continue in certain well-disposed locations. But most of the population in the coastal communities must have viewed the increasing time and energy required to hunt whales during cooling phases as decreasingly worthwhile. People shifted to other alternatives because they made more sense.

Previously less effective types of hunting now became more productive. Sealing and caribou hunting could be counted on to yield a more reliable return for the effort invested. A natural increase in the pinniped and caribou populations during Arctic cooling phases (see chapter 4), as well as the enduring complexity and variability of the coastal economy, fostered the shift to a new subsistence strategy.

But as ecological conditions inexorably came full circle, the hunting of large sea mammals once again recovered the ecological high ground, all the more so since, with each cycle, aboriginal whaling resumed at a higher technological level as the result of intervening cultural progress. Archeological data shows distinct progress in hunting weapons, and increases in sheer amounts of whale bones between the Old Whaling Culture and Old Bering Sea sites a thousand years later. Likewise, whaling was clearly much more intensive and productive during the Punuk–early Thule period than in Old Bering Sea times.

Thus, above and beyond a short-term tendency toward equilibrium between whaling and seal-and-caribou subsistence patterns, the role and efficiency of indigenous whaling clearly displays an absolute growth trend over time. Although the shape of the curves remains stable, the amplitude of each whaling cycle increases because knowledge and technology improve over time. Just recently, we have even witnessed the latest such technologically facilitated swell in native whaling—during the 1960s and 1970s. Owing to increased economic wealth among Alaskan Eskimos, the numbers of active boat crews, of native communities engaged in whaling, and of whales caught in northwestern Alaska increased two to three times in a period of ten to fifteen years (Braund et al. 1988, Durham 1979, Marquette and Bockstoce 1980).

Population Dynamics and Shifts on the Arctic Coast

Of course, the effects of any change in the preexisting game management system affected various communities differently, be it the abundance of hunting resources, their accessibility, or the community's ability to harvest them. Following those trends, some areas waned in importance, while the value of others increased with every resource change. This means that each phase in the history of maritime subsistence had its own unique hunting base that was valued the most at that time. North American archeologists have shown this pattern to hold throughout a wide range of prehistoric Eskimo settlements in

Alaska and the Canadian Arctic (see Anderson 1981, Bockstoce 1979, Fitzhugh 1972, Giddings and Anderson 1986, Kaplan 1986, Savelle and McCartney 1988, etc.). We can reconstruct a similar pattern on the Chukchi Peninsula as well.

Thus, for the Birnirk-type adaptation centered upon wild reindeer hunting and ice sealing, the best locations were situated on open coastlines with convenient access both to tundra hunting ranges and to lagoons that freeze early. The Punuk system of resource exploitation favored settlement in locations close to the whale and walrus seasonal migration routes, such as islands, peninsulas, and protruding capes. In the sixteenth to eighteenth centuries Eskimos gradually withdrew from large sections of the Siberian coast and concentrated into two mountainous extremities of the Chukchi Peninsula. Eskimo adherence to the subsistence settlement model of the Punuk was not the only reason for this. These promontories were removed and inaccessible from the main routes of the Chukchi reindeer herders, and thus provided some security from invasion by the latter as their subsistence system thrived.

When we compare the distribution of prehistoric and traditional Asiatic Eskimo settlements, certain areas clearly emerge along the coast as places of continuous inhabitation, where the population even accumulated during crisis situations. In general, the northeast and southeast tips of the Chukchi Peninsula served continuously as such refugia throughout the history of the Asiatic Eskimos. In contrast to these refuge areas, some regions along the coast evidently were used by maritime hunters only during certain periods. These include stretches of land at the margins of prehistoric Eskimo occupation on the Chukchi and East Siberian seas, the northern and western coasts of the Gulf of Anadyr, and, possibly, along the lowland shoreline of Mechigmen Bay. In these places we would expect to find extended interruptions in territorial use and abrupt shifts in cultural continuity.

Reserving certain hunting areas for "emergency" use was an important risk management strategy in the maritime subsistence system. As a result the geographical boundaries of the sedentary maritime hunting culture on the Chukchi Peninsula tended to "pulse" over time. During favorable periods, the territory occupied by coastal hunters expanded. Conversely, when hunting conditions deteriorated, the population drew in rapidly toward the most productive niches, where the largest and most stable villages stood. And the migration cycle could extend further. If hunting conditions grew still worse, people could redisperse along the coast in small groups to make the best use of what resources remained. However, such camps were short-term, as their inhabitants usually subsequently regrouped back into a few refugia niches. From there, once hunting conditions improved, they could begin the settlement cycle anew.

Information drawn from Asiatic Eskimo oral traditions in the communities of Chaplino (Ungazik) and Sireniki (Sirynykh) indicates that several such migration cycles occurred from the late 1700s up to the early 1900s (Chlenov and Krupnik 1983:132–39, Krupnik 1983:68–84). Many prehistoric and traditional coastal villages on the Chukchi Peninsula had a minimum of two (Uel'kal', Sianlik, Sinrak, Kynlirak, Imtuk, among others) to three (Sikliuk, Kiginin, Kivak, Yryrak) settlement waves, each with an extended hiatus in between. Later arrivals usually did not consider themselves to be genetically related to the former inhabitants, who might have abandoned the site decades or even centuries before.

Such a flexible settlement model, with continuous migrations, outflows, and displacements of maritime hunting groups along the coast, could be an extremely effective adaptive form given the instability of the Arctic environment. As noted in chapter 2, it had to be based on certain social norms of "openness," permitting people to migrate and new villages, hunting camps, and crews to congregate freely, in spite of relatively strict territoriality and close attachment of territories to specific communities. However, it remains unclear whether such openness was an original feature in the maritime subsistence system or whether it arose as an adaptation to increasing density and population growth during a particular period, to remain to be recorded in the postcontact society.

That such population growth actually occurred during the course of the two-thousand-year documented history of the Asiatic Eskimo, we know from extensive site surveys conducted on the southeast tip of the Chukchi Peninsula (Krupnik 1981a, 1983). The Old Bering Sea population of the area evidently consisted of a few hundred people in all, that is, two to three times less than in the late 1800s. This population was scattered among several far-flung small and medium-sized sites. From this, we can imagine Old Bering Sea society as one in which several small socially and economically autonomous communities existed along the coast, located at distances of one- to two-days' paddling from one another, separated by uninhabited stretches of shore in between.

Archeologists are in unanimous agreement that a noticeable increase occurred in the coastal population, and that the size and number of coastal villages grew during the Punuk period from 900 to 1000 C.E. (Ackerman 1984:112, Arutiunov 1982:95, Arutiunov and Sergeev 1975:196, Dikov 1979:219, etc.). Large communities appeared, with stable social structures and enough surplus production to support construction of ritual sites and intercommunity ritual centers like Whale Alley. Not coincidentally, we found more than 150 meat storage pits at Whale Alley, some of them still with the remains of unused food in them (Arutiunov et al. 1982:36–40).

But, even in the Punuk era when there were large clots of population, large spaces of empty coastline remained between them. Dense settlement of the Chukotka coast, with dozens of coastal villages and camps separated by short spaces of five to fifteen kilometers, as were observed in the early 1900s (see chapter 2), clearly belong to a later period, not earlier than the seventeenth to eighteenth centuries. This leads us to suppose that it was precisely at this time that the coastal niches on the Asiatic side of Bering Strait became overcrowded. Local coastal hunters turned into "overcrowded foragers," with all the ecological and social consequences that implied: greater sedentarization, fewer alternative resources, deeper vulnerability to periodic failures in their food supply, and so forth (see Cohen 1981). Since that time the coastal population has ranged from 800 to 1,200 people, with well-documented periodic declines followed by rapid recovery to or near its previous level.

Changes in Hunting Implements and Techniques

Technological shifts can be considered yet another adaptive mechanism of the maritime hunting economy to environmental instability. Concrete forms of such shifts on the Chukchi Peninsula have been examined several times, based on the evolution of harpoon heads found at the Uelen and Ekven burial sites (Arutiunov and Sergeev 1969, 1975, Arutiunov 1975, 1982). The main conclusion we may draw from these is that the evolution of weapons and technology in the Eskimo hunting economy moved in a spiral, not in a linear, progressive fashion. Although the entire traditional complex of Eskimo hunting equipment was essentially formed as early as the Old Bering Sea–Okvik cultures—that is some two thousand years ago—several clear periods can be defined in those two millennia when it was simplified or even reverted to original, more primitive forms. This developmental model of vivid explosions alternating with regression to seemingly more primitive, long-outmoded forms describes the history of Eskimo decorative art as well (Bronstein 1986, McGhee 1976).

During the hardest times some groups of Arctic coastal hunters could even experience complete eradication of certain procurement techniques and the loss of very important technological elements of polar maritime subsistence. The best-known example of this comes from the Polar Eskimo of northwest Greenland, who lost the umiak, bow and arrow, and fish spear when they were completely isolated from other societies during the "Little Ice Age." Attrition of important technological achievements caused a decline in previously thriving whaling and sealing, caribou hunting, and summer fishing (Gilberg 1974–75, 1984). The number of food products Polar Eskimos consumed was drastically reduced, while caribou meat and willow ptarmigan were generally considered among the Polar Eskimo to be "unclean" species, unusable for human food.

But the same example of the Polar Eskimo serves to show that once intercultural contacts were reestablished, lost skills could be recovered and the previous subsistence system reconstructed in a matter of a few years. Ethnographic materials from the eighteenth to early twentieth centuries from the Chukchi Peninsula to Greenland reveal the amazing resourcefulness of Eskimo hunters in adapting to new, more developed tools and hunting methods. This was true in the Thule period, when the appearance of dogsleds suddenly made it possible for Eskimos to travel long distances in winter. It was true again in the nineteenth and twentieth centuries when iron harpoons, firearms, wood-hulled boats with sails, and then motorized vessels were adopted in the course of a single generation, bringing about a complex linkage between technological and social innovations without changing the essence of the indigenous subsistence system (Freeman 1974–75, Gilberg 1974–75, Hall 1978)

While visiting Eskimo villages, I have had more than one occasion to listen to elder hunters tell stories of how, with the appearance of outboard motors in the 1930s, they began to hunt walrus, beluga, and gray whales from skinboats at sea. Until then, it had been impossible to chase and kill these animals using only oars or sails. But, in only two or three years, hunters had successfully picked up the new hunting methods. Such rapid incorporation of technological innovations into the traditional subsistence system attests to a deeply rooted aspect of the native culture: its receptiveness to reform using the entire wisdom of preceding generations.

Factors in Maritime Subsistence Transitions

From these and similar examples we can clearly see how three groups of factors constantly influence the transitions of maritime subsistence systems. These are the ecological dynamics in the surrounding environment, the internal evolution of hunting technologies, and "external" influence—either directly on the maritime hunting communities, or indirectly on the resources they used. At the same time, these factors most often acted independently and even on contrasting vectors to each other. Dynamic processes in the environment were mainly cyclical in nature, so that relatively adverse periods regularly alternated with more favorable ones. Development of the technological base of subsistence thanks to accumulated knowledge and skills was in general linear and, in a long-term historical perspective, focused on improving hunting productivity and optimizing resource use for a gradually increasing coastal population. For the Asiatic Eskimo this tendency led to an increase in the significance of whale and walrus hunting in their economy, which enabled accumulation of a food surplus, an increase in population, and expansion of the resource area.

It is harder to evaluate the influence of "external" social factors, especially when contact between the coastal hunters and members of nonindigenous societies was intense. Cross-cultural contact typically brought about many different innovations, with profoundly contradictory and often unforeseeable consequences. While more powerful hunting equipment was available and additional food sources appeared, imported epidemics caused widespread disease and the traditionally utilized resources were badly overhunted. Old forms of social organization disintegrated at the same time that new structures for maintaining relations with the outside world grew. All these contradictory processes of transformation in aboriginal societies following European and American contact have been documented for many Arctic regions, including the Chukchi Peninsula (see Gurvich 1966, 1982, Dikov 1989, Vdovin 1965).

Unfortunately, we have no ethnohistorical methodology readily available to evaluate the combined effects of these three groups of agents (ecological dynamics, internal technological development, and external social influence) on indigenous subsistence systems. However, certain criteria exist that are proxy indicators for the cumulative result of such multivariate development. The most obvious of these include the population growth curve, spatial dynamics of the utilized territory, and changes in subsistence productivity, that is, fluctuations in the balance between how much food the community needed and how much it produced.

And once more we see that the development of maritime subsistence was not linear and was defined by a layering of different, sometimes mutually contradictory, social and ecological trends. When favorable social and ecological circumstances coincided, as was the case in the 1930s, the coastal population grew up quickly, the communities used larger resource territories, and subsistence production increased. When unfavorable trends occurred congruently, as was the case, for example, in the early 1700s, resource territories shrank and the Eskimo population fell. When the vectors of ecological and social trends differed, they tended, as it were, to cancel each other out, although, in general, the negative impact of external social factors had a more pronounced effect. Thus, American overhunting of whales, walrus, and seals from the 1850s to the 1890s triggered a crisis in Eskimo subsistence even in a relatively favorable ecological environment, followed by introduction of more efficient hunting implements. It led to the onset of a catastrophic famine that gripped the population on both sides of Bering Strait around 1880.

This aspect of the indigenous maritime economy is fully explicable by its attachment to small, intensively exploited hunting areas and a huge dependency for well-being upon short seasonal peaks in food production. This means that, compared to the nomadic interior subsistence model, coastal systems turn out to be *more vulnerable* in conditions of intensive intercultural contact, even though the development of new implements and more effective hunting methods in response sometimes permitted them to neutralize or even shorten the crisis.

During temporary lessening of external influence, as occurred on the Chukchi Peninsula in the early 1900s, indigenous systems could partially regenerate, and then "secondary" traditional subsistence forms arose, when borrowed hunting technology was successfully used in combination with indigenous hunting methods. One example of this regeneration is the subsistence system of the Asiatic Eskimos in the early 1900s, described in chapter 2, where the indigenous foundation of resource utilization connected amazingly well with dependence upon an external market, use of European equipment, and commercial orientation of many hunting products.

Maritime Subsistence in the Western Eurasian Arctic

These conclusions about the multivariate and cyclical nature of development in maritime subsistence will help us to unravel yet another thread in the history of the Arctic—that of the indigenous sea-mammal hunting culture on the opposite end of northern Eurasia, on the Barents and Kara Sea coasts. Maritime hunting economies in the western sector of the Eurasian Arctic have been much less thoroughly studied than the history of Eskimo-type cultures in the Bering Sea region. But the ecological conditions in the former area were entirely adequate for human inhabitation, and the sea-mammal hunting stocks were, apparently, no less abundant than in Bering Strait, as we learn from descriptions left to us of walrus, seal, and whale herds numbering in the thousands during the 1600s to 1700s and even the 1800s (Chapskii 1939:62–65, Dergachev 1877:38, Latkin 1853:51, Van-Linshotten 1915:485, 488, etc.).

Archeological evidence of specialized maritime hunting in the western Eurasian Arctic dates far back. People from the Komsa culture in northern Norway actively engaged in maritime hunting and beach combing, as did hunters from the closely related "Arctic paleolithic" culture on the north coast of the Kola Peninsula, which was closely related to them (8000–6000 B.C.E.) (Gurina 1990a:9–12, Shumkin 1988:9–11). Remains of permanent settlements or multi-year seasonal hunting camps with a rich cultural layer and huge quantities of sea-mammal bones belong to the Neolithic and Early Bronze Age (3000 to 1000 B.C.E.). Judging by the osteological remains, harp seal hunting played the main role in subsistence, as well as hunting of bearded seal, ringed seal, walrus, beluga, narwhal, and the use of beached whales, together with fishing and hunting for tundra and forest animals and birds (Gurina 1990a:13–15, 1990b:28–30, Shumkin 1988:12–13). Neolithic petroglyphs in northern Norway and the White Sea coast preserve vivid scenes of prehistoric people hunting for beluga, walrus, and whales from large, multi-seat boats with oars and strikers, thrusting harpoons into the animals as they swim in the open sea (Ravdonikas 1938, Savvateev 1985).

The expansion of maritime hunting further east, along the Barents and Kara Sea coasts has been dated to a somewhat later time in the first millennium B.C.E. People from the sedentary Ust' Polui culture in the northern Ob' region, who conducted active hunting for walrus, beluga, and seals around the first centuries C.E./B.C.E. have often been compared or even directly connected with prehistoric residents of Alaska or even historical Eskimos and maritime Chukchi (Chernetsov 1953:237, Larsen and Rainey 1948:158, Moberg 1975:104).

It would appear that indigenous maritime hunting achieved its maximum extent in the western Eurasian Arctic around the beginning of the second millennium C.E. Archeological evidence corresponding to this time, which is analogous to the Punuk period in the North Bering Sea, shows it penetrating far to the east, into the Kara Sea basin. Excavation has unearthed maritime settlements on Vaigach Island and Cape Tiutei-Sale on the Yamal Peninsula, hunting camps in the Piasidai and Taz River estuaries and in Nakhodka Bay, and piles of walrus, polar bear, and seal skulls in historical Nenets sacrificial places on the Yamal Peninsula coast (see Chernetsov 1935, Khlobystin 1987, Lashook 1968, Zhitkov 1913, etc.).

Medieval sources further confirm the existence of some maritime population in the western Eurasian Arctic. Vague references appear in the writings of Old Norse and Arab geographers from the ninth to thirteenth centuries, followed by quite concrete narratives in the Russian Chronicles of "Yugra" and "Korela," who caught seals, whales, and walrus on the Arctic Ocean coast in the 1500s, and a whole cycle of Nenets folklore about the elflike "Sirtia" (Sikhirtia) (Alekseev 1932, Berg 1956b, Khomich 1966, Lashook 1958, Vasil'ev 1970, 1979b). Lastly, records of West European polar explorers in the 1500s and 1600s contain several direct references to sedentary maritime hunters supposedly encountered on the Barents Sea coast living in underground shelters and dwellings made from "the skins of fish" (DeLamartin'er 1912, Van-Linshotten 1915, Vasil'ev 1970).

These are all well-known facts (at least in the Russian and Scandinavian literature), and the existence in the western Eurasian Arctic of coastal sea-mammal hunters in the first and early second millennia C.E. can be considered proven. But it is just as well known that by the 1700s this society was no longer there. At that time, all indigenous inhabitants of the western Eurasian Arctic, the Saami and Nenets, were for the most part reindeer herders or fishers, with small herds of domestic reindeer for transportation. With the exception of certain groups of coastal Saami in Norway, the so-called "sea-going Saami," only Europeans—Norwegians, Finns, and Russian Pomors—engaged in fishing and maritime hunting in this area on a commercial scale. The evident death or gradual fading of indigenous maritime subsistence, and the radical shift in traditional resource use between 1600 and 1700, or, more broadly, 1500 and 1800, is in need of historical explanation.

Valeri Chernetsov was the first to discover this western Arctic maritime culture on Yamal Peninsula. In his words, maritime hunting was eclipsed here by a more efficient type of indigenous economy, which he termed "sled reindeer herding that is more refined, and provides more security with an equal amount of effort" (Chernetsov 1935 : 131). Therefore, the prehistoric Samoyed, who first introduced this "sled reindeer herding" to the Arctic, easily displaced hunters from the coastlands and islands of the Barents and Kara seas, such as Yamal, Vaigach, Novaia Zemlia, etc. Chernetsov believed that, for the most part, these hunters were wiped out or assimilated by the Samoyed by 1500 or so.

The most popular opinion at present is one originally advanced by Georgii Prokof'ev. In this view, the sedentary Arctic hunters fused with the Samoyed newcomers in an original two-component ethnicity, and transmitted some elements of their maritime culture to it (Prokof'ev 1940; see also Dolgikh 1970, Vasil'ev 1979b).

Both hypotheses explain the social mechanisms of cultural contact, but neglect to elucidate on what ecological basis the encounter between two such contrasting subsistence systems occurred. If large-scale intensive reindeer husbandry only appeared in northwestern Eurasia in the 1700s (see chapter 5), then the nomadic hunting-and-herding economy that the prehistoric Samoyed brought north into the tundra could hardly have been more "refined" than the Eskimo-type maritime economy. In addition, as we have seen, the number of people living on nomadic hunting and small-scale reindeer husbandry even in the 1600s was quite small.

Groups of tundra nomads could easily have made periodic raids on the coastal communities, as occurred, for example, on the Chukchi Peninsula, judging by innumerable legends in the oral traditions of both reindeer Chukchi and Eskimo, recounting wars between the two. But it does not make sense that nomadic reindeer hunters and herders would have evicted the coastal hunters from the ecological niche they occupied; even less could they have offered them alternative sources of survival. If anything, just the opposite process should have occurred, whereby some nomads would have decided to settle on the coast. Once again, we know this was the case on the Chukchi Peninsula, where the arrival of Chukchi nomads on the coasts generally led them to embrace the more efficient maritime subsistence pattern and join the Eskimo villages or establish sedentary communities of their own along the shore.

We may speculate on the historical demise of the indigenous maritime economy in the western Eurasian Arctic based on the models presented above for transitions of coastal and tundra nomadic resource utilization systems. Of course, written and especially archeological evidence for this area is painfully scarce, and rife with apparent contradictions, so our reconstruction will rest on hypothetical underpinnings to the customary degree. In addition, any general model is intrinsically incapable of expressing all local variations of this process throughout the huge territory from Scandinavia to the Yamal Peninsula. With these caveats in mind, however, we can certainly construct a plausible scenario as follows.[2]

Around the turn of the first millennium C.E., during the Medieval Climatic Optimum, a favorable setting for the indigenous maritime economy ensued throughout the entire Arctic. The ice conditions encouraged a northward shift in the marine-mammal migration routes into the higher latitudes and the very interior of the Arctic basin (see Bockstoce 1976, McCartney and Savelle 1985, McGhee 1969, 1972, 1984, etc.). During this time the Thule Eskimo whaling culture advanced well up into the Canadian Archipelago, and in the north Bering Sea the Punuk whaling culture was in full sway. Explorers from the West Greenland Norse colonies successfully sailed far to the north and hunted for walrus and seal right up to Disko Bay, at 70° N (McGovern 1979:178–80). In the western Arctic, the summer ranges of whales, walrus, and seals pushed eastward through the Barents Sea and beyond, into the Kara Sea, which provided fertile ground for a growing maritime population. Remains of this population were found in the hunting camps Chernetsov describes on the Yamal Peninsula coast, and in the recently discovered settlements and ritual sites on Vaigach Island. In the latter, metal implements, medieval Arab and Persian coins, and a Novgorod chest icon were discovered, all evidence of active contacts with people from more southerly regions.[3]

But, along with the coastal residents, groups of mobile hunters continued to live in the inland tundra, relying on caribou harvesting, fishing, and occasional maritime hunting. Such was apparently the subsistence system of people living in seasonal camps in the West Siberian Arctic (Nakhodka, Kheibidia-Pedar, *inter alia*), the interior Bol'shaia Zemlia tundra, and the Kola Peninsula (Chernov 1951:109, Lashuk 1968:191, Lashuk and Khlobystin 1986:49, Shaiakhmetova 1990). The closest parallel in the North American Arctic would probably be the nineteenth-century Nunatarmiut Eskimos of the northwest Alaskan interior, who journeyed out to the seacoast in the summer months and made their way up the river valleys into the inland tundra for the winter.

As prehistoric Samoyed pushed into the western Eurasian Arctic in the course of several migration waves during the first millennium C.E. (Vasil'ev 1980:52–53), they indubitably strengthened the interior tundra population. When reindeer husbandry for transportation appeared as part of one of these waves, even if at first only in very limited numbers, it increased the productivity of the nomadic economy, since now hunters or even whole communities could travel long distances more easily.

But until the end of the "warm" ecological phase, that is, until 1300–1400, C.E., maritime hunting was clearly a more reliable form of subsistence than nomadic hunting or fishing. The communities of maritime hunters may have undergone linguistic or cultural assimilation by the growing tundra population. But, most likely, the coastal and inland groups coexisted for a long time, supporting marriage and trade ties. One reflection of this may be Nenets legends telling of marriages in the past with "Sirtia." (Cherntsov 1935:125, Khomich 1970:66, Vasil'ev 1970). Coastal hunters and people of the inland tundra interacted in much the same way on the Chukchi Peninsula, where linguistic assimilation and mixed marriages engendered a gradual metamorphosis of some Eskimos into maritime Chukchi, who nonetheless retained their old subsistence ways.

With the onset of the next ecological-climatic phase in the Arctic and the gradual transition to the subsequent Little Ice Age, the situation changed. As the temperature crept downward, the web of sea-mammal migration routes totally changed, shifting largely toward the south and west, and the peri-Atlantic regions. All this must have disrupted the stability of maritime subsistence in the continental sector of the western Eurasian Arctic—on the Yamal Peninsula, in the Ob' Bay, and even in the eastern half of the Barents Sea. It evidently worked in much the same way as the crisis that befell the Chukchi

Peninsula or the islands of the Canadian archipelago around 1500 C.E., which led to a decline in the indigenous whaling economy, fragmentation of coastal communities, and the exodus of maritime hunters from the harsher, northernmost, and continental strips of coast (Arutiunov et al. 1982, McGhee 1969, 1984, Maxwell 1985).

But meanwhile, off the coast of the western Eurasian Arctic, Russian Pomors and European sailors were promoting the first commercial sea-mammal industry in the region. As early as the ninth century Norse hunters had made initial attempts to establish a sealing industry on the Arctic coast of Norway and the Kola Peninsula. Ottar of Norway is credited with taking the first step toward starting a Norse commercial hunt in the Barents Sea when he was the first to navigate around the northern tip of Scandinavia toward the Kola Peninsula in the late 800s and caught fifty-six walrus on the way (Perry 1976:77). Novgorod-based Russian expeditions became active in the White and Barents seas around 1200 C.E. (Belov 1956:28–31, Chapskii 1939:63, Tomilin 1957:55–56).

But the first pressure on the marine stocks was not great and probably had little impact on the indigenous hunting economy. Russian hunting fleets sprang into action in the early 1500s, then, by the late 1500s, Dutch and British ships stumbled upon huge pods of whales and herds of walrus off the coast of Spitsbergen, Novaia Zemlia, Vaigach Island, and the Pechora estuary, where Russian hunting crews had been operating for some time.

For a brief heyday, the waters of the Barents Sea became a world center for a commercial maritime hunting industry. In the early 1600s, dozens of schooners came here from many countries each year—from Holland, England, Denmark, France, and Germany—large ships, bringing thousands of sailors to the region.[4]

For two centuries, no small portion of the adult male population in the Russian North went to sea each summer to hunt whales, walrus, and seals along the shores of the White and Barents Sea as far north as Novaia Zemlia and Spitsbergen. In the late 1600s something on the order of eight thousand Russian whaleboats with thirty thousand men on board descended upon the Murmansk coast to hunt and fish each year (Zhilinskii 1917:16). At the same time, Norwegian fishermen and maritime hunters began to encroach on the coastal Saami's best hunting grounds, forcing them to retreat from the ocean coasts and islands deeper into inland fjords (Mériot 1984:380).

Naturally, the indigenous peoples of the western Eurasian Arctic could not compete with the well-organized European and Russian commercial whaling fleets. In the 1620s and 1630s, ships belonging to the Northern Holland Company alone caught three to four hundred bowhead whales near Spitsbergen each year. The walrus catch numbered in the hundreds and thousands. Russian Pomor fleets were no less intensive. To this day huge piles of shattered walrus skulls litter the beaches around their derelict camps on Spitsbergen in hundred-foot swaths (Starkov 1986:245, Stora 1987:130–31).

It is this combination of unfavorable ecological trends with powerful external pressures that led to the decline and then the demise of indigenous maritime subsistence on the Barents and Kara Sea coasts. The richest hunting grounds following the main migration routes along the Spitsbergen coasts, Bear Island, the Kola Peninsula, the Pechora estuary, and the straits from the Barents to the Kara Sea were staked out by European whalers and Russian Pomors. Native hunters from the eastern half of the western Eurasian Arctic, that is, the Ob' Bay, Yamal Peninsula, and Novaia Zemlia, found themselves the worst off, trying to hunt at the tail end of the whale and walrus migration paths. The burden of overhunting not only sharply depleted the number of walrus and seals, but caused them to vanish completely from the peripheral extents of their ranges. Coastal communities could no longer survive on sea hunting here.

Rapid decimation of the main marine resources as a result of overhunting by the Europeans was not the sole protagonist in the *dramatis personae* of native history in the western Eurasian Arctic. Close ties between the coastal communities and the tundra nomads played a role of their own. In this respect, the coastal peoples of the western Eurasian Arctic are more aptly compared with the maritime Chukchi, who could always "pass" back into the nomadic tundra economy more easily, than with the Eskimos of Chukotka or Alaska. As with the Chukchi, a sense of linguistic continuity and regular intermarriage with the inland tundra people, and the presence in the coastal villages of many people who themselves, or whose parents, until recently had been herders made it easier for coastal people to leave when maritime hunting fell on hard times, and to make the transition back inland.

We can apply this scenario by extension to the coastal Saami, and especially to the eastern regions of the western Eurasian Arctic (the Bol'shaia Zemlia tundra, Yamal Peninsula, and Novaia Zemlia), where the coastal population had already become part of the Samoyed ethnic world by 1600 or so. Therefore, I consider it less accurate to say that Samoyed herders assimilated autochthonous maritime hunters, as Chernetsov proposed, than to conclude that the coastal population shifted from a maritime to an inland subsistence system dominated by fishing and hunting wild reindeer.

A mass exodus of maritime hunters into the tundra no doubt added to the size of the nomadic communities. In turn, the increase in population density and hunting pressure on the tundra fueled the perennial conflagrations of intertribal conflicts frequently documented for this period. But, on the other hand, the sudden presence of surplus labor in the tundra also could have pushed the development of large-scale reindeer husbandry forward more rapidly. More herders meant better protection and fewer losses of reindeer; more reindeer meant larger and stronger herding communities (Lebedev 1980: 88–89).

On top of all this, more favorable ecological conditions seem to have settled upon the tundra during this time. As the cooling trend set in in earnest, the wild reindeer population began to climb, providing an additional niche for the growing tundra population. By the late 1700s, descendants of the first maritime hunters to have joined the inland tundra communities, only 100 to 150 years before, completed the transition to a large-scale reindeer economy (recounted in chapter 5).

Yet, as late as the 1900s, oral traditions of the European and Yamal Nenets and Kola Saami preserved memories associating certain clans and surnames with erstwhile maritime hunting traditions.[5] Apparently, indigenous maritime hunting in the western Eurasian Arctic never ceased completely. Its intensity, however, was determined more by the volume of competition from European commercial fleets than by the dynamics of purely ecological conditions.

Thus, when European whalers wiped out the Barents Sea bowhead whale stocks and stopped coming there in the mid- to late 1600s, and again when the Russian Pomor industry declined in the late 1700s, maritime hunting began a prompt revival among the native population. Russian sources confirm that in the late 1700s the European Nenets started to hunt sea mammals again, supposedly "under the influence of Russians" (Kolycheva 1956: 79, Lepekhin 1802: 242, Voprosy i otvety 1787: 32). I think that it is more accurate to consider this the revival of preexisting subsistence traditions, which were preserved sporadically in the area. We now have archeological as well as documentary evidence to confirm this (Shumkin 1987:44–45, Zuev 1947:80).

By the mid-1800s, European Nenets in fact made up most of the crews on Russian sealing boats in the east Barents Sea. Russian merchants considered the Nenets excellent sailors and actively sought them out for work in commercial walrus and seal hunting (Islavin 1847:91, Latkin 1853:53). In the 1800s Archangel'sk merchants helped Nenets sea-mammal hunters set up permanent settlements on Novaia Zemlia, Vaigach, and Kolguev islands (Grigorova 1936, Podekrat 1936, Vasil'ev 1979). Thus, 150 to 200 years after its demise, aboriginal maritime subsistence was reborn in the western Eurasian Arctic.

By the early 1900s, approximately 10 percent of the European Nenets, or 600 to 800 people, earned their living in the coastal hunting economy. Of these, 180 people were sedentary Nenets colonists on Novaia Zemlia, 150 on Kolguev Island, and 50 on Vaigach Island; 100 to 120 more people lived in the village of Khabarovo on the Yugor Peninsula. Another 150 families of Siberian Nenets were engaged in maritime hunting in the central Kara Sea region, on the Yamal, Yavai, and Gydan peninsulas (Golovnev 1986:94).

Additional information comes from elders I spoke with in Ust' Kara in 1974, who clearly recalled details of life among the Nenets sealers in the Yugor Strait region in the early 1900s. Most of the commercial seal hunters were former reindeer herders who had moved to the coast. Groups of families set up tents to live in along the shore. By this time, Nenets no longer hunted whales or beluga, so harvesting focused on bearded seal, smaller seals, and walrus. The coastal people also fished, caught moulting birds, and trapped Arctic fox. Nenets traded seal skins and blubber, and walrus blubber, skins, and tusks to Russian merchants, and kept the sea-mammal meat, fish, and fowl for themselves. In addition, they depended in large measure upon purchased food such as flour and bread, and traded with wealthy herders for reindeer meat (Krupnik 1976a:75–76; see also Grigorova 1936:163–64, I. M. 1907: 26–27, Podekrat 1936:88–91).

In addition to the semisedentary Nenets hunters, in the summer months, several reindeer herders from throughout the Bol'shaia Zemlia tundra and Russian Pomors streamed into Yugor Strait to hunt. They formed joint boat crews and traveled together in wooden whaleboats to hunting grounds near Vaigach Island and Novaia

Zemlia. These various seasonal hunters did not eat seal or walrus meat themselves. They either traded it for money and goods to the merchants along with walrus tusks, blubber, sealskins, and oil, or used it for dog food or as bait for trapping Arctic fox. The Kola Peninsula Saami did not use sea-mammal meat for food either, but were actively engaged in commercial hunting for harp seals in several villages as late as the early twentieth century (Luk'ianchenko 1971:52, 54). Nenets reindeer herders conducted a similar maritime economy on the Yamal and Gydan peninsulas, where they mainly hunted for harp seal, walrus, and polar bears (Golovnev 1986:94).

Of course, by the 1800s and 1900s, contact with European commercial hunters had left its mark on native subsistence systems. The Nenets and Saami maritime economies acquired many traditions and hunting methods from the Russian Pomors. Hunters now used firearms to harvest seals individually from land or the shorefast ice; boat crews traveled in wooden boats and Russian-style schooners. Large numbers of seals were injured or drowned. Those that were landed were often only partially butchered and utilized.

Nonetheless, in the 1920s, native hunters brought in four-fifths of the total sea-mammal catch in northeast Arkhangel'sk Province of northern Russia. On the average, Nenets hunters caught two to three times more walrus and seals than Russian Pomors did (Krupnik 1986:215–16, *Pokhoziaistvennaia Perepis'* 1929:46–47). This form of native economy remained profitable until the 1940s and 1950s, when large-scale Russian immigration, industrialization, and new village construction caused a rapid decrease in hunting resources in the western Eurasian Arctic. The Kola Saami no longer engage in maritime hunting. Some Nenets hunters in modern villages on the Barents and Kara Sea coasts still catch seals for their own use. In recent years, that activity may even be increasing slightly (Bogoslovskaia and Krupnik 1987:6–7).

The Dual Subsistence Model

In this comparative review of maritime subsistence systems at the eastern and western extremes of the Eurasian Arctic we have seen how dynamic and flexible use of the environment constitutes the chief adaptive strategy of Arctic communities, regardless of what they hunted and when they lived. The ultimate course of cultural and economic transition, however, was determined by the specific interface between ecological and social changes in progress at any particular moment. The protracted history of Arctic maritime hunting has illustrated the relative sensitivity and vulnerability of coastal subsistence compared, for example, to reindeer husbandry. Dependent upon slim zones or fleeting seasons of concentrated resources, maritime subsistence systems proved especially susceptible to exogenous intervention. And herein lies the source of the unique symbiosis between the sedentary and nomadic models of Arctic resource use, as mismatched as they might seem in their productive capacities.

These two main models of indigenous resource use in the Arctic reacted differently to similar changes in the ecological environment. In general, warming phases were more favorable for the coastal population, whose resources came primarily from marine ecosystems. During this time, migratory routes of marine mammals and anadromous fish made a general shift toward the north. New grounds opened, the seasons for open-water, ice-edge, or ice-lead hunting began earlier in the spring, and the wintertime lean-season gap in the subsistence cycle shrank. But the same warming phases brought hard times to the hunting and herding populations of the inland tundra inasmuch as the frequency of epizootics and tundra fires increased, grazing conditions deteriorated, and pasture recovery slowed. Warming phases led to nadirs in the reindeer population cycles.

Cooling phases in the Arctic had the opposite effect. The descending ice edge blockaded high-latitude and continental stretches of the coast. People who lived there were eventually forced to move into the tundra and adjust to a new way of life. Thus, on the coasts, cooling usually led to deterioration in hunting conditions, famines, and population decline, while, in the inland tundra, cooling rejuvenated the reindeer herds, both caribou and, in more recent centuries, domestic, and caused the nomads' welfare to improve.

These constant swings of the ecological pendulum had enormous significance for the human residents of the Arctic. They encouraged development of a unique subsistence strategy, in which two or more resource use models developed in tandem. The Arctic population actually has created an economic continuum between the nomadic and the sedentary models, ready to embrace either one in response to environmental change. Any changes in the environment augured poorly for one part of the spectrum but, by the same token, bolstered the range of species, harvestable biomass, and productivity for the other. Adherence to common overarching themes of flexibility and "omnivorousness" in both systems made adjustment to new daily activities and annual cycles less painful, and eased the indigenous community's transition from one way of life to the other.

We can visualize the history of indigenous economies in the Arctic as like a tide periodically shifting from nomadic to sedentary modes then back again according to prevailing trends in the social and ecological environment. In observing these separate-but-related ebbs and flows in nomadic and sedentary subsistence, the indigenous economies seem to shift like sand in an hourglass: from land-game hunting and reindeer herding to maritime hunting and fishing, then back again in response to social and/or environmental change. To illustrate, in his reference to the nomadic Chukchi from Kolyma district, Sergei Buturlin wrote, "I was amazed by the degree of spiritual and physical flexibility they . . . displayed in shifting without hesitation from their usual nomadic pastoralism to semi-sedentary fishing. Only a few years ago one could travel from Kolyma River to Chaun Bay without encountering a single Chukchi on the coast. Now, one sees their ruidy [*yarangas*] everywhere along the shore" (Buturlin 1907:71).

The Eskimo caribou hunters' migration toward the coast from the interior of northern Alaska during the caribou crash of the late 1800s was equally large-scale and sudden (see Amsden 1979:397–400, Burch 1972:356–58, Spencer 1959:134–35). Counterexamples exist, too: during the 1700s, and especially during the famine of 1880, part of the coastal population, both Eskimo and Chukchi, moved into the tundra, where they were assimilated by reindeer herders. During the cooling phase of the 1600s–1700s, groups of Canadian coastal Eskimos were being transformed into highly specialized caribou hunters (Burch 1978). In the same manner and at the very same time, native coastal hunters known as "the Shelagi" in early Russian records vanished from the East Siberian Sea coast at the opposite end of the Arctic littoral, and nomadic reindeer herding groups appeared in their place (see Bogoras 1934, Okladnikov and Beregovaia 1971, Vdovin 1965). To this list, we can now add the demise of the aboriginal maritime culture of the western Eurasian Arctic and the transition of its people first to nomadic hunting, and then to reindeer husbandry.

This constant flux of Arctic aboriginal populations from sedentary to nomadic subsistence strategies and back again represents a highly specific adaptive model which I call a *dual* or *paired economy*. A paired economy emerged as a preeminently efficient mechanism to reconcile two potentially antagonistic strategies in a mutually complementary way. This linkage enabled Arctic peoples to withstand the changes constantly confronting them in their shifting environment. Its *sine qua non*, however, was survival, in the general sense, of the entire subsistence spectrum, from purely nomadic and sedentary adaptations at the extremes to a variety of transitional, seminomadic forms in between. The more variety, the greater the sustainability: dozens of local subsistence patterns proliferated and survived bearing specific ethnic or cultural faces, in accordance with this central principle of human adaptation in the Arctic. Even a rudimentary or impure cultural adaptation provided a refuge in which a technological, demographic, and spatial seed could survive until and if the environmental trend reversed and the conditions necessary to revive the parent model were reestablished on another turn of the ecological wheel.[6]

In those areas of the Arctic where this adaptive mechanism prevailed—on the Chukchi Peninsula, in northwestern Alaska, in northern Scandinavia, and on the Kola Peninsula—we can generally trace an unbroken line of human occupation and subsistence continuities over a long-term time frame. In other areas—for example, in Greenland or in the Canadian High Arctic—narrowly limited ecological conditions permitted only one main subsistence strategy. There, as one would expect, huge chronological gaps occurred between successive ancient Eskimo cultures. In cases where extremely severe ecological or social conditions caused the extinction of one of the paired economies, the crucial balance was destroyed and the coupled model disappeared. Even a short time span was then sufficient to disrupt an aboriginal cultural continuity and for many technological advances—hunting tools, techniques, and subsistence knowledge—to be lost.

As we have seen, this is what happened in the 1600s in the western Eurasian Arctic. Climatic cooling and commercial whaling disrupted the Barents and Kara Sea maritime subsistence systems for no more than 150 to 200 years. But that brief hiatus was sufficient to cause irreversible damage to indigenous cultural adaptations essential for survival in the Arctic. The aboriginal population lost the skills for cooperative boat-crew hunting for beluga, gray, and bowhead whales. They stopped building semisubterranean dwellings from whalebone and driftwood. They probably also forgot how to make skinboats and

Fig. 14. Masik site, Mechigmen Bay, Chukchi Peninsula. (Drawing by Sergei Bogoslovskii, 1981.)

walrus-tusk harpoons and how to air-dry meat without salt. They no longer made pottery or heated their homes with seal-oil lamps—the list goes on.[7]

Of course, cultural evolution in any environment tends to be wavelike, with alternating periods of flowering and regression, advances and declines. In this respect, there is nothing unique about cultural development among Arctic peoples. But the frequency and sharpness of these waves vary in certain social and ecological circumstances. Our examination of the history of northern reindeer pastoralism and Arctic maritime hunting clearly shows the capacity of Arctic native peoples for rapid demographic and economic growth in auspicious times. But extreme instability of their environment and a limited resource base meant that phases of crisis conditions were more frequent and more acute here than in other regions of the world. In the particular conditions of the Arctic, the cyclical development typical for the evolution of culture anywhere became particularly pronounced.

Ivory-decorated carvings of the Bering Sea Eskimo, powerfully expressive yet delicate; impressive series of prehistoric rock paintings in Scandinavia and Chukotka; remains of bustling Punuk whaling villages; painstakingly designed stone labyrinths of the Kola Peninsula; the monumental Whale Alley; and now-abandoned whalers' settlements at Masik in Bering Strait and on Somerset Island in the Canadian Arctic where whale skulls lie piled by the hundreds and thousands (fig. 14)—these are but a few of the peaks we know of in "Arctic civilization," which were superseded during subsequent phases of decline, or disappeared completely from the aboriginal traditions of the centuries to follow.

Does this mean that the apparent long-term stability of Arctic societies is only an artifice created by scanning too many centuries at once in retrospect, the result of scanty knowledge and a paucity of sources? Or are we historians imprisoned by our own illusions about the retarded tempo of development among local indigenous peoples? After all, the exploitation of the Arctic by humans was not a brute struggle for survival, but the outcome of active, sequential peopling of the prehistoric ecumene. That process was clearly contingent upon expanded demographic reproduction and a surplus of essential subsistence resources. Having established in multiple ways the flexibility and fluidity of Arctic adaptations, we still lack a few components necessary to understand the sources of inner growth and energy within the Arctic societies. These are to be presented in the following chapter.

CHAPTER SEVEN

The Aboriginal Hunter in the Arctic Ecosystem

Population Continuity

In 1982, the so-called "Utqiagvik family," a group of frozen human mummies and skeletons, was discovered at a prehistoric Eskimo site in Barrow, Alaska. A multidisciplinary project was subsequently launched to study the natural and cultural environment, and the physical status of the prehistoric Inuit population of Barrow (Lobdell and Dekin 1984). Participating researchers in the Utqiagvik Archeology Project conducted an ethnohistorical household survey in the modern village of Barrow and interviewed a number of local elders as resource experts on Inupiat culture.

For those who had long taken the idea of long-term Eskimo cultural continuity in the area as fact, the survey yielded resoundingly disappointing results. In the entire village, which was the largest Inuit community in Alaska with a native population of three thousand or more, researchers found few, if any, people whose ancestors had lived in Barrow at the end of the nineteenth century (Hall 1984). In less than a hundred years, the entire Barrow community had experienced a complete cultural and genealogical turnover, even though the native population had continuously increased, swelling eightfold between 1900 and 1984 (Masnik and Katz 1976).

This revelation, which so shocked the archeologists, had been a matter of discussion among ethnographers in available narratives and records for quite some time. As Vilhjalmur Stefansson wrote in 1908:

> The village of Cape Smyth [Barrow] probably contained about four hundred inhabitants in 1880, and contains about that today. But only four persons

(sic!) are now living who are considered by the Eskimos themselves to belong to the [original] Cape Smyth tribe, and only twenty or twenty-one others who are descended from the Cape Smyth tribe through one parent. The fact is that the excessive death rate of the last thirty years would have nearly wiped out the village . . . , so that no more than seven percent [of the population] can now be considered to belong to it. The difference is made up by the immigrants . . . the majority of whom come from inland (Stefansson 1951:66–67).

The demographic scenario at Point Barrow thus hardly seems to qualify as a cultural continuity. Nor is Barrow the only place where such discontinuities occurred. Out of more than three hundred people living in the Eskimo village of Gambell on St. Lawrence Island, Alaska, in 1955, Charles Hughes's survey revealed only one person whose forebears on both sides had lived in the village continuously since the mid-1800s (Hughes 1960:250). All the others had moved to Gambell from other villages around the island in the late 1800s, or were descendants of emigrants from the Chukchi Peninsula, Siberia.

Similar instances are recorded outside of Alaska. For example, 2,000 to 2,500 Inuit lived in the Mackenzie Delta region in the mid-nineteenth century. Within a hundred years this number had fallen to 1,500, and all but two or three dozen of these people were descendants of the Inuit incomers who had moved there recently, primarily from northern Alaska (Smith 1975:7). In compiling genealogies and clan lists for the Asiatic Eskimo of the Chukchi Peninsula, I was frequently struck by their volatility. The most basic components of the community—powerful families, well-established boat crews and entire villages—could turn over completely in a matter of twenty or thirty years as a result of migration, epidemics, or uneven growth rates among various clans, a phenomenon also noted among the neighboring and closely related St. Lawrence Island Eskimo (Hughes 1960:79). A similarly dynamic social structure was recently discovered among the aboriginal Avam Nganasan population of Taimyr Peninsula in Arctic Siberia from the 1600s on. Their traditional clan system only arose in the mid-1800s, when several families died out while others amalgamated and swelled rapidly during a period of repeated epidemics, famines, and irregular population growth (Afanas'eva 1980b).

Of course, we cannot overlook that Euro-American contact may have exacerbated the volatility of traditional Arctic communities. Famines, imported diseases, drastic depletion of traditional game resources, and the appearance of missionary stations, trading posts, and other incentives to migration introduced from the outside, all triggered massive upheaval among the aboriginal population and caused profound transformation in its social structure. In many regions, fragments of previous ethnoterritorial groups mixed together and formed new, rapidly growing social entities. Much of the literature during the Soviet period focused on describing such postcontact transformations, or "ethnic processes," as they were called, among the peoples of northern Siberia (Dolgikh 1952a, b, 1960, 1970, Gurvich 1966, 1982, Vasil'ev 1979b, Vdovin 1973, etc.). Similar postcontact effects are also well documented among the Eskimos (Inuit) of Alaska, Greenland, and Labrador (e.g., Burch 1975, 1980, Ray 1975, Rowley 1985, Taylor 1974). As we recall from our earlier chapters on the Asiatic Eskimo, Nenets, and Chukchi, the social upheaval of this period became an important factor influencing demographic trends among native peoples of the Arctic.

We should not, however, imagine the precontact period to have been some kind of "Golden Age" of health, harmony, and tranquility, when Arctic people always had enough to eat, never fought one another, and never had to pick up and abandon their homes. As Ernest Burch has written, "Most of us think in terms of a 'tradition' or a 'contact' or an 'aboriginal' state of affairs as having been somehow immutable until massive European interference suddenly changed everything. This is a tendency we must resist" (Burch 1980:261).

At times the dearth or complete absence of hard data tempts us to view Arctic communities as static ethnic groups. Assuming long-term cultural continuities, fixed populations, and rigid social structures might certainly make for neater narratives and simplify our task. However, time after time, the archeological and paleoanthropological records provide us with indisputable evidence of frequent and profound disruption in prehistoric cultural traditions, which until recently were believed to have existed unchanged "since time immemorial."

Thus, paleoanthropological analysis of the Utqiagvik burial site with which we opened this chapter revealed that the actual population completely changed at Barrow between the Birnirk and Thule cultures (i.e., between the eighth and ninth centuries C.E.), even though the basic ethnocultural complex continued unchanged (Hall 1984:135). Human craniums found in ancient Eskimo burial sites on the northeast tip of Chukchi Peninsula and Point Hope, Alaska, illustrate the radical population change (at least in terms of its physical characteristics) between the prehistoric and contemporary periods, although even here we are also dealing with a cultural tradition that is usually presented as remaining intact to some degree (Debets 1975:199–201). Long gaps have been established between the basic phases of prehistoric Eskimo culture in Greenland (Independence I, Independence II, Sarqaq, Early and Late Dorset, and Thule). During these gaps, the population either abandoned Greenland for other areas or died out, leaving large areas of the island completely uninhabitated (Fitzhugh 1984). Multiple cultural complexes from the inland areas of Arctic Alaska form an even more impressive "layer cake," where Denbigh, Norton, Ipiutak, Kayuk, Tuktu, Kavik, and other traditions rose and fell in succession without any kind of genealogical overlap, as though at different times and from different directions migrating groups periodically penetrated the Alaskan interior, then after a time disappeared without leaving offspring behind (Amsden 1979). The illustrations go on and on.

Our experience in the course of ethnohistorically interpreting Whale Alley referred to the same sort of cultural traditions that were broken and lost through the turmoils of native history (Arutiunov, Krupnik, and Chlenov 1982:94–135). Built from dozens of bowhead whale skulls and jaws, this ancient memorial site on the Chukchi Peninsula stands totally outside any identified local cultural tradition of either Chukchi or Eskimo in the 1800s. Although Whale Alley was clearly built by Eskimos no more than four to six hundred years ago, it appears to be the mysteriously abandoned legacy of an earlier historical reality. Early-contact Eskimos shared a closely related subsistence base with this previous cultural community, but followed divergent ritual practices and spiritual beliefs. In attempting to determine why a religious site of such obvious stature as Whale Alley fell so precipitously into deep oblivion, we emphasized the role of drastic population change through migrations from St. Lawrence Island, cultural shifts, and the appearance of a new system of Eskimo tribal areas in Chukotka sometime between 1500 and 1750 (Arutiunov et al. 1982:155–57).

Health, Mortality, and Population Increase

Analysis of such cultural and demographic rifts contributes greatly to understanding the historical development of Arctic peoples. Prehistoric Eskimo villages on the Chukchi Peninsula originating during Old Bering Sea time are often interpreted by archeologists as a stable sociolocational continuum virtually right up until the historical period (Arutiunov and Sergeev 1975). They were seen as remaining more or less constant in size, increasing only over the course of centuries or millenia. A similar pattern has also been presented for the prehistoric Aleuts. Albert Harper (1980:55–56) even modeled the prehistoric Aleut population as steadily maintaining an average growth rate of about 0.0002–0.0003 a year for the past nine thousand years (Harper 1980:55–56). Thus, a community of a hundred would gain a single person in thirty years and increase by three after an entire century. Within this minimum-growth model, small, stable hunting bands could sustain a demographic equilibrium with their resources and environment over the course of many centuries.

On this basis, do we really dare to conclude that the prehistoric Arctic demographic model differed so blatantly from the population model reconstructed above (see chapters 2 and 3)—one of high birth rates, very high mortality, and jagged population trends established by the postcontact records? And how does the minimum-growth model account for the inevitable human costs of local and large-scale migration, as well as recovery of a population from epidemics, famine, wars, or natural disasters, all of which figured prominently in the human condition since the first arrival of people in the Arctic?

Nowadays, few take seriously such unattributed pronouncements as, "The health of the Eskimos prior to their prolonged contact with western culture was good if not exceptional. The Eskimos showed that they have reached a remarkably effective adjustment to an unkind world and seemed to be thriving, despite some of the usual kinds of ills that all mankind is heir to" (Fortuine 1971:114, cited in Martin 1978:46). Early European observers, for example, noticed that the Eskimos they encountered suffered from cataracts, respiratory diseases, mental retardation, neurological disorders, and musculoskeletal defects. Pathological indications suggest that 10 percent of the people buried in the Old Bering Sea Ekven cemetery on the Chukchi Peninsula were so afflicted by arthritis and spondylitis that they were effectively crippled and unable to hunt or work productively within the home (Lebedinskaia 1969:197).

Some late-Punuk burials on Saint Lawrence Island show signs of malnutrition and even actual physical degeneration (Bandi 1976). According to reconstructions of medical and sanitary conditions, the native population of northeastern Siberia suffered from numerous catarrhal, dermatological, and gastrointestinal diseases, as well as tuberculosis and possibly even veneral diseases long before the arrival of Russians (Volfson 1984:38–39). Lastly, cases are known throughout the Arctic when famines or food poisoning wiped out entire communities. Hunting expeditions went to sea never to return, and large groups of people died from accidents or natural disasters (e.g., Burch 1980:285, Fainberg 1971:229–32, Mikkelsen 1944:20–21, Rowley 1985:4–7). Burch calculates that sometime before 1880, one-third of the original Kotzebue Inuit community drowned in freak accidents, while Taylor refers to a skinboat fleet of more than two hundred Eskimos perishing in the summer of 1773 off the coast of Labrador (Burch 1980:290, Taylor 1974:8). Asiatic Eskimos even have a special word, *qawangakhtuqaghmiit* ("the ones who did not awaken"), for people who died from hunger or disease; and old, abandoned dwellings on the Chukchi Peninsula are strewn with their bones.

In light of these facts, then, "demographic stability" is not a term one should apply to the native populations of the Eurasian Arctic and their long-term cultural continuum. On the contrary, the human history of the Arctic is characterized by an abundance of disruptions, crises, shifting ethnocultural traditions, and deep ecological and social shockwaves. Reading the seventeenth- and eighteenth-century records on the Siberian, Canadian, or Alaskan natives, one visualizes this history as an unbroken chain of epidemics, famines, internecine conflicts, disasters in domestic stocks and wildlife populations, as well as enslavement, assimilation, and even outright massacre in the course of European colonial expansion. This woeful epic of victimization is a recurring litany in the research on numerous Arctic peoples, from the Yukagir, Nganasan, Kerek and Koryak, G'wichin and Yellowknife Athapaskan, to the Eskimo of St. Lawrence Island and the Alaskan interior (see Burch 1975, 1980, Burgess 1974, Gurvich 1966, Krech 1978, Leonti'ev 1983, Tugolukov 1979, Vdovin 1973, etc.).

But even in such difficult ecological conditions and under the additional pressure of heavy losses resulting from newly introduced epidemic diseases, starvation, and resource depletion, the total native population of the Arctic actually increased during European contact. A popular genre in the Western anthropological literature provides dramatic renditions of how European contact wiped out local bands or even entire tribes (e.g., Southampton Island Sadlermiut, St. Lawrence Island Eskimo, Mackenzie Delta Eskimo, Yellowknife Athapaskan, Western Aleut, etc.) Much less well-known, but equally eloquent, are records of contact with the native Siberians, that present a very different picture. Using tax lists and other sources, Dolgikh has estimated that in the mid-1600s, that is, in the early-contact phase, there were 207,000 native Siberians, while the First Russian Census in 1897 numbers the same native Siberian population at 822,000 (Dolgikh 1960:615–17, Patkanov 1912:159–67). Narrowing our focus to the Arctic proper, around 30,000 people lived in Arctic Eurasia by 1650, not including Kola and Scandinavian Saami and Russian Pomors. By the early 1900s the same population had increased more than twofold—up to some 63,000 people (calculated according to Dolgikh 1960, *Pokhoziaistvennaia Perepis'* 1929). As we saw in the preceding chapters, some Arctic peoples, such as Nenets, Chukchi, reindeer Koryak, Saami etc., not only doubled or tripled in numbers and expanded territorially, but even progressed to a more labor-intensive form of subsistence—large-scale reindeer husbandry.

Natives of the North American Arctic, especially Aleut and Inuit in northern Alaska and certain areas of Canada, suffered far greater losses from European expansion. In contrast, notwithstanding frequent famines and epidemics, the Inuit population of Greenland increased 2.5 times from the late eighteenth to the early twentieth centuries, from 5,000 to 12,500 (Kleivan 1984:597). My recent summary of indigenous population dynamics in the Bering Sea area elicited no universal pattern of demographic decline resulting from Euro-American contact on either the Siberian or American sides (Krupnik 1990).

Although the arrival of Europeans exposed all native groups in the area to introduced diseases, social stress, and disruption of traditional subsistence and land tenure, the demographic effects varied widely. Some groups, such as Itel'men, Yukagir, Aleut, Kerek, Eyak, and St. Lawrence Island Eskimo, suffered dramatic and unrecoverable losses, while others eventually restabilized (Koryak, southwestern Alaska, Seward Peninsula, and Labrador Eskimo prior to the influenza epidemic of 1918), and still others experienced rapid growth in population and expanded their territory at the expense of their weakened neighbors (e.g., Chukchi, Even, and Tlingit). Thus, the Arctic provides us with a somewhat different story from that of other hunter-gatherers faced with European contact, one that reemphasizes the great stamina, resilience, and vitality of its people.

More on Infanticide in the Arctic

Models of minimum population growth, limited carrying capacity, and homeostatic human-environment ecology do not, however, explain the origins of this vitality. Such frameworks have suggested only one mechanism regulating "stability" in traditional Arctic societies—deliberate population control via certain forms of socially condoned demographic behavior, and, first and foremost, infanticide. This dovetails closely with another popular thesis, according to which Arctic hunters always used their available resources in a maximally conservationist, rational way and carefully limited themselves to catching only as much food as they needed to survive.

We have already cited kindred concepts, such as the existence of infanticide among certain Eskimo groups in the American Arctic, the custom of "voluntary death" applied to invalid and aging members among the Eskimo and Chukchi, the great respect shown for slaughtered animals among all northern peoples as well as ritual or rational traditions aimed at conserving game resources, etc. No one argues that these traditions did not exist. All are confirmed by a vast number of reliable ethnographic sources and direct observation (e.g., Birket-Smith 1929:95, 101, Bogoras 1934:106–12, Carr-Saunders 1922:146, Jochel'son 1898:152, Kjelström 1974/75:117–22, Krzywicki 1934:151, Nansen 1937:279–80, 375, Popov 1948:95, Weyer 1932, Zolotarev and Levin 1940:175, etc.). However, other contrasting traditions are equally well documented, and have been presented in the pages of this book.

At certain times in their history, Arctic peoples did exhibit a high birthrate and rapid population growth. Weyer has correctly noted that Eskimo sexual norms always were consonant with a desire to maintain as high a birthrate as possible (Weyer 1932:139). Notwithstanding an ongoing struggle for survival, where every unproductive member placed an additional burden on the community, Arctic peoples show great care and concern for children, elders, and invalids. As is well known, among all Arctic peoples childlessness traditionally was considered the greatest misfortune possible, while having lots of children usually enhanced a family's prestige. We constantly find references to families with many small children in Siberian household surveys, tax lists, and parish records from the 1700s up to the early 1900s. Such large families would not have been possible if strict population control was the rule.

Previously, I conducted a special examination of the effect of infanticide on the demographic structure of native peoples in the Eurasian Arctic, based on documentary sources from the eighteenth to early twentieth centuries (Krupnik 1985). To judge by the shelves of anthropological literature on the subject, infanticide would seem to be *the* focal point of indigenous "Arctic demography." Weyer (1932:131–32), following Carr-Saunders (1922), identified selective female infanticide as the principal mechanism of demographic "policy" and population control among Eskimos. Subsequent researchers were even moved to declare female infanticide a fundamental adaptive strategy for ensuring survival in the extreme Arctic environment (Balikci 1967:624–25), and, therefore, of necessity a universal practice among indigenous Arctic populations, and among all hunter-gatherer societies in general. According to the most extreme view, systematic infanticide formed the basic means of population control for all prehistoric and traditional societies, which deliberately destroyed anywhere from fifteen to fifty percent of their newborn infants, preferably girls (Birdsell 1968:239, 243).

In fact, as I have shown elsewhere, indications of infanticide among Siberian indigenous groups are infrequent, and testify mainly to the sporadic and random nature of the practice (Krupnik 1985:127; see also Pika 1986:42). Such was the case among the Asiatic Eskimo, Chukchi, and Nenets as discussed in chapters 2 and 3. Furthermore, my total sample of twenty-five native populations throughout the Eurasian Arctic yielded scant evidence of any practices of deliberate population control. My findings not only do not confirm the supposed existence of a universally "Arctic-type" age-sex structure, whether genetic or environmentally adaptive in origin—they reveal a rich spectrum of highly variable demographic patterns. Since native family records became available in Siberia, that is, from the 1700s onward, we find no traces of active infanticide among the peoples of the Eurasian Arctic, or, more precisely, no indication in the age-sex structures that it was practiced on a sex-selective basis.

Seen in a broad, circumpolar perspective, infanticide, and especially its selective female-focused aspect appear to have been primarily an idiosyncratically local phenomenon. Infanticide, where and when it occurred, was no more remarkable and no less illogical, intellectually or ecologically, than, for example, the Nenets custom of expelling women in labor from the heated family tent to give birth outdoors, even in winter, when many died as a result. Among Eskimo societies, infanticide clearly seems to have emerged only as a local cultural development (Riches 1974:359–61, Freeman 1971) reported primarily for the Central Canadian Arctic and some places in Alaska. Its absence or highly sporadic nature anywhere among the Asiatic Eskimo or Greenland and Labrador Inuit (Holm 1914:62, Taylor 1974:60) further emphasizes the local character of so peculiar a form of family "planning." Without denying that infanticide existed in the Arctic in the past (as in many other traditional societies, from Australian aborigines to medieval Iceland), we do well to regard this beloved wrench in the toolbox of proponents of steady-state human-environment relations in the Arctic much more critically. As Schrire and Steiger sagely noted, selective infanticide can hardly be considered an optimal ecological strategy, since, as in any society, "It is always possible to teach a woman to earn a livelihood, but impossible to teach a man how to bear a child" (1974:179–80).

Ecopopulation Strategies

The results of our investigation lead us to the following conclusion. Logically, the human-environment relationship in the Arctic could have varied, such that periods of "harmony" and "expansion" alternated in accordance with social and ecological change. More plausible, however, is that in an environment that changes so regularly and radically as the Arctic, an equilibrium between humans and their environment is effectively impossible.

As discussed in chapter 4, living organisms in the Arctic find the ecological homeostasis typical of lower latitudes difficult to achieve and jeopardizing to their survival. In the complex and constantly changing Arctic ecosystem, any "equilibrium" state is inherently unstable, short-lived, and inevitably tips in one direction or the other. If Arctic animals can compensate for crisis-period population losses with a surge in productivity during auspicious times (*r*-factor selection), then much slower-reproducing human beings in the same environment ought to have corresponding means for ecological and community survival.

Under these conditions, I believe that a constant high growth rate among Arctic aboriginal communities proved to be an adaptive form that yielded better results than any kind of drive toward stabilization and equilibrium with the environment. In the face of inevitable environmental disturbances, limiting the population would have been a luxury the aboriginal community could ill afford, especially at times when social and ecological circumstances supported a surge in growth. Out of this practical consideration stem many aspects of traditional Arctic community dynamics: tendencies toward territorial expansion, maximum resource utilization, and high birthrates which served to replenish the population rapidly in spite of ubiquitously short life-expectancy and high death rates.

A Moscow biologist, Vadim Mokievskii, pointed out to me that these behavioral features of Arctic human communities actually approximate the strategy described by the *r*-factor model, and thus narrow the differential between human adaptations and those of other large Arctic mammals.[1]

The ability to expand reproduction in the human community at any propitious moment, however brief, created a vital reserve in traditional Arctic societies. This hidden source of strength enabled Arctic communities to weather crises, game shortages, and even cultural declines, then to restore and even exceed their former number whenever positive environmental conditions returned. As the recorded histories of certain populations, such as the Nenets, Chukchi, and Greenland Inuit show, Arctic peoples were fully capable of three- or even fourfold population growth in the space of a few generations.

Migrations and Population Growth

We should not forget that, by modern standards, only a modest increase in the ratio of births to deaths was enough to swell the Arctic population rapidly. With a net rate of increase of 0.3 percent a year, or 3 per 1,000, the population doubles after 230 years, while with a net growth rate of 0.5 percent the community will increase tenfold in about 500 years. Annual growth of 0.4 percent is enough for the community to expand its territory ten times in 577 years, assuming the population density remains the same (Bottino 1987:115, Cowgill 1975:510). Clearly, we do not need centuries and millenia to explain instances of Arctic population and territorial expansion: the same effect could be achieved in a relatively short period of time favorable for human survival from both an environmental and social perspective. A few decades of increased growth then produced enough of a population "explosion" to resume exploitation of neglected hunting grounds, to reinhabit abandoned villages, and eventually to push some members of the community to look elsewhere in search of new habitats.

According to the late Russian archeologist Leonid Khlobystin, some unknown number of boreal Siberian people moved northward to the Eurasian Arctic six to eight thousand years ago. Along a broad front several thousand kilometers wide, scattered bands of caribou hunters left the taiga for the northern coastline and began to exploit the tundra zone from the Kola Peninsula to northern Yakutia and the Bering Sea (Khlobystin 1982:287–88). Minimum population growth and equilibrium theory models offer no means to comprehend how this flow could have begun and led to the formation of an established Arctic population of thirty thousand people by the time Russians arrived in the region.

By four to five thousand years ago, a similar migratory wave may have ultimately expanded into settlement of the American Arctic. Archeologists agree that the similar profile and nearly identical age of aboriginal encampments throughout the Arctic from northeast Siberia, through Alaska, Canada, Greenland, and into Labrador offer proof of an extremely fast migration occurring along the Arctic coasts of Siberia and North America (Maxwell 1985:48–50, Powers and Jordan 1989:14). The people of this culture, which we now call the Arctic Small Tool Tradition, primarily hunted caribou and musk-ox, engaged in ice sealing, and fished. To occupy, or even pass through, this expanse from Bering Strait to Greenland, leaving many dozens of hunting camps behind, was something only a society with a reliable subsistence system and the ability to sustain reproduction within each of many small, mobile groups could have done. The minimum population growth model is cognitively dissonant with this.

Canadian archeologist Robert McGhee has recently advanced the hypothesis that ancestral Eskimo may have reached Greenland and the Arctic coast of North America not only from the west via Bering Strait, but also from the east, making their way along the Siberian Arctic shore, and island-hopping across the icebound polar basin. McGhee traces this second route from the mouth of the Lena River to Taimyr Peninsula of the central Siberian Arctic, then along the island chain of Severnaia Zemlia, Franz Josef Land, and the Svalbard archipelago to the northeast coast of Greenland (McGhee 1988).

Such a journey across the islands and ice of the High Arctic along the eighty-second parallel was certainly unprecedented in the history of arduous migrations humans have made in expanding the limits of the ecumene. Not that prehistoric hunting peoples would have found this realm an icy wasteland—many familiar hunting species lived here in abundance: seals, polar bears, caribou, seabirds. But even if—or precisely because—migrating bands were few in number, the stability conferred by a reliable subsistence system and steady population growth would be a requisite precondition for Arctic population dispersal, whether by McGhee's proposed second route from Siberia west to Greenland or by the traditional route to North America via Bering Strait. Without such demographic resiliency and ecological flexibility, it would have been well-nigh impossible to compensate for the inevitable losses and hardships encountered on the dangerous trek.

Evidently, we need to reassess the demographic assumptions upon which we have customarily based the history of Arctic peoples, as well as other variables of more recent import. For example, could there have been a substantial migration path from St. Lawrence Island to the Chukchi Peninsula that interrupted the intertribal linkage to the Whale Alley sanctuary mentioned above? In order to overwhelm and obliterate the society from which Whale Alley's several-score builders were drawn, the wave of new arrivals must have numbered at least in the dozens, and more likely in the hundreds. Similarly, Thule colonization of the Canadian Arctic, Greenland, and Labrador from 1000 to 1500 C.E., which involved assimilation or displacement of Dorset-culture populations encountered there, was hardly the work of a single or a few isolated hunting bands. In my opinion, we should assume that several hundred people participated in this process, setting out in successive small bands from a threshold in the Bering Strait–northern Alaska area in a generally eastward flow (McGhee 1969–70, 1984, Maxwell 1985). Moreover, in both cases, "surplus" population apparently formed the groups that set out further upon the trail, since the settlements they left behind firmly maintained their cultural integrity and continuity.

Rapid population growth, sustaining communities in the hardship conditions of transit, could be expected in the new areas as well, and archeological data confirm such growth in some regions. Susan Kaplan claims that, after occupying the resource-rich coast of Labrador, the Thule Eskimo population grew sixfold from the fifteenth to the early eighteenth centuries, transforming the semi-deserted shores into one of the most densely populated areas of the Arctic (Kaplan 1983:303–82, 1985:60–61). Archeologists believe there were no Eskimos in central and southern Greenland when Norse colonists arrived there in 985. Within four or five hundred years after Eskimos resettled the west coast of Greenland in the thirteenth century, they achieved a population of over five thousand by the 1700s, a figure that already includes substantial losses from epidemics in the earlier phases of contact (see Gulløv 1985:74–91, McGovern 1979:179–81).

Population Models

Unfortunately, there are no direct data for a reconstruction of demographic processes in Arctic communities during this era of mass migrations, but intriguing computer simulations have been compiled and published. Taking Bering Strait as the point of origin, Robert Bottino modeled six alternative computer scenarios of Thule expansion across the North American Arctic based on variable rates of travel, fertility, mortality, and infanticide. Bottino found the scenario that most closely resembled historical reality was based on high fertility, moderate mortality, and no infanticide (Bottino 1987:118–20). Of course, computer models do not prove that one demographic practice or another actually was the norm in Eskimo society. But, in various ways, Bottino's analysis represents a valuable counter-argument to the minimum growth and equilibrium models as either primary or universal for Arctic peoples.

A population history of the Avam Nganasan reconstructed from Russian tax records from the 1600s to the 1800s provides greater insight (Afanas'eva 1979, 1980a, 1980b; see also Dolgikh 1952b, 1960:124–28, Simchenko 1982). The Avam Nganasan of the Taimyr Peninsula are the northernmost aboriginal group in the Eurasian Arctic. Over the past three hundred years, their population has alternately risen quickly, then fallen abruptly, usually as a result of catastrophic epidemics and famine. As Boris Dolgikh so eloquently writes, "In Nganasan folklore one senses that the life granted to the ancestral residents of northern Siberia was never an easy one. Death from famine and sickness, drowning in rivers and lakes, attacks by wild animals and human foes lay in wait at each step along the way. Entire families, clans and villages may die, but those who survive fight their environment and their enemies with even greater vigor"

(Dolgikh 1976:33). "Population booms" among the Nganasan were clearly restorative in nature: at least three times since the late 1600s the Nganasan population increased one-and-a-half times in twenty to thirty years. Such rapid growth compensated for prior losses due to devastating epidemics and famines (Afanas'eva 1980b).

The ability of the Nganasan to recover their numbers in such a short time attests to the absence of a population control mechanism among these Arctic people. According to the census data of the late 1700s, Nganasan families were amazingly large. No less than 30 percent had five or more living children, up to a maximum of twelve. During this phase of quick recovery, children and teenagers accounted for 45 to 50 percent of the population, that is, even more than among the Eskimo, Nenets, and Chukchi in the early 1900s, as described in building our model of native reproductive strategy in the Arctic. Future research will show to what degree this demographic behavior was typical in other Arctic groups, especially for those who managed to increase their populations rapidly during the last centuries, such as the Nenets, Chukchi, Even, and Eskimo of Greenland.

In short, the general model of demographic behavior among Arctic peoples fundamentally rests on two related tenets of population growth and territorial expansion. With this in view, we should not be surprised to find cases where these principles led to intensive exploitation of subsistence resources, with at times disastrous results. The environmental instability that prompted a maximum growth strategy dictated the tendency toward intensive resource use as well. This pattern emerges clearly when we compare Arctic resource management systems to those of foragers in less erratic environments, such as the hunters of the boreal forest—the Evenk and Ket in Siberia or Athapaskans in the American Subarctic—or the coastal fishing peoples of the Pacific Northwest, Aleutian Islands, Kamchatka Peninsula, and Sakhalin Island.

Harvest Techniques in the Arctic

Arctic resource use stands apart from the boreal and temperate-zone models in two main respects. The first is that available resources are highly seasonal, and those seasons are themselves extremely brief.

Arctic hunting was crucially dependent upon very short runs of abundant game throughout the annual cycle. These few weeks, sometimes days, or even hours had to provide hunters, their families, and the entire community with the bulk of food and supplies for a fairly long period. Second, in the Arctic ecosystem, future resources are extremely difficult to predict—nothing like the virtual clockwork of annual Pacific salmon runs. Taken together, such contingencies highlighted the crucial significance of surplus food storage in Arctic hunting systems (Testart 1982:527). An Arctic hunter could never be sure what game availability and harvest success awaited in the next season or coming year.

Many traditional Arctic hunting techniques were designed to seize an entire herd or stock of animals when it was encountered, so as to obtain the maximum catch (Tret'iakov 1935:245). Although this pattern originally referred to prehistoric and traditional indigenous hunting in northern Eurasia, it applies to many other members of the Arctic ecumene. Hester cites several examples of the "pointless" destruction by American Eskimos and Indians of entire herds of game (Hester 1967:178–79). Other authors see a similar pattern in native harvests of musk-ox and beluga in the Alaskan and Canadian Arctic (e.g., Burch 1977:140–41, McGhee 1974:19–22, Nelson 1969:207, Wilkinson 1975:21). Massive slaughters took place when caribou were hunted at river crossings, and also when, in summer, netting was broadcast for flightless, moulting birds. At times the community might take so much more than it could use, preserve, or transport that much of the catch simply rotted and went to waste. There is evidence of massive overhunting of birds, and animals killed by the hundreds and thousands, from throughout northeastern Siberia, the Canadian boreal forest, coastal Greenland, and the Alaskan interior.[2]

At times, native maritime hunting could be as destructive as the land-game harvest. "I saw a walrus rookery on the Gek Spit near the mouth of the Anadyr river," writes one observer. "Chukchi herders who hunt here were confident that they would kill every walrus in the rookery by the end of the year, (about eighty). They based this on planning to use no more than twenty; the remaining sixty they expected would simply be injured and drown" (Olsuf'ev 1896:126).

The subsistence balances we calculated in chapter 2 show that Asiatic Eskimo hunters sometimes caught up to twice as much meat as the community could use. During the spring migration, the crews hunted and butchered the meat continuously to the point of complete exhaustion. Huge amounts of meat and blubber were laid into the storage pits up to the top; scraps were fed to the dogs or left to rot on the beach. Eskimo elders recall that more than enough meat was stored to last until the next spring hunt, and if the next year's season began on time and the hunt was successful, the old meat was simply thrown away into garbage pits or abandoned houses.

Eskimo hunters used to pursue all large sea mammals that approached the shore—old, young, nursing calves, and mothers—although they could usually discern what type of animal it was from a long way off. But, as noted in chapter 2, the majority of the walrus, whale, and beluga catch consisted of immature animals or mothers with calves (Perri 1976:85, Silook 1976:32, Sivuqam 1985:139, etc.).

Eskimo whaling typically focused on juveniles, calves, and even nursing mothers. Alaskan Eskimos considered it good fortune to come across a female whale with its calf, because the crew could easily kill both animals at once. The meat of newborn calves and embryos was considered a great delicacy; during times of abundant food, hunters made a point of pursuing only young whales and newborns, and even chased full-grown whales away from shore back out to sea (Durham 1979a:27, McCartney 1984:96–97, Maher and Wilimovski 1963:19, Rainey 1947:261). Legends are told on both sides of the Bering Strait how in "the old days" hunters would often wait patiently in the ice around a female whale in labor as she gave birth, so as to kill the helpless newborn, and then the exhausted mother (Durham 1979a:27, S. Arutiunov, personal communication 1982, author's field data 1979, 1981).

Bones of calves and immature whales predominate in the remains of prehistoric Eskimo whaling villages throughout the Arctic from Baffin Island to Bering Strait (e.g., Cargill 1990:266, Maxwell 1985:284, Sabo, personal communication regarding Lake Harbour 1991). Archeologists unearthed the bones of 1,000 to 1,500 bowhead whales from several dozen Thule Eskimo encampments on Somerset Island in Arctic Canada. Judging by their size, most of the bones (97 to 99 percent) belonged to immature whales, yearlings, and even calves (McCartney and Mitchell 1988, McCartney and Savelle 1985). The few skulls and jaws belonging to adult whales stood out clearly because of their visibly larger size. The entire southern coast of Somerset Island appeared to have been a gigantic "butchering site," where small, easily accessible, and less dangerous whale calves and juveniles were pursued, caught, butchered, and stored by hunters from about 1,000 to 1,300 C.E.

At Point Hope, Alaska, photographs of the ancient Eskimo burial ground show how bowhead whale mandibles collected from collapsed graves and houses were recycled to build a cemetery fence; almost all came from very young animals (see pictures in Burch 1981:46, 47, Durham 1979a:27). Further down the coast of northwest Alaska, in the summer of 1991, I observed very small skulls and jawbones apparently belonging to similarly young calves near the village of Wales, on Cape Prince of Wales, Seward Peninsula.

But by far the most eloquent evidence that the ancient maritime hunting culture was targeted to immature whales and calves comes from archeological remains in the Mechigmen Bay region on the east coast of the Chukchi Peninsula, Siberia. A highly developed maritime culture flourished here for centuries, whose members specialized in hunting juvenile gray whales, primarily nursing calves and yearlings. The Masik village site at the head of Mechigmen Bay has survived as the most sobering monument to date of this "slaughter of calves." In 1981 we surveyed six abandoned settlements in Mechigmen Bay and calculated that they contained the remains of no less than 2,000 to 3,000 gray whale calves, as well as many tens of bowhead and other baleen whales. Hunting was evidently active through the 1600s to 1800s and probably much earlier. We calculated that no less than 1,500 juvenile whales were killed at the Masik site only, their skulls packed into the foundations of dug-out homes and built into fences for meat pits or laid out in circles and lines on the ground for some kind of ritual purpose. The native hunt for gray whale calves continued right up until the mid-1900s. Local hunters we interviewed considered adult whales too dangerous and cumbersome to transport and slaughter, and never attempted to hunt them with harpoons and lances.[3]

Cases of Indigenous Overkill

Objectively, hunting techniques such as slaughtering entire groups of animals and focusing on easier, more accesible prey such as juveniles and nursing females increased the impact of Arctic aboriginal hunting on game resources. It is inconceivable that the indigenous inhabitants of the Arctic, widely believed to possess intimate knowledge of their habitat, did not realize the impact selective hunting of whale calves or nursing females would have on the population. Burch claims that Inuit believed that animate resources existed in essentially unlimited supply and that, from their point of view, the problem was not the size of the fish and game populations but the extent to which spirits controlled access to those populations (Burch 1991a:5). I only partially agree with this assessment: in my opinion, Arctic people fully comprehended the impact they had on game resources, at least locally. The numerous hunting rituals intended to preserve and "replenish" wildlife attest to this, as well as the generally conservationist nature of hunting ethics among Arctic peoples. Chukchi, Yukagir, Even, Nganasan, and Alaskan Eskimos were equally reported to believe that a sudden shortage of wild reindeer or fish was always a punishment for excessive hunting in the past, or neglecting to fulfill social norms of showing respect for one's prey (Bogoras 1975:133, Dolgikh 1952b:23, Jochel'son 1898:141, Spenser 1959:264–67).

In the past, authors often attempted to find the causes of native overhunting in the impacts of Russian or Anglo-American colonization, the introduction of firearms or the onslaught of European settlers from the south (Amsden 1979:402–403, Hester 1967:178–79, Kertselli 1925:18–20, Muir 1917:127–28, Nansen 1937:375, Wilkinson 1975:33, etc.). While this may have been true in some instances, we now know of numerous cases in which prehistoric Arctic hunters as well as postcontact traditional bands with no ties to the commercial hunting economy engendered ecological crises on a local scale. Native subsistence patterns were fully capable of diminishing hunting grounds, decimating game populations, or even extinguishing certain species in a broad area without any assistance from the consequences of European contact.

In the mid-1800s, groups of Caribou Inuit encountered the inland herds of musk-ox near the headwaters of the Telon and Kazan rivers in the central Canadian Arctic. Musk-ox were an easy prey—unlike caribou, they do not flee when alarmed, but form a protective circle around the females and calves and stand their ground instead. Hunters could walk right up to the herd and kill the animals point-blank. Drastic overhunting immediately ensued, and, by the early 1900s, the musk-ox population was wiped out, with no aspersions cast upon the traditional Eskimo value system and hunting traditions whatsoever (Burch 1977:143–48).

The extermination of musk-ox by Eskimo hunting is often invoked as a classic example of wanton human depredation upon fragile Arctic resources (Macpherson 1981:104–105). Nor were bows and arrows or spears any less effective weapons than flintlocks or rifles. A group of Canadian Inuit who relocated to Banks Island around 1850 completely wiped out the local musk-ox population by 1900 with no access to firearms or European contact whatsoever. Archeologists unearthed the remains of more than 3,000 musk-ox in 150 hunting camps on the island (Vincent and Gunn 1981). Eskimo hunters killed off all the musk-ox in the Alaskan Brooks Range two hundred years before Europeans set foot in the area (Campbell 1978:201–202).

Long before European contact, Aleuts exterminated the slow-moving Steller's sea cow (*Rythina Stelleri*) from the subarctic fringe. By the mid-eighteenth century, the species had vanished from the Aleutian Islands, and survived only on uninhabited Bering Island near the Siberian shore (Laughlin and Harper 1979:2). In addition to musk-ox and Steller's sea cow, several other game species proved remarkably vulnerable to the impacts of aboriginal hunting. As Macpherson notes, these were all species harvested by "mass slaughter" techniques, including, for example, the Barren Ground caribou, especially its island populations, the great auk (*Pinguinus impennis*), exterminated in Greenland and the Canadian Arctic during the nineteenth century,[4] some larger species of moulting geese, anadromous fish, such as Arctic char, and others (Macpherson 1981:104–105). Then, as internal population cycles or overhunting thinned the ranks of the more vulnerable species, hunting pressure shifted to other species, as occurred in the late nineteenth century in northern Alaska, when Eskimo hunters killed off the Dall sheep (*Ovis dalli*) population when reduced numbers of caribou deprived them of their usual means of survival (Campbell 1979).

Overkill and Harvest Strategies

We can regard these and other such cases as anomalies—deviations explained by occasional confluences of extreme circumstances in a long and relatively enduring history of human-environment interactions in the Arctic. But we also know of certain aboriginal adaptations in which regular overkill constituted an immanent element in the subsistence system. One such adaptation is illustrated by the annual cycle and hunting strategies of the Canadian Caribou Eater Chipewyan. These hunters lived at the edge of the forest and tundra, and relied heavily on the skins and meat of migrating caribou, who crossed through their territory twice a year. In the fall, just before the migrating herds arrived, the Chipewyan communities split up into numerous smaller hunting bands and set up a continuous barricade perpendicular to the north-south migration route. No matter where along this line the migrating herd first crossed, it encountered one or another of the watchful bands, who then set about killing as many animals as they could until more herds arrived and spread out more evenly among the other hunting encampments set up along the migration front (Sharp 1977, Smith 1978). In a very short, intense period of days or weeks, a single successful hunting band of five to ten hunters and their families had to kill, slaughter, and prepare for storage hundreds or even thousands of caribou, enough to feed the entire community. Huge losses were unavoidable, and figure in Chipewyan hunting ethics.[5]

Elements of the same game procurement strategy can be identified among many groups of Arctic and Subarctic caribou hunters: the Nganasan, Yukagir, northern Yakut, Even, and mixed-Russian populations in the Indigirka, Kolyma, and Anadyr' River basins in the Eurasian Arctic, and the Chipewyan, G'wichin, and Dogrib of northern North America, along with Eskimo/Inuit of northern Alaska, Canada, and Greenland. The descriptions of these groups' traditional mass harvests, when hundreds and thousands of animals were slaughtered and a huge proportion of them wasted are amazingly similar (Campbell 1978, Gurvich 1977, Ingold 1980, Meldgaard 1986, Popov 1948, Portenko 1941, Simchenko 1976, Tret'iakov 1935, Tugolukov 1979, Vibe 1967, etc.). This is hardly a coincidence. Each year, the size of the caribou population, the migration route, and exactly when the animals will arrive are all hard to predict. Thus, episodic overkill apparently becomes a reasonable risk management technique where highly unstable game resources such as caribou are concerned. In contrast, an overkill hunting strategy appears to have no parallel among the hunters and fishers of the northern forest or the temperate coastal zone, because the resources of the river valleys and maritime ecosystems are far less marked by instability and unpredictability.

In the Arctic coastal zone, however, we find similar evidence of overhunting as an integral element in a number of models of maritime subsistence. Archeologist Dennis Stanford has reconstructed a subsistence model for the Birnirk Eskimo culture in northwest Alaska and the Chukchi Peninsula around C.E. 500 to 900, which reveals that they conducted intensive harvesting of seal and caribou. In a very short time, Birnirk hunters completely dispatched the entire seal population within a ten to twenty kilometer radius of a band encampment, then proceeded further up or down the coast to work their way through a fresh herd with equal thoroughness. Ernest Burch has pithily named this hunting strategy the "search and destroy" technique (Burch 1972:347). It is a strategy that creates a highly mobile hunting culture, but one with voracious capacities for territorial expansion whenever the population swells. Therefore, Stanford believes that the transition from Birnirk to Thule culture occurred when Birnirk overhunting eventually resulted in extermination of the coastal seal population in northern Alaska, so that Birnirk hunters were forced to abandon those hunting grounds and find a new means of survival (Stanford 1976:114).

Overkill and "Rationality" in Aboriginal Subsistence

Once again, we encounter an apparent contradiction here: the actual impact of native hunting on game resources did not correspond either to a norm of "rational" resource use, or to the ethic of aboriginal hunting behavior. The last thing I want is to portray Arctic hunters as merciless predators blindly destroying their own ecosystem. However, neat presentations in ecology textbooks that endeavor to contrast the "harmonious" and "intuitively ecological" human-environment relationships of indigenous people with the wholesale destruction of nature by modern industrial societies are more an attempt to compare apples and oranges for polemical purposes than a realistic conceptual framework for analysis of traditional Arctic subsistence. Such stereotypes are obviously a product of modern environmentalist idealization. As Tim Ingold states, "The rationality of conservation is totally alien to a predatory subsistence economy, which rests on the fundamental premise that the herds are responsible for the existence of Man, rather than men . . . for the perpetuation of the herds" (Ingold 1980:71).

The aboriginal hunter never regulated hunting resources in the contemporary sense of ecosystem management. He was first and foremost a consumer of those resources, who had full and unquestioned self-confidence in his ethical and physical ability to kill whatever animals he needed for his own survival. Whether intuitively or quite consciously, he could on occasion arrive at more or less rational techniques to exploit game resources in ways that would simultaneously conserve them. At times such rational use would be coincidental, or was rational for utilitarian reasons quite divorced from intentional game conservation, such as making use of the most accessible resources, minimizing the hunting effort, and reducing the distance and time any game would be subsequently transported for use.

We find the best example of Arctic hunters as fortuitous conservationists in their emphasis on targeting juveniles of many species. According to the model first established for the California condor (*Gymnogyps californianus*), among most large animals, reproducing adults in fact constitute the most vulnerable part of the population, not newborns and juveniles. Due to the slow rate of reproduction among large mammals, survival of mature cohorts of reproductive age is critical to the welfare and stable recruitment of the herd, because any sudden increase in mortality—always a possibility in the rapidly shifting Arctic environment—can arrest the herd's growth (Järvinen and Varvio 1986). From an ecological standpoint, therefore, selective hunting of calves among such species is actually the most rational form of hunting, because hunters eke out as much food as possible with minimum disruption to the game population.[6]

Thus, although the Eskimo hunt for sea-mammal juveniles and calves may seem merciless to some, objectively speaking, and however fortuitously it may have developed, it appears to represent an intuitively discovered form of resource exploitation that in some aspects coincides with principles of sustainable game management. And we can locate a similar "intuitively rational" basis to many other forms of Arctic native resource utilization. However, as one long-time observer of traditional Nenets subsistence concludes, "conservation occurs as long as it doesn't involve food. Where resource conservation goes against the grain of human survival, it loses its priority" (Evladov 1929 : 58). The latter approach appears to be the most objective one by which we can seek to understand the hunting ethics and behavior of indigenous people coping with the extreme uncertainty of the Arctic ecosystem.

Therefore, in analyzing the role of the traditional hunter in the Arctic ecosystem, we must distinguish his *ecological experience* from his actual *ecological behavior*. The former concerns a hunter's accumulated sum total of beliefs and observation-based knowledge of the environment and the place of human beings within it. This intimately experiential and well-defined body of knowledge includes a wide range of detailed data and keen empirical observations on all aspects of the Arctic environment, far exceeding the bounds of strictly utilitarian knowledge needed for everyday existence (Nelson 1969:373–75, 1973:301–307). Information on past resource fluctuations and community adaptations was encoded in both historical and oral traditions, including folktales and myths (Minc 1986).

Quite to the contrary, what I will call here the "ecological behavior" of Arctic peoples—that is, their actual resource management practices—was multifaceted, sometimes contradictory, and, as our examples above illustrate, in many cases downright destructive. It stands in need of dispassionate appraisal in light of what we now know about wildlife ecology, game conservation, and rational environmental practices.

Arctic versus Boreal Subsistence

In comparing the ecological experience and behavior of various groups of traditional hunters, we should bear in mind that both are always heavily imprinted with the local circumstances prevailing in the hunter's environment. Thus, obvious differences exist between the harvesting methods and behavior of tundra as opposed to boreal forest hunters (i.e., Eskimo/Inuit vs. Tungus, Ket, and Athapaskan), and we readily trace their origins in the differing natural cycles of the two biomes. In conditions of greater game diversity found in the boreal forest/taiga environment, a local hunter encountered relatively predictable though highly patchy distribution of hunting resources in both space and time. He could choose and use alternative resources to a far greater degree than an Arctic hunter. This condition held consistently true except for very rare anomalies of shortages due to unusually severe weather, game fluctuations, or simultaneously coincident lows in the long-term cycles of several species at once.[7]

Herein lies, in my opinion, an explanation for the more "conservationist" and, at the same time, profoundly spiritual ecological belief system of the boreal forest hunters compared to hunters in the Arctic. The idea of "equilibrium" is fully applicable to the relationship that boreal forest peoples maintained with their resources and environment via rational ecological knowledge and ostensibly magical practices and rituals found within their traditional animistic framework. Humans, various species of animals, and even plants were visualized as possessing equal rights and equal power within a single cooperative community, whose relations were based upon mutual respect and strict codes of deeply spiritual etiquette. This worldview and its components have been thoroughly described among North American Indians, but can also be traced among most native peoples of the Siberia boreal zone, including the Evenk, Khanty, Ket, Sel'kup, Nivkh, and Nanay.[8]

In contrast, Arctic inland and coastal hunters lived in extremely unstable natural environments. These subsistence harvesters perforce developed a more aggressive ecological ideology. Their actual management practices were constantly in contradiction with a conservationist hunting culture and rituals, which on the whole appear to reflect a similarly animistic belief system (see Gurvich 1975:78–79, Popov 1984:56–59, Simchenko 1976:239–41, Vdovin 1976:22). Compared to the deeply ritualized traditions of the boreal forest societies, the harvesting ethic of Arctic hunters appears highly simplified, in part because lower species diversity required definition of the human stance toward a much smaller number of game animals in the Arctic. For example, among the North Alaskan Inuit only the bowhead whale, grizzly bear, and wolf hunts were associated with elaborate ritual practices, while the vast majority of animals (seals, beluga, walrus, caribou, birds, and fish) were harvested with a minimum of ritual (Spencer 1959:267–76).

The greater simplicity of Arctic belief systems, however, does not prevent some authors from maintaining that Arctic hunters have achieved more resilient and technologically more successful harvesting practices than the hunters of the boreal forest (Nelson 1973, 301–16). However, we can suppose that the Arctic hunter's ecological "aggressiveness" was by no means an invariable component of his ecological ethics and behavior. It seemingly remained dormant until provoked in times of scarce game or deteriorating hunting conditions. But, when game was plentiful and catches reliable, practices tended to be more ritualized, or at least people had more time for elaborate hunting rituals and festivals. In all likelihood, the monumental sanctuary of Whale Alley and the dozens of ritual arrangements of juvenile gray whale skulls at Masik and other sites on the Bering Strait represent just such a phase in the aboriginal spiritual traditions of the Arctic.

CHAPTER EIGHT

Arctic Adaptations and Paleolithic Society

In modern social sciences, each discipline has its own field of inquiry, the boundaries of which are generally well defined in space and time. The "field" of Arctic ecological anthropology focuses upon interactions between circumpolar peoples and their environments. This means that its geographical boundaries are fairly strictly defined, and venturing beyond can be at times a risky business. As we saw in chapter 7, the ecological experience and behavior of boreal hunters derived from different principles of environmental interaction than those of people who lived in the barren tundra and Arctic coastlands. Therefore, in attempting to draw broad generalizations we should do so in full awareness that there are many "ethnoecologies"—Arctic, boreal, tropical, mountainous, desert, and so forth—each with its own parameters, internal logic, and models of development.

We have far more *temporal* flexibility in our use of Arctic ecological anthropology. At present, the archeologically established history of Arctic aborigines is thirteen to fourteen millenia long, if one counts apparently highly reliable dates from the Berelekh settlement, at 71° N in the lower course of the Indigirka River in northern Yakutia. But even these data are clearly not limiting. Ever since the English geologist William Boyd Dawkins hypothesized a relationship between contemporary Eskimos and Upper Paleolithic hunters of Western Europe, it has been clear that the culture of circumpolar peoples has broad historical parallels. Although Dawkins's hypothesis was subsequently disproved, for many decades Arctic ethnography has been considered an invaluable source for archeological and historical studies of prehistoric society.[1]

Thus opens yet another field of scientific inquiry in which models of aboriginal Arctic subsistence prove highly useful. As is well known, in economic-cultural terms the Upper Paleolithic hunters of the northern Eurasian late Pleistocene glacial plains (25,000 to 12,000 years B.P.) are considered the closest historical analogue to indigenous circumpolar peoples. According to recent reconstructions, these hunters settled the open spaces of the periglacial "tundra-steppe zone," where a harsh, cold climate prevailed.[2] They based their subsistence on hunting several of the late Pleistocene so-called big-game species, including woolly mammoth, caribou, and bison.

Long ago, archeologists pointed out the direct parallels in material culture between Upper Paleolithic mammoth hunters in the Central Russian Plain and southern Siberia and several modern circumpolar groups, first and foremost Eskimo. The high productivity of prehistoric hunting allowed many periglacial prehistoric bands to conduct a sedentary or semisedentary way of life and even to build, as the Eskimo did, large settlements of permanent dwellings. Other archeologically confirmed direct cultural parallels include construction of permanent framed winter dwellings made from wood poles or large mammal bones (whale or mammoth); use of permafrost meat-storage pits; straight-cut outer garments made from fur; use of animal bones for fuel, and as raw materials for hunting and digging tools; and use of large stone knives to butcher large animals.[3]

In addition, many scholars discern vivid parallels in decorative art, elements of social organization, rituals, counting systems, ornamentation, and, of course, in overall principles of ecological behavior.[4] In all these respects the prehistoric residents of the northern Eurasian glacial plains, in the words of American paleontologist Arthur Jellinek, ". . . are the most comparable to the Eskimos—the only surviving culture with a carnivorous orientation as extreme as the Eurasian Upper Paleolithic" (Jellinek 1967:195).

Until now the search for such cultural analogies between paleolithic and Arctic aboriginal societies was mainly the work of archeologists. Russian ethnographers, in contrast, are presently highly skeptical of directly extrapolating from eighteenth- or nineteenth-century sources to the Upper Paleolithic (see Pershits 1979:32–35, Fainberg 1986:136). Even given the apparent resemblances (or similarities) in many aspects of material or spiritual culture, not one traditional Arctic group can be compared with Upper Paleolithic mammoth-hunting peoples in terms of the former's much longer historical development and richer patchwork of cultural contacts. But the truth of this general premise does not negate the possibility of using carefully selected ethnographic analogues for historical or archeological reconstructions. Many characteristics of Paleolithic hunting behavior and everyday life truly are extremely hard to comprehend on the basis of available archeological records alone.

And here our knowledge of indigenous Arctic subsistence and ecology can prove of great value. Direct ethnographic observation, or models that include use of local oral tradition, are capable of recapturing methods of hunting, butchering, preserving and preparing food, making household items, building homes on permafrost, or making use of local resources to adapt to a cold, glacial environment. Although socially and even ecologically the historical Bering Sea Eskimo is far removed from the Paleolithic mammoth hunter of the Central Russian Plain, such details are crucial to meaningful interpretation of archeological materials. Several archeologists have long recognized and made use of the ecological knowledge of Arctic residents in seeking to understand life in Upper Paleolithic societies.[5]

What contribution to this debate can we glean from the preceding analysis of forms of traditional subsistence among northern Siberian people? I would like to illustrate the possibilities with just a few of the most striking examples concerning general principles of hunting, resource use, population and settlement dynamics, and the characteristics of demographic reproduction in prehistoric communities. This range of topics thus recapitulates the essential elements of subsistence among Arctic natives presented in earlier chapters, including the ethics and practice of resource utilization. I should stipulate that, where possible, I have confined myself to examples from within the geographical territory of northern Eurasia, since all the suggested parallels are by no means equally applicable to the Paleoindian Clovis mammoth hunters of North America, another highly successful adaptation of Upper Paleolithic hunting culture.

Prehistoric Hunting Tactics

At numerous points Russian archeologists have emphasized that the semisedentary way of life and comparatively large size of Upper Paleolithic communities in the periglacial zone of Eastern and Central

Europe were the direct result of a highly productive prehistoric hunting economy (Bibikov 1969:17–18, Ermolova 1978:195, Efimenko 1931:58–60, Gladkikh et al. 1985:73–74, Grigor'ev 1968:155–56, Pidoplichko 1976:44, etc.). The harvest of mammoths and other large herbivorous animals amply sufficed to meet the community's needs for food, fuel, and raw materials for clothing, tools, and housing. In this respect Upper Paleolithic hunting truly resembled the subsistence systems of Arctic whale and walrus hunters of the Bering Strait region, which were characterized by an equally high level of "sufficiency" and specialization.

But the Upper Paleolithic hunting equipment, as we know, was markedly inferior to that of the historical Eskimo. The former had neither complex toggling harpoons with attached floats nor swift, tillered skinboats. When hunting on open water, Eskimo hunters carried or towed the carcasses of harvested animals home by boat, and used dog teams or pull-sleds to transport meat caught on ice or land. With the possible exception of primitive sledges, we have no knowledge of any comparable Paleolithic means for transporting game.

This strongly suggests that ancient hunters focused their efforts on harvesting quarry as close to the village as possible. Otherwise, dragging the meat, blubber, and bones back to the village from the hunting site would have consumed a disproportionate amount of labor. This would have increased the creative pressure to refine the harvesting process itself to an extremely efficient art, since a hunter traveling on foot knew he could carry back only a small portion of an animal killed far from home: "The greater the distance over which meat is to be transported, . . . [and] the greater the bulk of material to be transported per unit of time, . . . the more radical will be the culling of low-utility anatomical parts along the transport route" (Binford 1978:459).

Analogies with Eskimo whaling may help to explain the subsistence strategies of the Upper Paleolithic big-game hunters. To reiterate briefly, Eskimos harvested large sea mammals in two ways. The first consisted of timing the hunt to coincide with periods and places when the animals' mobility was naturally constricted, such as seal and walruses at rookeries or ice fields, or whales migrating through narrow leads, sleeping on the water's surface, or trapped in shallow water, inlets, or bays. The second strategy relied upon multiple, rapid strikes to weaken the animal as quickly as possible from loss of blood, compounded by floats that increasingly dragged on the animal as it tired. In both cases, the key weapon was not the harpoon (an analogue to the Paleolithic dart) but a heavy killing lance. In the whale and walrus hunt, this long, sharpened, bone-tipped lance was not hurled at the target, but held firmly with both hands to kill the animal with a deep, penetrating blow once it had weakened sufficiently to approach it directly.

Hunting with a heavy, killing lance requires close physical contact between hunter and prey. Although Arctic aborigines could not swim at all, they did not fear such close contact with the hulking sea mammals. We would expect to find indications of a similar attitude in reconstructions of Upper Paleolithic mammoth hunters.

Hence, popular imagery depicting bands of prehistoric hunters tracking or clustered around woolly mammoths, armed with light spears or hefting stone axes, clubs, or even big rocks should be dismissed as unrealistic. In all likelihood, well-organized hunting parties preferred to lie in wait for the animals, or even to drive them closer to the community's camp, or toward river crossings, ravines, or shallow water thinly covered with ice—that is, to areas where the game's mobility was naturally constrained. Then, hunters could use artificial means to limit the prey's mobility still further by wounding, distracting, frightening, or physically overwhelming it.

A strong and experienced hunter ("harpooner") probably delivered the mortal blow to the mammoth or other large animal at an appropriate moment with a heavy lance, tipped with a long, bayonet-like point of mammoth tusk or horn.[6] Fragments of such points or even whole spears made from mammoth tusk have been found in excavations of many Paleolithic mammoth-hunter settlements on the Central Russian Plain and in southern Siberia.[7]

Only such an efficient and well-thought-out strategy could explain the discovery in some of these camps of large chunks of whole mammoth carcasses, piles of ribs and vertebrae of too little value to warrant transportation, and even entire undismembered skeletons (Efimenko 1931:59–60, Ermolova 1985:11, Gerasimov 1958:42, Gladkikh et al. 1985, illustration in Pidoplichko 1976, Klein 1969, Soffer 1985). Collective hunting, butchering, and conveyance of the catch to camp clearly point to a high degree of social organization in Paleolithic communities, and a refined and conscientiously observed system of cooperation and division of labor. The analogies with cooperative whale hunting among the Eskimo are obvious. Behind these analogies lie the accumulated weight of experience of many professional hunters, and a distribution of labor, painstakingly developed over the course of centuries and observable even today among contemporary Eskimo boat crews and Yukagir, Nganasan, and Chipewyan caribou-hunting groups. We can hypothesize that elements of these relationships existed among Upper Paleolithic mammoth-hunting communities, including communal ecological knowledge, harvest ethics, and resource utilization systems.

Settlement Patterns of the Prehistoric Population

Given similar harvest tactics, selection of optimal settlement sites was crucially important to Paleolithic subsistence. Once again we can look for analogies with traditional Arctic ecology. In chapter 2, we reviewed the basic locational criteria for Eskimo settlements: proximity to the most productive hunting areas, a variety of easily accessible resources, good visibility of surrounding waters and lands, and location where two or more resource ecosystems converge. All hold true for many identified Upper Paleolithic hunting sites. Thus, it would seem that ecological locational stereotypes existed for Paleolithic communities just as for Arctic residents.

Upper Paleolithic encampments on the Russian Plain and in Siberia show a well-established tendency to be located close to river valleys, especially on capes and spits formed by lateral ravines or hollows (Boriskovskii 1963:26–27, Efimenko 1953:419–20, Pidoplichko 1976:15, Rogachev 1957:18–19, Soffer 1985:235–38, Velichko et al. 1977:46–49). Even considering the relatively low density of the Paleolithic population, however, such ecologically ideal niches were limited in number. Therefore, hunters might frequently or even preferentially reuse the territories of old, abandoned communities. Eskimos often did the same when selecting new settlement sites. The remains of previous inhabitation served as visual reminders that the site was an ecologically advantageous one, and created a sense of both real and imagined continuity of resource use in that place. Not least important, evidently, was the opportunity to recycle the remains of abandoned dwellings as building materials for a new settlement (see Abramova 1964:177, Bader 1977:37, 1978:189, Bibikov 1981:48, Grigor'ev 1972:19–21, Pidoplichko 1976:107, Sergin 1974:7, etc.). This tradition is well recorded among the Chukchi Peninsula Eskimo and ancient Eskimo whalebone-dwelling settlements in the Canadian Arctic.

Analysis of Whale Alley and of the remains of other large Eskimo constructions indicates the impressive engineering capabilities of ancient residents of the Arctic. How they accomplished such large-scale construction with a minimum of tools in permafrost conditions remains a mystery. The capacious dimensions of ancient semisubterranean dwellings and the sheer mass of building materials such as whalebone, huge boulders, and wood beams, continue to confound not only the archeologists, but contemporary native people as well, who have lost the skills and knowledge of such construction techniques. "People used to be stronger than they are today," was the response from our Eskimo guides when we unearthed whale jaws five meters long or skulls weighing almost a ton at such sites. Evidently, the same comment would be forthcoming in regard to the Paleolithic builders of mammoth-bone dwellings, which in some cases consist literally of hundreds of specially chosen, at times even hand-tooled, bones from many animals. Although the bones of a mammoth weigh considerably less than a whale's—the skull, for example, weighs about one hundred kilograms, and a tusk about two hundred (Soffer 1985:280)—the total weight of "building materials" used in construction could be as much as fifteen to twenty tons per site (Bibikov 1981:40, Gladkikh et al. 1985:71, Pidoplichko 1976:41, Soffer 1985:379–81).

The possibility that Paleolithic communities made repeated use of abandoned dwellings and camp sites makes it difficult to estimate the population of these sites accurately. After all, even a small group that changed its location and reinhabited unused dwellings periodically or even seasonally could create the archeological illusion that the area was intensively used on a protracted basis. We encountered this with Arctic hunters as well: on the southeast coast of the Chukchi Peninsula, almost every bay contains archeological remains of ancient Eskimo dwellings and campsites, but it is well known that they were never inhabited simultaneously (Krupnik 1981a:105).

In this case, the Arctic data can be used quite successfully to adjust for the artificial effect of repeated inhabitation on archeologically derived Paleolithic population estimates, as well as the estimated territorial dimensions and statistics on population and density of inhabitation across large regions. It is usually believed that Upper Paleolithic periglacial hunting communities consisted of 50 to 100 people, with a resource area of 500 to 720 square kilometers, although lower and much higher estimates exist as well (Bibikov 1969:13–14, Efimenko 1931:59, 1953:437, Grigor'ev 1968:152, 1970:59, Hassan 1979:140, Masson 1976:31, 104, Shnirel'man 1986:432, etc.). By traditional Arctic standards, a residential community of 50 is already quite large, while a group of 100 or more is a rare exception indeed. Such "clots" of population were possible only in the most resource-rich locations and always coincided with seasonal migration routes of various game species. The entire remainder of the community's territory was used only a few months a year, or episodically during emergencies.

If we now follow the Pleistocene geographers in supposing that groups of prehistoric hunters were closely tied to river valleys—the migration routes and zones of increased game concentrations (Vereshchagin 1971:206–207, 1979:32, Pidoplichko 1976:24), then aggregate estimates of the average density and population for wide regions during the Paleolithic era appear fairly uninformative. As with the coastal hunters of the Arctic, the actual determinant of settlement among prehistoric communities was not the absolute amount of territory accessible from that location, but rather the number of intensively used ecological niches dotting the river's edge or shoreline. Areas of high population density were thus separated by huge, virtually uninhabited watersheds.

Archeologists sometimes try to use game estimates to determine how long a Paleolithic site was occupied, and by how many people (see Bibikov 1969:14–18, 1981:36–37, Ermolova 1978:176–77, Klein 1969:220–25, Pidoplichko 1969:151–54, Soffer 1985:292–302, etc.). Notwithstanding large discrepancies and margins of error, this method appears quite reliable, especially when it is adjusted to subsistence balances, as has been done for some historical groups of Arctic hunters. If a juvenile mammoth, to use Pidoplichko's figure, provided 1,000 kilograms of meat (Pidoplichko 1969:152)—that is, the approximate equivalent of 2 or 3 walrus and 2 to 3 times less than a juvenile gray or bowhead whale,[8]—then a prehistoric community of 50 had to kill 12 to 15 small mammoths each year. Based on the total caloric content of one reindeer carcass, reindeer hunting would have had to yield for the same community no less than 600 to 800 animals a year, or, according to other estimates, as much as 900 reindeer a year (Ermolova 1978:176–77). Vereshchagin calculated that the Upper Paleolithic hunters of the Central Russian Plain and the

Crimean Peninsula, a population of about 15,000 required approximately 10,500,000 kilograms of meat a year. To meet these demands, hunters would thus have had to kill 80,000 horses (100 kilograms of butchered meat per animal), 30,000 bison (300 kilograms of butchered meat per animal), 120,000 reindeer, or 10,000 mammoths a year (Vereshchagin 1967a:381, Vereshchagin and Baryshnikov 1984:508). All these calculations were based on an assumption that the catch was fully and efficiently utilized, which was highly unlikely to have been the case.

A huge number of animal bones must thus have accumulated at Paleolithic sites in only a few years, even considering that some part of these may have been burned for fuel in cooking fires. And here again we can draw from an Arctic parallel. Fifty to eighty people could easily have resided in the ancient settlement of Masik on Mechigmen Bay, where the skulls of approximately two thousand juvenile gray whales were found, the largest such accumulation reported anywhere on the Chukchi Peninsula. In order to accumulate this many bones over the course of two to three centuries, the community would have had to catch five to eight whales a year.

We can assume that Paleolithic sites with large layers of bone remains were inhabited for much shorter periods of time. The 1,000 aurochs killed at Amvrosievka site would have fed a community of 100 to 120 for 3 to 5 years, if the entire carcass was fully used, which, as we know, was not the case. The remains of 600 reindeer found at the Malta site in southern Siberia, and of 400–500 animals at Schussenreed, Switzerland, would hardly have met the full annual requirements of a Paleolithic hunting band of some 50 people if they lived exclusively on reindeer. Even the largest Paleolithic reindeer bone accumulations in Western Europe, at Stellmoore site in northern Germany (about 1,200 animals) and at Gourdan site in southern France (more than 3,000), could represent deposits of only a few successful hunting seasons (see bone estimates in: Ermolova 1978:176; Mongait 1973:142; Okladnikov 1941:25; Sturdy 1975:64, etc.). At present, the duration of residence at Paleolithic sites is determined by archeologists mainly on the basis of a so-called "minimum number" of harvested animals, recalculated to fulfill estimated human needs. By introducing ethnographic realities from the experience of Arctic native people—their methods of butchering and transporting meat, the seasonality of hunting, their ways of preserving and using food, etc.—we may alter such calculations profoundly.

Natural Resource Utilization

We have much evidence that Upper Paleolithic hunting was extremely wasteful and irrational (Bader 1978:192, Boriskovskii 1979:186, Zamiatnin 1960:97, 100, Masson 1976:30). Some archeologists are fairly categorical on this issue. "In general, paleolithic harvest was rapacious at all times, including calving and nursing seasons. No limits were set for harvesting particular game populations and frequently, the catch exceeded actual food consumption" (Liubin and Baryshnikov 1985:7).

Bone remains in archeological sites indicate that the basic catch consisted of seasonal groupings of animals made up of young individuals and females with offspring, that is, the most vulnerable part of the game population (Boriskovskii 1953:325, Pidoplichko 1969:69, 1976:78, 91, Pidoplichko et al 1972:190, Vereshchagin 1971:213). Cases of overhunting are well known in the European and Russian Upper Paleolithic, leading to decimation of entire herds of large herbivores (at Soliutre, Amvrosievka, Starosel'e, and several other sites). In such cases, many carcasses were completely untouched (Zamiatnin 1960:100, Boriskovskii 1984:178, Pidoplichko 1953:64–65, Vereshchagin 1971:208, 215). A similar model of cropping an entire family unit, intended for the slaughter of calves and subadults but resulting in enormous wastes of meat, was introduced recently for Clovis Paleoindian mammoth hunters in North America (Saunders 1980).

Although remains of small "household pits" (for meat storage?) have been found in some Paleolithic archeological sites on the Russian Plain (Efimenko 1953:429–30, Zamiatnin 1960:100, Rogachev 1970:72–76, Sergin 1983:28–29), it is hard to say how effectively a prehistoric hunter was able to lay in stores of game. Arctic residents had a tradition of creating huge food reserves, and even they were unable to preserve anywhere near all the catch for subsequent use before it rotted. Even in the cold northern climate, the meat of various animals does not keep and spoil equally. The Asiatic Eskimo maintain, for example, that walrus meat is the most suitable for frozen storage underground, while the meat of bearded and other seals works best for summer air drying. The time of the hunt is critical, since even under permafrost conditions only some of the catch could be preserved if the weather was warm. The same Eskimos tell that a bowhead whale killed in the fall migration had to be fully butchered right away, because it would go bad within two to three days. The meat of gray whales killed in summer spoiled even faster. Therefore, periods of intense storage activity were very short among Arctic peoples, and usually took place in early spring or late fall (see chapter 2).

Evidently, residents of Paleolithic settlements also laid in most of their food reserve in the fall, when they had a better chance of storing it in frozen form.[9] During the warmer months of the year, Upper Paleolithic hunters' subsistence was apparently based on episodic harvesting of large herbivores. Only part of the fresh meat was consumed after the hunt, and most of the harvest went to waste. In this case, to save labor, the most accessible animals were killed the fastest—juveniles, pregnant females, and, of course, calves. Arguments in favor of selective extraction of calves and juvenile animals by mammoth hunters of the Central Russian Plain remain rather contradictory (Soffer 1985:303–308), and harvest strategies might differ significantly from one area to another, as well as among Upper Paleolithic Russia, Siberia, and Paleoindian North America.

But we are hard pressed to find an alternative explanation for the obvious differences between the age-sex structure of the natural, "catastrophic" accumulations of entire mammoth herd remains such as the Berelekh "cemetery" on the lower Indigirka River in Arctic Siberia, and those of the Paleolithic settlements in the Central Russian Plain. Hence at the Mezhirich Paleolithic site in Ukraine, which has the largest counted number of mammoth remains known (109 animals), calves and juveniles constitute 80 to 85 percent, while old animals were all but absent. In contrast, only about half the Berelekh herd, which apparently died of natural causes, was made up of calves and juveniles, while mature and older mammoths constituted 21 percent (Pidoplichko 1976:77–78, Soffer 1985:306–307, Vereshchagin 1977, Zherekhova 1977:56). The largest Paleolithic mammoth-hunting camps in North America, at Dent and Lehner Ranches, also contain only or primarily calf and juvenile remains (Haury et al. 1959:27–28, Saunders 1980:90, Soffer 1985:306–308).

The unsparing, rapacious character of prehistoric hunting must have had a destructive effect on the game resources of the tundra-steppe and on the Paleolithic hunter's environment in general. The active role of Upper Paleolithic big-game hunters in wiping out many large Pleistocene mammals of the Eurasian periglacial plains has been emphasized many times (Bader 1978:186–88, Budyko 1967:33–35, 1974:246–49, Vereshchagin 1971:215, 224–30, Vereshchagin and

Baryshnikov 1984:507–509). The crux of the debate appears to center on the *relative* effect of human predation compared to various ecological factors in the disappearance of Eurasian mammoth fauna, as was the case with other large Pleistocene herbivorous mammals in North and South America, Africa, and Australia (see Grayson 1980:1967a,b:387–91, Masson 1976:30–31, Martin 1967a,b, 1973, 1982, 1984, and several papers in Martin and Klein 1984 and Martin and Wright 1967).

A culture in which big-game hunting forms the basis of subsistence cannot help but be aggressive toward the environment. The accumulated weight of social and technological adaptation in such a culture permits a human community to break the laws of biological balance, and irrevocably prods the community into destruction of equilibrium in the environment. The community's technical capabilities and the stability of its habitat, however, are another matter. In some places, intensive human predation consisting of selective extermination of calves or of cropping entire family units comprised of females, calves, and subadults could continue for a long time without threatening the well-being of a game population. This is exactly what may have occurred among the hunters of juvenile gray whales at Masik site on the Chukchi Peninsula, or the Thule whalers on Somerset Island in the Canadian Arctic. However, if the environment is unstable and the community's biological resources experience sharp cyclical fluctuations, the pressure of such hunting can rapidly lead to catastrophic results. This conclusion, though formulated here based upon analysis of prehistoric and early-contact Arctic hunters, is fully applicable to the Paleolithic ecumene as well (McDonald 1984:426–27, Soffer 1985:209–11).

We should not overlook the fact that, in addition to direct extermination of animals, prehistoric man also had a powerful indirect effect on game stocks. The consequences of artificial barricades, scaring game away from watering holes or "refuge" pastures, destruction of traditional migration routes, splitting up grazing areas, or dividing large herds could be just as pernicious (Haynes 1980:115, Jelinek 1967:119, Vereshchagin 1971:215, Zamiatnin 1960:100). Of course, parallels with the Arctic hunting techniques cannot directly answer the question troubling Pleistocene archeologists and zoologists the most: who or what caused the extinction of mammoths in the periglacial plains of Eurasia and North America? But the basic fact that, at certain times, Upper Paleolithic hunters, like their historic Arctic counterparts, could utilize resources in such a way as to destroy the equilibrium in these ecosystems is no longer in doubt.

Mobility and Migration in the Paleolithic Community

Given this hunting strategy, instability was endemic to prehistoric resource utilization. It is true that certain paleogeographical reconstructions indicate that the Pleistocene tundra-steppe was biologically very productive, immeasurably more so than the modern landscapes of the Arctic realm (Butzer 1964:374–75, Masson 1976:38, Vereshchagin 1979:166, Vereshchagin and Kuz'mina 1977:77). However, available calculations of biomass and reproduction rates for large Pleistocene mammals are usually conducted by analogy with the modern African savanna and therefore may be inherently flawed.

We have already noted that the hunters of the periglacial tundra-steppe, like the traditional occupants of the Arctic, could conduct sedentary, or, more precisely, semisedentary lives only in areas of elevated biological productivity—on migration routes or in places of seasonal accumulation of large herds of game. But this analogy is incomplete: Upper Paleolithic hunters most likely lacked the "Eskimo"-style techniques for building large food reserves that lent subsistence some stability. Therefore, another model of resource exploitation seems more likely for them: expansion or migration, harvesting the new territory until its resources were quickly exhausted, then moving on to another ecological niche.

This model is reminiscent of the subsistence system of Arctic tundra hunters or, to an even greater degree, that of the traditional hunters of the boreal forest such as Athapaskan Indians, Ket, or Sel'kup. It can only exist where population density is extremely low, small hunting bands are constantly on the move, and each community has a large territory of its own. In addition, this model requires quite modern means of transportation, including boats, sled or pack dogs, skis, hand-sledges, and so forth. The hunters of the periglacial Eurasian plains do not appear to have possessed any of these technological means.

Residents of the periglacial zone seem to have discovered that the most efficient adaptive form for human life there was constant mobility, or, more precisely, the capacity for constant mobility and rapid territorial shifts. This does not mean that the ancient mammoth hunters conducted a nomadic way of life, following the game herds wherever they went. A prehistoric community might have several settlement sites within its use area and shift sequentially between them throughout the year or at certain intervals. A similar way of life was found among the Inuit of the Canadian Arctic, who maintained a very complicated system of seasonal resource use with several types of stationary or semistationary dwellings. A Paleolithic community could disperse seasonally into a number of smaller hunting bands, each with their own hunting trails and fixed campsites, as was the case in the past among the Eskimos of northwestern Alaska or the southeastern Chukchi Peninsula. Lastly, when necessary, a community was capable of rapid segmentation and separation into several "daughter" subgroups, that could relocate flexibly, and could thus expand the larger group's residence area through migration.

We have already seen how effectively this mechanism functioned within the traditional subsistence systems of the Eurasian Arctic. I will only reemphasize that, among Arctic communities, migration was by no means always the consequence of famine, overpopulation, or any other crisis. As some Eskimo cases illustrate, these migrations frequently originated at times when food was in relatively good supply, and reflected the group's attempt to increase its territory, bolster its resource base, search for new hunting sites, or defuse personal rivalries and social tensions brewing within the community (Rowley 1985). But the traditional residents of the Arctic were also fully capable of purely human curiosity, wanderlust, or dreams of a "better life" to be found over the next pressure-ridge.

I think it is fair to expect that all of these motives influenced the people of the Upper Paleolithic as well. Like traditional Arctic residents, Paleolithic hunters could believe in the existence of "unspoiled lands" rich in game with plentiful offspring that retreated there each year to escape the predations of humans. Therefore, in the search for new, untouched hunting areas, prehistoric bands gradually pushed further along the game animals' seasonal migration routes. Of course, people moved much more slowly than animals, but each year they would catch up with the migration routes of game and birds and thus verify their course.

As we saw in the preceding chapters, this is in fact how archeologists reconstruct the settlement process of the Canadian Arctic by Thule Eskimos at the end of the first millennium C.E. Entire hunting communities, more mobile "daughter" bands, and even individual families of intrepid travelers, could pour eastward behind the sea-mammal herds in a migration wave. Evidently, human settlement of the polar extremes of Eurasia occurred in the same way, after the retreat of the last glaciers or during the Holocene optimum, when groups of inland reindeer hunters advanced into the Arctic tundra from the Kola Peninsula to the Pacific Ocean (see chapter 7).

In both of the aforementioned cases, migration took place during ecologically favorable periods across a front of hundreds or even thousands of kilometers. This means that large expansions in the Arctic ecumene usually occurred as the result of fairly massive population influxes, not because of the coincidental survival of isolated bands of refugees from famine or a more populous competitor. According to recent reconstructions, this was true of the successive waves of settlement in northeast Asia, Beringia, and northern North America by the distant ancestors of Eskimo, Aleut, Athapaskan, and Paleosiberian (Paleoasiatic) peoples (Turner 1985:50–57). Apparently, the multiple Upper Paleolithic inhabitations of the Central Russian Plain concurred with retreat and advance phases during the most recent glaciation. I wonder whether the same model may be applicable even to the original peopling of North America by proto-Paleoindians. Paul Martin called this massive settlement "the discovery of the largest productive unexploited landmass in human history," comparable in the modern imagination only to discovery of a new habitable planet (1973:969). And here, by way of confirmation, one might recall the proud words of the American geographer Carl Sauer: "Folk who stuffed or starved, who took no heed of the tomorrow, could not have possessed the Earth or [and!—*I. K.*] laid the foundations of human culture" (Sauer 1956:50).

Demographic Processes in Prehistoric Communities

As the preceding examples show, expansion of the prehistoric ecumene and exploitation of new, larger use areas would have been impossible without stable population growth in Upper Paleolithic hunting societies. After all, migration is not merely the simple relocation of a human unit from one ecological niche to another. Amidst the continual fluctuations of birth and death, migration appears to include three independent demographic processes: decline (or demise) of former age-sex structure, human losses in the process of migration itself, and reviving a lasting economic-demographic unit in a new habitat.

Memories and stories of Asiatic Eskimo migrations during the nineteenth and twentieth centuries provide evidence of elevated death risks for the migrants, rapid successions of unsuccessful intermediate settlement sites, and the periodic return of entire groups or certain families to the old residence site. At all stages, survival and successful adaptation in the new location was crucially dependent upon the rate of natural increase among the migrants, and their ability to replenish the loss of life incurred en route. This means that in acknowledging the important role of migrations in Upper Paleolithic subsistence hunting we must clearly recognize their capacity for rapid growth as well, at least during certain periods of time.

Meanwhile, most academic reconstructions paint a very different picture of demographic processes in Upper Paleolithic hunting societies. They assert that prehistoric communities maintained small, relatively stable populations and extremely low growth rates. Some authors even reconstruct "statistical-average" indicators of Paleolithic population growth of approximately 0.015 percent a year, or one to two people per thousand for an entire decade (Budyko 1967: 31, Bunak 1980:202–204, Coale 1974:43, Deevey 1960:198–200, Dumond 1975:717, Hassan 1980:305, etc.). Such low growth rates attempt to strengthen the theoretical proposition that Pleistocene hunting communities supposedly lived in a constant state of K-selection; that is, they were compelled to support a stable and relatively low population in accordance with the "carrying capacity" of their habitat (Bettinger 1980:206, Hayden 1981:526–30).

Of course, "average" figures for tens and hundreds of millennia can represent the possible growth rate of the Paleolithic human population only in the most general way. The inaccuracy of these calculations in any short-term models for estimating of population growth among Arctic residents is quite obvious.

The proposed explanations of demographic "stability" in the Paleolithic population are very similar as well. Based on the assumption that prehistoric communities were in environmental "homeostatic equilibrium," one has but to identify artificial means of population control as the chief determinant of this stability, including infanticide, abortion, regulation of sexual activity, and intertribal wars.[10] In contrast, some authors believe that demographic equilibrium in Paleolithic hunting groups was maintained by natural means:

depressed birth rates owing to poor nutrition, the rigors of life, and early female death; or a high overall death rate from starvation, intertribal warfare, and epidemics (Averbukh 1967:20–24, Boughey 1973:161, Deevey 1960:195, Weiner 1968:410–16; for a review of available models of demographic reproduction in the prehistoric era, see Hassan 1980:307–11).

Basically, the gist of both views is that, until the Mesolithic transition to more productive economic patterns, population growth was very slow and for brief periods almost imperceptible. Therefore, when represented in graphic form, the Paleolithic growth rate usually appears as a straight line running almost parallel to the time axis (see Boughey 1971:226–27, Coale 1974:42, Deevey 1960:198, Hassan 1980:306).

Such a global "statistical-average" reconstruction reflects only the most general trend. Analogy with the demographic history of peoples of the Arctic can develop the reconstruction more fully. As we have discussed, their apparently retarded growth rate and stable population as seen from a distant historical perspective are an illusion resulting from a lack of sufficient or reliable data. The paucity of available information obscures the true dynamism of development: the alternations of population spurts during favorable periods with catastrophic declines at moments of ecological crisis, mutual hostility, or epidemics.

To an even greater degree, this inequity was characteristic for demographic trends in the prehistoric era. That the death rate was very high in prehistoric society is hardly in doubt, nor that huge population losses occurred periodically from repeated famines, epidemics, and natural disasters. But in places where specialized big-game hunting provided surplus production and the possibility of stable settlement, the conditions were right for rapid population growth. In part, this could have been the case during the Upper Paleolithic era in the periglacial tundra-steppe, as several authors insist (Bibikov 1969:17–22, Gladilin 1974:73, Hassan 1980:311–12, Turner 1985:52, Vereshchagin 1971:216).

According to some estimates, during periods of favorable development, natural increase in Upper Paleolithic hunting communities quite possibly could have reached 1.2 to 1.4 percent a year, that is, one hundred times greater than the "average" level reconstructed for the entire prehistoric era! (see Birdsell 1958:192, Deevey 1960:200, Dumond 1975:718, Martin 1973:970–71, Shnirel'man 1986:434).

These periods probably did not last very long, but such growth rates could result in the doubling of some communities in fifty to seventy years. This means that relative overpopulation, substantial migration flows, and rapid restitution of human losses were all fully realistic possibilities in Paleolithic society.

A particularly favorable situation developed, evidently, when Paleolithic hunters moved into new, previously uninhabited territory, where game had not yet adapted to sophisticated techniques of human predation. The best-known example of this is the "Pleistocene Overkill" model suggested by Paul Martin (Martin 1967a, 1967b, 1973, 1982, 1984). According to this scenario in its several computer-simulated versions (Martin 1973, Mosimann and Martin 1975), ten to twelve thousand years ago the glaciated plains of North America became the epicenter of a "population explosion" never before witnessed in the history of humankind, when an originally small group of "initial migrants" swelled to as many as six hundred thousand people. Such a rapidly growing population, with an estimated annual growth rate of 3.5 percent, that is, doubling every twenty years, required only around a thousand years to occupy the gigantic ecological niche of North and South America, an area of more than forty million square kilometers, and to destroy 85 percent of its big-game fauna.

Paul Martin remains the most consistent proponent of this "Pleistocene Overkill" model (and of its latest "hunting blitzkrieg" version—see Martin 1982, 1984), along with its ecological and demographic corollaries. In spite of widespread criticism and evident inaccuracy in the suggested parameters of human reproduction success in his North American "population explosion" model (Whittington and Dyke 1984), this model is rightfully called "the first detailed explanation of Pleistocene extinctions ever to have been forwarded [and] . . . presented in such a powerful way" (Grayson 1984:821). Of course, the Upper Paleolithic birth, death, and natural-increase indicators used in North American computer scenarios (like the very idea of unchecked exponential population growth in these different ecological conditions) can hardly be applied directly to the big-game hunters of the Central Russian Plain. But, on the other hand, repeated human migrations northward in northern Eurasia during the late Pleistocene, as well as occupation of the entire circumpolar tundra zone and the richest hunting niches on Arctic islands and coasts during postglacial times, cannot be imagined without an assumption of rapid, stepwise population growth. We find analogies to such rapid population leaps in entirely similar ecological conditions in the ethnographic past of the people of the Arctic.

Ecological Crises and the Development of Paleolithic Society

In that case, is the same cyclical model that we proposed above for development of the traditional Arctic peoples applicable to Upper Paleolithic big-game hunting societies? During the 1960s and 1970s it was popular in archeological literature to stress the impact of ecological crises on the development of human cultures in prehistory. As is often cited, overexploitation of hunting resources by Paleolithic hunters should unavoidably have disrupted their economy, destroyed the society's equilibrium with its environment, and at times even led to a reduction in population and direct cultural-economic regression (Bibikov 1969:22, Budyko 1967:35, 1977:251–54, Gladilin 1974:72, Martin 1973:793).

On the other hand, some suggest that ecological crises could have motivated early Paleolithic hunters to search for other means of subsistence and a transition to new, more productive economic patterns. A well-established "catastrophic" approach maintains that, since ancient times, ecological crises of overpopulation or resources have accompanied the development of human society at every step, constituting an important factor in migrations, and providing a catalyst to historical progress (Gladilin 1974:73–76, Hayden 1981:528, Lapin 1974:84–85).

In this case, the truth by no means lies somewhere in the middle. Any beneficial effects that ecological crises may have had on prehistoric social development occurred only on the most general, global-historical level. As the experience of Arctic peoples shows, within any concrete community, an ecological crisis did not lead to progress, but to hunger, traumatic demographic shocks, and disintegration of existing social and economic networks. Where serious crises occurred on a regular basis, as they did among traditional Arctic societies, they inevitably impeded the process of cultural development, destroyed any population increases achieved, and voided incipient forms of more complex social relations.

The history of Eskimo hunting culture on the Chukchi Peninsula provides an especially clear illustration of such a scenario. For two thousand years, this culture went through several periods of expansion, accompanied by a boom in social achievements. At the far edge of the ecumene, under conditions of a semiprehistoric foraging economy, we find complex forms of social organization, spiritual activity, and large-scale ritual construction that were previously considered possible only in early-agricultural civilizations (Arutiunov, Krupnik, and Chlenov 1981). But as soon as the environmental pendulum swung the other way, this progress was replaced by an equally rapid cultural decline, such that even memories of these achievements faded within a few centuries.

The victims of rises and falls in human culture in the Arctic sank into historical invisibility, obscured by the depths of centuries and by the countless generations of people that followed, exploiting the polar limits of the ecumene. Therefore, in our descriptions and reconstructions we actually refer to the "lucky" few who survived to leave us fairly clear traces of their cultures or progeny, and whom we have encountered directly in historical times. The true history of the Arctic, according to Christian Vibe, is more a chronicle of numberless disturbances and "explosions" than of continuity and survival, and thus is only minimally accessible by means of the accumulated tools and knowledge of science.

I believe that we must acknowledge this to an even greater degree in our efforts to reconstruct the history of Paleolithic societies. All our parallels with Arctic ecological anthropology indicate that these were exceptionally dynamic human communities that experienced an endless succession of slumps and discoveries, regressions and advances into unexplored areas of the planet. The generally "ecophobic," aggressive character of Upper Paleolithic hunting communities, and their active behavior directed toward expanded reproduction correlate well with this conclusion.

It is precisely our experience of Arctic peoples that most resoundingly refutes the model so popular in the 1960s and 1970s, of primitive hunting societies as stable, balanced groups living according to the laws of ecological homeostasis with their environments (see Birdsell 1968, Deevey 1960, Divale 1972, Dumond 1975, Hayden 1972, Narr 1956, etc.). The ancient history of humankind knows too many instances in which the equilibrium of ecosystems has been disrupted by human overpredation or other unchecked economic activity to call the attempt to maintain ecological stability a "universal mechanism" of adaptation, the "archetype" of behavior in prehistoric societies.

The "equilibrium approach" to the Paleolithic societies has been thoroughly subjected to critical analysis (Cohen 1981:276, Henneberg 1975:87, Shnirel'man 1986:427, 434–35), not least for its aspirations to acceptance as a universal explanatory model. It appears more accurate to consider the "equilibrium" option as one of many possible modes of adaptation rather than as the sole, and certainly not as the optimal, one. Such an adaptation might have functioned effectively in a relatively stable environment, in which resources were well known and could not be increased rapidly within a given subsistence strategy. But it would have been of little use in an unstable environment with sharp, cyclical fluctuations in game populations.

Not coincidentally, some authors believe that although artificial means of population control, such as infanticide, abortion, sexual taboos, etc., may have existed in prehistoric societies, they were not widely practiced until *after* the transition to more intensive food-producing economies (Boughey 1971:228–29, 289). As such they were more typical of early-agricultural and pastoral societies, and were firmly retained in antiquity, in the medieval period, and, of course, in modern methods of "demographic planning."

This perspective is confirmed in the general trend in human use of the environment. With the transition from highly unreliable big-game hunting in the Upper Paleolithic to more stable Mesolithic fishing, gathering, and sea-mammal hunting, with the subsequent appearance of food-producing economies, and then irrigated agriculture and indoor stock breeding, humankind successively reduced the instability of its existence. The productive capacities of the environment became more and more defined, and the lows and highs in subsistence resources increasingly predictable. Thus, the possibilities for planning grew, along with regulation and even artifical limitation of a society's own needs.

We should, however, view the primary *ecological* aspect of human evolution as the human species' capacity to inhabit and appropriate nearly the entire known range of environments on earth in a relatively short period of time. Thanks to this, humankind acceded to a truly unique place in the global biosphere. To attain this position, human beings had to possess extraordinary evolutionary mechanisms, which clearly distinguished them from the rest of the natural world.

These mechanisms were the use of fire, toolmaking, social organization, and the retention and transmission of culture. We can also add a specific type of *ecological behavior* to this list, one directed toward continual population growth and, objectively speaking, toward destruction of equilibrium with the environment. Lacking much in the way of technology, prehistoric people were compelled to "overcome" nature to a far greater degree than were their more powerful descendants. But it was precisely this demand made on the environment by human economy and reproduction, documented by the archeological remains of traditional Arctic societies, that permitted Paleolithic communities still at the hunter-gatherer economic stage to occupy, appropriate, and transform practically the entire planet.

Epilogue

As our investigation and this book come to an end, I want only to add a few words in closing about the future prospects for "Arctic adaptations." What is the significance of this concept for Arctic researchers and residents today? And do the principles established herein have any application outside of purely academic research on the history and anthropology of native Arctic peoples?

It is possible to show that the role of the traditional adaptations I have presented in this book is steadily eroding. Before the eyes of one or two generations of anthropologists, the way of life, subsistence, and the entire lattice of relationships between Arctic peoples and their environment has been deeply transformed. Although according to official statistics the great majority of Arctic natives are considered "rural residents"—about 70 percent in Alaska and 75 percent in Siberia (Levin 1991:11, *Itogi* 1989:73, Statistics 1991:8–9)—most of them now live in large modernized communities firmly situated within the contemporary cash economy. This process began long before our time. But in the late twentieth century it acquired a precipitous and, it now appears, irreversible character.

Of course, whaling, sealing, land-game hunting, fur trapping, fishing, and family reindeer herding are still important in many communities. They play an enormous role in supporting cultural continuity and ethnic identity among the native population, and in maintaining occupations and the customary diet. But they are based on completely different principles than those of the traditional economies, and usually constitute a livelihood supplementary to wage-employment or public subsidies, or a source of cash income for buying other goods. In the best case, we can call this system a mixed subsistence-market economy (Wolfe and Walker 1987:68, Brown and Burch 1992:211).

Modernization has had even more dramatic consequences. Industrial civilization penetrated the Arctic and Subarctic later than other regions of the planet, but did so with the accumulated strength of a history of expansion, and armed with the might of modern technology. Europeans introduced commercial methods of exploiting natural resources to the Arctic in the 1600s, creating terrific pressure on the most valuable species of fur-bearing animals and sea mammals, such as beaver, Arctic fox, sable, bowhead whale, walrus, etc. By 1900, exploitation turned to mineral resources, as the starting gun set off the rush for gold on Seward Peninsula and in the Yukon and Klondike valleys in Alaska, as well as in Yakutia and on the Chukchi Peninsula of Siberia.

Massive-scale industrial construction in Siberia in the 1930s and 1940s by thousands of Stalin-era gulag prisoners, and the discovery of Arctic oil and gas in the middle of the century radically changed the situation there. The native population began to experience growing social and ecological pressure now not only on individual species of local resources, but all across their lands. An especially tragic situation developed in the Russian (formerly Soviet) Arctic, where industrial, transportation, and military construction were a state monopoly and were often carried out without any concern for the health of the local environment and people whatsoever. As a result, many ecosystems were devastated by technogenic impacts and pollution.

In the struggle between industrial civilization and traditional forms of native subsistence, the forces turned out to be wildly unequal. Under the stress of state-financed mining, logging, military programs, and road construction, seizure of the local populations' grazing areas and hunting grounds proceeded almost unrestricted. Siberian peoples, who had no power to resist the industrial expansion, left or moved out of their native lands. The new owners built legions of multistory cement towns and villages, pipelines, and oil wells . . . and left in their path an ecological wasteland.

But the Arctic was fated to play a different role. It was here that the limits of industrial expansion were first to be recognized and tested in the late twentieth century. Unlike the Third World, however, where decolonization was achieved through force and political resistance, emancipation for the Arctic is emerging from the evolution of ecological and humanitarian values within Western culture itself. "Limits to growth" in the Arctic were erected in the form of new ecological and social priorities, most of all environmental protection and minority rights. This new ethic was first asserted successfully in the Scandinavian countries and Greenland and emerged in Alaska and Canada in the 1970s. Only by the very end of the 1980s did a comparable phenomenon appear in the former Soviet Union and rise swiftly to popularity in Siberia.

The aboriginal peoples of Siberia, state institutions, and social movements in Russia embarked on this course very late. The struggle for native land claims is really only now getting off the ground. Protected by the planned economy of a huge state, Siberian minorities did not experience the problems of other Arctic minorities in the 1980s, such as the antisealing and antitrapping campaigns by international animal rights organizations (see *Arctic Environment* 1991, Wenzel 1991, Woods 1986). Until very recently no native organizations existed in Siberia that were capable of standing up for subsistence rights. This entire layer of accumulated political experience, so essential for contemporary survival of Arctic minorities in the West, was virtually nonexistent in the former Soviet Union.

But the Siberian case is interesting in and of itself, because of its unique feature of maximum participation of an authoritarian paternalistic state in the development of Arctic regions. Quite recently, this state seemed omnipotent in its programs to industrially expand and modernize the native population. Most notably, it encountered the same limits to industrial growth that other Arctic nations encountered, and it repeated many of the same patterns in solving the problems of its northern territories.

The critical turning point in the Russian Arctic came in 1988, under the influence of increased liberalization in political life in the former USSR, growing independence among scholars and the press, and new social movements. This was the first time that official state policy of industrial development and modernization for the Arctic (and for Siberia, in general) and its native people was criticized openly, and ultimately condemned. In public debates and newspapers it was announced that the uncontrolled industrial expansion of the 1970s and 1980s had caused the destruction of ecological balance in many parts of Siberia, and its continuation was leading to sure catastrophe for the local environment and native peoples.[1]

Two gigantic development projects emerged as symbols for the new opposition: opening up gasfields on Yamal Peninsula, including a new railroad and several pipelines; and erection of the Turukhansk hydroelectric plant in Evenkiia. Both were ultimately set aside by government decisions, and not least because they threatened the culture and livelihood of the native population (Aipin 1989, Pika and Prokhorov 1988, Prokhorov 1989, Savoskul and Karlov 1988).

Starting in mid-1988, the Soviet press, for the first time since the 1920s, began to publish materials about the alarming situation of native Siberian peoples and the crisis in their economies, cultures, and resource management systems.[2] This stream of information soon completely washed away the illusion, carefully cultivated since the 1930s, of Siberian peoples "flowering" under the paternalistic care of the socialist state.

Lastly, also in 1988, the question was first raised of creating special social and political organizations of native Siberians to protect their rights and give them political representation (see Pika and Prokhorov 1988:82–83, Na Perelome 1989:3, Alia 1991:24). Local cultural groups and regional associations formed rapidly throughout Siberia. Activists in the new associations began to demand the return of lands appropriated by the state, the reinstatement of traditional forms of resource utilization, and preferential rights to the biological resources of their lands.[3] This trend was fully evidenced in the activities of the Association of Minority Peoples of the North, formed in March 1990 in Moscow (Alia 1991, *Indigenous Peoples* 1990, Sangi 1990, Sokolova 1990a, Convention 1991, etc.).

In all social systems, popular ecological movements cleave to a particular kind of developmental logic. Starting from isolated challenges and petitions, they then gather momentum in mass protests against concrete technological projects and in the end arrive at ideas of sustainable development and self-determination. The struggle for clean air and water, for conservation of hunting grounds and pasturelands, becomes inseparable from calls for cultural survival and self-government. This was the case among Alaskan and Canadian Inuit, American Indians, and Scandinavian Saami during the 1960s–1980s. The same process is gathering force now in Siberia, right up to demanding the creation of local reservations for protecting traditional lands, and picketing industrial plants on native populations' territories (Aipin 1991, Petrunenko 1991, *The Arctic* 1991).

As experience in the American Arctic has shown, such situations stimulate interest in native traditions of resource use and cultural heritage. As a result, native people develop new political and ideological programs. In the first stage, they declare the priority of traditional subsistence values, reject industrial expansion, and identify with a "native lifestyle." This life, far from the big settlements with their alcoholism, unemployment, and domination by European newcomers, is increasingly regarded as the genuine way of life, embodying a former self-sufficiency and freedom. Active participation in traditional subsistence activities, such as hunting, fishing, and family reindeer herding, is one of the basic conditions of this life.

Of course, individual families can live off subsistence activities in hunting camps or small villages, especially in conjunction with elements of a cash economy. But, in order for this model to stabilize and open up to significant numbers of people, it must reflect traditional adaptive principles of Arctic peoples. The most important of these are flexibility and variability in the resource utilization system, sequential distribution of hunting pressure in time and space, and the parallel existence of several subsistence strategies with differential responses to environmental change, all described in the preceding pages of this book.

Ecological movements of Arctic residents to protect their land and subsistence traditions are only one sphere in which we can identify contemporary instances of "Arctic adaptations." Another such realm lies in the appearance of commercial hunting and reindeer-herding economies, which in Siberia were squelched for many years by the monolithic priority on industrial development. Modern biology can drastically improve the efficiency of commercial game use through resource inventories, stock assessment, and reliable monitoring of recruitment rates.

But even the most rationally organized commercial use of resources will take place in a ubiquitously unstable Arctic environment of sharp fluctuations and periodic crashes. To survive in these conditions, a commercial Arctic economy must draw upon several different strategies and a series of interchangeable, alternative resources. It will badly "need space" and also time, and must achieve very rapid growth rates in an auspicious period in order to recover more easily from losses during the inevitable lulls. In other words, it must come to approximate the organizational principles of the traditional subsistence systems developed by native Arctic peoples.

Overall, these principles appear to be no less meaningful for strategies of industrial development in the polar regions. The ecological experience of northern peoples demonstrates to us the *cost* of stability and the *laws* of long-term existence in the Arctic. The cost of stability is increased loss and constant disruptions in economic-cultural continuity, and the periodic disappearance of certain models as environments or resources shift. The *law* of long-term survival is rejection of any one-track development (which dooms any one model to inevitable death) and a return to multifaceted economic systems, which facilitate rapid transition from one form of production to another.

In the language of contemporary economics this means that, notwithstanding all its technological achievements, monopolistic industrial development of the Arctic in theory has no lasting future. But industrialized civilization does poorly at absorbing the knowledge of local cultures, even though it pays dearly for this neglect. Once they dig up all the available mineral resources, people will be forced to leave the Arctic barrenland and to abandon the cement cities and ready-made infrastructure they have built, now bereft of alternative sources of survival. To sustain a stable economy in the north, it is crucial to preserve a new set of "dual" economic models—the indigenous and the commercial. In any shift of orientation, either one can absorb part of the resources and labor force. And this, too, is something we have learned from the history of Arctic adaptations.

There is one more sphere in the contemporary Arctic in which a consideration of indigenous subsistence models has enormous significance: the conservation and monitoring of biological resources, or even of entire areas. More precisely, in most cases this means the *interaction* of national and international conservation regimes with various forms of local resource utilization.

The huge spatial dimensions of Arctic ecosystems was always the source of their vitality, allowing them to recover ecologically damaged areas quickly. In traditional subsistence systems, uninhabited lands, lands belonging to migratory communities, or abandoned settlements together with their resource territories, played the role of unique temporal "reservoirs." Falling temporarily out of use, they periodically were used by neighboring communities as a reserve if any environmental changes occurred. In any future systems of environmental protection and rational resource management the same functional role will be played by territories with various conservation regimes and native subsistence priority-use areas.

Comanagement is one of the most attractive new strategies for flexible protection of game resources (Osherenko 1988). In this system, responsibility for a game population's welfare is divided between the game management agencies and native users, and with time is placed increasingly on the latter. Several such comanagement regimes have already proved effective in exploiting populations of bowhead whale, caribou, beluga, waterfowl, polar bear, and other valuable or vulnerable game resources of the Arctic (Osherenko 1988).

This approach can ultimately lead to a complex system of reciprocal responsibility among groups of native users, game management agencies, and even entire governments. And here the sides should understand each other well. Nationally or internationally established conservation regimes are usually very rigid. They attempt to adhere to ideas of "ecosystem equilibrium," "minimal allowable" natural impact, "average" population growth rates, "rationally determined" game quotas, and so forth.

As I have attempted to show in this book, native resource management was always based upon a completely different set of principles. Therefore, it is impossible to require native residents to hold their lives and welfare hostage to the fluctuating dynamics of certain game populations. This would be immoral and unnatural, most of all from an ecological point of view. Flexibility and pluralism, mobility and a high hunting pressure for short periods of time, aggressiveness and a rapid growth rate are the result of historical adaptation to a specific environment. We are only now beginning to understand the laws of this adaptation. It would be premature indeed to evaluate them according to our views of what constitutes "rational" resource management.

On the eve of the twenty-first century, society overall stands faced with the necessity of searching for a new ideology to guide development of polar regions. The Arctic can no longer be regarded as the "last frontier," an inexhaustible storehouse of resources for modern industry. Equally, it can never again become a region of "white silence," which will belong only to its ancient inhabitants, returned to some kind of ideally balanced, traditional forms of survival. In the late twentieth century, both these visions are unrealistic.

Perhaps it is in the Arctic that we will manage to find some other, third way, based on values of a new ecological thinking. The Arctic states are looking for ways to cooperate, to articulate the interests and rights of minorities with the needs of modern society. The new model of economic development will apparently be built upon the recognition of *equality* and *equivalence*—economic, ideological, and cultural—among many forms of resource utilization. It awaits for us to find an intelligent compromise among preferential indigenous zones of land use, the industrial wastelands of mass-scale resource development, various forms of protected natural and historical-cultural territories, areas for commercial hunting, reindeer herding, recreation, and tourism.

The road to compromise, no doubt, will be long and difficult. And, in that process, Arctic ethnoecology will acquire its own new, contemporary resonance—as the science of traditional adaptations and the ecological experience of native peoples of the Arctic.

Notes

1. Arctic Context and Research Design (pp. 1–27)

1. All ethnic names of the Siberian native peoples are spelled, throughout the text, according to the latest version of the National Geographic Society's map "Peoples of the Soviet Union" (1989).

2. The same term had a differen history in Russian anthropology. Subsistence, or *zhizneobespechenie*, literally "providing life," was first used by Sergei Arutiunov in reference to a research project on Armenian rural culture in the late 1970s (Arutiunov 1989, Arutiunov et al. 1983). Here, *zhizneobespechenie* was used primarily in the sense of "livelihood." A special term was suggested, "*kul'tura zhizneobespecheniia*," to denote all the elements of culture that support human daily life, specifically including food, clothing, housing, villages, and so forth (Arutiunov 1989:201–202, Arutiunov and Mkrtumian 1985:20–22, Arutiunov et al. 1983:8–9).

3. These projects included, for example, Robert Spencer's "Human Ecology in Arctic Alaska from 1953–1955," the results of which appeared in his well-known monograph (Spencer 1959); Joseph Sonnenfeld's "Changes in Subsistence Among the Barrow Eskimos," Office of Naval Research Project ONR-140 (Arctic Institute of North America, 1956); A. J. Kerr's report, "Subsistence and Social Organization in a Fur Trade Community," an anthropological report on the Rupert's House Indians prepared for the National Committee for Community Health Studies (Ottawa, 1950); Dimitri Shimkin's, "The Economy of a Trapping Center: the Case of Fort Yukon, Alaska," *Economic Development and Cultural Change* 3, no. 3 (1955):219–40; etc.

4. In considering peacetime uses of nuclear power, the Atomic Energy Commission chose a site in northern Alaska on the Chukchi Sea coast for the first experimental explosion. The test was never conducted, but, from 1959 to 1962, one hundred scientists in various specialties were dispatched to

the Alaskan Arctic to conduct reconnaisance and feasibility studies in tundra geography, ecology, and cultural history. Don Foote was one of these, who subsequently continued his research after the project was discontinued.

5. Among these are several excellent works: Dolgikh 1952, Levin 1941, Popov 1948, 1952, Vasilevich and Levin 1951, etc.

6. For a long time, my work on reconstructing subsistence balances (Krupnik 1976c, 1978, 1988a) was the sole Siberian analogue to this trend, and just recently has been taken up by another author (Shnirel'man 1990).

7. See also Weiner 1964:500–503. In more recent work, "optimal population" is more frequently used to convey the same meaning (see Freeman 1970:145).

8. Even a regional sample of the American Arctic conveys the breadth of this work (Burch 1985, Burgess 1974, Denniston 1974, Foote 1965, Foote and Greer-Wootten 1966, Hall 1971, Kemp 1971, Riewe 1977, Smith 1991, Wenzel 1991, etc.), especially when we add the many technical reports on contemporary native communities in Alaska and Canada (see additional references in *Abstracts* 1986, Brown and Burch 1992, Usher and Wenzel 1987, Wolfe and Walker 1987, etc.).

2. *Sea-Mammal Hunters of the Arctic Coast (pp. 28–85)*

1. Most of the documentary data used in this chapter were assembled in the course of collaborative research by the author and Mikhail Chlenov from 1971 to 1987. For preliminary reviews of these sources see Krupnik 1980, 1981b, and 1983.

2. The first name is a modern Russian spelling. The name in parenthesis is the original Eskimo (Siberian Yupik) form.

3. For diagrams of the trophic relationships within Eskimo ecosystems see Boughey 1973:159, Freeman 1984:37, Kemp 1971:108–109. See the most recent analysis of energy flow and trophic relations in the Arctic ecosystem in Welch et al. 1992:345–54.

4. "The spirits, it seems, take care that the people of this country shall not multiply. In olden times war was sent down to ward off increase. After that, in spite of the abundant variety of sea-game, famine would come and carry off the surplus. At present, with the fulsome supply of American food, the disease comes down, and the result is exactly the same" (Bogoras 1904:36).

5. In the spring of 1908 the ship's log of the American schooner *Herman* gives a complete account of 114 different types of goods that were supplied to the residents of Imtuk and Sireniki, everything from wooden prefabricated houses, whaleboats, and guns to mirrors, irons, and opera glasses, for a total sum of $5,400 (SS *Herman* Trade Book, 1909, copy kindly provided by John Bockstoce).

6. Knopfmiller 1940:211, 800 kilograms; Razumovskii 1931:106, 840 kilograms; Karaev 1923:11, "blubber from one hundred seals"; Zenkovich 1938:61, "three kilograms a day," e.g., 1,095 kilograms, etc. For the American Arctic, see Kemp 1971:108, Mikkelsen 1944:165, etc.

7. The most knowledgeable local experts who assisted me in this process

deserve special gratitude: Aleksandr Ratkhugwi (1907–1977, Sireniki), Vladimir Nutaugwi (1914–?, Sireniki), Utykhtykak (1914–1976, Imtuk), Andrei Kukil'gin (1922–1985, Imtuk), Mikhail Iukhak (1927–1979, Imtuk), Petr Napaun (1912–1983, Avan), Iurii Pukhluk (1922, Avan), Vasilii Ankatagin (1925–1979, Avan), Vladimir Akka (1922–1988, Ureliki), Nikolai Anagikak (1922–1976, Ureliki), Ivan Ashkamakin (1911, Chaplino), Vladimir Tiiato (1922–1985, Chaplino), Vladimir Tagitutkak (1922, Sikliuk), Petr Nutatagin (1921, Kivak), Tnanufan (1911–1984, Naukan), Vladimir Gukhugwi (1922–1989, Naukan). In each case the experts are referred to by their date of birth (and death, if relevant) and by their original village of birth.

8. The calculated caloric value of imported food products received by the Eskimos of Avan in 1895 was more than 22 million kcal (Gondatti 1898: xxiii), or 20 percent of the annual energy needs of the community. In Chaplino in 1900 400 sacks of flour were purchased for local consumption, which could supply 17 percent of annual energy needs. In 1908 the residents of Imtuk and Sireniki obtained food items with an estimated total caloric value of 60.8 million kcal from the schooner *Herman* (45 percent of the communities' estimated annual needs).

9. According to field investigations by Liudmila S. Bogoslovskaia from 1981 to 1987.

10. Only 2,000 to 2,500 guillemot pairs now nest on the entire area of Cape Dezhnev (Tomkovich and Sorokin 1983:134). If, earlier, the Eskimos of Naukan used to gather fifty to sixty eggs per family a year, their annual harvest could have exceeded 3,000 to 3,500 eggs, or the total recruitment of the bird colony.

11. In the winter of 1934, seventeen out of fifty-five Eskimos who had relocated to Wrangell Island died from starvation or illness (Mineev 1946), the majority of them adults. In 1900, a year of epidemics, catarrhal illnesses, and hunting accidents on St. Lawrence Island, forty-five people or about 15 percent of the local population died there. Of these there were thirty-two adults (twenty-three women and nine men), but only twelve children (Lerrigo 1901:101). The list of similar instances goes on.

3. Reindeer Pastoralists of the Inland Tundra (pp. 86–127)

1. The latter are usually called the reindeer Chukchi to differentiate them from the maritime Chukchi, who lived in coastal villages and maintained a sea-mammal economy highly similar to that of the Eskimos.

2. The most complete accounts of the Bol'shaia Zemlia Nenets reindeer economy are contained in Babushkin 1926, 1930, Kertselli 1911, Plettsov 1925, and Ekonomika Bol'shezemel'skoi tundry 1934. On the Chukchi pastoralist economy, see Arkhincheev 1957, Bogoras 1904, Druri 1936, Ioffe 1937, Orlovskii 1928a, b, and Schmit 1939.

3. This kind of partnership, including its causes and motivations, was extensively researched and analyzed by several authors in the 1930s: Arkhincheev 1957, Bogoras 1931, *Krainii Sever* 1935, Maslov 1934, Terletskii 1934.

4. For the Nenets area, see Andreev, Igoshina, and Leskov 1935:179,

Arteev 1926:141–43, Babushkin 1930:7, 65, Kertselli 1911:91, 97, Kuratov 1925:40, Lepekhin 1805:225, Vitiugov 1923:10–11, and Verbov 1939:45, 63–64. For the Chukchi, see Anadyrskii krai 1935:39–40, Bogoras 1934:12, Shmit 1939:116, 140, and Vdovin 1965:160.

5. For more detail, see Brodnev 1959:71, Efimenko 1878:217, and Minenko 1975:39.

6. For the areas covered here, see Andreev 1933, Andreev, Igoshina, and Leskov 1935, Druri 1933, 1936, Gorodkov 1926, Ioffe 1937, Orlovskii 1928b, and Shmit 1939.

7. For the Nenets, these were: December to early April (winter pastures), July to September (summer and early autumn pastures), and two transitional periods of migrations, April to June, and October to November.

8. Calculated from Bunakov 1934:57–58, Gassovskii 1939:26, *Itogi Perepisi* 1929, *Naselennye Punkty* 1928:xxxvii, *Pokhoziaistvennaia Perepis'* 1929:30, 114, and Semerikov 1933:29. Among the Nenets of the Kara River, population density reached 0.037 per square kilometer, while among the Chaun Chukchi, it fell as low as 0.007 to 0.011.

9. According to data that were evidently less than complete, the Chukchi infant mortality rate was 30 percent in 1925 and 32 percent in 1939 (*Itogi Perepisi* 1929:iv, Svedeniia 1939:1, V. A. 1935:60–64).

10. For data on the structure and dynamics of reindeer stock among the Nenets and Chukchi nomads, see Ekonomika Bol'shezemel'skoi tundry 1934:121–24, *Krainii Sever* 1935:72, Plettsov 1925:13–14, Shmit 1939:11–12, Sokolov 1935:63–66, and Terletskii 1930:56–57.

11. For the Nenets, this was 28 percent men, 22 percent women, 7 percent elders, and 43 percent children. For the Chukchi, this was 23 percent men, 28 percent women, 6 percent elders, and 43 percent children (see tables 12 and 13).

12. These figures were derived from my calculations based upon slaughter-weight data, and the production and caloric content of the meat from various age-sex groups of domestic reindeer (see Krupnik 1976c:62–63). The original indicators are available in Anadyrskii krai 1935:32, Arkhincheev 1957:57, Kudelia 1973:44, Makridina 1956:57, Mukhachev 1969:111, and Zhigunov 1961:320–25.

13. This amount was arrived at as follows: among the Nenets, sixteen skins for clothing, ten for *chum* repair, fourteen for bedding and household items; for the Chukchi, twelve skins for clothing, sixteen for dwellings and the *yaranga*, and twelve for household needs (Krupnik 1976c:61).

14. Since we omitted tea and several other infrequently used items such as candy and alcohol, the calculated weight of imported foods in consumption falls slightly short of the actual figure.

15. Marine-mammal meat and especially blubber has a substantially higher caloric content (1,400 to 1,700 kcal/kg and 7,500 kcal/kg, respectively) than the meat of the domestic reindeer killed by the herders for their own use (1,000–1,200 kcal/kg).

16. For a list of ethnic groups and their subsistence systems useful for such a comparison, see Ellen 1982:126–27).

4. *The Challenge of Change in the Arctic Environment (pp. 128–159)*

1. Arutiunov et al. 1982, Dikov 1989, Dolgikh 1960, 1970, Gurvich 1966, Lashuk 1958, Vasil'ev 1979b, Vdovin 1965, 1973, etc.

2. But see a directly opposing view in Minc 1986 and Minc and Smith 1989.

3. "As soon as the water dropped, dead fish appeared everywhere, especially pike; then the magpies began to fall (they are the most common bird here), then foxes, wolverines, wolves, bears, and all that year, we found their corpses everywhere by the dozen, such that, by the following year, there was almost no game to be found" (Gondatti 1897a:140).

4. See Kertselli 1911:48–50 for Bol'shaia Zemlia tundra, Fitzhugh 1972:173 for Labrador, and Martin 1978 for a general discussion of "game crises."

5. *The Rise of Reindeer Pastoralism in the Arctic (pp. 160–184)*

1. As noted above in chapter 4, this interpretation concurs with my analysis first published in 1975 (Krupnik 1975) and stands in opposition to the view endorsed recently (Minc 1986:70, Minc and Smith 1989:15).

2. See Andreev 1947:100, Vdovin 1973:230, 1974:118, Voprosy i otvety 1787:IX:4–6, Georgi 1777:7–9, Kolonial'naia politika 1935:157, Krasheninnikov 1949:453, Steller 1938:130, Mériot 1980:55, Lundmark 1989:38.

3. This view is supported by native folk stories in which some domestic reindeer fall into the hands of hunters who had no herds before. Inevitably, the stories end with the ill fate and rapid destruction of the stolen herds. See Vasil'ev 1979b:56.

4. Lennart Lundmark estimated the entire transition to pastoralism to have taken about 150–200 years among the Saami of northern Sweden—from the late 1500s up to the late 1700s (Lundmark 1989:39).

6. *The Evolution of Maritime Hunting (pp. 185–215)*

1. See a similar explanation for the Canadian Arctic in McCartney and Savelle 1985:51.

2. The first outlines of this transition were introduced in Krupnik 1981c.

3. Vladimir Pitul'ko has directed my attention to the fact that this period actually may have been unfavorable for the maritime hunting economy on the Kola Peninsula. Pitul'ko suggests that medieval sea-mammal migration routes shifted not only east, but further north into the Barents Sea toward Spitsbergen, Franz Joseph Land, and the north island of Novaia Zemlia (V. V. Pitul'ko, letter to the author, 1990). Whales, walrus, and seals moved beyond reach for the indigenous hunters, but, with advancements in European Arctic navigation technology, became easy prey for the Russian Pomors and European whalers.

4. Details on European commercial maritime hunting in the Western Eurasian Arctic are provided in *Angliiskie puteshestvenniki* 1938, Belov 1956, Braat 1984, Chapskii 1939, Hacquebord 1981, Kit 1973, Perry 1976, Scammon 1968, Van-Linshotten 1915.

5. For example, the Vylka clan in the Bol'shaia Zemlia tundra and the Iaptik on the Yamal Peninsula (Islavin 1847:132, 134, Chernetsov 1935:132, Vasil'ev 1979:55–57); also, the Kharlins, among the Kola Saami, who considered themselves to be "from the seal clan" (Luk'ianchenko 1971:50).

6. This model has recently been challenged by a comparable paleoenvironmental reconstruction developed by Leah Minc for the northwestern Alaskan Arctic (Minc 1986, Minc and Smith 1989). Minc's model, which was built without knowledge of my earlier Russian publications, conversely connects "bad subsistence times" on the Alaskan coast and successful caribou hunting in the interior with warmer climatic conditions, and, alternately, scarce caribou resources and abundant coastal whaling with climatic cooling trends. However, the basic theoretical proposition is virtually identical: when there is temporal alternation in the availability of marine and terrestrial faunal resources, humans must respond to these fluctuations by emigration, intergroup alliances, and/or by rapidly adopting the alternative subsistence orientation (Krupnik 1989:187, Minc and Smith 1989:20).

7. All these cultural adaptations lost by 1800 were documented in the western Eurasian Arctic by early European sources or have been reconstructed by anthropologists based on folklore and local traditions. On cooperative whale and beluga hunting among the Nenets in the 1600s–1700s, see Alekseev 1936:273, Golovnev 1986:95, Zuev 1947:80; on dwellings made from whalebone and logs, Alekseev 1936:285 (ca. 1647), Van-Linshotten 1915:576 (ca. 1595), DeLamartin'er 1912:46, 53 (ca. 1653); on the presence of dogsleds and dog transportation, Golovnev 1986:98–99; for wood-framed, kayak-like skinboats, see Beliavskii 1825:258.

7. *The Aboriginal Hunter in the Arctic Ecosystem (pp. 216–240)*

1. "In a highly variable environment, a continuously high number of younger age groups greatly facilitates accelerated population recovery during favorable periods. In other words, lacking the ability to transform their highly unstable environment substantially, Arctic aborigenes were compelled to pursue both social and biological population management strategies that were consonant with the organizational principles of the overall ecosystem" (Vadim Mokievskii, personal correspondence, September 25, 1990).

2. See references in Bogoras 1975:133, Campbell 1978:190, Grønnow 1986:60–63, Ingold 1980:69–70, Jochelson 1898:41, Martin 1978:164–65, Nellemann 1969:150–52, Nelson 1973:311, Portenko 1941:83, Tugolukov 1979:47–48, etc.

3. Surveys by Mikhail Chlenov, Liudmila Bogoslovskaia, and the present author in the summer of 1981. Our data were briefly published in Chlenov

and Krupnik 1984, Bogoslovskaia and Votogrov 1982, Krupnik et al. 1983, Krupnik 1987a.

4. On the extinction of great auk in Greenland by Eskimo overhunting around 1500 B.C.E., see Meldgaard 1988:160–61, 167.

5. For the most recent and a slightly different interpretation of the Caribou Eater Chipewyan subsistence system see Burch 1991b:441–42.

6. I am indebted to Liudmila Bogoslovskaia for directing my attention to this aspect of aboriginal maritime ecology.

7. On the influence of boreal ecological cycles on aboriginal hunting behavior, see Nelson 1980:223–28, also Rogers and Black 1976, Waisberg 1975, Winterhalder 1983.

8. For details on the hunting ethics and beliefs of boreal hunting peoples, see Martin 1978:34–39, 71–74, 150–51, Nelson 1973:311, 1980:229–31, Tanner 1979, and, in Siberia, Alekseenko 1974:226, Kulemzin 1984:155–56, Smoliak 1976:143–44, Taksami 1976:204–06, Tugolukov 1969:148, 152–53, Vasilevich 1969:216–20, etc.

8. Arctic Adaptations and Paleolithic Society (pp. 241–262)

1. Originally published in W. B. Dawkins, "Eskimaux in the South of Gaul," *Saturday Review* 13 (London, 1866): 6. For further detail, refer to Okladnikov 1941:30–31, also Binford 1978, David 1973, Efimenko 1931, Sturdy 1972, 1975, Wilkinson 1972, 1975, etc.

2. For descriptions of the environmental conditions of the glacial tundra-steppe and sparsely forested zone, see Bader 1977, Gladkikh et al 1985, Soffer 1985, Stanley 1980, Velichko et al. 1977, Vereshchagin 1979, etc.

3. See Bader 1977:33, 1978:185, Bibikov 1981:36–38, Boriskovskii 1953:225, 1963:24–27, 1979:192–94, 1984:190, Clark 1953:34–37, Ermolov 1985:41–42, Efimenko 1953:369–71, Okladnikov 1941:26–31, Pidoplichko 1969:12–16, 1976:35–40, Sergin 1983:28–30, etc.

4. Arutiunov and Sergeev 1975:183, Bader 1978:172, Bibikov 1981:83, Frolov 1974:112–24, Soffer 1985:416–18, also Abramova 1966, etc.

5. See the publications of Lewis Binford and his colleagues concerning the results of field investigations among the Nunamiut Eskimo in northern Alaska from 1969 to 1972 (Binford 1978, 1980, Binford and Chasko 1976, etc.), also research in Greenland and the Canadian Arctic (Sturdy 1972, Wilkinson 1975).

6. On the use of heavy lances in the Paleolithic, see Ermolov 1985:451; on killing prey from a short distance, see Abramova 1964:179, Abramova and Grechkina 1985:46; for entrapment in shallow pits, see Boriskovskii 1953:208, 1979:165, Vereshchagin and Kuz'mina 1977:89.

7. Abramova and Grechkina 1985:47–49, Bader 1977:35, 1978:186, 204–205, Ermolov 1985:41, Petrin 1986:62–64, Pidoplichko 1969:137–38, 1976:159–63, Vereshchagin 1977:40.

8. Olga Soffer (1985:294) estimates the yield of adult mammoth at 1,800 kilograms, though she does not include animal fat in her caloric calculations.

In the cold climate of the periglacial steppe, fat must have been an important element in the Paleolithic hunting diet. If one includes only the meat, then a large mammoth was approximately equal to a juvenile whale.

9. This conclusion is fully confirmed by the recent seasonal analysis of American mastodon deaths (*Mammut americanum*) resulting from Paleoindian hunting in the Great Lakes region (Fisher 1987:360–61). All ten animals displaying indisputable evidence of human butchering died in the late fall or early winter, while mastodon found without any marks of human activity primarily died in the spring and summer. If this reconstruction is accurate, the predominance of young males among mastodon killed in the fall is fully explicable, since these provided their human predators with a maximum utilizable food supply for winter storage.

10. Birdsell 1968:238–39, Divale 1972:224–25, Dumond 1975:717, Hayden 1972:216, Stott 1969:103, Vishnevskii 1976:25, etc.

Epilogue (pp. 263–270)

1. Significant milestones in this process included the conference on "Rational Use and Protection of Natural Systems in Island and Coastal Zone Areas of the Arctic Seas" (Leningrad, March 1988, *Bogoslovskaia* 1991); public hearings on ecological problems in the North (Moscow, April 1988) and the fate of northern peoples (Moscow, August 1988, Na Perelome 1989); discussion concerning the future of native peoples at the International Conference of Arctic States to Coordinate Arctic Scientific Research (Leningrad, December 1988); the first conferences on ethical problems of northern development, which opened a whole series of similar discussions and publications (Bakshtanovskii 1988, 1989, 1990, 1991); the creation of a public watch-group, "The Troubled Arctic" (Moscow, February 1989); a series of articles in the journals, *Severnye prostory* and *Sovetskaia etnografiia* (Oborotova 1988); publication of two official proposals for modernizing Siberian minorities (*Etnokul'turnoe Razvitie* 1988, *Kontseptsiia* 1989) and public response to them; and so forth. See the updated review in: Fondahl 1993.

2. Aleksandr Pika and Boris Prokhorov, "Big Problems for Minority Peoples" (in Russian), *Kommunist* (1988), n. 16 (see Pika and Prokhorov 1989); Valeri Sharov, "Is the Land Too Small for Small Ethnic Groups?" (in Russian) *Literaturnaia gazeta* (1988), n. 33; Ivan Levshin, "Harsh Reality of a Harsh Land" (in Russian) *Pravda* (1988), n. 360; "At the Turning Point" (in Russian) *Sovetskaia kul'tura* (1989), n. 18; see more references in Sokolova 1990a, 1990b.

3. Eremei Aipin, "Not by Oil Alone" (in English) *Moscow News* (1989), n. 2, pp. 9–10; Alitet Nemtushkin, "Hanging in the Balance" (in Russian), *Severnye prostory* (1988), n. 3; Anna Nerkagi, "The Death of Any Ethnic Group, Be it Nenets, Khanty or Sel'kup, Will Eventually be Reflected in the Health of All Humanity" (in Russian) *Severnye prostory* (1989), n. 1; Vladimir Sangi, "The Land Should Regain Its True Owners" (in Russian) (Sangi 1990), etc.

References Cited

Abramova, Zoia A. 1964. K voprosy ob okhote v verkhnem paleolite [On the Issue of Hunting in the Upper Paleolithic]. *Sovetskaia Arkheologiia* 4:177–80. Moscow.

———. 1966. *Izobrazheniia cheloveka v paleoliticheskom iskusstve Evrazii* [The Image of Man in Eurasian Paleolithic Art]. Moscow-Leningrad: Nauka.

Abramova, Zoia A., and Tatiana Yu.Grechkina. 1985. Ob okhote i okhotnichiem vooruzhenii v pozdnem paleolite Vostochnoi Sibiri [On the Hunting and Hunting Ammunition in the Late Paleolithic of Eastern Siberia]. *Kratkie soobshcheniia Instituta Arkheologii* 181:44–49. Moscow.

Abstracts. 1986. *Abstracts of Technical Papers* series. Juneau: Alaska Department of Fish and Game, Division of Subsistence.

Ackerman, Robert E. 1984. Prehistory of the Asian Eskimo Zone. *Arctic*, D. Damas (ed.), 106–18. *Handbook of North American Indians* 5. Washington, D.C.: Smithsonian Institution.

———. 1988. Settlements and Sea Mammal Hunting in the Bering-Chukchi Sea Region. *Arctic Anthropology* 25(1): 52–79.

Adamenko, V. N. 1963. Opyt izucheniia sushchestvovaniia lednikov Poliarnogo Urala za 260-letnii period po dannym dendrokhronologicheskogo analiza [Study in Existence of the Polar Ural' Mountain Glaciers During the 260-Year Record, According to Dendroclimatic Analysis]. *Gliatsiologicheskie issledovaniia* 9:103–18.

Adamenko, V. N., and N. V. Lovelius. 1976. Anomalii prirosta derev'ev i izmenenia barico-tsirkulyatsionnykh uslovii poslednego tysyacheletiia [Anomalies in Tree-Growth and Changes in the Baro-Circulation Conditions of the Last Millennium]. *Izvestiia Geograficheskogo Obshchestva* 108(4): 290–96.

Adams, C. 1935. The Relation of General Ecology to Human Ecology. *Ecology* 16(3): 316–35.

Agenbroad, Larry D. 1984. New World Mammoth Distribution. In *Quaternary Extinctions: A Prehistoric Revolution*, P. S. Martin and R. G. Klein (eds.), 90–108. Tucson: University of Arizona Press.

Afanas'eva, Galina M. 1979. Nganasanskii rod po documental'nym materialam XVII v. [The Nganasan Clan According to the Documentary Records of the Seventeenth Century]. In *Etnokul'turnye protsessy v sovremennykh i traditsionnykh obshchestvakh*, I. I. Krupnik and G. A. Aksyanova (eds.), 3–15. Moscow: Institute of Ethnography.

———. 1980a. Demograficheskaia kharakteristika avamskikh nganasan po istochnikam XVII–XIX vv. [Demographic Characteristics of the Avam Nganasan According to the Records of the Seventeenth to the Nineteenth Centuries]. *Sovetskaia etnografiia* 2:25–35.

———. 1980b. Etnodemograficheskie osobennosti razvitiia nganasan v XVII–XX vv. (K voprosu o kharaktere formirovaniia obosoblennykh populyatsii severnykh samodiitsev) [Ethnodemographic Features of the Nganasans from the Seventeenth to the Twentieth Centuries (On the Type of Formation of the Isolated Populations of the Northern Samoyedic Peoples)]. Abstract of Ph.D. diss., 24 pp. Moscow: Institute of Ethnography.

Aigner, Jean. 1985. Early Arctic Settlements in North America. *Scientific American* 253(5): 160–69.

Aipin, Yeremei. 1989. Not by Oil Alone. *IWGIA Newsletter* 57:138–43. Copenhagen.

———. 1991. U.S.S.R.: Road of Discord. *IWGIA Newsletter* 1:36–39.

Aivangu. 1985. *Nash rodnoi Ungazik* [Our Native Ungazik]. Magadan: Knizhnoe Izdatel'stvo.

Akimov, Anatolii T., and L. A. Bratsev. 1957. Dinamika severnoi granitsy lesa v pravoi chasti basseina reki Usy [Dynamics of the Northern Tree-Line in the Right-Bank Section of the Usa River Basin]. *Izvestiia Komi filiala Vsesoyuznogo Geograficheskogo Obshchestva* 4:83–91. Syktyvkar.

Aleksandrova, Vera D. 1977. Geobotanicheskoe raionirovanie Arktiki i Antarktiki [The Geobotanical Divisions of the Arctic and Antarctic]. *Komarovskie Chteniia* 29. Leningrad.

Alekseenko, Evgeniia A. 1974. Narodnye znaniia ketov [Folk Knowledge of the Kets]. In *Sotsial'naia organizatsia i kul'tura narodov Severa*, I. S. Gurvich (ed.), 218–30. Moscow: Nauka.

———. 1976. Predstavleniia ketov o mire [The Ket's beliefs on the universe]. In *Priroda i chelovek v religioznykh predstavleniiakh narodov Sibiri i Severa*, I. S. Vdovin (ed.), 67–105. Leningrad: Nauka.

Alekseev, Mikhail P. 1932. *Sibir' v izvestiakh zapanoevropeiskikh puteshestvennikov i pisatelei* [Siberia through the records of Western travelers and writers]. 2 vols., Irkutsk: Irkutskoe obl. izdatel'stvo, vol. 1 (1932), vol. 2 (1936).

Alekseev, Valerii P. 1975. Antropogeotsenozy: sushchnost', tipologiia, dinamika [Anthropogeocenosis: Essence, Typology, Dynamics]. *Priroda* 7:19–23.

Alekseeva, Tatiana I., et al. 1972. Antropologicheskoe izuchenie lesnykh nentsev (morfologiia, fiziologiia i populiatsionnaia genetika) [Anthropological Survey of the Forest Nenets (Morphology, Physiology, and Population Genetics)]. *Voprosy antropologii* 41:19–35. Moscow.

Alia, Valerie. 1991. Aboriginal Perstroika. *Arctic Circle* (Nov.–Dec.): 23–29.

Alland, Alexander, Jr. 1975. Adaptation. *Annual Review of Anthropology* 5:59–73.

Alland, Alexander, Jr., and Bonnie McCay. 1973. The Concept of Adaptation in Biological and Cultural Evolution. In *Handbook of Social and Cultural Anthropology*, J. J. Honigmann (ed.), 143–78. Chicago: Rand McNally.

Amsden, Charles W. 1979. Hard Times: A Case Study from Northern Alaska and Implications for Arctic Prehistory. In *Thule Eskimo Culture: An Anthropological Perspective*, A. P. McCartney (ed.), 395–410. *Archaeological Survey of Canada* 88. Ottawa.

Anadyrskii krai. 1935. Anadyrskii krai [The Anadyr Region]. Manuscript, F.K-II, op.1, no.193. St. Petersburg: Institute-Museum of Anthropology and Ethnography.

Andersen, David B. (comp.). 1984. Regional Subsistence Bibliography. III. Northwest Alaska. *Technical Paper* 94. Anchorage: Alaska Department of Fish and Game, Division of Subsistence.

Anderson, Douglas D. 1981. Ob izmeneniiakh doistoricheskikh modelei zhizneobespecheniia eskimosov: predvaritle'naia razrabotka [On the Changes in Eskimo Prehistoric Subsistence Patterns: A Working Paper]. In *Traditsionnye kul'tury Severnoi Sibiri i Severnoi Ameriki*, I. S. Gurvich (ed.), 67–82. Moscow: Nauka.

———. 1984. Prehistory of North Alaska. In *Arctic*, D. Damas (ed.), 80–93. *Handbook of North American Indians* 5. Washington, D.C.: Smithsonian Institution.

Anderson, Douglas D., et al. 1977. *Kuuvangmiit Subsistence: Traditional Eskimo Life in the Latter Twentieth Century*. Washington, D.C.: U.S. National Park Service.

Anderson, James N. 1973. Ecological Anthropology and Anthropological Ecology. In *Handbook of Social and Cultural Anthropology*, J. J. Honigmann (ed.), 179–239. Chicago: Rand McNally.

Anderson, Rudolph M. 1921. Report on the Natural History Collections of the Expedition. In V. Stefansson, *My Life with the Eskimo*, 436–527. New York: Macmillan.

Andreev, Alexandr I. 1947. Opisaniia o zhizni i uprazhnenii obitaiushchikh v Turukhanskoi i Berezovskoi okrugakh raznogo roda iasachnykh inovertsakh [Description of the Life and Activity of the Various Tribute-Paying Aliens of the Turukhan and Berezovo District]. *Sovetskaia etnografiia* 1:84–103.

Andreev, Vladimir N. 1933. Kormovye resursy olenevodstva v zapadnoi chasti Bol'shezemel'skoi tundry [Grazing Resources for the Reindeer Industry in the Western Part of the Bol'shaia Zemlia Tundra]. *Olen'i pastbishcha Severnogo Kraia* 2:119–84.

———. 1956. Zaselenie tundry lesom v sovremennuyu epokhu [The Forestation of Tundra in Recent Times]. *Rastitel'nost' Krainego Severa SSSR i eye osvoenie* 1:27–45. Moscow.

Andreev, V. N., K. N. Igoshina, and A. I. Leskov. 1935. Olen'i pastbishcha i rastitel'nyi pokrov Poliarnogo Priural'ia [Reindeer Pastures and Vegetation of the Polar Urals]. *Sovetskoe olenevodstvo* 5:171–407.

Andrews, J. T., P. T. Davis, W. H. Mode, N. Nichols, and S. K. Short. 1981. Relative Departures in July Temperature in Northern Canada for the Past 6000 Years. *Nature* 289:164–67.

Andrews, John T., and Gifford H. Miller. 1979. Climatic Change over the last 1000 Years, Baffin Island, N.W.T. In *Thule Eskimo Culture: An Anthropological Perspective*, A. P. McCartney (ed.), 541–556. *Archaeological Survey of Canada* 88. Ottawa.

Andrianov, Boris V. 1985. *Neosedloe naselenie mira (istoriko-etnograficheskoe issledovanie)* [Non-Sedentary Population of the World (A Historical-Ethnografic Study)]. Moscow: Nauka.

Andrianov, Boris V., and Nikolai N. Cheboksarov. 1972. Khozyaistvenno-kul'turnye tipy i problemy ikh kartogragirovaniia [The Economic-Cultural Types and Some Issues in Their Cartography]. *Sovetskaia etnografiia* 2:3–16.

Angliiskie puteshestvenniki. 1938. *Angliiskie puteshestvenniki v Moscovskom gosudarstve v XVI veke* [British Travelers in Moscovia during the Sixteenth Century. Translation of Records]. Leningrad.

The Arctic. 1991. *The Arctic. IWGIA Yearbook* 1990, 37–45. Copenhagen.

Arctic Environment. 1991. *Arctic Environment: Indigenous Perspectives. IWGIA Document* 69:3–46.

An Arctic Obligation. 1992. Report of the U.S. Arctic Research Commission to the President and the Congress of the United States of America (October 1990–September 1991). Washington, D.C.: U.S. Arctic Research Commission.

Argentov, Andrei. 1850. Pervaia narodnaia perepis' chukchei naseliaiushchikh Chavanskii krai [The First Population Census of the Chukchis Peopling the Chaun Area]. Manuscript, F.64, op.1, no.32. Archive of the Russian Geographic Society, St. Petersburg.

Arkhincheev, Il'ia S. 1957. Materialy dlia kharakteristiki sotsial'nykh otnoshenii chukchei v sviazi s sotsialisticheskoi rekonstruktsiei khoziaistva [Data Describing the Social Relationships among the Chukchis with Regard to the Socialist Reconstruction of the Economy]. *Trudy Instituta etnografii* 35:38–98.

Armand, David L. 1947. Osnovy metoda balansov v fizicheskoi geografii [Principles of the Balance Approach in Physical Geography]. *Izvestiia Vsesoiuznogo Geograficheskogo Obshchestva* 79(6): 629–46.

Arsen'ev, Vladimir K. 1927. *Tikhookeanskii morzh* [Pacific Walrus]. Khabarovsk and Vladivostok: Knizhnoe Delo.

Arteev, G. I. 1926. Kochev'e olenevodov severo-zapadnoi chasti Obdorskogo raiona [Nomadic Patterns of the Reindeer Herders in Northwest Section of the Obdorsk District]. *Ural* 8 (Pt.1, Ural'skii Sever): 141–45. Sverdlovsk.

Arutiunov, Sergei A. 1975. Rol' sredy v formirovanii variatsii drevneeskimosskoi kul'tury [Role of the Environment in Ancient Eskimo Cultural Variability]. In *Karta, skhema i chislo v etnicheskoi geografii*, M. A. Chlenov (ed.), 22–26. Moscow: Geograficheskoe Obshchestvo.

———. 1982a. Problemy primorskoi adaptatsii v Beringomorskom regione [Issues in Maritime Adaptation in the Bering Sea Region]. In *Paleometall severo-zapadnoi chasti Tikhogo okeana*, A. V. Aleksandrov, S. A. Arutiunov, and D. L. Brodianskii (eds.), 78–97. Vladivostok: Izdatel'stvo DVGU.

———. 1982b. Etnicheskie obshcnosti doklassovoi epokhi [Ethnic Entities of the Pre-Class Age]. In *Etnos v doklassovom i ranneklassovom obshchestve*, A. I. Pershits (ed.), 55–82. Moscow: Nauka.

———. 1989. *Narody i kul'tury. Razvitie i vzaimodeistvie* [Peoples and Cultures. Evolution and Interaction]. Moscow: Nauka.

Arutiunov, Sergei A., Igor I. Krupnik, and Michail A. Chlenov. 1979. Kitovaia alleia—drevneeskimosskii kul'tovyi pamiatnik na ostrove Ittygran ["Whale Alley"—Ancient Eskimo Memorial on the Ittygran Island]. *Sovetskaia etnografiia* 4:12–28.

———. 1981. Istoricheskie zakonomernosti i prirodnaia sreda (na primere pamiatnikov drevneeskimosskoi kul'tury) [Historical Rules and Natural Environment (As Seen from the Example of Ancient Eskimo Cultural Monuments)]. *Vestnik Akademii Nauk SSSR* 2:91–102. Moscow.

———. 1982. *Kitovaya alleia. Drevnosti ostrovov proliva Seniavina* [Whale Alley. Antiquities of the Senyavin Strait Islands]. Moscow: Nauka.

Arutiunov, Sergei A., Eduard S. Markarian, and Yuri I. Mkrtumian. 1983. *Kul'tura zhizneobespechenia i etnos. Opyt etnokul'turologicheskogo issledovania (na materialakh armianskoi sel'skoi kul'tury)* [Subsistence Culture and Ethnos. An Attempt at Ethnocultural Study (on the Database of the Armenian Peasant Culture)]. Erevan: Armenian Academy of Sciences.

Arutiunov, Sergei A., and Yuri I. Mkrtumian. 1985. Problemy tipologicheskogo isledovaniia mekhanizmov zhizneobespecheniia v etnicheskoi kul'ture [On the Typological Study of the Subsistence Mechanisms in an Ethnic Culture]. In *Tipologiia osnovnykh elementov traditsionnoi kul'tury*, 19–33. Moscow: Nauka.

Arutiunov, Sergei A., and Dorian A. Sergeev. 1969. *Drevnie kul'tury aziatskikh eskimosov (Uelenskii mogil'nik)* [Ancient Cultures of the Asiatic Eskimos (The Uelen Cemetery)]. Moscow: Nauka.

———. 1975. *Problemy etnicheskoi istorii Beringomor'ia (Ekvenskii mogil'nik)* [Questions in Ethnic History of the Bering Sea Area (The Ekven Cemetery)]. Moscow: Nauka.

Astrinskii, D. A., and S. M. Navasardov. 1970. O structure potrebleniia productov pitaniia korennym naseleniem Chukotskogo natisonal'nogo okruga [On the Structure of Food Consumption by the Natives of the Chukchi National Area]. *Problemy Severa* 14:204–208. Moscow.

Atlas. 1964. *Atlas Geograficheskikh Otkrytii v Sibiri i v Severo-Zapadnoi Amerike* [Atlas of the Geographic Discoveries in Siberia and Northwest America. Seventeenth and Eighteenth Centuries]. A. V. Efimov, M. I. Belov, and O. M. Medushevskaya (comps.). Moscow: Nauka.

Averbukh, Mikhail S. 1967. *Zakony narodonaseleniia dokapitalisticheskikh formatsii* [Population Demography Laws of the Precapitalistic Stages]. Moscow: Nauka.

Babushkin, A. I. 1926. Tundrovoe khoziaistvo (olenevodstvo) [The Tundra Economy (Reindeer Herding)]. In *Komi oblast'. Ekonomicheskii obzor*, Pt.1, 134–49. Ust'Sysol'sk.

———. 1930. *Bol'shezemel'skaia tundra* [Bolshaia Zemlia Tundra]. Syktyvkar: Komi Oblstatotdel.

Bader, Otto N. 1977. Paleoekologiia i liudi stoyanki Sungir' [Paleoecology and People of the Sungir' Site]. In *Paleoekologiia drevnego cheloveka*, I. K. Ivanova and N. D. Praslov (eds.), 31–40. Moscow: Nauka.

———. 1978. *Sungir'. Verkhnepaleoliticheskaia stoyanka* [Sungir'. An Upper Paleolithic Site]. Moscow: Nauka.

Bakhrushin, Sergei V. 1925. Samoedy v XVII veke [The Samoyeds during the Seventeenth Century]. *Severnaia Aziia* 5–6:85–94. Reprinted in: S. V. Bakhrushin, *Izbrannye trudy* [Selected Papers], vol. 1. Moscow: Academy of Sciences, 1956.

Bakshtanovskii, Vladimir I. (ed.). 1988. *Samotlorskii practicum—2* [Samotlor Workshop—2: Humanitarian Aspects of the Industrial Development of the Tyumen' Oil Region]. Tyumen': Institute of the Problems of the North.

———. 1989. *Osvoenie bez otchuzhdeniia* [Settling without Estrangement: Humanitarian Aspects of the Industrial Development in the Tyumen' Oil Region]. Tyumen': Institute of the Problems of the North.

———. 1990. *Arkticheskaia politika: chelovecheskoe izmereniie* [Arctic Politics: The Human Dimension]. Tyumen': Institute of the Problems of the North.

———. 1991. *Yamal'skii konflict: gumanitarnaia expertiza* [The Yamal Confrontation: A Humanitarian Expertise]. Tyumen': Institute of the Problems of the North.

Balikci, Asen. 1967. Female Infanticide on the Arctic Coast. *Man* n.s. 2(4): 615–25.

Bandi, Hans-Georg. 1969. *Eskimo Prehistory*. College: University of Alaska Press.

———. 1976. Arkheologiia ostrova Sviatogo Lavreniia, Aliaska [The Archaeology of St. Lawrence Island, Alaska]. In *Beringiia v kainozoe*, V. L. Kontrimavichus (ed.), 485–91. Vladivostok: U.S.S.R. Academy of Sciences.

Banfield, Alexander W. F. 1975. Are Arctic Ecosystems Really Fragile? In

Proceedings of the 1st Reindeer and Caribou Symposium, J. Luick et al. (eds.), 545–51. Fairbanks: University of Alaska.

Bank, Theodore P., II. 1952. Botanical and Ethnobotanical Studies in the Aleutian Islands, I: Aleutian Vegetation and Aleut Culture. *Papers of the Michigan Academy of Science, Arts, and Letters* 37:13–30. Ann Arbor.

Barry, R. G., W. H. Arundale, J. T. Andrews, R. S. Bradley, and H. Nichols. 1977. Environmental Change and Cultural Change in the Eastern Canadian Arctic During the Last 5000 Years. *Arctic and Alpine Research* 9(2): 193–210.

Beach, Hugh. 1981. Reindeer Herd Management in Transition: The Case of Tuorpon Saameby in Northern Sweden. *Uppsala Studies in Cultural Anthropology* 3. Stockholm.

Beliavskii, F. 1825. *Poezdka k Ledovitomy moriu* [Trip Toward the Polar Sea]. Moscow.

Belikov, Sergei M. 1927. Zametki o Chukotke [Sketches about Chukotka]. *Ekonomicheskaia zhizn' Dal'nego Vostoka* 9:115–25.

Belov, Mikail I. 1956. *Arkticheskoe moreplavanie s drevneishikh vremyon do serediny XIX veka* [Arctic Navigation from Ancient Times until the mid-1800s]. Moscow: Morskoi Transport.

Belykh, V. I., and G. K. Konechnykh. 1976. O dinamike chislennosti borovoi dichi v Yakutii [On the Population Dynamics of the Grouse Species in Yakutiia]. In *Biologicheskie osnovy i opyt prognozirovaniia izmenenii chislennosti okhotnich'ikh zhivotnykh*, 46–47. Kirov.

Bennett, John W. 1946. An Interpretation of the Scope and Implications of Social Scientific Research in Human Subsistence. *American Anthropologist* 48 (4, pt. 1): 553–73.

———. 1969. *Northern Plainsmen: Adaptive Strategy and Agrarian Life*. Chicago: Aldine.

Berg, Lev S. 1938. *Osnovy klimatologii* [The Fundamentals of Climatology]. Leningrad: Uchpedgiz.

———. 1943. Uroven' Kaspiiskogo moria i usloviia plavaniia v Arktike [The Level of the Caspian Sea and Navigation Conditions in the Arctic]. *Izvestiia Vsesoyuznogo Geograficheskogo Obshchestva* 75(4): 16–20.

———. 1956a. Drevneishie svedeniia o Krainem Severe Sibiri [The Most Ancient Records on the Siberian Far North]. In L. S. Berg. *Selected Works* 1:211–19. Moscow: Academy of Sciences.

———. 1956b. Lomonosov i pervoe russkoe plavanie dlya otyskaniia severo-vostochnogo prokhoda [Lomonosov and the First Russian Voyage in Search for the North-East Passage]. In Ibid.

———. 1958. Nedavnee izmenenie klimata v storony potepleniia [Recent Warming Climatic Trend]. In Ibid. 2:146–59.

Bergerud, A. T. 1974. Decline of Caribou in North America Following Settlement. *Journal of Wildlife Management* 38(4): 757–70.

———. 1980. A Review of the Population Dynamics of Caribou and Wild Reindeer in North America. In *Proceedings of the Second Reindeer and Caribou Symposium*, E. Reimers et al. (eds.), 556–81. Trondheim.

Bergerud, A. T., R. D. Jakimchuk, and D. R. Carruthers. 1984. The Buffalo of the North: Caribou (*Rangifer tarandus*) and Human Developments. *Arctic* 37(1): 7–22.

Betin, V. V. and Yu. V. Preobrazhenskii. 1962. *Surovost' zim v Evrope i ledovitost' Baltiki* [Severity of Winters in Europe and Ice Conditions of the Baltic Sea]. Leningrad: Gidrometeoizdat.

Bettinger, Robert L. 1980. Explanatory/Predictive Models of Hunter-Gatherer Adaptation. In *Advances in Archaeological Method and Theory* M. B. Schiffer (ed.), 3:189–255. New York: Academic Press.

Bezumov, K. Ia. 1960. *Promysel morskogo zveria* [Sea-Mammal Harvesting]. Magadan: Knizhnoe Izdatel'stvo.

Bianki, V. V., T. D. Gerasimova, and V. N. Karpovich. 1967. Sovremennoe sostoianie gnezdovii obyknovennoi gagi na Evropeiskom Severe [Recent Status of Nesting Areas of the Arctic Eider over the European North (of Russia)]. *Problemy Severa* 11: 218–23.

Bibikov, Sergei N. 1969. Nekotorye aspecty paleoekonomicheskogo modelirovaniia paleolita [Some Aspects of Paleoeconomic Modeling of the Paleolithic]. *Sovetskaia arkheologiia* 4:5–22.

———. 1981. *Drevneishii muzykal'nyi kompleks iz kostei mamonta. Ocherk material'noi i dukhovnoi kul'tury paleoliticheskogo cheloveka* [A Very Ancient Musical Complex of Mammoth Bones: Essay in Material and Spiritual Culture of the Paleolithic Man]. Kiev: Naukova Dumka.

Bilibin, N. N. 1933. Batratskii trud v kochevom khoziaistve koriakov [Farm Laborers' Work in the Koryak Reindeer Economy]. *Sovetskii Sever* 1:36–46.

Binford, Lewis R. 1978. *Nunamiut Ethnoarchaeology*. New York: Academic Press.

———. 1980. Willow Smoke and Dog's Tail: Hunter-Gatherer Settlement System and Archaeological Site Formation. *American Antiquity* 45(1): 4–20.

Binford, Lewis R., and W. J. Chasko, Jr. 1976. Nunamiut Demographic History: A Provocative case. In *Demographic Anthropology. Quantitative Approach*, E. Zubrow (ed.), 63–143. Albuquerque: University of New Mexico Press.

Birdsell, Joseph B. 1953. Some Environmental and Cultural Factors Influencing the Structuring of Australian Aboriginal Populations. *American Naturalist* 87(834): 171–207.

———. 1958. On Population Structure in Generalized Hunting and Collecting Populations. *Evolution* 12(2): 189–205.

———. 1968. Some Predictions for the Pleistocene Based on Equilibrium Systems among Recent Hunter-Gatherers. In *Man the Hunter*, R. B. Lee and I. DeVore (eds.), 229–40. Chicago: Aldine.

Birket-Smith, Kaj. 1929. The Caribou Eskimos: Material and Social Life and Their Cultural Position. *Report of the 5th Thule Expedition (1921–1924)* 5(1–2). Copenhagen.

———. 1936. *The Eskimos*. London: Methuen

Bishop, R. H., and R. A. Rausch. 1974. Moose Population Fluctuations in Alaska, 1950–1972. *Natuarlist Canadien* 101(3–4): 559–93.

Bockstoce, John R. 1973. A Prehistoric Population Change in the Bering Strait Region. *Polar Record* 16(105): 793–803.

———. 1976. On the Development of Whaling in the Western Thule Culture. *Folk* 18:40–46.

———. 1979. *The Archaeology of Cape Nome, Alaska. University Museum Monograph* 38. Philadelphia: University of Pennsylvania.

Bockstoce, John R., and Daniel B. Botkin. 1980. *The Harvest of the Pacific Walrus by the Pelagic Whaling Industry, 1848–1914.*

———. 1983. *The Historical Status and Reduction of the Western Arctic Bowhead Whale* (Balaena mysticetus) *Population by the Pelagic Whaling Industry, 1848–1914. Report of the International Whaling Commission, Special Issue* 5:107–41.

Bogolepov, Mikhail A. 1908. Kolebaniia klimata v Zapadnoi Evrope s 1000 po 1500 gg. [Climatic Fluctuations in Western Europe, A.D. 1000–1500]. *Zemlevedenie* 2:41–58.

———. 1921. *Nastupayushchie vozmushcheniia klimata* [The Up-Coming Climatic Disturbances]. Moscow: Novaia Derevnia.

———. 1928. *Periodocheskie vozmushchenia klimata* [The Periodic Climatic Disturbances]. Moscow: Novaia Derevnia.

Bogoras, Waldemar G. (a.k.a.) Bogoraz-Tan, Vladimir G.) 1901. Dnevnik 1901 g. vo vremia puteshestviia i prebyvaniia v Unyine [Diary of the Year of 1901 During Trip and Stay at Unuin]. Manuscript, F.250, op.1, no.116. Archive of the Russian Academy of Sciences, St. Petersburg.

———. 1904. The Chukchee: Material Culture. *Memoirs of the American Museum of Natural History. The Jesup North Pacific Expedition*, vol. 7, pt. 1(1). Reprinted in 1975 by AMS Press.

———. 1907. The Chukchee: Religion. Ibid., vol. 7, pt. 2.

———. 1925. K voprosu o priroste severosibirskikh tuzemnykh plemyon (po povodu stat'i Mikh. Plotnikova) [On the Growth of the North Siberian Native Tribes (with Regard to the Paper by Mikh. Plotnikov)]. *Severnaia Aziia* 4:27–29.

———. 1929. Elements of the Culture of the Circumpolar Zone. *American Anthropologist* 31(4): 579–601.

———. 1930. New Data on the Type and Distribution of Reindeer Breeding in Northern Eurasia. In *Proceedings of the 23rd International Congress of Americanists*, 403–10. New York.

———. 1931. Klassovoe rassloenie u chukoch olenevodov [Class Stratification among the Reindeer Chukchi]. *Sovetskaia etnografiia* 1–2:93–116.

———. 1932. Severnoe olenevodstvo po dannym khoziaistvennoi perepisi 1926–1927 g. [Northern Reindeer Industry according to the Data of the Economic Census of 1926–1927]. *Sovetskaia Etnografiia* 4:26–62.

———. 1933. Olenevodstvo. Vozniknovenie, razvitie i perspektivy [Reindeer Herding: Its Origin, Development, and Prospects]. *Trudy Laboratorii Genetiki* 1:219–51. Leningrad: Academy of Sciences.

———. 1934. Yuitskii (aziatsko-eskimosskii yazyk) [The Yuit (Asiatic

Eskimo) Language]. In *Yazyki i pis'mennost' narodov Severa* 3:105–28. Moscow-Leningrad.

———. 1941. Ocherki kul'tury narodov Severa [Essays in the Cultures of the Northern Peoples]. Unpublished Manucript, F. K-1, Op.1. Archive of the Institute-Museum of Anthropology and Ethnography, St. Petersburg.

Bogoslovskaia, Liudmila S. 1990. Mezhdunarodnyi park v Beringii [International Park in Beringia Area]. *Poliarnik* (Provideniia) 94:3.

Bogoslovskaia, Liudmila S. (ed.). 1991. Problemy ekologii poliarnykh oblastei [Issues in Ecology of the Polar Areas]. vol. 2. Moscow: Nauka.

Bogoslovskaia, Liudmila S., and Leonard M. Votrogov. 1982. Gruppirovki serykh kitov na mestakh letne-osennego nagula [Groupings of the Gray Whales on Summer-Fall Feeding Grounds]. In *Izuchenie, Okhrana i Ratsional'noe Ispol'zovanie Morskikh Mlekopitaiushchikh*. V. A. Zemski (ed.), 36–37. Astrakhan': KaspNIRO.

Bogoslovskaia, Liudmila S., Leonard M. Votrogov, and Igor I. Krupnik. 1982. The Bowhead Whale off Chukotka: Migrations and Aboriginal Whaling. *Report of the International Whaling Commission* 32:391–99.

Bogoslovskaia, Liudmila, and Igor Krupnik (comps.). 1987. O promysle morzveroboinom [On Sea-Mammal Hunting]. *Severnye prostory* 1:5–9. Moscow.

Borisenkov, E. P., and V. M. Pasetskii. 1983. *Extremal'nye prirodnye iavleniia v russkikh letopisiakh XI–XVII vv.* [Extremal Natural Phenomena as Revealed from the Russian Chronicles of the Eleventh to Seventeenth Centuries]. Leningrad: Gidrometeoizdat.

Boriskovskii, Pavel I. 1953. Paleolit Ukrainy [The Paleolithic of Ukraine]. *Materialy i issledovanniia po arkheologii SSSR* 40. Moscow-Leningrad: Izdatel'stvo AN SSSR.

———. 1963. Ocherki po paleolitu basseina Dona [Essays in the Paleolithic of the River Don Basin]. *Materialy i issledovanniia po arkheologii SSSR* 121. Moscow-Leningrad: Izdatel'stvo AN SSSR.

———. 1979. *Drevneishee proshloe chelovechestva* [The Most Ancient Past of Mankind]. Leningrad: Nauka.

Boriskovskii, Pavel I. (ed.). 1984. *Paleolit SSSR* [The Palaeolithic of the USSR]. Moscow: Nauka.

Bottino, Robert. 1987. Peopling of the Arctic: A Computer Simulation. *Arctic* 40(2): 111–22.

Boughey, Arthur. 1971. *Man and the Environment: An Introduction to Human Ecology and Evolution*. New York: Macmillan.

———. 1973. *Ecology of Populations*. New York: Macmillan.

Braat, J. 1984. Dutch Activities in the North and the Arctic during the Sixteenth and Seventeenth Centuries. *Arctic* 37(4): 473–80.

Bradley, R. S. 1973. Seasonal Climatic Fluctuations on Baffin Island during the Period of Instrumental Records. *Arctic* 26(3): 230–43.

Braerstrup, Fritz W. 1941. A Study on the Arctic Fox in Greenland. Immigrations, Fluctuations in Numbers Based Mainly on Trading Statistics. *Meddelelser om Grønland* 131(4): 1–102.

Braham, Howard W. 1984. The Bowhead Whale, *Balaena mysticetus*. *Marine Fisheries Review* 46(4): 45–53.

Braund, Stephen R., Sam W. Stoker, and John A. Kruse. 1988. *Quantification of Subsistence and Cultural Need for Bowhead Whales by Alaskan Eskimo*. Special Report submitted to the International Whaling Commission, IWC TC/40/AS2. Anchorage.

Braund, Stephen R., William E. Simeone, and Lisa Moorehead. 1991. *Subsistence and Cultural Need for Bowhead Whales by the Village of Little Diomede, Alaska*. Special Report prepared for the Alaska Eskimo Whaling Commission. Anchorage.

Breiwick, J. M., L. L. Eberhardt, and H. W. Braham. 1984. Population Dynamics of Western Arctic Bowhead Whales (*Balaena mysticetus*). *Canadian Journal of Fisheries and Aquatic Sciences* 41(3): 484–96.

Brice-Bennett, Carol (ed.). 1977. *Our Footprints Are Everywhere*. Nain: Labrador Inuit.

Briffa, K. R., P. D. Jones, J. R. Pilcher, and M. K. Hughes. 1988. Reconstructing Summer Temperatures in Northern Fennoscandia Back to A.D. 1700 Using Tree-Ring Data from Scots Pine. *Arctic and Alpine Research* 20(4): 385–94.

Briffa, K. R., T. S. Bartholin, D. Eckstein, P. D. Jones, W. Karlen, F. H. Schweingruber, and P. Zettenberg. 1990. A 1,400-Year Tree-Ring Record of Summer Temperature in Fennoscandia. *Nature* 346:434–39.

Brodnev, Mikhail M. 1959. Iz istorii zemel'nykh i imushchestvennykh otnoshenii u iamal'skikh nentsev [On the History of Pasture-Ownership and Property Relations among the Yamal Nenets]. *Sovetskaia etnografiia* 6:69–79.

Bronstein, Mikhail M. 1986. Tipologicheskie varianty drevneeskimosskogo graficheskogo ornamenta (K probleme etnokul'turnoi istorii Beringomor'ia) [Typological Variations of the Ancient Eskimo Ornamental Styles (On the Question of Ethnocultural History in the Bering Sea Area, 1000 B.C.–1000 A.D.)]. *Sovetskaia etnografiia* 6:46–57.

Brown, Thomas C., and Ernest S. Burch, Jr. 1992. Estimating the Economic Value of Subsistence Harvest of Wildlife in Alaska. In *Valuing Wildlife Resources in Alaska*, G. Peterson, C. S. Swanson, D. W. McCollum, and M. H. Thomas (eds.), 203–54. Boulder: Westview Press.

Brush, Stephen B. 1975. The Concept of Carrying Capacity for Systems of Shifting Cultivation. *American Anthropologist* 77(4): 799–811.

Bryson, Reid A., and W. M. Wendland. 1967. Tentative Climatic Patterns for Some Late Glacial and Post-Glacial Episodes in Central North America. In *Life, Land, and Water*, W. J. Mayer-Oakes (ed.), 271–98. Winnipeg.

Budagian, Fyodor E. (ed.). 1961. *Tablitsy khimicheskogo sostava i pitatel'noi tsennosti pishchevykh produktov* [Tables to Estimate Chemical Composition and Caloric Value of Various Food Items]. Moscow: Medgiz.

Budyko, Mikhail I. 1967. O prichinakh vymiraniia nekotorykh zhivotnykh v kontse pleistotsena [On the Causes of Extinction of Some Animals at the End of the Pleistocene]. *Izvestiia Akademii Nauk SSSR (Seriia Geographicheskaia)* 4:28–36.

———. 1974. *Izmeneniia klimata* [The Climate Change]. Leningrad: Gidrometeoizdat.

———. 1977. *Global'naia ekologiia* [Global Ecology]. Moscow: Mysl'.

Bunak, Victor V. 1980. *Rod* Homo, *ego vozniknovenie i posleduiushchaia evolutsiia* [The Genus of *Homo*: Its Origin and Further Evolution]. Moscow: Nauka.

Bunakov, E. V. 1936. Nenetskii natsionalnyi okrug Severnogo kraia [Nenets National Area of the Northern Province]. *Trudy Poliarnoi Komissii AN SSSR* 29. Moscow.

Burch, Ernest S., Jr. 1972. The Caribou/Wild Reindeer as a Human Resource. *American Antiquity* 37(3): 339–68.

———. 1975. *Eskimo Kinsmen: Changing Family Relationships in Northwest Alaska. Monographs of the American Ethnological Society* 59. St. Paul: West Publishing Company.

———. 1977. Muskox and Man in the Central Canadian Subarctic, 1689–1974. *Arctic* 30(3):135–54.

———. 1978. Caribou Eskimo Origins: An Old Problem Reconsidered. *Arctic Anthropology* 15(1): 1–35.

———. 1979. The Ethnography of Northern North America: A Guide to Recent Research. *Arctic Anthropology* 16(1): 62–146.

———. 1980. Traditional Eskimo Societies in Northwest Alaska. In *Alaska Native Culture and History*, Y. Kotani and W. B. Workman (eds.), 253–304. *Senri Ethnological Studies* 4. Osaka.

———. 1981. *The Traditional Eskimo Hunters of Point Hope, Alaska: 1800–1875*. Barrow: North Slope Borough.

———. 1983. *Peoples of the Arctic*. Illustrative Map. Washington, D.C.: National Geographic Society.

———. 1985. *Subsistence Production in Kivalina, Alaska: A Twenty-Year Perspective. Technical Paper* 128. Alaska Department of Fish and Game, Division of Subsistence.

———. 1991a. Herd Following Reconsidered. *Current Anthropology* 32(4): 439–45

———. 1991b. Rationality and Resource Use among the Hunters. Paper presented to the International Conference on Religion and Ecology in Northern Eurasia and North America. University of Hokkaido, Sapporo.

Burgess, Stephen M. 1974. The St. Lawrence Islanders of Northwest Cape: Patterns of Resource Utilization. Unpublished Ph.D. Diss., University of Alaska, Fairbanks. Ann Arbor: University Microfilms.

Burke, A. 1936. O periodichnosti v ledovom rezhime [On the Periodism in the Sea-Ice Regime]. *Sovetskaia Arktika* 5:86–88.

Burns, John J. 1984. Living Resources. In *United States Arctic Interests: The 1980s and 1990s*. W. W. Westermeyer and K. M. Shutsterich (eds.), 75–104. New York, etc.: Springer-Verlag.

Buturlin, Sergei A. 1907. *Otchyot upolnomochennogo Ministerstva vnu-*

trennikh del po snabzheniiu prodovol'stviem v 1905 g. Kolymskogo i Okhotskogo kraia [Report of the Special Officer Sent by the Department of Interior to Supervise the Food Supply to the Kolyma and Okhotsk Areas in the Year of 1905]. St. Petersburg.

———. 1928. Nekotorye soobrazheniia o edinom tsennostnom vyrazhenii severnogo khoziaistva [Some Considerations on the Universal Price Equivalent in the Northern Economy]. *Severnaia Aziia* 2:46–52.

Butzer, Karl W. 1964. *Environment and Archaeology*. Chicago: Aldine.

Byard, Pamela Joy. 1981. Population History, Demography, and Genetics of the St. Lawrence Island Eskimos. Unpublished Ph.D. diss., University of Kansas. Ann Arbor: University Microfilms.

Campbell, John M. (ed.). 1962. Prehistoric Cultural Relations between the Arctic and Temperate Zones of North America. *Arctic Institute of North America. Technical Papers* 11.

Campbell, John M. 1968. Territoriality among Ancient Hunters: Interpretations from Ethnography and Nature. In: *Anthropological Archeology in the Americas*, B. Meggers (ed.), 1–21. Washington, D.C.: Anthropological Society of Washington.

———. 1978. Aboriginal Human Overkill of Game Populations: Examples from Interior Northern Alaska. In *Archaeological Essays in Honor of Irving B. Rouse*, R. Dunnel and E. S. Hall (eds.), 179–208. The Hague: Mouton.

Cargill, Jody. 1990. Analysis of Mammal Faunal Remains. In *The 1981 Excavations at the Utqiagvik Archaeological Site, Barrow, Alaska.* E. S. Hall, Jr., and L. Fullerton (eds.), 1:263–79. Barrow: North Slope Borough.

Carr-Saunders, Alexandr M. 1922. *The Population Problem. A Study in Human Evolution*. Oxford: Oxford University Press.

Cashdan, Elizabeth. 1983. Territoriality among Human Foragers: Ecological Models and an Application to Four Bushman Groups. *Current Anthropology* 24(1): 47–55.

Casteel, R. W. 1972. Two Static Maximum Population Density Models for Hunter-Gatherers: A First Approximation. *World Archaeology* 4(1): 19–40.

Chapskii, K. K. 1939. Kratkii istoricheskii analiz sovremennogo sostoianiia zapasov morzha v Barentsevom i Karskom moriakh [A Brief Historical Analysis of the Recent Status of Walrus Resources in the Barents and Kara seas]. *Problemy Arktiki* 3:62–69. Leningrad.

Charnolusskii, V. V. 1930. *Materialy po bytu loparei. Opyt opredeleniia kochevogo sostoianiia loparei vostochnoi chasti Kol'skogo poluostrova* [Data on the Daily Life of the Lapps: An Attempt to Estimate the State of Nomadism among the Lapps of the Eastern Kola Peninsula]. Leningrad: Russkoe Geograficheskoe Obshchestvo.

Chernetsov, Valerii N. 1935. Drevniaia primorskaia kul'tura na poluostrove Iamal [Ancient Maritime Culture on the Yamal Peninsula]. *Sovetskaia etnografiia* 4–5:109–133.

———. 1953. Ust'-Poluiskoe vremia v Priob'e [The Ust-Polui Period in the

Ob Region]. *Materialy i issledovaniia po arkheologii SSSR* 35:221–41. Moscow. Reprinted in V. N. Chernetsov and W. Moszynska, *Prehistory of Western Siberia*, 113–38. Montreal and London: Arctic Institute of North America.

Chernov, Georgii A. 1951. Stoianki drevnego cheloveka v severnoi chasti Bol'shezemel'skoi tundry [Sites of Prehistoric Man in the Northern Part of the Bol'shaia Zemlia Tundra]. *Kratkie soobshcheniia Instituta istorii material'noi kul'tury* 36:96–114.

Chesemore, D. L. 1968. Occurrence of Moose near Barrow, Alaska. *Journal of Mammology* 49(3): 528–29.

Chesnov, Yan V. 1970. O sotsial'no-ekonomicheskikh i prirodnykh usloviiakh vozniknoveniia khoziaistvenno-kul'turnykh tipov (V sviazi s rabotami M. Levina) [On Socioeconomic and Environmental Grounds in the Development of Economic-Cultural Types (In Connection with M. Levin's Publications)]. *Sovetskaia etnografiia* 6:15–26.

Chirkova, A. F. 1967. K voprosu o vzaimootnosheniiakh pestsa i lisitsy na Krainem Severe [On the Relationships Between Arctic and Red Fox in the Polar North]. *Problemy Severa* 11:111–13.

Chitty, Helen. 1950. Canadian Arctic Wildlife Enquiry 1943–1949, with a Summary of Results since 1933. *Journal of Animal Ecology* 19(1): 180–93.

Chizhevskii, Aleksei L. 1973. *Zemnoe ekho solnechnykh bur'* [The Earth's Echo of the Sun's Storms]. Moscow: Mysl'.

Chizhov, Oleg P. 1976. *Oledenenie severnoi poliarnoi oblasti* [Glaciation of the Northern Polar Area]. Moscow: Nauka.

Chlenov, Michael. 1973. Distinctive Features of the Social Organization of the Asiatic Eskimos. Paper Prepared for Distribution in Advance at the Ninth International Congress of Ethnological and Anthropological Sciences. Chicago-Moscow.

Chlenov, Mikhail A., and Igor I. Krupnik. 1983. Dinamika areala aziatskikh eskimosov v XVIII–XIX vv. [Dynamics of the Asiatic Eskimo Area during the 1700s and 1800s]. In *Areal'nye issledovaniia v yazykoznanii i etnografii*. 129–39. Leningrad: Nauka.

———. 1984. Whale Alley. A Site on the Chukchi Peninsula, Siberia. *Expedition* 26(2): 6–15.

Clark, J. G. D. 1953. *Doistoricheskaia Evropa. Ekonomicheskii ocherk* [Prehistoric Europe: An Economic Survey]. Moscow: Inostrannaia Literatura.

Clarke, Janet T., Sue E. Moore, and Donald K. Ljungblad. 1987. Observations of Bowhead Whale (*Balaena mysticetus*) Calves in the Alaskan Beaufort Sea during the Autumn Migration, 1982–1985. *Report of the International Whaling Commission* 37:287–93.

Coale, Ansley. 1974. The History of the Human Population. *Scientific American* 231(3): 41–51.

Cohen, Mark N. 1981. Pacific Coast Foragers: Affluent or Overcrowded? In *Affluent Foragers: Pacific Coast East and West*, Sh. Koyama and D. Thomas (eds.), 275–95. *Senri Ethnological Studies* 9. Osaka.

Collins, Grenold. 1940. Habits of the Pacific Walrus (Odobenus divegens). *Journal of Mammology* 21:138–44.
Convention. 1991. Convention of the 26. *IWGIA Newsletter* 2:17–18.
Cowgill, George L. 1975. On Causes and Consequences of Ancient and Modern Population Change. *American Anthropologist* 77(3): 505–25.
Cropper, John P. 1982. Climate Reconstructions (1801 to 1938) Inferred from Tree-Ring Width Chronologies of the North American Arctic. *Arctic and Alpine Research* 14(3): 223–41.
Damas, David. 1969. Environment, History, and Central Eskimo Society. In *Contributions to Anthropology. Ecological Essays*, D. Damas (ed.), 40–64. *National Museum of Canada Bulletin* 230. Ottawa.
———. 1984. Introduction. In *Arctic*, D. Damas (ed.), 1–7. *Handbook of North American Indians* 5. Washington, D.C.: Smithsonian Institution.
Danishevskii, G. M. 1968. *Patologiia cheloveka i profilaktika zabolevanii na Severe* [Human Pathology and Disease Prophylaxis in the North]. Moscow: Meditsina.
David, N. 1973. On Upper Palaeolithic Society, Ecology and Technological Change: The Noaillian Case. In *The Explanation of Cultural Change*, C. Renfrew (ed.), 277–303. London: Duckworth.
Davydov, A. F. 1960. O fiziologicheskikh prisposobleniiakh i povedenii severnykh olenei pri teplovom vozdeistvii vneshnei sredy [On the Physiological Adaptation of Reindeer under the Heat Stress of the Environment]. In *Reguliatsiia obmena tepla i drugikh fisiologicheskikh funktsii u sel'skokhozyaistvennykh zhivotnykh v usloviiakh vysokikh temperatur*, 71–74. Krasnodar.
Debets, Georgii F. 1975. Paleoantropologicheskie materialy iz drevene-beringomorskikh mogil'nikov Uelen i Ekven [Paleoanthropological Data from the Old Bering Sea Eskimo Cemeteries at Uelen and Ekven]. In S. A. Arutiunov and D. A. Sergeev, *Problemy etnicheskoi istorii Beringomor'ia: Ekvenskii mogil'nik*, 198–240. Moscow: Nauka.
Deevey, Edward S., Jr. 1960. The Human Population. *Scientific American* 203(3): 194–203.
Dekin, Albert A., Jr. 1972. Climatic Change and Cultural Change: A Correlative Study from Eastern Arctic Prehistory. *Polar Notes* 12(1): 11–31.
DeLamartin'er P. 1912. Puteshestvie v severnye strany (1653) [Voyage to the Northern Countries]. *Zapiski Moskovskogo Arkheologicheskogo Instituta* 15. Moscow.
Denniston, Glenda B. 1974. The Diet of the Ancient Inhabitants of Ashishik Point, an Aleut Community. *Arctic Anthropology* 11 (suppl.): 143–52.
Denton, G. H., and W. Karlen 1973. Holocene Climatic Changes, Their Pattern and Possible Cause. *Quaternary Research* 3:155–205
Dergachev, N. 1877. *Russkaia Laplandiia. Statisticheskii, geograficheskii i ethnograficheskii ocherk* [The Russian Lappland: Statistical, Geographic and Ethnographic Outlines]. Arkhangel'sk.
Diaz, Henry F., John T. Andrews, and Susan K. Short. 1989. Climate Variations in Northern North America (6000 B.P. to Present) Reconstructed

from Pollen and Tree-Ring Data. *Arctic and Alpine Research* 21(1): 45–59.

Dikov, Nikolai N. 1977. *Arkheologicheskie pamiatniki Kamchatki, Chukotki i Verkhnei Kolymy. Aziia na styke s Amerikoi v drevnosti* [Archaeological Monuments of Kamchatka, Chukotka, and Upper Kolyma: Asia Joining America in Prehistory]. Moscow: Nauka.

———. 1979. *Drevnie kul'tury severo-vostoka Azii. Aziia na styke s Amerikoi v drevnosti.* [Ancient Cultures of Northeast Asia: Asia Joining America in Prehistory]. Moscow: Nauka.

Dikov, Nikolai N. (ed.). 1989. *Istoriia Chukotki s drevneishikh vremyon do nashikh dnei* [History of the Chukotka from the Ancient Times to the Present]. Moscow: Mysl'.

Divale, W. T. 1972. Systematic Population Control in Middle and Upper Paleolithic: Inferences Based on Contemporary Hunter-Gatherers. *World Archaeology* 4(2): 222–43.

Dmitriev, D. 1925. Severnoe olenevodstvo i ego ekonomika [Northern Reindeer Herding and Its Economy]. *Severnaia Aziia* 5–6:105–14.

Dobronravova, N. P. and N. N. Kuindzhi. 1962. Pitanie i nekotorye storony obmena veshchestv u korennogo naseleniia Krainego Severa [Nutrition and Some Aspects of Metabolism among the Indigenous Population of the North]. *Problemy Severa* 6:112–14.

Dokumenty. 1946. Dokumenty ekonomicheskogo obosnovaniia motorno-zveroboinykh stantsii (MZS) Chukotskogo natsional'nogo okruga [Papers in Economic Foundation of the Motor-Hunting Stations in the Chukchi National Area]. Manuscript, F.470, op.1, no.9. State Archive of the Kamchatka Province, Petropavlovsk-Kamchatskii.

Dolgikh, Boris O. 1946. Rodovoi i plemennoi sostav narodnostei Severa Srednei Sibiri [Clan and Tribal Composition of the Peoples of the Central Siberian North]. Unpublished Ph.D. diss. Moscow: Institute of Ethnology.

———. 1949. Rodovoi i plemennoi sostav narodnostei Severa Srednei Sibiri [Clan and Tribal Composition of the Peoples of the Central Siberian North]. *Kratkie soobshcheniia Insituta ethnografii* 5:70–85.

———. 1952a. O nekotorykh etnogeneticheskikh protsessakh (pereseleniiakh narodov i rasprostranenii iazykov) v Severnoi Sibiri [On Some Ethnogenetic Processes (Migrations of Peoples and Diffusion of Languages) in Northern Siberia]. *Sovetskaia etnografiia* 1:51–59.

———. 1952b. Proiskhozhdenie nganasanov [The Origin of the Nganasans]. *Trudy Instituta Etnografii* 18:5–87. Reprinted in *Studies in Siberian Ethnogenesis. Arctic Institute of North America. Translations from Russian Sources*, H. Michael (ed.), 2:220–99. Toronto: University of Toronto Press.

———. 1954. Starinnye obychai entsev sviazannye s rozhdeniem rebyonka i vyborom emu imeni [Ancient Customs of the Enets Connected with Childbirth and Name-Giving]. *Kratkie soobshcheniia Instituta etnografii* 20:35–43.

———. 1960. Rodovoi i plemennoi sostav narodov Sibiri v XVII veke

[Clan and Tribal Composition of the Siberian Indigenous Peoples in the Sixteenth Century]. *Trudy Instituta Etnografii* 55. Moscow.

———. 1964. Problemy etnografii i arkheologii Arktiki [Questions in Ethnography and Anthropology of the Arctic]. *Sovetskaia etnografiia* 4:76–90.

———. 1970. *Ocherki po etnicheskoi istorii nentsev i entsev* [Essays in Ethnic History of the Nenets and Enets]. Moscow: Nauka.

Dolgikh, Boris O. (comp.). 1976. *Mifologicheskie skazki i istoricheskie predaniia nganaşan* [Mythological Tales and Historical Legends of the Ngananansan]. Moscow: Nauka.

Dolgikh, Boris O., and Il'ia S. Gurvich. 1970. Karta rasseleniia sosedskikh territorial'nykh gruppirovok narodov Severa na 1926–1927 gg. [Map of the Residential Communities of the Northern Peoples in Siberia in the Years 1926–1927]. In *Obshchestvennyi stroi u narodov Severnoi Sibiri. XVII-nachalo XX v*, I. S. Gurvich and B. O. Dolgikh (eds.), 437–52. Moscow: Nauka.

Dolgikh, Boris O., and Maksim G. Levin. 1951. Perekhod ot rodo-plemennykh sviazei k territorial'nym v istorii narodov Severnoi Sibiri [Transition from Kinship to Territorial Relationships in the History of the Peoples of Northern Siberia]. *Trudy Instituta Etnografii* 14:95–108. Reprinted in *Studies in Siberian Ethnogenesis. Arctic Institute of North America. Translations from Russian Sources*, H. Michael (ed.), 2:300–13. Toronto: University of Toronto Press.

Draper, H. H. 1977. The Aboriginal Eskimo Diet in Modern Perspective. *American Anthropologist* 79(2): 309–16.

Driver, Harold E. 1969. *Indians of North America*. Chicago: University of Chicago Press.

Driver, Harold E., and William C. Massey. 1957. Comparative Studies of North American Indians. *Transactions of the American Philosophical Society*, n.s. 47(2): 165–456.

Druri, I. V. 1933. Anadyrskoe olenevodstvo [The Anadyr Reindeer Economy]. *Sovetskii sever* 5:74–77.

———. 1936. Pastbishchnoe khozyaistvo i vypas olenei u chukoch Anadyrskogo raiona [Pasture Economy and Reindeer Herding among the Chukchis of the Anadyr District]. *Trudy Arkticheskogo Instituta* 62:105–24.

———. 1949. Dikii severnyi olen' Sovetskoi Arktiki i Subarktiki [Wild Reindeer of the Soviet Arctic and Subarctic]. *Trudy Arkticheskogo Instituta* 200. Leningrad.

Dumond, D.A. 1975. The Limitation of Human Population: A Natural History. *Science* 187(4178):713–21.

Dumond, Don E. 1980. A Chronology of Native Alaskan Subsistence Systems. In *Alaska Native Culture and History*, Y. Kotani and W. B. Workman (eds.), 23–47. *Senri Ethnological Studies* 4. Osaka: National Museum of Ethnology.

Dunbar, Maxwell J. 1973. Stability and Fragility in Arctic Ecosystems. *Arctic* 26(3): 179–86.

Durham, Floyd. 1979a. Recent Trends in Bowhead Whaling by Eskimos in the Western Arctic with Emphasis on Utilization. Paper Published by the Whale Protection Fund.

———. 1979b. The Catch of Bowhead Whales (*Balaena mysticetus*) by Eskimos with Emphasis on the Western Arctic. *Natural Museum of Los Angeles County, Contribution* 314, 14 pp.

Efimenko, P. Ia. 1878. Iuridicheskie obychai loparei, korelov i samoedov Arkhangel'skoi gubernii [Judicial Customs of the Lapps, Karelians, and Samoyeds of the Arkhangel'sk Province]. *Zapiski Russkogo Geograficheskogo Obshchestva* 8(2): 1–233.

Efimenko, P. P. 1931. Znachenie zhenshchiny v orinyakskuiu epokhy [The Role of Woman in the Orignac Age]. *Izvestiia GAIMK* 11(3–4). Leningrad.

———. 1953. *Pervobytnoe obshchestvo. Ocherki po istorii paleoliticheskogo vremeni* [Primordial Society: Essays in the History of the Paleolithic Age]. Kiev: Izdatel'stvo AN USSR.

Ekonomicheskie Obzory. 1939. Ekonomicheskie obzory i godovye pokazateli razvitiia narodnogo khozyaistva okruga za 1930–1960 gg. [Economic Reviews and Annual Data on the Economic Development of the (Chukchi National) Area, 1930–1960]. Manuscript, F.15, no.3. State Archive of the Chukchi Autonomous Area, Anadyr.

Ekonomicheskii Ocherk. 1939. Ekonomicheskii ocherk Chukotskogo raiona [Economic Review of the Chukchi District]. Manuscript, F.15, op.15, no.7. State Archive of the Chukchi Autonomous Area, Anadyr.

Ekonomika Bol'shezemel'skoi tundry. 1934. Ekonomika Bol'shezemel'skoi tundry [Economy of the Bol'shaia Zemlia Tundra]. Manuscript, F.197, op.2, no.125. State Archive of the Nenets Autonomous Area, Nar'ian-Mar.

Ellana, Linda J. 1983. Bering Strait Insular Eskimo: A Diachronic Study of Ecology and Population Structure. *Technical Paper* 77. Alaska Department of Fish and Game, Division of Subsistence.

———. 1988. Skin Boats and Walrus Hunters of Bering Strait. *Arctic Anthropology* 25(1): 107–19.

Ellana, Linda J., George K. Sherrod, and Steven Langdon. 1986. Subsistence Mapping: An Evaluation and Methodological Guidelines. *Technical Paper* 125. Alaska Department of Fish and Game, Division of Subsistence.

Ellen, Roy. 1978. Problems and Progress in the Ethnographic Analysis of Small-Scale Human Ecosystems. *Man* 13:290–303.

———. 1982. *Environment, Subsistence and System: The Ecology of Small-Scale Social Formations*. Cambridge: Cambridge University Press.

Elton, Charles S. 1931. Epidemics among Sledge Dogs in the Canadian Arctic and Their Relation to Disease in the Arctic Fox. *Canadian Journal of Research* 5 (December): 673–92.

———. 1934. *Ekologiia zhivotnykh* [Animal Ecology]. Moscow and Leningrad: Biomedgiz.

Ermolov, Leonid B. 1985. Okhotnich'ia deiatel'nost' i ekologiia v kamennom veke Severnoi i Tsentral'noi Azii [Hunting Activity and Ecology During the Stone Age in Northern and Central Asia]. *Kratkie soobshcheniia Instituta Arkheologii* 181:40–44.

Ermolova, Nina N. 1978. *Teriofauna doliny Angary v pozdnem antropogene* [The Teriofauna of the Angara Valley in the Late Anthropogene]. Novosibirsk: Nauka.

———. 1985. Okhotnich'ia deiatel'nost' cheloveka [Human Hunting Activity]. *Kratkie soobshcheniia Instituta Arkheologii* 181:9–12.

Etnokul'turnoe Razvitie. 1988. *Etnokul'turnoe razvitie narodnostei Severa v usloviiakh nauchno-technicheskogo progressa na perspectivu do 2005 goda (kontseptsiia razvitiia)* [Ethnocultural Perspectives on the Peoples of the North under the Scientific-Technological Progress up to the Year of 2005 (The Concept for the Development)]. Moscow: Institute of Ethnography.

Evladov, V. P. 1927. Samoedskii tovarnyi nabor i nekotorye zadachi nastupaiushchego pushno-zagotovitel'nogo sezona v tundre [The Samoyed Shopping List and Some Tasks for the Upcoming Fur-Harvesting Season in the Tundra]. *Ural'skii okhotnik* 8–9:7–10.

———. 1929. Yamal'skaia ekspeditsiia Uraloblzemupravleniia [The Yamal Expedition of the Ural Province Surveyor Agency]. Manuscript. Copy in the personal archive of Dr. Alexandr Pika.

Fainberg, Lev A. 1971. *Ocherki etnicheskoi istorii Zarubezhnogo Severa (Aliaska, Kanadskaia Arktika, Labrador, Grenlandiia)* [Essays in Ethnic History of the Foreign North (Alaska, Canadian Arctic, Labrador, Greenland)]. Moscow: Nauka.

———. 1986. Rannepervobytnaia obshchina okhotnikov, sobiratelei i rybolovov [The Early Primordial Community of Hunters, Gatherers, and Fishermen]. In *Istoriia pervobytnogo obshchestva*. A. I. Pershits (ed.), 2:130–235. Moscow: Nauka

Fay, Francis H. 1982. Ecology and Biology of the Pacific Walrus, *Odobenus divergens Illiger*. *North American Fauna* 74. Washington, D.C.: U.S. Fish and Wildlife Service.

Fedoseev, Georgii A. 1965. Sravnitel'naia kharacteristika populiatsii kol'chatoi nerpy pribrezhnykh vod Chukotskogo poluostrova [On the Comparative Characteristics of the Ringed Seal Populations offshore the Chukchi Peninsula]. *Izvestiia TINRO* 59:194–212. Magadan.

———. 1974. Nekotorye itogi i sovremennye problemy izucheniia lastonogikh [Some Results and Current Issues in the Study of Pinnipeds]. *Zoologiia pozvonochnykh* 6 (Morskie mlekopitayushchie): 87–137. Moscow: VINITI.

———. 1984. Populiatsionnaia structura, sovremennoe sostoianie i perspectivy ispol'zovaniia ledovykh form lastonogikh v severnoi chasti Tikhogo okeana [On the Population Structure, Current Status, and Prospects for Utilization of the Pagophilic Pinnipeds of the Northern Pacific]. In *Morskie mlekopitaiushchie*, A. V. Yablokov and V. A. Zemskii (eds.), 130–46. Moscow: Nauka.

Fisher, Daniel C. 1987. Mastodont Procurement by Paleoindians of the

Great Lakes Region: Hunting or Scavenging? In *The Evolution of Human Hunting*, M. H. Nitecki and D. V. Nitecki (eds.), 309–421. New York: Plenum Press.

Fitzhugh, William W. 1972. Environmental Archaeology and Cultural Systems in Hamilton Inlet, Labrador (A Survey of the Central Labrador Coast from 3000 B.C. to the Present. *Smithsonian Contributions to Anthropology* 16. Washington, D.C.

———. 1975. A Comparative Approach to Northern Maritime Adaptations. In *Prehistoric Maritime Adaptations of the Circumpolar Zone*, W. W. Fitzhugh (ed.), 339–86. Paris and The Hague: Mouton.

———. 1984. Paleo-Eskimo Cultures of Greenland. In *Arctic*, D. Damas (ed.), 528–39. *Handbook of North American Indians* 5. Washington, D.C.: Smithsonian Institution.

———. 1988. Economic Patterns in Alaska. In *Crossroads of Continents: Cultures of Siberia and Alaska* W. W. Fitzhugh and A. Crowell (eds.), 191–93. Washington, D.C.: Smithsonian Institution.

Fitzhugh, William W., and H. F. Lamb. 1986. Vegetation History and Culture Change on the Central Labrador Coast. *Annals of the New York Academy of Sciences* 288(9): 481–97.

Fondahl, Gail. 1993. Siberia: Native Peoples and Newcomers in Collision. In *Nations and Politics in the Soviet Successor State*. I. Bremmer and R. Taras (eds.), 477–510. Cambridge: Cambridge University Press.

Foote, Don C. 1960. *The Eskimo Hunter at Pt. Hope, Alaska*. U.S. Atomic Energy Commission. Pub. PNE-441. Oak Ridge, Tenn.

———. 1961. *The Eskimo Hunter at Pt. Hope, Alaska*. II. U.S. Atomic Energy Commission. Pub. PNE-442. Oak Ridge, Tenn.

———. 1965. Exploration and Resource Utilization in Northwestern Arctic Alaska before 1855. Unpublished Ph.D. diss., McGill University, Montreal.

———. 1967. *The East Coast of Baffin Island, N.W.T.: An Area Economic Survey*. Ottawa: Department of Indian Affairs and Northern Development.

———. 1970a. Changing Resource Utilization by Eskimos in North-Western Arctic Alaska, 1850–1962. *Proceedings of the 7th Congress of Anthropological and Ethnological Sciences* 10: 308–13. Moscow: Nauka.

———. 1970b. An Eskimo Sea-Mammal and Caribou-Hunting Economy: Human Ecology in Terms of Energy. *Proceedings of the 8th Congress of Anthropological and Ethnological Sciences* 3: 262–67. Tokio and Osaka.

Foote, Don C., and B. Greer-Wootten. 1966. Man-Environment Interactions in an Eskimo Hunting Systems. Paper presented at the Symposium "Man-Animal Linked Cultural Sub-systems." 133rd Annual Meeting of the AAAS.

Foote, Don C., and H. A. Williamson. 1966. A Human Geographical Study. In *Environment of the Cape Thompson Region, Alaska*, N. J. Wilimovsky and J. N. Wolfe (eds.), 1041–1109. Oak Ridge, Tenn.: U.S. Atomic Energy Commission.

Forde, Daryll C. 1934. *Habitat, Economy and Society: A Geographical Introduction to Ethnology*. London: Methuen.

Formozov, Alexandr N. 1935. *Kolebaniia chislennosti promyslovykh zhivotnykh* [Fluctuations in Animal Game Populations]. Moscow and Leningrad: KOIZ.

———. 1946. Snezhnyi pokrov kak faktor sredy, ego znachenie v zhizni mlekopitayushchikh i ptits SSSR [The Snow Cover and Its Role in the Life of Mammals and Birds of the USSR]. *Materialy k poznaniyu fauny i flory SSSR* 5. Moscow.

———. 1959. Izmeneniia granits rasprostraneniia mlekopitayushchikh i ptits [Changes in the Areal Boundaries of Mammals and Birds]. In *Geografiia naseleniia nazemnykh zhivotnykh i metody eye izucheniia*, 172–196. Moscow: Academy of Sciences.

Fraker, M. 1984. Balaena mysticetus: *Whales, Oil, and Whaling in the Arctic*. Anchorage.

Freeman, Milton M. R. 1967. An Ecological Study of Mobility and Settlement Patterns among the Belcher Island Eskimos. *Arctic* 20(3): 154–75.

———. 1969–70. Studies in Maritime Hunting, I: Ecologic and Technologic Restraints on Walrus Hunting, Southampton Island, N.W.T. *Folk* 11–12:155–71.

———. 1970. Not by Bread Alone: Anthropological Perspectives on Optimum Populations. In *The Optimum Population for Britain*, L. R. Taylor (ed.), 139–49. London and New York: Academic Press.

———. 1971. A Social and Ecological Analysis of Systematic Female Infanticide among the Netsilik Eskimos. *American Anthropologist* 73(5): 1011–18.

———. 1974–75. Studies in Maritime Hunting, II: An Analysis of Walrus Hunting and Utilisation: Southampton Island, N.W.T., 1970. *Folk* 16–17:147–58.

———. 1984. Arctic Ecosystems. In *Arctic*, D. Damas (ed.), 36–48. *Handbook of North American Indians* 5. Washington, D.C.: Smithsonian Institution.

Freeman, Milton M. R. (ed.). 1976. *Inuit Land Use and Occupancy Project*. 3 vols. Ottawa: Department of Indian and Northern Affairs.

Frolov, Boris A. 1974. *Chisla v grafike paleolita* [Numbers in the Paleolithic Graphic Arts]. Novosibirsk: Nauka.

Gapanovich, Ivan I. 1923. Promysel lastonogikh i kitoobraznykh na Dal'nem Vostoke [Pinniped and Cetacean Harvesting in the Far East]. In *Rybnye i pushnye bogatstva Dal'nego Vostoka*, 316–41. Vladivostok.

———. 1925. Kamchatskoe tuzemnoe naselenie kak kul'turno-ekonomicheskii faktor [The Native Population of Kamchatka as a Cultural and Economic Factor]. *Severnaia Aziia* 5–6.

Gardner, James S. 1981. General Environment. In *Subarctic*, J. Helm (ed.), 5–14. *Handbook of North American Indians* 6. Washington, D.C.: Smithsonian Institution.

Garusov, I. S. 1967. O sotsial'noi prinadlezhnosti krupnogo olenevoda severo-vostoka nakanune kollektivizatsii [On the Social Affiliation of Rich Herdsmen Before the Collectivization]. *Zapiski Chukotskogo Kraevedcheskogo muzeia* 4:52–57. Anadyr.

Gassovskii, G. N. 1939. Okhotnichii promysel basseina reki Anadyria i ego rekonstruktsiia [Hunting Economy of the Anadyr River Basin and its Reconstruction]. *Trudy Instituta Polyarnogo Zemledelia, Zhivotnovodstva i Promyslovogo Khozyaistva. Series "Hunting Economy"* 4. Moscow.

George J. C., L. M. Philo, G. M. Carroll, and T. F. Albert. 1988. 1987. Subsistence Harvest of Bowhead Whales (*Balaena mysticetus*) by Alaskan Eskimos. *Report of the International Whaling Commission* 38:389–92.

Georgi, Iogann G. 1777. *Opisanie vsekh v Rossiiskom gosudarstve obitaiushchikh narodov, takzhe ikh zhiteiskikh obriadov, ver, obyknovenii, zhilishch, odezhd i prochikh dostoprimechatel'nostei* [Description of all the Peoples of the Russian Empire, and Also of Their Life Rituals, Beliefs, Traditions, Dwellings, Clothing, and Other Peculiarities]. Vol. 3. St. Petersburg.

Geptner, Vladimir G. 1960. Dinamika areala nekotorykh kopytnykh i antropokul'turnyi factor [Dynamics of the Area of Certain Ungulates as Influenced by the Anthropocultural Factor]. *Voprosy Geografii* 58:24–54. Moscow.

Geptner, V. G., A. A. Nasimovich, and A. G. Bannikov. 1961. *Mlekopitaiushcie Sovetskogo Soiuza* [Mammals of the Soviet Union]. Vol. 1, *Artiodactyls and Perissodactyls*. Moscow: Vysshaia Shkola.

Gerasimov, Mikhail M. 1958. Paleoliticheskaia stoianka Mal'ta [Mal'ta Paleolithic Site]. *Sovetskaia etnografiia* 3:28–52.

Giddings, James L., Jr. 1960. The Archaeology of Bering Strait. *Current Anthropology* 1(2): 121–38.

———. 1961. Cultural Continuities of Eskimos. *American Antiquity* 27(2): 155–73.

Giddings James L., Jr., and Douglas D. Anderson. 1986. *Beach Ridge Archeology of Cape Krusenstern. Eskimo Settlements around Kotzebue Sound, Alaska*. Washington, D.C.: National Park Service.

Gilberg, Rolf. 1974–75. Changes in the Life of the Polar Eskimos Resulting from a Canadian Immigration into the Thule District, North Greenland, in the 1860s. *Folk* 16–17:159–70.

———. 1984. Polar Eskimo. In *Arctic*, D. Damas (ed.), 577–94. *Handbook of North American Indians* 5. Washington, D.C.: Smithsonian Institution.

Gjessing, Gutorm. 1975. Maritime Adaptations in Northern Norway Prehistory. In *Prehistoric Maritime Adaptations of the Circumpolar Zone*, W. W. Fitzhugh (ed.), 87–100. Paris-The Hague: Mouton.

Gladilin, V. N. 1974. Rol' narodonaseleniia v protsesse vzaimodeistviia prirody i obshchestva v kamennom veke [Role of the Population in the Interaction between Environment and Society during the Stone Age]. In *Pervobytnyi chelovek, ego material'naia kul'tura i prirodnaia sreda v pleistotsene i golotsene*, A. A. Velichko (ed.), 71–78. Moscow: Institut Geografii AN SSSR.

Gladkikh, Mikhail I., Ninel' L. Korniets, and Ol'ga Soffer. 1985. Zhilishcha iz kostei mamonta na Russkoi ravnine [Dwellings of Mammoth Bones on the Russian Plain]. *V mire nauki* 1:68–74.

Golitsyn, Nikolai D. 1888. *Zapiska Arkhangel'skogo gubernatora . . . kniazia N. D. Golitsyna po obozreniiu Pechorskogo kraia letom 1887 g.* [Report of the Arkhangel'sk Governor, Prince N. D. Golitsyn, with the Review of the Pechora Area, as of Summer 1887]. Arkhangel'sk.

Golovnev, Andrej V. 1986a. Istoricheskaia tipologiia traditsionnykh form khoziaistva u narodov Severo-Zapadnoi Sibiri (XVII-nachalo XX v.) [Historical Typology of the Traditional Economies of the Peoples of Northwest Siberia (the 1600s–early 1900s). Abstract of Ph.D. diss., 19 pp. Moscow: Institute of Ethnography.

———. 1986b. Sistema khoziaistva sibirskikh tundrovykh nentsev v kontse XIX-nachale XX vv. [Economic System of the Siberian Tundra Nenets in the Late Nineteenth to Early Twentieth Century. In *Genesis i Evoliutsia Etnicheskikh Kul'tur Sibiri*, 180–90. Novosibirsk.

———. 1988. Etnograficheskaia rekonstruktsiia khoziaistvennogo oblika primorskoi kul'tury na severe Zapadnoi Sibiri [An Ethnographic Reconstruction of the Economy of Aboriginal Maritime Culture in Northwestern Siberia]. In *Istochniki i metody isledovaniia sotsial'nykh i kul'turnykh protsessov*, 92–103. Omsk: Omsk University. Reprinted in *Arctic Anthropology* 29(1):96–103.

Gondatti, Nikolai L. 1897a. Osedloe naselenie reki Anadyra [Sedentary Population along the Anadyr River]. *Zapiski Priamurskogo Otdela Russkogo Geograficheskogo Obshchestva* 3(1): 111–65. Khabarovsk.

———. 1897b. Sostav naseleniia Anadyrskoi okrugi [Population Structure of the Anadyr District]. Ibid. 166–78.

———. 1898. Poezdka iz sela Markova na reke Anadyre v bukhtu Provideniia (Beringov Proliv) [A Trip from the Village of Markova, Anadyr River to the Providenya Bay, Bering Strait]. Ibid. 4(1).

Gorodkov, Boris N. 1926. Olen'i pastbishcha na severe Ural'skoi oblasti [Reindeer Pastures of the Northern Ural Province]. *Ural* 8. Pt. 1, *Ural'skii Sever*, 145–56. Sverdlovsk.

Govorukhin, V. S. 1947. Dinamika landshaftov i klimaticheskie kolebaniia na Krainem Severe [Landscape Dynamics and Climatic Fluctuations in the Polar North]. *Izvestiia Vsesoiuznogo Geograficheskogo Obshchestva* 79(3): 317–24.

Gracheva, Galina N. 1983. *Traditsionnoe mirovozzrenie okhotnikov Taimyra (na materialakh nganasan XIX-nachala XX v.)* [Traditional World View of the Taimyr Peninsula Hunters (As Based on the Data on the Nganasans of the 1800s and early 1900s]. Leningrad: Nauka.

Graumlich, Lisa J. 1991. High Lattitude Tree-Ring Data: Records of Climatic Change and Ecological Response. In *Proceedings of the International Conference on the Role of the Polar Regions in Global Change*, G. Weller (ed.), 565–69. Fairbanks: Geophysical Institute.

Grayson, Donald K. 1980. Vicissitudes and Overkill: The Development of Explanations of Pleistocene Extinctions. In *Advances in Archaeological Method and Theory*, M. B. Schiffer (ed.), 3:357–403. New York: Academic Press.

———. 1984. Explaining Pleistocene Extinctions: Thoughts on the Structure of a Debate. In *Quaternary Extinctions: A Prehistoric Revolution*, P. S. Martin and R. G. Klein (eds.), 807–23. Tucson: University of Arizona Press.

Gribbin, J., and H. H. Lamb. 1980. Izmenenie klimata za istoricheskii period [Climate Change through Historic Time]. In *Izmeneniia klimata*, 102–21. Leningrad: Gidrometeoizdat.

Grigor'ev, Gleb P. 1968. *Nachalo verkhnego paleolita i proiskhozhdenie* Homo sapiens [Beginning of the Upper Paleolithic and Origin of the *Homo sapiens*]. Leningrad: Nauka.

———. 1970. Verkhnii paleolit [The Upper Paleolithic]. *Materialy i issledovanniia po arkheologii SSSR* 166:43–63.

———. 1972. Vosstanovlenie obshchestvennogo stroiia paleoliticheskikh okhotnikov i sobiratelei [Reconstruction of the Social Organization of the Paleolithic Hunter-Gatherers]. In *Okhotniki-sobirateli-rybolovy*, A. M. Reshetov (ed.), 11–26. Leningrad: Nauka.

———. 1974. Metodicheskie osnovaniia dlia razresheniia voprosa sootnosheniia prirodnogo okruzheniia i kul'tury cheloveka [Methodical Grounds to Determine the Relationship between the Environment and Man's Culture]. In *Pervobytnyi chelovek, ego material'naia kul'tura i prirodnaia sreda v Pleistotsene i Golotsene*, A. A. Velichko (ed.), 65–70. Moscow: Institute Geografii AN SSSR.

Grigorova, Ol'ga P. 1934. Kartina krovi v sviazi s usloviiami zhizni i avitaminozom u russkogo i nenetskogo naseleniia Novoi Zemli [Blood Picture as Seen in regard to Life Conditions and Avitaminosis among the Russian and Nenets Residents of the Novaia Zemlia]. *Anthropologicheskii zhurnal* 1–2:163–77.

Grønnow, Bjarne. 1986. Recent Archaeological Investigations of West Greenland Caribou Hunting. *Arctic Anthropology* 23(1): 57–80.

Gulløv, Hans G. 1985. Whales, Whalers, and Eskimos: The Impact of European Whaling on the Demography and Economy of Eskimo Society in West Greenland. In *Cultures in Contact: The European Impact on Native Cultural Institutions in Eastern North America,* A.D. *1000–1800*. W. W. Fitzhugh (ed.), 71–98. Washington, D.C., and London: Smithsonian Institution.

Gurina, Nina N. 1990a. Osnovnye etapy razvitiia kul'tury drevnego naseleniia Kol'skogo poluostrova [Main Stages in Cultural Development of the Ancient Population of the Kola Peninsula]. *Kratkie soobshcheniia Instituta Arkheologii* 200:8–16.

———. 1990b. O progressivnykh formakh khoziaistva drevnikh plemyon Zapoliar'ia (po materialam Kol'skogo poluostrova) [On Progressive Economic Patterns of the Ancient Tribes of the High Arctic (Based on Data from the Kola Peninsula)]. Ibid. 27–33.

Gurvich, Il'ia S. 1966. Etnicheskaia istoriia severo-vostoka Sibiri [Ethnic History of Northeast Siberia]. *Trudy Instituta Etnografii* 89. Moscow.

———. 1970. Sosedskaia obshchina i proizvodstvennye ob'edineniia malykh narodov Severa [Residential Community and Economic Groupings of the Northern Minorities]. In *Obshchestvennyi Stroi u Narodov Severnoi Sibiri*, I. Gurvich and B. Dolgikh (eds.), 384–417. Moscow: Nauka.

———. 1977. *Kul'tura severnykh yakutov-olenevodov* [Culture of the Northern Yakuts-Reindeermen]. Moscow: Nauka.

———. 1983. Problema etnogeneza olennykh grupp chukchei i koriakov v svete etnograficheskikh dannykh [Question of Ethnogensis of the Reindeer Divisions of the Chukchi and Koryak under the Light of Ethnographic Data]. In *Na styke Chukotki i Aliaski*, V. P. Alekseev (ed.), 143–67. Moscow: Nauka.

Gurvich, Il'ia S. (ed.). 1975. *Yukagiry. Istoriko-etnograficheskii ocherk* [The Yukaghirs: Historical-Ethnographic Review]. Novosibirsk: Nauka.

———. 1982. *Etnicheskaia istoriia narodov Severa* [Ethnic History of the Peoples of the North]. Moscow: Nauka.

Gurvich, Il'ia S., and Boris O. Dolgikh (eds.). 1970. Obshchestvennyi stroi u narodov Severnoi Sibiri. XVII-nachalo XX v. [Social System of the North Siberian Peoples: Sixteenth to early Twentieth Century]. Moscow: Nauka.

Gurvich, Il'ia S., Boris O. Dolgikh, and Anna V. Smoliak. 1970. Khoziaistvo narodov Severa v 17-nachale 20 vv. [Economy of the North Siberian Indigenous Peoples from the 1600's to early 1900's]. In *Obshchestvennyi stroi u narodov Severnoi Sibiri*, I. S. Gurvich and B. O. Dolgikh (eds.), 38–70. Moscow: Nauka.

Haber, G. C., and C. J. Walters. 1980. Dynamics of the Alaska-Yukon Caribou Herds and Management Implications. In *Proceedings of the 2nd Reindeer-Caribou Symposium*, E. Reimers et al. (eds.), 665–69. Trondheim.

Hacquebord, Louwrens. 1981. The Rise and Fall of a Dutch Whaling-Settlement on the West Coast of Spitsbergen. In *Early European Exploitation of the Northern Atlantic. 800–1700.* 79–132. Groningen: University of Groningen.

Hall, Edwin S., Jr. 1971. Kangiguksuk: A Cultural Reconstruction of a Sixteenth Century Eskimo Site in Northern Alaska. *Arctic Anthropology* 8(1): 1–101.

———. 1978. Technological Change in Northern Alaska. In *Archaeological Essays in Honor of Irving B. Rouse*, R. C. Dunnel and E. S. Hall (eds.), 209–29. The Hague: Mouton.

———. 1984. A Clear and Present Danger: The Use of Ethnohistoric Data for Interpreting Mound 44 at the Utqiagvik Site. *Arctic Anthropology* 21(1): 135–39.

Halstead, Paul, and John O'Shea. 1989. Introduction: Cultural Responses to Risk and Uncertainty. In *Bad Year Economics: Cultural Responses to*

Risk and Uncertainty, P. Halstead and J. O'Shea (eds.), 1–7. Cambridge: Cambridge University Press.

Hardesty, Donald L. 1977. *Ecological Anthropology*. New York: John Wiley and Sons.

Harper, Albert B. 1979. Istoriia aleutskoi populiatsii [History of the Aleut Population]. *Sovetskaia etnografiia* 6: 50–60.

Hassan, Fekri. 1979. Demography and Archaeology. *Annual Review of Anthropology* 8: 137–60.

———. 1980. The Growth and Regulation of Human Population in Prehistoric Times. In *Biosocial Mechanisms of Population Regulation*, M. Cohen et al. (eds.), 305–19. New Haven and London: Yale University Press.

Hatch, Elvin. 1973. The Growth of Economic, Subsistence, and Ecological Studies in American Anthropology. *American Anthropologist* 29(4): 221–43.

Haury, Emil W., E. B. Sayles, and William W. Wasley. 1959. The Lehner Mammoth Site, Southeastern Arizona. *American Antiquity* 25(1): 2–30.

Hayden, Brian. 1972. Population Control among Hunter-Gatherers. *World Archaeology* 4(2): 205–21.

———. 1981. Research and Development in the Stone Age: Technological Transitions among Hunter-Gatherers. *Current Anthropology* 22(5): 519–48.

Haynes, Vance C., Jr. 1966. Elephant-hunting in North America. *Scientific American* 214(6): 104–12.

———. 1980. The Clovis Culture. *Canadian Journal of Anthropology* 1(1): 115–21.

Helm, June. 1962. The Ecological Approach in Anthropology. *The American Journal of Sociology* 67 (6): 630–39.

Hemming, J. E. 1975. Population Growth and Movement Patterns of the Nelchina Caribou Herd. In *Proceedings of the 1st Reindeer-Caribou Symposium*. J. Luick et al. (eds.), 162–69. *Biological Papers of the University of Alaska. Special Report* 1. Fairbanks.

Henneberg, M. 1975. Notes on the Reproduction Possibilities of Human Prehistoric Populations. *Przeglad Anthropologizny* 41. Warsaw.

Hertz, Ole, and Finn O. Kapel. 1986. Commercial and Subsistence Hunting of Marine Mammals. *AMBIO* 15(3): 144–51.

Hester, J. 1967. The Agency of Man in Animal Extinction. In *Pleistocene Extinctions: The Search for a Cause*, P. S. Martin and H. E. White (eds.), 169–92. New Haven and London: Yale University Press.

Hickey, Clifford G. 1976. An Economic View of Adaptation. In *Contribution to Anthropology: The Interior Peoples of Northern Alaska*, E. S. Hall, Jr. (ed.), 235–98. *National Museum of Man. Mercury Series*. 49. Ottawa.

Hooper, William H. 1976. *Ten Months among the Tents of the Tuski*. 2d ed. New York: AMS Press.

Hughes, Charles C. 1960. *An Eskimo Village in the Modern World*. Ithaca, N.Y.: Cornell University Press.

———. 1984. Siberian Eskimo. In *Arctic*. D. Damas (ed.), 247–61. *Handbook of North American Indians*. 5. Washington, D.C.: Smithsonian Institution.

Hughes, J. D. 1983. *American Indian Ecology*. El Paso: Texas Western Press.

Iakobii, A. I. 1893. Ugasanie inorodcheskikh plemyon Severa [Extinction of Native Tribes of the North]. St. Petersburg.

I. M. 1907. Iz poezdki na Novuiu Zemliu (o novozemel'skikh samoedakh) [Sketches from the Trip to Novaia Zemlia (on the Novaia Zemlia Samoyeds)]. *Zemlevedenie* 1–2:23–36. Moscow.

Indians of North America. 1979. Indians of North America. Map Produced by the Cartographic Division, National Geographic Society. Washington, D.C.: National Geographic Society.

Indigenous Peoples. 1990. *Indigenous Peoples of the Soviet North. IWGIA Document* 60. Copenhagen.

Ingold, Tim. 1980. *Hunters, Pastoralists, and Ranchers: Reindeer Economies and Their Transformations*. Cambridge: Cambridge University Press.

Ioffe, E. G. 1937. Opisanie Chaunskogo raiona [Description of the Chaun District]. Manuscript, F.K-V, op.1, no.35. Institute-Museum of Anthropology and Ethnography, St. Petersburg.

Ionin, A. S. 1959. *Berega Beringova moria* [The Coastlines of the Bering Sea]. Moscow: Academy of Sciences.

Islavin, Vladimir. 1847. *Samoedy v domashnem i obshchestvennom bytu* [The Samoyeds in Their Home and Daily Social Life]. St. Petersburg.

Itin, Vivian A. 1936. Kolebaniia ledovitosti [The Sea-Ice Fluctuations]. *Sovetskaia Arktika* 1:178–85.

Itin, Vivian, and N. Sibirtsev. 1936. *Severnyi morskoi put' i Karskie ekspeditsii* [The Northern Sea-Route and the Kara Expeditions]. Novosibirsk: Zapadno-Sibirskoye Kraevoe Izdatel'stvo.

Itogi. 1989. *Itogi Vsesoiuznoi Perepisi Naseleniia 1979 goda* [Results of the All-Union Population Census of 1979]. Vol. 4, pt. 1, fasc. 1, *National Composition of the Population of the USSR*. Moscow: Goscomstat.

Itogi Perepisi. 1929. *Itogi perepisi severnykh okrain Dal'ne-Vostochnogo kraia, 1926–1927* [Census Data for the Northern Margins of the Far-East Province, 1926–1927]. Blagoveshchensk: Dal'nevostochnyi Kraevoi Statisticheskii Otdel.

Iudin, A. M. 1969. *Ocherk izucheniia olenevodstva Chukotki* [Review of the History of Studies of Reindeer Herding in Chukotka]. Magadan: Knizhnoe Izdatel'stvo.

Jacoby, G. C., and E. R. Cook. 1981. Past Temperature Variations Inferred from a 400-Year Tree-Ring Chronology from Yukon Territory, Canada. *Arctic and Alpine Research* 13:409–18.

Janes, Robert R. 1983. Archaeological Ethnography among Mackenzie Basin Dene, Canada. *The Arctic Institute of North America. Technical Papers* 28.

Järvinen, O., and S.-L. Varvio. 1986. Proneness to Extinction of Small

Populations of Seals: Demographic and Genetic Stochasticity vs. Environmental Stress. *Finnish Game Research* 44:6–18. Helsinki.

Jellinek, Arthur J. 1967. Man's Role in the Extinction of Pleistocene Faunas. In *Pleistocene Extinctions: The Search for a Cause*, P. S. Martin and H. E. White (eds.), 193–200. New Haven and London: Yale University Press.

Jochelson, Waldemar/Vladimir I. 1898. *Ocherk zveropromyshlennosti i torgovli mekhami v Kolymskom okruge* [Review of Game Industry and Fur Trade in the Kolyma District]. St. Petersburg.

———. 1908. The Koryak. *The Jesup North Pacific Expedition. Memoir of the American Museum of Natural History* 10. Reprint. New York: AMS Press, 1975.

Kabo, Vladimir R. 1986. *Pervobytnaia dozemledel'cheskaia obshchina* [The Primordial Pre-Agricultural Community]. Moscow: Nauka.

Kalinnikov, Nikolai F. 1912. Nash Krainii Severo-Vostok [Our Far Northeast]. *Zapiski po gidrografii* 34 (suppl.). St. Petersburg.

Kaplan, Susan A. 1983. Economic and Social Change in Labrador Neo-Eskimo Culture. Ph.D. diss. Ann Arbor: University Microfilms.

———. 1985. European Goods and Socio-Economic Change in Early Labrador. In *Cultures in Contact. The European Impact on Native Cultural Institutions in Eastern North America,* A.D. *1000–1800*, W. W. Fitzhugh (ed.), 45–70. Washington, D.C. and London: Smithsonian Institution.

Karaev, Aleksandr I. 1926. Chukotsko-Anadyrski krai (ocherki mestnogo zhitelia) [The Chukchi-Anadyr' Area: Notes of a Local Resident]. *Ekonomicheskaia Zhizn' Dal'nego Vostoka* 4 (4): 136–56, (5): 137–46.

Karaev, Fyodor I. 1923. Dokladnaia zapiska upolnomochennogo po Chukotskomy uezdu F. Karaeva [Report by the Chukchi District Officer, F. Karaev]. Manuscript, Fund P-2333, Op.1, n.113, pp.259–64. Central State Archive of the Far East, Tomsk.

Kelly, P. M., J. H. W. Karas, and L. D. Williams. 1984. Arctic Climate. In *Arctic Whaling. Proceedings of the International Symposium*, 25–38. Groningen: University of Groningen.

Kemp, William B. 1971. The Flow of Energy in a Hunting Society. *Scientific American* 225(3): 104–15.

Kertselli, Sergei V. 1911. *Po Bol'shezemel'skoi tundre s kochevnikami* [Along the Bol'shaia Zemlia Tundra with the Nomads]. Arkhangel'sk.

———. 1925. O prave na okhotu u promyslovogo naseleniia [On Hunting Rights among the Local Hunting Population]. In *Okhota i okhotnik*, 14–32. Moscow.

Khlobystin, Leonid P. 1973. O drevnem zaselenii Arktiki [On Ancient Peopling of the Arctic]. *Kratkie soobshcheniia Instituta Arkheologii* 136:11–16.

———. 1982. Pervonachal'noye zaselenye Rossiiskogo Zapolyar'ya [The Initial Peopling of the Russian Arctic]. *Proceedings of the Eleventh INQUA Congress* 1:286–88. Moscow.

———. 1985. Raboty na ostrove Vaigach i Iugorskom poluostrove [Surveys on the Vaigach Island and the Iugor Peninsula]. *Arkheologicheskie otkrytiia 1984*. Moscow: Nauka.

———. 1987. Raboty v Arkhangel'skom Zapoliar'e [Surveys in the Arkhangelsk High Arctic]. In *Arkheologicheskie otkrytiia 1986*. 40–42. Moscow: Nauka.

Khlobystin, Leonid P., and Galina N. Gracheva. 1974. Poiavlenie olenevodstva v tundrovoi zone Evropy, Zapadnoi i Srednei Sibiri [The Appearance of Reindeer Breeding in the Tundra Zone of Europe, Western and Central Siberia]. In *Formy perekhoda ot prisvaivaiushchego khoziaistva k proizvodiashchemy. Proceedings of a Conference*, 81–86. Leningrad.

Khlobystin, Leonid P., and Galina M. Levkovskaia. 1974. Rol' sotsial'nogo i ekologicheskogo faktorov v razvitii arkticheskikh kul'tur Evrasii [Role of Ecological and Social Factors in the Development of Arctic Cultures in Eurasia]. In *Pervobytnyi chelovek, ego material'naia kul'tura i prirodnaia sreda v Pleistotsene i Golotsene*, A. A. Velichko (ed.), 235–42. Moscow: Institut Geografii.

Khlobystin, Leonid P., I. V. Vereshchagina, and V. Ia. Shumkin. 1988. Issledovaniia zapoliarnoi expeditsii [Surveys of the High Arctic Expedition]. In *Arkheologicheskie otkrytiia 1986*, 41–43. Moscow: Nauka.

Khomich, Liudmila V. 1966. *Nentsy. Istoriko-etnograficheskie ocherki* [The Nenets: Historical and Ethnographic Essays]. Moscow and Leningrad: Nauka.

———. 1970. *Problemy etnogeneza i etnicheskoi istorii nentsev* [Problems in the Ethnogenesis and Ethnic History of the Nenets]. Moscow: Nauka.

Khotinskii, N. A. 1977. *Golotsen Severnoi Evrazii. Opyt transcontinental'noi korreliatsii etapov razvitiia rastitel'nosti i klimata* [Holocene of Northern Eurasia: An Attempt at a Transcontinental Correlation of Major Periods in Climate and Vegetation Evolution]. Moscow: Nauka.

Kibal'chich, Arkadii A. 1984. Biologiia razmnozheniia i estestvennye zapasy tikhookeanskogo morzha [Reproductive Biology and Natural Resources of the Pacific Walrus]. Abstract of unpublished Ph.D. diss., 25 pp. Moscow.

Kilmarx, J. 1986. Archaeological and Ethnohistoric Evidence for Material Acculturation in Barrow, Alaska. *Études/Inuit/Studies* 10(1–2): 203–31.

Kirch, Patrick V. 1980. The Archaeological Study of Adaptation: Theoretical and Methodological Issues. *Advances in Archaeological Method and Theory* 3:101–56.

Kirikov, Sergei V. 1960. *Izmeneiia zhivotnogo mira v prirodnykh zonakh SSSR (lesnaia zona i lesotundra)* [Changes in the Animal Life of the Environmental Zones of the USSR (Forest and Forest-Tundra Zones)]. Moscow: Izdatel'stvo AN SSSR.

———. 1966. *Promyslovye zhivotnye, prirodnaia sreda i chelovek* [Game Animals, Natural Environment, and Man]. Moscow: Nauka.

Kirillov, Nikolai V. 1908. Sanitarnaia obstanovka i bolezni poliarnykh stran (preimushchestvenno severo-vostoka Azii) [Sanitary Conditions and Diseases of the Polar Area (Northeast Asia in Particular)]. *Vestnik obshchestvennoi gigieny, sudebnoi i practicheskoi meditsiny* 11:1769–99.

Kishchinskii, Alexandr A. 1967. Materialy o rasprostranenii dikikh kopytnykh v Severo-Vostochnoi Sibiri [Data on the Distribution of Wild Ungulates in Northeastern Siberia]. *Problemy Severa* 11:142–48.

———. 1975. Ostrovnye populiatsii severnogo olenia v vostochnom sektore Sovetskoi Arktiki i puti ikh ratsional'noi ekspluatatsii [Insular Reindeer Populations in the Eastern Sector of the Soviet Arctic and Techniques of Rational Management]. In *Dikii severnyi olen' v SSSR*, E. E. Syroechkovskii (ed.), 164–68. Moscow: Sovetskaya Rossiia.

Kit. 1973. *Kit* [The Whale]. Leningrad: Gidrometeoizdat.

Kjellström, Rolf. 1974–75. Senilicide and Invalidicide Among the Eskimos. *Folk* 16–17:117–24. Copenhagen.

Klein, Richard G. 1969. *Man and Culture in the Late Pleistocene: A Case Study*. San Francisco: Chandler.

———. 1973. *Ice-Age Hunters of the Ukraine*. Chicago: University of Chicago Press.

Kleivan, Inge. 1984. West Greenland Before 1950. In *Arctic*. D. Damas (ed.), 595–621. *Handbook of North American Indians* 5. Washington, D.C.: Smithsonian Institution.

Knopfmiller, Margarita O. 1940a. Morskoi zveroboinyi promysel Chukotki [The Sea-Mammal Hunting Industry of Chukotka]. Unpublished Ph.D. diss., F. K-II, op. 1, no. 284. Archive of the Institute-Museum of Anthropology and Ethnography, St. Petersburg.

———. 1940b. Unpublished Field Data and Notes for the Ph.D. Dissertation. Ibid. no. 239, 286.

Kolonial'naia Politika. 1935. Kolonial'naia politika tsarizma na Kamchatke i Chukotke v XVIII veke [Colonial Policy of the Tsarist Government in Chuktoka and Kamchatka during the 1700s]. Collection of archival records. Leningrad: Institut Narodov Severa.

Kolycheva, Elena I. 1956. Nentsy Evropeiskoi Rossii v kontse XVII-nachale XVIII veka [The Nenets of European Russia during the late 1600s and early 1700s]. *Sovetskaia etnografiia* 2:76–88.

Konakov, Nikolai D. 1983. *Komi okhotniki i rybolovy vo vtoroi polovine XIX-nachale XX v.* [Komi Hunters and Fishermen during the Second Half of the 1800s and early 1900s]. Moscow: Nauka.

———. 1986. Stanovlenie krupnotabunnogo olenevodstva na Kol'skom poluostrove [Development of the Large-Herd Reindeer Economy on the Kola Peninsula]. In *Traditsiia i sovremennost' v kul'ture sel'skogo naseleniia Komi ASSR*, 42–56. Syktyvkar: Komi Filial AN SSSR.

———. 1987. *Drevnekomi promyslovyi kalendar'* [Ancient Komi Hunting Calendar]. Syktyvkar.

Kontseptsiia. 1989. *Kontseptsiia sotsial'nogo i economicheskogo razvitiia narodnostei Severa na period do 2010 goda* [Concept for the Social and Economic Development of the (small) Peoples of the North up to the Year 2010]. V. I. Boiko (ed.). Novosibirsk: Institute of History, Philology, and Philosophy.

Kopylov, I. P. 1928. *Tungusskoye khoziaistvo Leno-Kirengskogo kraia po dannym statistiko-economicheskogo obsledovaniia 1927 g.* [Tungus Economy of the Lena-Kirenga Area, according to the Economic Inventory of 1927]. Novosibirsk: Pereselencheskoe Upravlenie.

Kosarev, Mikhail F. 1974. *Drevnie kul'tury Tomsko-Narymskogo Priob'ia* [Ancient Cultures of the Tom'-Narym Cisob' Region]. Moscow: Nauka.

———. 1984. *Zapadnaia Sibir' v drevnosti* [West Siberia in Prehistory]. Moscow: Nauka.

Kosven, Mark O. 1962. Iz istorii etnografii koryakov v XVIII veke [On the History of the Koryak Ethnography of the 1700s]. *Trudy Instituta Etnografii* 78:276–91.

Kotliakov, V. M., and L.S. Troitskii. 1985. Novye dannye ob oledenenii Shpitsbergena [New Data on Glaciation in Spitsbergen]. *Vestnik Akademii Nauk* 2:128–36.

Koviazin, N. M. 1936. Olenevodstvo v Evenkiiskom natsional'nom okruge [Reindeer Industry in the Evenk National Area]. In *Ocherki po Promyslovomu Khoziaistvu i Olenevodstvu Krainego Severa*, 3–38. Leningrad: Institut Narodov Severa, Nauchno-Issledovatel'skaia Assotsiatsiia.

Koz'min, Valerian A. 1980. K voprosy o vremeni poiavleniia olenevodstva u obskikh ugrov [On the Developmental Period of the Ob' Ugrian Reindeer Economy]. In *Etnografiia Severnoi Azii*, 163–71. Novosibirsk: Nauka.

———. 1981. Ekologicheskie faktory slozhenya zapadnosibirskogo olenevodstva [Ecological Factors in the Origin of Northwestern Siberian Reindeer Breeding]. In *Metodologicheskie aspekty arkheologicheskikh i etnograficheskikh issledovanii v Zapadnoi Sibiri*, 150–53. Tomsk: Tomskii Universitet.

Krainii Sever. 1935. *Krainii Sever. Itogi perepisi khoziaistv v tryokh raionakh* [The Far North: Economic Census Data for the Three Areas]. Vol. 1. Moscow: Upravlenie Narodno-Khozyaistvennogo Ucheta RSFSR.

Krasheninnikov, Stepan. 1948. *Opisanie zemli Kamchatki* [Description of the Land of Kamchatka]. Moscow and Leningrad: Glavsevmorput'. Translated as: *Explorations of Kamchatka*. Portland: Oregon Historical Society, 1972.

Krasil'nikov, Mikhail. 1928. K voprosy ob ugasanii severnykh narodnostei [On the Extinction of the Northern Tribes]. *Statisticheskoe obozrenie* 3:97–100.

Kratkaia. 1960. *Kratkaia geograficheskaia entsiklopediia* [Abridged Geographical Encyclopedia]. Vol. 1. Moscow: Sovetskaia Entsiklopediia.

Krech, Shepard III. 1978. On the Aboriginal Population of the Kutchin. *Arctic Anthropology* 15(1): 89–104.

Krechmar, A. V., A. V. Andreev, and A. Ya. Kondrat'ev. 1978. *Ekologiia i rasprostranenie ptits na severo-vostoke SSSR* [Ecology and Ranges of Bird Species in the Northeastern USSR]. Moscow: Nauka.

Kroeber, Alfred L. 1939. *Cultural and Natural Areas of Native North America. University of California Publications in American Archae-*

ology and Ethnology 38. Berkeley: University of California Press.
Krupnik, Igor I. 1975. Prirodnaia sreda i evolyutsiia tundrovogo olenevodstva [The Natural Environment and the Evolution of Reindeer Economy]. In *Karta, skhema i chislo v etnicheskoi geografii*, M. Chlenov (ed.), 26–47. Moscow: Geograficheskoe Obshchestvo SSSR.
———. 1976a. Pitanie i ekologiia khozyaistva nentsev Bol'shezemel'skoi tundry v 20-kh godakh XX v. [Nutrition and the Ecological Basis of the Economy of the Bol'shaia Zemlia Nenets in the 1920s]. In *Nekotorye problemy etnogeneza i etnicheskoi istorii narodov mira*, P. I. Puchkov (ed.), 64–95. Moscow: Institute of Ethnography.
———. 1976b. Stanovlenie krupnotabunnogo olenevodstva u tundrovykh nentsev [The Rise of Large-Scale Reindeer Herding among the Tundra Nenets]. *Sovetskaia Etnografiia* 2:57–69.
———. 1976c. Faktory ustoichivosti i razvitiia traditsionnogo khozyaistva narodov Severa (k metodike izucheniia etnoekologicheskikh sistem) [Factors in the Stability and Evolution of the Northern Peoples' Traditional Economies (Toward a Method of Studying Ethnoecological Systems)]. Unpublished Ph.D. diss. Moscow: Institute of Ethnology and Archaeology.
———. 1977. Osvoenie sredy i ispol'zovanie promyslovykh ugodii u aziatskikh eskimosov [Environmental Exploitation and Use of Hunting Grounds by the Asiatic Eskimos]. In *Nekotorye voprosy izucheniia etnicheskikh aspektov kul'tury*, S. B. Rozhdestvenskaia (ed.), 4–17. Moscow: Institute of Ethnography.
———. 1978. K kolichestvennoi otsenke traditsionnogo khoziaistva aziatskikh eskimosov [Toward a Quantitative Approach to the Traditional Asiatic Eskimo Economy]. In *Problemy etnografii i etnicheskoi anthropologii*. V. V. Pimenov (ed.), 26–39. Moscow: Nauka.
———. 1980. Morskoi zveroboinyi promysel aziatskikh eskimosov v 1920–1930 gg. [Asiatic Eskimo Sea-Mammal Harvest during the 1920s and 1930s]. In *Morskie mlekopitaiushchie*, V. A. Zemskii (ed.), 66–79. Moscow: Pishchevaia Promyshlennost'.
———. 1981a. Drevnie poselki i demograficheskaia istoriia aziatskikh eskimosov yugo-vostoka Chukotskogo poluostrova (vkliuchaia ostrov Sviatogo Lavrentiia) [Ancient Settlements and Demographic History of the Asiatic Eskimo of the Southeastern Chukchi Peninsula (Including St. Lawrence Island)]. In *Traditisionnye kul'tury Severnoi Sibiri i Severnoi Ameriki*, I. S. Gurvich (ed.), 97–118. Moscow: Nauka.
———. 1981b. Asiatic Eskimo Traditional Subsistence Model: Cultural Continuity and Possibilities for Reconstruction. *Études/Inuit/Studies* 5(2): 3–28.
———. 1981c. K istorii aborigennoi primorskoi kul'tury v zapadnom sektore Arktiki [On the History of Aboriginal Maritime Culture in the Western Part of the Arctic]. In *Metodologicheskie aspekty arkheologicheskikh i etnograficheskikh issledovanii v Zapadnoi Sibiri*, 70–73. Tomsk: Tomskii Universitet.
———. 1983. Drevnie i traditsionnye poseleniia eskimosov na yugo-

vostoke Chukotskogo poluostrova [Ancient and Traditional Eskimo Settlements on the Southeastern Chukchi Peninsula]. In *Na styke Chukotki i Alyaski*, V. P. Alekseev (ed.), 65–95. Moscow: Nauka.

———. 1984a. Mestnyi beregovoi promysel lastonogikh na yugo-vostoke Chukotskogo poluostrova (1940–1970'e gg.) [Local Shore-Based Hunting for Pinnipeds off the Southeastern Chukchi Peninsula (from the 1940s to the 1970s)]. In *Morskie mlekopitaiushchie*, A. Yablokov and V. Zemskii (eds.), 212–23.

———. 1984b. Gray Whaling and the Aborigines of the Pacific Northwest: The History of Aboriginal Whaling. In *The Gray Whale*. Eschrichtius robustus, M. L. Jones, S. L. Swartz, and S. Leatherwood (eds.), 103–20. Orlando: Academic Press.

———. 1985. The Male-Female Ratio in Certain Traditional Populations of the Siberian Arctic. *Études/Inuit/Studies* 9(1): 115–40.

———. 1986. Aborigennyi morskoi promysel v zapadnom sektore Sovetskoi Arktiki (istoriia i traditsii) [Aboriginal Sea-Mammal Hunting in the Western Part of the Soviet Arctic (History and Cultural Traditions)]. In *Morskie mlekopitaiushchie*, V. Zemskii (ed.), Moscow.

———. 1987a. Bowhead vs. Gray Whale in Chukotka Aboriginal Whaling. *Arctic* 40(1): 16–32.

———. 1987b. Demograficheskoe razvitie aziatskikh eskimosov v 1970-e gody (Osnovnye tendentsii i etnosotsial'nye usloviia) [Demographic Transitions of the Asiatic Eskimos during the 1970s (Major Trends and Ethnosocial Conditions)]. In *Regional'nye problemy sotsio-demograficheskogo razvitiia*. B. B. Prokhorov (ed.), 85–110. Moscow: Institute of Sociology.

———. 1987c. Komandorskie ostrova: istoriia osvoeniia i traditsii prirodopol'zovaniia [The Commander Islands: History of Settling and Traditions of Resource Management]. In *Ratsional'noe prirodopol'zovanie na Komandorskikh ostrovakh*, V. E. Sokolov (ed.), 14–23. Moscow: Moskovski Universitet.

———. 1987d. Traditsii v sovremennoi zaniatosti komandorskikh aleutov [Cultural Traditions in Modern Employment among the Commander Island Aleuts]. Ibid. 174–86.

———. 1988a. Asiatic Eskimos and Marine Resources: A Case of Ecological Pulsations or Equilibrium. *Arctic Anthropology* 25(1): 94–106.

———. 1988b. Economic Patterns in Northeastern Siberia. In *Crossroads of Continents: Cultures of Siberia and Alaska*, W. W. Fitzhugh and A. Crowell (eds.), 183–91. Washington: Smithsonian Institution.

———. 1988c. Infantitsid v traditsionnykh obshchestvakh Arktiki: adaptivnaia strategiia ili kul'turnyi mekhanizm [Infanticide in Traditional Arctic Societies: Adaptive Strategy or Cultural Mechanism?]. In *Ekologiia amerikanskikh indeitsev i eskimosov*, V. A. Tishkov (ed.), 76–84. Moscow: Nauka.

———. 1988d. Osnovnye napravleniia etnoekologii Amerikanskoi Arktiki [Main Directions in the Ethnoecology of the American Arctic]. Ibid. 55–63.

———. 1990. Cultures in Contact: The Population Nadir in Siberia and North America. *European Review of Native American Studies* 4(1): 11–18.

Krupnik, Igor I., Lyudmila S. Bogoslovskaya, and Leonard M. Votrogov. 1983 Gray Whaling off Chukotka Peninsula: Past and Present Status. *Report of the International Whaling Commission* 33:557–62.

Krupnik, Igor I., and Michail A. Chlenov. 1979. Dinamika etnolingvisticheskoi situatsii u aziatskikh eskimosov (konets 19 veka-1970'e gody) [Dynamics of the Ethnolinguistic Situation among the Asiatic Eskimo (from the late Nineteenth Century and up to the 1970's)]. *Sovetskaia etnografiia* 2:19–29.

Krylov, V. M. 1936. Olenevodstvo Penzhinskogo raiona (Koriakski natsional'nyi okrug) [Reindeer Herding in the Penzhina District (Koryak Autonomous Area)]. In *Ocherki po promyslovomy khoziaistvu i olenevodstvu Krainego Severa*, 39–70. Leningrad: Institut Narodov Severa, Nauchno-Issledovatel'skaia Assotsiatsiia.

Kryuchkov, Vasili V. 1976. *Chutkaia Subarktika* [A Sensitive Subarctic]. Moscow: Nauka.

Krzywicki, Ludwik. 1934. *Primitive Society and Its Vital Statistics*. London: Macmillan.

Kudelia, E. I. 1973. Izuchenie produktivnosti pogolov'ia olenei lesotundrovoi zony Magadanskoi oblasti [A Study of Productivity among the Reindeer Population of the Tundra-Forest Zone of Magadan Province]. *Trudy Magadanskogo Instituta Sel'skogo Khoziaistva Dal'nego Vosotka* 2:43–46. Magadan.

Kulemzin, Vladislav M. 1984. *Chelovek i priroda v verovaniiakh khantov* [Man and Nature in the Traditional Beliefs of the Khanty]. Tomsk: Tomskii Universitet.

Kuratov, A. F. 1925a. K voprosy o zemleustroistve v tundrakh Evropeiskoi Rossii v sviazi s obshchim polozheniem "inorodtsev" na Severe [On Pasture Allocation in the Tundra Zone of European Russia with Regard to the General Situation of the Natives in the North]. *Komi-Mu* 3–4 (13–14): 33–47. Syktyvkar.

———. 1925b. Sostoianie olenevodstva v Bol'shezemel'skoi i Malozemel'skoi tundrakh i na Novoi Zemle [On the Status of the Reindeer Economy in the Bol'shaia and Malaia Zemlia Tundras and on the Novaia Zemlia Islands]. *Komi-Mu* 1(11): 5–9.

Lack, David. 1957. *Chislennost' zhivotnykh i eye regulyatsya v prirode* [Animal Population Numbers and Their Natural Regulation]. Moscow: Inostrannaya Literatura.

Lamb, Hubert H. 1977. *Climate: Present, Past and Future*. Vol. 2. London: Methuen.

Lantis, Margaret. 1955. Problems of Human Ecology in the North American Arctic. *Arctic Institute of North America Special Publications* 2:195–208.

Lapin, V. V. 1974. Sreda i samoreguliatsiia sotsial'nykh sistem v pervobytnuiu epokhy [Environment and Self-Regulation of Social Systems during the Primordial Age]. In *Pervobytnyi chelovek, ego material'naia kul'tura i prirodnaia sreda v pleistotsene i golotsene*, 73–86. Moscow: Institut geografii.

Larsen, Helge E., and Froelich Rainey. 1948. Ipiutak and the Arctic Whale Hunting Culture. *Anthropological Papers of the American Museum of Natural History* 42.

Lashook, Lev P. 1958. *Ocherk etnicheskoi istorii Pechorskogo kraia* [Essay in Ethnic History of the Pechora Area]. Syktyvkar.

———. 1968. "Sirtia"—drevnie obitateli Subarktiki ["Sirtia"—Ancient Residents of the Subarctic]. In *Problemy anthropologii i istoricheskoi etnografii Azii*, 178–83. Moscow: Nauka.

Lashook, Lev P., and Leonid P. Khlobystin. 1986. Sever Zapadnoi Sibiri v epokhu bronzy [The Western Siberian North during the Bronze Age]. *Kratkie soobshcheniia Instituta Arkheologii* 185:43–50.

Latkin, Vasilii N. 1853. Dnevnik vo vremia puteshestviia na Pechoru v 1840 i 1843 gg. [Diary of the Trip to Pechora River in 1840 and 1843]. Vol. 1–2. St. Petersburg.

Laughlin, William S. 1963. Eskimos and Aleuts: Their Origins and Evolution; Physiological and Cultural Adaptation to Facilitate the Evolutionary Success of Eskimo-Aleut Stock. *Science* 142(3593): 633–45.

———. 1966. Genetical and Anthropological Characteristics of Arctic Populations. In *The Biology of Human Adaptability*, P. T. Baker and J. S. Weiner (eds.), 469–95. London: Oxford University Press.

———. 1972. Ecology and Population Structure in the Arctic. In *Structure of Human Populations*, G. A. Harrison and A. J. Boyce (eds.), 379–92. Oxford: Clarendon Press.

———. 1980. *Aleuts: Survivors of the Bering Land Bridge*. New York: Holt, Rinehart, and Winston.

Laughlin, William S., and Jean S. Aigner. 1975. Aleut Adaptation and Evolution. In *Prehistoric Maritime Adaptations of the Circumpolar Zone*, W. W. Fitzhugh (ed.), 181–201. The Hague and Paris: Mouton.

Laughlin, William S., and Albert B. Harper. 1979. Demographic Diversity, Length of Life and Aleut-Eskimo Whaling. Paper prepared for Panel on Aboriginal Subsistence Whaling, Seattle.

Lebedev, Vladimir V. 1978. Rol' olenevodstva v khoziaistvennom komlekse tazovskikh sel'kupov (k probleme stanovleniia proizvodiashchego olenevodcheskogo khoziaistva) [The Role of Reindeer Herding in the Economy of the Taz Sel'kups (On the Rise of a Food-Producing Reindeer Economy)]. In *Problemy etnografii i etnicheskoi anthropologii*, V. V. Pimenov et al. (eds.), 14–25. Moscow: Nauka.

———. 1980. Sem'ia i proizvodstvennyi kollektiv u naseleniia pritundrovoi polosy severo-zapada Turukhanskogo kraia v XIX v. [Family and Productive Unit among the Tundra Residents of the Northwestern Turukhan Area in the 1800's]. *Sovetskaia etnografiia* 2:82–91.

Lebedev, Vladimir V., and Elena A. Oborotova. 1991. K voprosu ob ecologicheskom gomeostaze v traditisionnykh obshchestvakh Arktiki i

Subarktiki [On Ecological Homeostasis in Traditional Societies in the Arctic and Subarctic]. In *Etnicheskaia ekologiia*, V. V. Kozlov (ed.), 270–86. Moscow: Nauka.

Lebedeva, L. S. 1972. Los' Severnoi Ameriki [The North American Moose]. In *Okhotovedenie*, 299–316. Moscow.

Lebedinskaia, Galina V. 1969. Patologicheskie izmeneniia na skeletakh iz Ekvenskogo mogil'nika [Pathological Modifications on the Ancient Skeletons from the Ekven Cemetery]. In S. A. Arutiunov and D. A. Sergeev, *Drevnie kul'tury aziatskikh eskimosov. Uelenskii mogil'nik*, 195–200. Moscow: Nauka.

Lee, Richard B., and Irven DeVore (eds.). 1968. *Man the Hunter*. Chicago: Aldine.

Leeds, Anthony. 1965. Reindeer Herding and Chukchi Social Institutions. In *Man, Culture, and Animals. The Role of Animals in Human Ecological Adjustment*, A. Leeds (ed.), 87–128. Washington: American Association for the Advancement of Science.

———. 1976. Economics and Subsistence. In *Encyclopedia of Anthropology*, D. Hunter and P. Whitten (eds.), 138–40. New York: Harper & Row.

Leont'ev, Vladilen V. 1983. *Etnografiia i fol'klor kerekov* [Ethnography and Folklore of the Kereks]. Moscow: Nauka.

Lepekhin, Ivan. 1805. Dnevnye zapiski puteshestviia po raznym provintsiiam Rossiiskogo gosudarstva [Diary Notes of a Journey through Various Provinces of the Russian State]. Vol. 4. Petersburg.

Le Resche, R. E., R. H. Bishop and J. W. Coady. 1974. Distribution and Habitats of Moose in Alaska. *Naturaliste Canadien* 101(1): 143–78.

Lerrigo, P. H. J. 1901. Report from St. Lawrence Island. In *10th Annual Report on Introduction of Domestic Reindeer into Alaska*, 98–132. Washington, D.C.: Government Printing Office.

Levin, Maksim G. 1947. K probleme istoricheskogo sootnosheniia khozyaistvenno-kul'turnykh tipov Severnoi Azii [On the Historical Sequence of Economic-Cultural Types in Northern Asia]. *Kratkie soobshcheniia Instituta etnografii* 2:84–86.

———. 1958. Etnicheskaia antropologiia i problemy etnogeneza narodov Dal'nego Vostoka [Ethnic Anthropology and the Problems of Ethnogenesis of the Peoples of the Far East]. *Trudy Instituta Etnografii* 36. Moscow. Reprinted as: Ethnic Origins of the Peoples of Northeastern Asia. *Arctic Institute of North America. Translations from Russian Sources* 3. Toronto: University of Toronto Press, 1963.

———. 1960. Problems of Arctic Ethnology and Ethnogenesis. *Acta Arctica*, fasc 12. Proceedings of the Circumpolar Conference in Copenhagen, 47–60.

Levin, Maksim G., and Nikolai N. Cheboksarov. 1955. Khoziaistvenno-kul'turnye tipy i istoriko-etnograficheskie oblasti [Economic-Cultural Types and Historical-Ethnographic Areas]. *Sovetskaia etnografiia* 4:3–17.

———. 1957. Obshchie svedeniia (rasy, yazuki, narody) [General Setting

(Races, Languages, and Peoples)]. In *Ocherki obshchei etnografii*, vol. 1, S. P. Tolstov, M. G. Levin, and N. N. Cheboksarov (eds.), 6–55. Moscow: Academy of Sciences.

Levin, Maksim G., and Leonid P. Potapov (eds.). 1956. *Narody Sibiri* [Peoples of Siberia]. Moscow and Leningrad: Academy of Sciences. Reprinted as: *The Peoples of Siberia*. Chicago: University of Chicago Press, 1964.

Levin, Michael J. 1991. Alaska Natives in a Century of Change. *Anthropological Papers of the University of Alaska*. 23(1–2): XX, 1–217.

Liprandi, K. 1933. Syr'evye resursy Chukotki [Natural Resources of the Chukchi Peninsula]. *Sovetskii Sever* 6:58–59.

Liubin, V. P., and G. F. Baryshnikov. 1985. Okhotnich'ia deiatel'nost' drevneishikh (ashelo-must'erskikh) obitatelei Kavkaza [Hunting Activity of the Most Ancient (Ashell-Moustier) Inhabitants of the Caucasus]. *Kratkie soobshcheniia Instituta arkheologii* 181:5–9.

Lobdell, John E., and Albert A. Dekin, Jr. 1984. Introduction. *Arctic Anthropology* 21(1): 1–4.

Lotz, Jim. 1976. Area Economic Surveys: Critique and Assessment. In *Inuit Land Use and Occupancy Project*, M. Freeman (ed.), 2:23–30. Ottawa: Department of Indian and Northern Affairs.

Lovelius, N. V. 1970. Teploobespechennost' gor Putorana i ledovitost' Baltiki [The Warming Conditions of the Putorana Mountains and the Baltic Sea-Ice]. *Izvestiia Vsesoiuznogo Geograficheskogo Obshchestva* 102(1): 63–65.

———. 1979. *Izmenchivost' prirosta derev'ev. Dendroindikatsiia prirodnykh protsessov i antropogennykh vozdeistvii* [Fluctuations in Tree-Ring Growth. The Dendro-Indication of Natural Processes and Human Agents]. Leningrad: Nauka.

Lowie, Robert H. 1938. Subsistence. In *General Anthropology*, F. Boas (ed.), 282–326. Boston, etc.: D. C. Heath and Company.

Luk'ianchenko, Tat'iana V. 1971. *Material'naia kul'tura saamov Kol'skogo poluostrova kontsa XIX–XX v.* [Material Culture of the Kola Saami of the late 1800s and 1900s]. Moscow: Nauka.

Lundmark, Lennart. 1989. The Rise of Reindeer Pastoralism. In *Readings in Saami History, Culture, and Language*, N. Broadbent (ed.), 31–44. *Center for Arctic Cultural Research. Umea University. Miscellaneous Publications* 7. Umea.

McCartney, Allen P. 1975. Maritime Adaptation in Cold Archipelagoes: An Analysis of Environment and Culture in the Aleutian and Other Island Chains. In *Prehistoric Maritime Adaptations of the Circumpolar Zone*, W. W. Fitzhugh (ed.), 281–338. The Hague and Paris: Mouton.

———. 1980. The Nature of Thule Eskimo Whale Use. *Arctic* 33(3): 517–41.

———. 1984. History of Native Whaling in the Arctic and Subarctic. In *Arctic Whaling*, 79–112. Groningen: University of Groningen.

McCartney, Allen P., and Edward D. Mitchell. 1988. Marine Megafauna: Human Ecology and Thule Eskimo Whaling. Paper Presented at the 53rd Annual Meeting of the Society for American Archaeology. Phoenix, Ariz.

McCartney, Allen P., and James Savelle. 1985. Thule Eskimo Whaling in the Central Canadian Arctic. *Arctic Anthropology* 22(2): 37–58.

McDonald, Jerry N. 1984. The Reordered North American Selection Regime and Late Quaternary Megafaunal Extinctions. In *Quaternary Extinctions: A Prehistoric Revolution*, P. S. Martin and R. G. Klein (eds.), 404–39. Tucson: University of Arizona Press.

McGhee, Robert. 1969–70. Speculations on Climatic Change and Thule Cultural Development. *Folk* 11–12:173–84. Copenhagen.

———. 1972. Climatic Change and the Development of the Canadian Arctic Cultural Traditions. In *Climatic Changes in the Arctic Areas during the last 10,000 Years*, Y. Vasari et al. (eds.), 39–60. *Acta Universitatis Ouluensis. Series A. Geologica* 1. Oulu, Finland.

———. 1974. Beluga Hunters. An Archaeological Reconstruction of the History and Culture of the Mackenzie Delta Kittegaryumiut. *Newfoundland Social and Economic Studies* 13. Toronto: University of Toronto Press.

———. 1984. Thule Prehistory of Canada. In *Arctic*, D. Damas (ed.), 369–76. *Handbook of North American Indians* 5. Washington, D.C.: Smithsonian Institution.

———. 1988. Proiskhozhdenie eskimosov: vozmozhna li al'ternativnaia gipoteza [Origin of the Eskimos: an Alternative Hypothesis]. With Comments by Igor Krupnik. *Sovetskaia etnografiia* 3:110–17.

McGovern, Thomas. 1979. Thule-Norse Interaction in Southwest Greenland; A Speculative Model. In *Thule Eskimo Culture: An Anthropological Retrospective*, A. P. McCartney (ed.), 171–88. *Archaeological Survey of Canada* 88. Ottawa.

Macpherson, A. H. 1981. Commentary: Wildlife Conservation and Canada's North. *Arctic* 34(2): 103–107.

Maher, William I., and Norman J. Wilimovsky. 1963. Annual Catch of Bowhead Whales by Eskimos at Point Barrow, Alaska, 1928–1960. *Journal of Mammology* 44(1): 16–20.

Makridin, K. V. 1962. O severnoi granitse rasprostraneniia losia [On the Northern Limit of Elk/Moose Distribution]. *Zoologicheskii zhurnal* 41(7): 1090–94.

Makridina, K. V. 1956. Kaloriinost' olen'ego miasa [The Caloric Content of Reindeer Meat]. *Karakulevodstvo i zverovodstvo* 1:57.

Maksimov, A. A. 1984. *Mnogoletnie kolebaniia chislennosti zhivotnykh, ikh prichiny i prognoz* [Long-Term Fluctuations in Animal Populations: Their Causes and Forecast]. Novosibirsk: Nauka.

Maksimov, Aleksandr N. 1929. Proiskhozhdenie olenevodstva [The Origin of Reindeer Breeding]. *Uchenye zapiski Instituta istorii* 6.

Maksimov, I. V. 1954. Vekovye kolebaniia ledovitosti severnoi chasti Atlanticheskogo okeana [Age-Old Sea-Ice Fluctuations in the Northern Atlantic]. *Trudy Instituta okeanologii* 8:41–91. Moscow.

Malaurie, Jean-Noel. 1973. *Zagadochnyi Tule* [The Mysterious Thule]. Moscow: Mysl'. Russian translation from the original French edition: "Les Derniers rois du Thule; une annee parmi les Eskimos polaires du Groenland." Paris: Plon, 1955.

Mamadyshskii, N. N. 1910. *Usinskii krai. Podvorno-ekonomicheskoe issledovanie poselenii r.Usy v 1909 g.* [The Usinsk Area: A Household Economic Inventory along the Usa River in 1909]. Arkhangel'sk.

Marquette, Willman M., and John Bockstoce. 1980. Historical Shore-Based Catch of Bowhead Whales in the Bering, Chukchi, and Beaufort Seas. *Marine Fisheries Review* 42(9–10): 5–19.

Marquette, Willman M., and Howard W. Braham. 1982. Gray Whale Distribution and Catch by Alaskan Eskimos: A Replacement for the Bowhead Whale? *Arctic* 35(3): 386–94.

Martin, Calvin. 1978. *Keepers of the Game: Indian-Animal Relationships and the Fur Trade*. Berkeley: University of California Press.

Martin, Paul S. 1967a. Prehistoric Overkill. In *Pleistocene Extinctions: The Search for a Cause*, P. S. Martin and H. E. Wright, Jr. (eds.), 75–120. New Haven: Yale University Press.

———. 1967b. Pleistocene Overkill. *Natural History* 76(1): 32–38.

———. 1973. The Discovery of America. *Science* 179(4077): 969–74.

———. 1982. The Pattern and Meaning of Holarctic Mammoth Extinction. In *Paleoecology of Beringia*, D. M. Hopkins, et al. (eds.), 399–408. New York: Academic Press.

———. 1984. Prehistoric Overkill: The Global Model. In *Quaternary Extinctions: A Prehistoric Revolution*, P. S. Martin and R. G. Klein (eds.), 354–403. Tucson: University of Arizona Press.

Martin, Paul S., and H. E. Wright (eds.). 1967. *Pleistocene Extinctions: The Search for a Cause*. New Haven: Yale University Press.

Martin, Paul S., and Richard G. Klein (eds.). 1984. *Quaternary Extinctions: A Prehistoric Revolution*. Tucson: University of Arizona Press.

Maserang, C. H. 1977. Carrying Capacity and Low Population Control. *Journal of Anthropological Research* 33(4): 474–92.

Maslov, P. P. 1934. Kochevye ob'edineniia edinolichnykh khoziaistv v tundre Severnogo kraia [Nomadic Groupings of Individual Families in the Northern Province Tundra]. *Sovetskii Sever* 5:27–34.

Masnik, G. S. and S. H. Katz. 1976. Adaptive Childbearing in a North Slope Eskimo Community. *Human Biology* 48(1): 37–58.

Mason, Otis T. 1896. Influence of Environment Upon Human Industries or Arts. *Annual Report of the Smithsonian Institution for 1895*, 639–65. Washington, D.C.: Smithsonian Institution.

———. 1907. Environment. In *Handbook of North American Indians North of Mexico*, F. W. Hodge (ed.), 427–30: *Bureau of American Ethnology Bulletin* 30. Washington, D.C.

Masson, Vadim M. 1976. *Ekonomika i sotsial'nyi stroi drevnikh obshchestv* [Economy and Social Structure of Ancient Societies]. Leningrad: Nauka.

Materialy Anadyrskoi expeditsii. 1950. Materialy Anadyrskoi zemexpeditsii MSKH RSFSR o khoziaistvennom, agrotekhnicheskom i zootechnicheskom obsledovanii kolkhozov Chuktoskogo raiona, 1946–1950 [Report of the Anadyr Surveying Expedition, Russian Ministry of Agriculture, on the Economic, Agro- and Zootechnical Survey of the Collective Farms of the Chukchi District, 1946–1950]. Manuscript, F.3, op. 1. no. 21, 24, 34, 37. State Archive of the Chukchi Autonomous Area, Anadyr.

Materialy Chukotskoi zemekspeditsii. 1938. Materialy Chukotskoi zemexpeditsii Narkomzema RSFSR o khoziaistvenno-ekonomicheskom obsledovanii Chukotskogo raiona [Report of the Chukchi Surveying Expedition of the Russian Comissariat of Agriculture on the Economic Survey of the Chukchi District]. Manuscript, F.3, op. 1, no. 7. State Archive of the Chukchi Autonomous Area, Anadyr.

Materialy po statistike. 1925. *Materialy po statistike Kamchatskoi gubernii* [Data on the Statistics of the Kamchatka Province]. Khabarovsk: Upravlenie Statistiki.

Materialy Pripoliarnoi. 1929. *Materialy Pripoliarnoi perepisi 1926–1927 gg. v Sibirskom krae* [Data of the 1926–1927 Polar North Census in the Siberian Province]. Vols. 1–3. Krasnoyarsk-Novosibirsk: Sibirskii Kraevoi Statisticheskii Otdel.

Maxwell, Moreau S. 1985. *Prehistory of the Eastern Arctic*. Orlando, Florida: Academic Press.

Meldgaard, Morten. 1986. The Greenland Caribou—Zoogeography, Taxonomy, and Population Dynamics. *Meddelelser om Grønland. Bioscience* 20. Copenhagen.

———. 1987. Human Implications of Arctic Animal Population Fluctuations: Caribou in Greenland. In *Arctic Heritage. Proceedings of a Symposium*, J. G. Nelson, R. Needham, and L. Norton (eds.), 242–51. Banff, Canada.

———. 1988. The Great Auk, *Pinguines impennis* (L) in Greenland. *Historical Biology* 1:145–78.

Mel'nikov, V. I. 1925. K voprosu o pomoshchi brodiachim i kochevym narodnostiam [On the Issue of Aid to the Nomad and Wandering Populations]. *Severnaia Aziia* 5–6:160–64.

Menovshchikov, Georgii A. 1956. Eskimosy [The Eskimos]. In *Narody Sibiri*, M. G. Levin and L. P. Potapov (eds.), 934–49. Moscow: Academy of Sciences. English translation: The Eskimos. In *The Peoples of Siberia*, M. Levin and L. Potapov (eds.), 836–50. Chicago and London: University of Chicago Press.

———. 1959. *Eskimosy* [The Eskimos]. Magadan: Knizhnoe Izdatel'stvo.

———. 1982. Otrazhenye polozhitel'nykh narodnykh znanii v yazyke aziatskikh eskimosov [Rational Knowledge of the Environment as Reflected in the Language of the Asiatic Eskimos]. *Kraevedcheskie zapiski* 11:154–64. Magadan.

Mériot, Christian. 1980. *Les Lapons et leur société: Étude d'ethnologie historique*. Paris: Privat.

———. 1984. The Saami People from the Time of the Voyage of Otter to Thomas fon Westen. *Arctic* 37(4): 373–84.

Mikhel', N. M. 1938. *Promyslovye zveri severo-vostochnoi Yakutii* [Game Animals of Northeastern Yakutia]. Leningrad: Glavsevmorput'.

Mikkelsen, Ejnar. 1944. The East Greenlanders' Possibilities of Existence, Their Production and Consumption. *Meddelelser om Grønland* 134(2).

Miller, Vsevolod F. 1897. Ob eskimosskikh narechiiakh Anadyrskogo okruga [On the Eskimo Dialects of the Anadyr District]. *Zhivaia starina* 2:133–59. Moscow.

Minc, Leah D. 1986. Scarcity and Survival: The Role of Oral Tradition in Mediating Subsistence Crises. *Journal of Anthropological Archaeology* 5:39–113.

Minc, Leah D., and Kevin P. Smith. 1989. The Spirit of Survival: Cultural Responses to Resource Variability in North Alaska. In *Bad Year Economics: Cultural Responses to Risk and Uncertainty*, P. Halstead and J. O'Shea (eds.), 8–39. Cambridge: Cambridge University Press.

Mineev, Aref I. 1946. *Ostrov Vrangelia* [Wrangell Island]. Moscow and Leningrad: Glavsevmorput'.

Minenko, Nina A. 1975. Materialy po obychnomu pravu narodov Severo-Zapadnoi Sibiri 1-oi poloviny XIX v. [Data on the Traditional Law of the Natives of Northwest Siberia during the First Half of the Nineteenth Century]. In *Arkheografiia i istochnikovedenie Sibiri*, 30–46. Novosibirsk: Nauka.

Mitusova, R. P. 1925. Materialy po biudzhetam krestianskikh samoyedskikh i ostiatskikh khoziaistv [Budget Data on Samoyed and Ostyak Peasant Households]. *Statistika Urala. Series V.* 5:104–28.

Moberg, Carl-Axel. 1975. Circumpolar Adaptation Zones East-West and Cross-Economy Contacts North-South: An Outsider's Query, Especially on Ust'-Poluj. In *Prehistoric Maritime Adaptations of the Circumpolar Zone*, W. W. Fitzhugh (ed.), 101–12. The Hague and Paris: Mouton.

Molchanov, A. A. 1976. *Dendro-klimaticheskie osnovy prognozov pogody* [Dendro-Climatic Grounds for Weather Forecasts]. Moscow: Nauka.

Mongait, A. L. 1973. *Arkheologiia Zapadnoi Evropy. Kamennyi vek* [Archaeology of Western Europe: The Stone Age]. Moscow: Nauka.

Moran, Emilio F. 1982. *Human Adaptability: An Introduction to Ecological Anthropology*. Boulder: Westview Press.

Morzveroboinyi Promysel. 1934. Morzveroboinyi promysel i morzveroboinaia promyshlennost' [Sea-Mammal Hunting and the Sea-Mammal Industry]. Manuscript, F. R-94, op.1, no.11, pp.29–72. State Archive of the Magadan Province, Magadan.

Mosimann, James E., and Paul S. Martin. 1975. Simulating Overkill by Paleoindians. *American Scientist* 63(3): 304–13.

Muir, John. 1917. *The Cruise of the Corwin: Journal of the Arctic Expedition of 1881 in Search of De Long and the Jeannette*. Boston and New York: Houghton and Mifflin Co.

Mukhachev, A. D. 1969. Miasnaia produktivnost severnogo olenia v zavisimosti ot pola, vozrasta i upitannosti [Meat Productivity of Domestic Reindeer with Regard to Their Age, Gender, and Fatness]. *Trudy Vsesoiuznogo Sel'skokhoziastvennogo Instituta zaochnogo obrazovaniia* 31:108–11.

Murdock, George P. 1967a. The Ethnographic Atlas: A Summary. *Ethnology* 6(2): 109–236.

———. 1967b. *Social Structure*. New York: The Free Press.

Murdock, George P., and Timothy J. O'Leary (comps.). 1975. *Ethnographic Bibliography of North America*. 4th ed. Vol. 2, *Arctic and Subarctic*. New Haven: Human Relations Area Files Press.

Murdock, George P., and Douglas R. White. 1969. Standard Cross-Cultural Sample. *Ethnology* 8(4): 329–69.

Na Perelome. 1989. Na Perelome [At the Turning Point]. A round-table discussion. *Sovetskaia kul'tura* 18:3.

Nansen, Fridtjof. 1937. *Zhizn' eskimosov* [The Eskimo Life]. Leningrad. Russian Translation from the original Norwegian edition *Eskimoliv*. Kristiania, 1891.

Narodnoe khoziaistvo. 1972. *Narodnoe khoziaistvo SSSR. 1922–1972 gg.* [State Economy of the USSR, 1922–1972]. Moscow: Statistika.

Narr, Karl J. 1956. Early Food-Producing Populations. In *Man's Role in Changing the Face of the Earth*, W. L. Thomas, Jr. (ed.), 134–51. Chicago: University of Chicago Press.

Naselennye Punkty. 1928. *Naselennye Punkty Ural'skoi oblasti* [Settlements of the Ural Province]. Vol. 12 (Tobol'sk District). Sverdlovsk.

Nasimovich, A. A. 1955. *Rol' snezhnogo pokrova v zhizni kopytnykh zhivotnykh na territorii SSSR* [The Role of Snow-Cover in the Life of Ungulates throughout the Territory of the USSR]. Moscow: Academy of Sciences.

Native Livelihood. 1979. *Native Livelihood and Dependence. A Study of Land-Use Values Through Time*. Anchorage.

Naumov, Nikolai P. 1933. *Dikii severnyi olen'* [Wild Reindeer]. Moscow and Leningrad: KOIZ.

———. 1934. Mlekopitaiushchie Tungusskogo okruga [Mammals of the Tungus Area]. *Trudy Poliarnoi Komissii AN SSSR* 17.

Naumov, Sergei P. 1939. Kolebaniia chislennosti u zaitsev [Population Fluctuations among the Arctic Hare]. *Voprosy ekologii i biogeotsenologii* 5–6:40–82. Leningrad.

Nazarov, A. A. 1979. Raspredelenie i ispol'zovanie resursov pestsa [Distribution and Management of Arctic Fox Game Resources]. In *Okhotnich'e-promyslovoe khoziaistvo Severa*, 88–109. Moscow.

Nazarov, V. S. 1947. Istoricheskii khod ledovitosti Karskogo moria [Historical Trends in the Kara Sea Ice]. *Izvestiia Vsesoyuznogo Geograficheskogo Obshchestva* 79(6): 653–55.

———. 1949. *Kolebaniia ledovitsti morei* [Fluctuations in Sea Ice]. Moscow and Leningrad: Gidrometeoizdat.

Nechiporenko, G. P. 1927. Morzhovyi promysel na Chukotke [Walrus

Hunting off the Chukchi Peninsula]. *Ekonomicheskaia zhizn' Dal'nego Vostoka* 6–7:169–77.
Nellemann, George. 1969. Caribou Hunting in West Greenland. *Folk* 11–12:133–54. Copenhagen.
Nelson, Richard K. 1969. *Hunters of the Northern Ice*. Chicago: University of Chicago Press.
———. 1973. *Hunters of the Northern Forest*. Chicago: University of Chicago Press.
———. 1980. Athapaskan Subsistence Adaptations in Alaska. In *Alaska Native Culture and History*, Y. Kotani and W. B. Workman (eds.), 205–32. *Senri Ethnological Studies* 4. Osaka.
Nichols, Harvey. 1972. Summary of the Palynological Evidence for Late-Quaternary Vegetation and Climate Change in the Central and Eastern Canadian Arctic. In Climatic Changes in Arctic Areas During the Last 10,000 Years, Y. Vasari et al. (eds.), 309–39. *Acta Universitatis Ouluensis. Series A. Geologica* 1. Oulu.
———. 1975. Palynological and Paleoclimatic Study of the Late Quaternary Displacement of the Boreal Forest-Tundra Ecotone in Keewatin and Mackenzie, N.W.T., Canada. *Institute of Arctic and Alpine Research, Occasional Paper* 15.
Nikkul', K. 1975. Nekotorye osobennosti olenevodstva u saamov [Some Peculiarities of Saami Reindeer Breeding]. *Sovetskaia etnografiia* 4:131–37.
Nikulin, P. G. 1941. Chukotskii morzh [Walrus of Chukotka]. *Izvestiia TINRO* 20:21–60. Vladivostok.
Norin, Boris N. 1974. Nekotorye problemy izucheniia vzaimootnoshenii lesnykh i tundrovykh ekosistem [On the Issue of Studies of Interrelationships Between Forest and Tundra Ecosystems]. *Botanicheskii zhurnal* 59(9): 1254–68.
Norin, B. N., I. V. Ignatenko, A. V. Knorre, and N. V. Lovelius. 1971. Rastitel'nost' i pochvy lesnogo massiva Ary-Mas (Taimyr) [Vegetation and Soils of the Ary-Mas Forest (Taimyr Peninsula)]. *Botanicheskii zhurnal* 56(9): 1272–83.
Oborotova, Elena A. 1988. Narody Severa v sovremennom mire: vzglyady i pozitsii [The Peoples of the North in the Modern World: Perspectives and Viewpoints]. *Sovetskaia etnografiia* 5:146–49.
O'Brien, McMillan P. (comp.). 1982. *Alaska Subsistence Bibliography*. Anchorage.
Obukhov, P. 1967. Dikii olen' v nizov'iakh Kolymy [Wild Reindeer in the Kolyma River Low Reaches]. *Okhota i okhotnich'e khoziaistvo* 5:17. Moscow.
Odum, Howard T. 1967. Energetics of World Food Production. In *The World Food Problem: A Report to the President's Science Advisory Committee*, 3:55–94. Washington, D.C.
———. 1971. *Environment, Power, and Society*. New York etc.: Wiley-Interscience.

Øgrim, M. 1970. The Nutrition of Lapps. *Arctic Anthropology* 7(1): 49–52.

Okladnikov, Aleksei P. 1941. Paleoliticheskie zhilishcha v Bureti (po raskopkam 1936–1940 gg.) [Palaeolithic Dwellings at the Buret' Site (According to the Excavations of 1936–1940)]. *Kratkie soobshcheniia Instituta istorii material'noi kul'tury* 10:16–31. Leningrad.

Okladnikov, Aleksei P., and Nina A. Beregovaya. 1971. *Drevnie poseleniia Baranova mysa* [Ancient Settlements of Cape Baranov]. Novosibirsk: Nauka.

Olenevodstvo. n.d. Olenevodstvo. Chukotskoe olenevodstvo [Reindeer Breeding. Chukchi Reindeer Breeding]. Manuscript, F.K-V, op. 1, no. 525. Institute-Museum of Anthropology and Ethnography, St. Petersburg.

Olson, Dean Fransis. 1969. Alaska Reindeer Herdsmen. A Study of Native Management in Transition. *Institute of Social, Economic and Government Research, Special Report* 22. College, Alaska.

Olsuf'ev, A. V. 1896. Obshchii ocherk Anadyrskoi okrugi, eyo ekonomicheskogo sostoianiia i byta naseleniia [General Review of the Anadyr District, Its Economic Situation and Lifestyles of the Residents]. *Zapiski Priamurskogo Otdela Russkogo Geograficheskogo Obshchestva* 2(1). Khabarovsk.

Orlova, Elena P. 1936. "Yupigyty" (aziatskie eskimosy) ['Yupigyt' (The Asiatic Eskimos)]. Manuscript, F.K-II, op. 1, no. 179. Institute-Museum of Anthropology and Ethnology, St. Petersburg.

———. 1941. Aziatskie eskimosy [The Asiatic Eskimo]. *Izvestiia Russkogo Geograficheskogo Obshchestva* 73(2): 201–22. Moscow.

Orlove, Benjamin S. 1980. Ecological Anthropology. *Annual Review of Anthropology* 9:235–73.

Orlovskii, P. N. 1928a. Anadyrsko-chukotskoye olenevodstvo [The Reindeer Industry of the Anadyr-Chukchi Area]. *Severnaia Aziia* 1:45–54.

———. 1928b. God anadyrsko-chuktoskogo olenevoda [The Yearly Cycle of an Anadyr-Chukchi Reindeer Herdsman]. *Severnaia Aziia* 2:61–70.

Osherenko, Gail. 1988. Can Comanagement Save Arctic Wildlife? *Environment* 30(6): 7–13, 29–33.

Panin, G. 1930. Vliianie klimaticheskikh izmenenii na severnogo olenia [The Influence of Climatic Change on Reindeer]. *Sovetskii Sever* 7–8: 60–64.

Parmuzin, Iurii P. 1967. Landshaftnoe raionirovanie lesotundr i severnykh redkolesii zaeniseiskikh territorii [Landscape Typology of the Forest-Tundra and Shrub Zones of the Trans-Enisei Area]. In *Rastitel'nost' lesotundry i puti eyo osvoeniia*, 20–28.

Parovshchikov, V. Ia. 1959. Izmeneniia arealov mlekopitaiushchikh severa Evropeiskoi chasti SSSR [Changes in the Ranges of Mammals of the Northern Section of the European Part of the USSR]. In *Geografiia rasseleniia nazemnykh zhivotnykh i metody eye izucheniia*, Moscow: 217–26. Academy of Sciences.

Parrack, Dwain W. 1969. An Approach to the Bioenergetics of Rural West Bengal. In *Environment and Cultural Behavior: Ecological Studies in Cultural Anthropology*, A. P. Vayda (ed.), 29–46. Garden City, N.Y.: The Natural History Press.

Patkanov, Serafim K. 1911. *O priroste inorodcheskogo naseleniia Sibiri. Statisticheskie materialy dlia osveshcheniia voprosa o vymiranii tuzemnykh plemyon* [On the Growth of the Native Population of Siberia: Statistical Data Regarding the Issue of Extinction of the Native Tribes]. St. Petersburg.

———. 1912. Statisticheskie dannye pokazyvaiushchie plemennoi sostav naseleniia Sibiri, iazyk i rody inorodtsev [Statistical Data on the Tribal Composition of the Siberian Population, on Language and Clan Structure of the Aliens]. *Zapiski Russkogo Geograficheskogo Obshchestva (Otdelenie statistiki)* 11(1).

Pavlov, P. N. 1972. *Pushnoi promysel v Sibiri v 17 v.* [Fur Harvesting in Siberia during the Seventeenth Century]. Krasnoiarsk: Krasnoiarskoye Knizhnoe Izdatel'stvo.

Perri, R. 1976. *Mir morzha* [The World of the Walrus]. Leningrad: Gidrometeoizdat.

Pershits, Abram I. 1979. Etnografiia kak istochnik pervobytnoistoricheskikh rekonstruktsii [Ethnography as a Source for Prehistoric Reconstructions]. In *Etnografiia kak istochnik rekonstruktsii istorii pervobytnogo obshchestva*, A. I. Pershits (ed.), 26–42. Moscow: Nauka.

Petrin, V. T. 1986. *Paleoliticheskie pamiatniki Zapadno-Sibirskoi ravniny* [Palaeolithic Monuments of the West Siberian Plain]. Novosibirsk: Nauka.

Petrunenko, Oksana. 1991. A Soviet Reservation? Yes! *IWGIA Newsletter* 1:40–41.

Petrukhin, S. 1926. Rybnye i morskie promysly Okhotsko-Kamchatskogo kraia [Fish and Sea-Mammal Industries of the Okhotsk-Kamchatsk Region]. *Severnaia Aziia* 1:53–59. Moscow.

Pidoplichko, Ivan G. 1953. Amvrosievskaia paleoliticheskaia stoianka i eye osobennosti [The Amvrosiev Paleolithic Site and Its Features]. *Kratkie soobshcheniia Instituta arkheologii Ukrainy* 2:63–65.

———. 1964. Vliianie cheloveka na razvitie fauny v pleistotsene i golotsene [Man's Impact on the Development of Animal Life in the Pleistocene and Holocene]. Paper presented at the 7th International Congress of Anthropological and Ethnological Sciences. Moscow: Nauka.

———. 1969. *Pozdnepaleoliticheskie zhilishcha iz kostei mamonta na Ukraine* [Upper Paleolithic Mammoth-Bone Dwellings in the Ukraine]. Kiev: Naukova Dumka.

———. 1976. *Mezhirichskie zhilishcha iz kostei mamonta* Mammoth-Bone Dwellings at Mezhirich]. Kiev: Naukova Dumka.

Pika, Alexandr I. 1981. Biologicheskie resursy Sos'vinskogo Priob'ia i ikh ispol'zovanie aborigennym naseleniem v 17–19 vv. [Biological Resources of the Sos'va-Ob' Area and Its Exploitation by the Indigenous Residents from the 1600s to the 1800s]. In *Metodologicheskie aspekty arkheo-*

logicheskikh i etnograficheskikh issledovanii v Zapadnoi Sibiri. Tomsk: Tomskii Universitet.

———. 1986. Gomeostaz v demograficheskoi istorii narodov Severa (XVII–XIX vv.): real'nost' ili illiuziia? [Homeostasis in the Demographic History of the Northern Peoples (Seventeenth to Nineteenth Centuries): A Reality or An Illusion?]. *Sovetskaia etnografiia* 3:36–46.

———. 1988. Bioresursy zapadno-sibirskogo Severa i ikh ispol'zovanie korennyn naseleniem v XVII–XIX vv. [The Biological Resources of the West Siberian North and Their Utilization by the Aborigines in the Seventeenth to Nineteenth Centuries]. In *Sotsial'no-Economicheskie Problemy Drevnei Istorii Sibiri*, 131–41. Tobol'sk: Tobol'sk Pedagogical Institute.

Pika, Alexandr I., and Boris B. Prokhorov. 1989. The Big Problems of Small Ethnic Groups. *IWGIA Newsletter* 57:123–35. Originally published in *Communist* 16 (1988).

Pletsov, N. 1925. Samoyedy Bol'shezemel'skoi i Malozemel'skoi Tundr (po dannym perepisi 1924 goda) [The Samoyeds of the Bol'shaia and Malaia Zemlia Tundras (According to the Census Data of 1924)]. *Severnoe khoziaistvo* 2–3. Arkhangel'sk.

Podekrat, A. G. 1936. Promysly ostrova Kolgueva [Hunting Economies of the Kolguev Island]. In *Ocherki po promyslovomu khoziaistvu i olenevodstvu Krainego Severa*. 71–115. Leningrad: Institut Narodov Severa, Nauchno-Issledovatel'skaia Assotsiatsiia.

Pokhoziaistvennaia Perepis'. 1929. *Pokhoziaistvennaia Perepis' Pripoliarnogo Severa SSSR 1926–27 g. Territorial'nye i gruppovye itogi perepisi* [Economic Census of the Polar North of the USSR, 1926–1927. Areal and Group Results]. Moscow: Statizdat.

Polozova, L. G., and S. G. Shiyatov. 1976. Vekovye kolebaniia klimata na osnove analiza godichnogo prirosta derev'ev vdol' poliarnoi granitsy lesa [Age-Old Climate Fluctuations Based on the Analysis of Annual Tree-Ring Growth along The Polar Tree Line]. In *Istoriia biotsenozov SSSR v golotsene*, 14–23. Moscow: Nauka.

Popov, Andrei A. 1935. Olenevodstvo u dolgan [Reindeer Economy of the Dolgans]. *Sovetskaia etnografiia* 4–5:185–205.

———. 1946. Semeinaia zhizn' u dolgan [Family Life among the Dolgans]. *Sovetskaia etnografiia* 4:50–74.

———. 1948. Nganasany. Material'naia kul'tura [The Nganasans: Material Culture]. *Trudy Instituta Etnografii* 4. Moscow.

———. 1952. Kochevaia zhizn' i tipy zhilishch u dolgan [Nomadic Life and the Typology of Dwellings among the Dolgans]. *Trudy Instituta Etnografii* 18:142–72.

———. 1984. *Nganasany. Sotsial'noe ustroistvo i verovaniia* [The Nganasans: Social Structure and Beliefs]. Leningrad: Nauka.

Portenko, Leonid A. 1941. Fauna Anadyrskogo kraia [The Fauna of the Anadyr Area]. *Trudy Instituta poliarnogo zemledelya, zhivotnovodstva i promyslovogo khoziaistva* (*Series "Promyslovoe khoziaistvo"*) 14. Leningrad.

Poselennye itogi. 1928. *Poselennye itogi tuzemnoi perepisi 1926 g. Kamchatskii okrug* [Population Data of the Native Census of 1926: Kamchatsk District]. Vladivostok.

Powers, Roger W., and Richard H. Jordan. 1989. Post Pleistocene Human Biogeography and Climate Change in Siberia and Northern North America. Paper Submitted to the International Conference on "The Earth's Climate and Variability of the Sun over Recent Millenia: Geophysical, Astronomical, and Archaeological Aspects." London.

Preobrazhenskii, B. V. 1953. *O povyshenii produktivnosti olenei v Nenetskom Natsional'nom okruge* [On the Increase of Productivity of Reindeer in the Nenets National Area]. Arkhangel'sk: Knizhnoe Izdatel'stvo.

Prik, Z. M. 1968. O kolebaniiakh klimata Arktiki i ikh prichinakh [On Fluctuations in the Arctic Climate and Their Causes]. *Trudy Arkticheskogo i Antarkticheskogo Insituta* 274:10–21.

Prokhorov, Boris B. 1989. USSR: How to Save Yamal. *IWGIA Newsletter* 58:113–28.

Prokof'ev, Georgii N. 1940. Etnogoniia narodnostei Ob'-Eniseiskogo basseina [Ethnogony of the Population of the Ob'-Enisei Basin]. *Sovetskaia etnografiia* 3:67–76.

Prozorov, A. A. 1902. *Ekonomicheskii obzor Okhotsko-Kamchatskogo kraia* [An Economic Review of the Okhtosk-Kamchatsk Province]. St. Petersburg: Trud.

Qiniqtuagaksrat. 1980. *Qiniqtuagaksrat Utuqqanaat Inuuniagninisiqun: The Traditional Land Use Inventory for the Mid-Beaufort Sea*. Vol. 1. Barrow: North Slope Borough Commission on History and Culture.

Rainey, Froelich. 1947. The Whale Hunters of Tigara. *Anthropological Papers of the American Museum of Natural History* 41(2).

Rakhillin, V. K. 1970. Kolebaniia chislennosti osnovnykh vidov ptits arkhipelaga "Sem' ostrovov" [Fluctuations in the Major Bird Populations of the "Seven Islands" Archipelago]. In *Produktivnost' biotsenozov Subarktiki*, 164–67. Sverdlovsk: Sverdlovskii Universitet.

Rappaport, Roy A. 1967. *Pigs for the Ancestors: Ritual in the Ecology of a New Guinea People*. New Haven and London: Yale University Press.

———. 1971. The Flow of Energy in an Agricultural Society. *Scientific American* 225(3): 116–132.

Ravdonikas, V. I. 1938. *Naskal'nye izobrazheniia Onezhskogo ozera i Belogo moria* [Rock Paintings of the Onega Lake and the White Sea]. Vol. 2. Moscow and Leningrad: Academy of Sciences.

Ray, Dorothy J. 1975. *The Eskimos of Bering Strait*. Seattle and London: University of Washington Press.

———. 1983. *Ethnohistory in the Arctic: The Bering Strait Eskimo. Alaska History Series* 23. Kingston, Ont.: the Limestone Press.

Razumovski, V. I. 1931. Lastonogie Chukotki [The Pennipeds off the Chukotka Peninsula]. *Sotsialisticheskaia rekonstruktsiia rybnogo khoziaistva Dal'nego Vostoka* 11–12:100–107.

Reimers, Nikolai F. 1972. Ekologicheskie suktsessii i promyslovye zhivotnye [Ecological Successions and Animal Game Populations]. In *Okhotovedenie*, 67–108. Moscow.

Reimers, Nikolai F., and Alexei V. Yablokov. 1982. *Slovar' terminov i poniatii, sviazannykh s okhranoi zhivoi prirody* [A Glossary of Terms Related to Natural Conservation]. Moscow: Nauka.

Reeves, Randall R., and Edward Mitchell. 1988. Current Status of the Gray Whale, *Eschrichtius robustus*. *Canadian Field-Naturalist* 102(2): 369–90.

Report. 1979. Report of the Panel to Consider Cultural Aspects of Aboriginal Whaling in North Alaska. Submitted to the International Whaling Commission's Special Meeting on Aboriginal Whaling. Seattle, Wash.

———. 1983. Report on Nutritional, Subsistence, and Cultural Needs Relating to the catch of Bowhead Whales by Alaskan Natives. Submitted to the 35th Meeting of the International Whaling Commission. IWC TC/35/AB3.

———. 1988. Report of the Sub-Committee on Protected Species and Aboriginal Subsistence Whaling. *Report of the International Whaling Commission* 38:109–16.

Riches, David. 1974. The Netsilik Eskimo: A Special Case of Selective Female Infanticide. *Ethnology* 13(4): 351–61.

Riewe, Roderick R. 1977. The Utilization of Wildlife in the Jones Sound Region by the Grise Fiord Inuit. In *Truelove Lowland, Devon Island, Canada: A High Arctic Ecosystem*, L. C. Bliss (ed.), 623–44. Edmonton: University of Alberta Press.

Rochev, P. A. 1969. Biologicheskaia produktivnost' severnogo olenevodstva [Biological Productivity of the Northern Reindeer Industry]. *Nar'iana-Vynder* 127:3. Nar'ian-Mar.

Rodahl, Karl. 1954. Eskimo Methabolism. A Study of Racial Factors in Basal Methabolism. *Norsk Polarinstitutt Skriffter* 99. Oslo.

Rogachev, A. N. 1957. Mnogosloinye stoianki Kostenko-Borshevskogo raiona na Donu i problema razvitiia kul'tury v epokhu verkhnego paleolita na Russkoi ravnine [Multicomponent Sites of the Kostenki-Borshevo Area on the River Don and Questions in Cultural Development during the Upper Paleolithic of the Russian Plain]. *Materialy i issledovaniia po arkheologii SSSR* 59:9–134.

———. 1970. Paleoliticheskie zhilishcha i poseleniia [Paleolithic Dwellings and Sites]. *Materialy i issledovannia po arkheologii SSSR* 166:64–77.

Rogers, Edward S., and Mary B. Black. 1973. Subsistence Strategy in the Fish and Hare Period, Northern Ontario: The Weagamow Ojibwa, 1880–1920. *Journal of Anthropological Research* 32(1):1–43.

Romanov, A. A. 1941. Pushnye zveri Lensko-Khatangskogo kraiya i ikh promysel [The Fur Animals of the Lena-Khatanga Area and their Exploitation]. *Trudy Instituta poliarnogo zemledeliia, zhivotnovodstva i promyslovogo khoziaistva (Series "Promyslovoe khozyaistvo")* 6. Leningrad.

Roots, F. E. 1985. Severnaia nauchnaia set': regional'noe sotrudnichestvo v tseliakh razvitiia i okhrany prirody [Northern Research Network:

Regional Cooperation Focused on Natural Development and Conservation]. *Priroda i resursy* 21(2): 2–10. Moscow.

Rowley, Susan. 1985. Population Movements in the Canadian Arctic. *Études/Inuit/Studies* g(1):3–22.

Rozanov, Mikhail P. 1931. Promysel morskogo zveria na Chukotskom poluostrove [Sea-Mammal Hunting off the Chukchi Peninsula]. *Sovetskii Sever* 6:44–59.

Rudenko, Sergei I. 1947. *Drevniaia kul'tura Beringova moria i eskimosskaia problema* [The Ancient Culture of the Bering Sea and the Eskimo Problem]. Moscow and Leningrad: Glavsevmorput'. Reprint. Arctic Institute of North America, 1961.

Ryabtseva, K. M. 1970. Dinamika oledeneniia Khibin v golotsene v sviazi s ritmami uvlazhnennosti Severnogo polusharya [Dynamics of the Khibin Mountain Glaciation through the Holocene as Related to the Humidity Rhythms of the Northern Hemisphere]. In *Ritmy i ziklichnost' v prirode*. 105–20. *Voprosy geografii* 79. Moscow.

Sabo, George III. 1991. *Long Term Adaptations Among Arctic Hunter-Gatherers: A Case Study from Southern Baffin Island*. New York and London: Garland Publishing.

Salisbury, Richard F. 1975. Non-Equilibrium Models in New Guinea Ecology: Possibilities of a Cultural Extrapolation. *Anthropologica* 17(2): 127–49.

Sangi, Vladimir. 1990. Land Should Regain Its Genuine Owners. *IWGIA Newsletter* 62:116–23.

Saprykin, N., and M. Sinel'nikov. 1926. Samoyedy Kaninskoi i Timanskoi tundr [The Samoyeds of the Kanin and Timan Tundra]. *Severnoe khoziaistvo* 2–3:60–79. Arkhangel'sk.

Sarychev, Gavriil A. 1952. *Puteshestvie flota kapitana Sarycheva po severovostochnoi chasti Sibiri, Ledovitomu moriu i Vostochomu okeanu* [The Journey of the Navy Captain Gavriil Sarychev along the Northeastern Edge of Siberia, the Icy Sea, and the East Ocean]. Moscow: Glavsevmorput'.

Sauer, Carl O. 1956. The Agency of Man on the Earth. In *Man's Role in Changing the Face of the Earth*, W. L. Thomas (ed.), 49–69. Chicago: University of Chicago Press.

Saunders, Jeffrey J. 1980. A Model for Man-Mammoth Relationships in Late Pleistocene North America. *Canadian Journal of Anthropology* 1(1): 87–98.

Savelle, James M., and Allen P. McCartney. 1988. Geographical and Temporal Variation in Thule Eskimo Subsistence Economies: A Model. *Research in Economic Anthropology* 10: 21–72.

———. 1991. Thule Eskimo Subsistence and Bowhead Whale Procurement. In *Human Predators and Prey Mortality*, M. C. Stiner (ed.), 201–16. New York: Westview Press.

Savoskul, Sergei, and Viktor Karlov. 1988. Turukhanskaia GES i sud'ba Evenkii [The Turukhan Hydroelectric Plant and the Fate of Evenkiya. Letter to the Editorial Board]. *Sovetskaia etnografiia* 5:166–68.

Savvateev, Iurii A. 1985. Osobennosti sredy i okhotnich'ia deiatel'nost' v kamennom veke na territorii Karelii [Environmental Features and Human Hunting Activity during the Stone Age in Kareliia]. *Kratkie soobshcheniia Instituta Arkheologii* 181:30–36. Moscow.

Scammon, C. 1968. *The Marine Mammals of the Northwestern Coast of North America, Together with an Account of the American Whale-Fishery*. New York: Dover.

Sdobnikov, V. M. 1933. Nekotorye dannye po biologii olenia i olenevodstvu v severo-vostochnoi chasti Malozemel'skoi tundry [Some Data on Reindeer Biology and the Reindeer Economy in the Northeastern Part of the Malaia Zemlia Tundra]. *Olen'i pastbishcha Severnogo Kraia* 2:185–229. Arkhangel'sk.

Segal', A. N. 1960. Osobennosti termoreguliatsii u domashnego olenia v usloviiakh povysheniia letnikh temperatur [Thermoregulation in Domestic Reindeer under the Condition of Summer Temperature Increase]. In *Reguliatsiia obmena tepla i drugikh fiziologicheskikh funktsii u sel'skokhoziaistvennykh zhivotnykh v usloviiakh vysokikh temperatur*, 239–42. Krasnodar.

Semenov-Tian'-Shan'skii, Orest I. 1938. Ekologiia borovoi dichi Laplandskogo zapovednika [Ecology of the Grouse Species of the Lapland Game Reserve]. *Trudy Laplandskogo Goszapovednika* 1:213–305.

———. 1948a. Dikii severnyi olen' na Kol'skom poluostrove [Wild Reindeer on the Kola Peninsula]. Ibid. 2:3–90.

———. 1948b. Los' na Kol'skom poluostrove [Elk on the Kola Peninsula]. Ibid. 2:91–162.

Semerikov, P. P. 1933. *Olenevodstvo tundr Nenetskogo okruga* [The Reindeer Industry in the Tundras of the Nenets Area]. Arkhangel'sk: Sevkraigiz.

Sergeev, Mikhail A. 1934. *Koriakskii natsional'nyi okrug* [The Koryak National Area]. Leningrad: Institut Narodov Severa.

———. 1955. Nekapitalisticheskii put' razvitiia malykh narodov Severa [Noncapitalistic Ways of Development among the Small Peoples of the North]. *Trudy Instituta Etnografii* 27. Moscow.

Sergin, Viktor Ia. 1974. O khronologicheskom sootnoshenii zhilishch i prodolzhitel'nosti obitaniia na pozdnepaleoliticheskikh poseleniiakh [On the Chronological Sequence of Dwellings and Length of Residence at Late Paleolithic Sites]. *Sovetskaia arkheologiia* 1:3–11.

———. 1983. O naznachenii bol'shikh iam na paleoliticheskikh poseleniiakh [On the Function of Large Pits at Paleolithic Sites]. *Kratkie soobshcheniia Instituta Arkheologii* 173:23–31.

Severtsev, S. V. 1941. *Dinamika naseleniia i prisposobitel'naia evolutsiia zhivotnykh* [Population Dynamics and the Adaptive Evolution of Animal Species]. Leningrad: Academy of Sciences.

Shaiakhmetova, L. G. 1990. Novye dannye o drevnem naselenii tsentral'noi chasti Kol'skogo poluostrova [New Data on the Ancient Population of the Interior of the Kola Peninsula]. *Kratkie soobshcheniia Instituta Arkheologii* 200:33–38.

Sharp, Henry S. 1977. The Caribou-Eater Chipewyan; Bilaterality, Strategies of Caribou Hunting and Fur Trade. *Arctic Anthropology* 14(2): 35–40.

Shinkwin, Anne, and Mary Pete. 1984. Yup'ik Eskimo Societies: A Case Study. *Études/Inuit/Studies* (Supplement Issue, 2): 95–112.

Shiyatov, S. G. 1967. Kolebaniia klimata i vekovaia struktura drevostoev listvennichnykh redkolesii v gorakh Poliarnogo Urala [Climate Fluctuations and the Ancient Forest Structure of the Larch Woodland in the Polar Ural Mountains]. In *Rastitel'nost' lesotundry i puti eye osvoeniia*, 271–78. Leningrad: Nauka.

———. 1975. Sverkhvekovoi tsikl v kolebaniiakh indeksov prirosta listveniitsy (*Larix sibirica*) na poliarnoi granitse lesa [Over-Age Fluctuations in Tree-Growth Indices for the Siberian Larch (*Larix sibirica*) along the Northern Tree Line]. In *Biologicheskie osnovy dendrokhronologii*, 47–53. Leningrad and Vil'nius.

———. 1979. Rekonstruktsiia kolebanii klimata i dinamiki poliarnoi granitsy lesa na severe Zapadnoi Sibiri za poslednie 900 let na osnove analiza radial'nogo prirosta derev'ev [A Reconstruction of Climate Change and Polar Tree-Line Fluctuation in Northern West Siberia During the Last 900 Years, Based on an Analysis of Tree-Width Growth]. In *Osobennosti estestvenno-geograficheskoi sredy i istoricheskie protsessy v Zapadnoi Sibiri*, 21–23. Tomsk: Tomskii Universitet.

Shmit, E. V. 1939. Kratkii ocherk Zemekspeditsii Narkomzema RSFSR o sostoianii razvitiia olenevodstva i sobakovodstva v Chaunskom raione [Brief Report of the Surveying Expedition of the RSFSR Ministry of Agriculture on the Status of Reindeer and Dog-Breeding in the Chaun District]. Manuscript, F. 3, op.1, no.9. State Archive of the Chukchi Autonomous Area, Anadyr.

Shnakenburg, Nikolai B. 1939. Eskimosy (istoriko-etnograficheskii ocherk) [The Eskimos (Historical and Ethnographic Sketch)]. Manuscript, F. K-I, op.1, no.557. Institute-Museum of Anthropology and Ethnography, St. Petersburg.

Shnirel'man, Victor A. 1977. Rol' domashnikh zhivotnykh v periferiinykh obshchestvakh (na primere traditsionnykh obshchestv Sibiri i Ameriki) [The Role of Domesticated Animals in Marginal Societies (as Derived from the Data on Traditional Societies in Siberia and America)]. *Sovetskaia etnografiia* 2:29–49.

———. 1980. *Proiskhozhdenie skotovodstva (kul'turno-istoricheskaia problema* [The Origin of Animal Husbandry (A Cultural and Historical Issue)]. Moscow: Nauka.

———. 1986. Demograficheskie i etnokul'turnye protsessy epokhi pervobytnoi rodovoi obshchiny [Demographic and Ethnocultural Processes during the Era of Primordial Clan Community]. In *Istoriia pervobytnogo obshchestva*, A. I. Pershits et al. (eds.), 2:427–89. Moscow: Nauka.

———. 1990. Cherchez le Chien: Perspectives on the Economic Survival of Traditional Fishing-Oriented People of Kamchatka in Modern Times.

Paper presented at Sixth Hunter-Gatherers Conference, Fairbanks, Alaska.

Shnitnikov, Aleksei V. 1969. *Vnutrivekovaia izmenchivost' komponentov obshchei uvlazhnionnosti* [Intracentenary Variability of the Components of General Humidity]. Leningrad: Nauka.

Shreiber, Sergei E. 1931. *Mediko-sanitarnoe obsledovanie naseleniia Viliuiskogo i Olekminskogo okrugov* [A Medical and Sanitary Inventory of the Population of Vilui and Olekma Districts]. Leningrad: USSR Academy of Sciences.

Shrire, Carmel, and William L. Steiger. 1974. A Matter of Life and Death: An Investigation into the Practice of Female Infanticide in the Arctic. *Man* 9(2): 161–84.

Shumkin, V. Ia. 1987. Issledovanie Kol'skogo poluostrova [A Survey of the Kola Peninsula]. *Arkheologicheskie otkrytiia 1985* 44–45. Moscow.

———. 1988. K voprosy o formirovanii khoziaistvenno-kul'turnykh tipov u drevnego naseleniia Kol'skogo poluostrova [On the Origin of Economic-Cultural Types among the Prehistoric Population of the Kola Peninsula]. *Kratkie soobshcheniia Instituta Arkheologii* 193:9–14.

Siivonen, L. 1950. Some Observations on the Short-Term Fluctuations in Numbers of Mammals and Birds in the Sphere of the Northernmost Atlantic. *Papers on Game Research* 4:4–31.

Silook, Roger. 1976. *Seevookuk: Stories the Old People Told on St. Lawrence Island*. Anchorage: Alaska Publishing Co.

Simchenko, Yuri B. 1976. *Kul'tura okhotnikov na olenei Severnoi Evrazii. Etnograficheskaia rekonstruktsiia* [Culture of the Reindeer-Hunters of Northern Eurasia: An Ethnographic Reconstruction]. Moscow: Nauka.

———. 1978. Severnaia Aziia [Northern Asia]. In *Pervobytnaia periferiia klassovykh obshchestv do nachala Velikikh geograficheskikh otkrytii*, A. I. Pershits (ed.), 146–61. Moscow: Nauka.

———. 1982. Nganasany [The Nganasans]. In *Etnicheskaia istoriia narodov Severa*, I. S. Gurvich (ed.), 81–99. Moscow: Nauka.

Sirina, Anna A. 1992. Preemstvennost' v organizatsii sredy zhiznedeiatel'nosti (na primere evenkov verkhov'ev r. Nizhniaia Tunguska) [Continuity in Organization of the Life-Supporting Environment (as Instanced by the Evenks of the Upper Reaches of the Low Tunguska River)]. *Etnograficheskoe obozrenie* 2:77–88.

Sivuqam. 1985. *Sivuqam Nangaghnegha: Lore of St. Lawrence Island*. Vol. 1, *Gambell*. Unalakleet: Bering Strait School District.

Skrobov, V. D. 1958. Prodvizhenie zhivotnykh lesnoi zony v tundru [The Expansion of the Boreal Game Animals to the Tundra Area]. *Priroda* 11:104–105.

———. 1967. Sovremennoe rasprostranenie i chislennost' dikogo severnogo olenia na severe Zapadnoi Sibiri [Present Distribution and Numbers of Wild Reindeer in Northern West Siberia]. *Problemy Severa* 11:124–28.

Slonim, A. D. 1966. *Fiziologiia termoreguliatsii i termicheskoi adaptatsii u sel'skokhozyaistvennykh zhivotnykh* [Physiology of the Thermoregulation and Thermal Adaptation of Domesticated Animals]. Moscow and Leningrad: Nauka.

Slyunin, Nikolai V. 1900. *Okhotsko-Kamchatskii krai [Okhotsk-Kamchatsk Province]*. Vols. 1 and 2. St. Petersburg: Ministerstvo Finansov.

Smirnov, V. S. 1967. Analiz dinamiki chislennosti pestsa na Yamale i puti intensifikatsii ego promysla [Analysis of the Arctic Fox Population Dynamics in the Yamal Peninsula and Ways to Intensify its Management]. *Problemy Severa* 11:70–90.

Smith, Derek G. 1975. *Natives and Outsiders: Pluralism in the Mackenzie River Delta, Northwest Territories*. Mackenzie Delta Research Project 12. Ottawa: Dept. of Indian Affairs and Northern Development.

Smith, Eric Alden. 1979. Human Adaptation and Energetic Efficiency. *Human Ecology* 7(1): 53–74.

———. 1981. The Application of Optimal Foraging Theory to the Analysis of Hunter-Gatherer Group Size. In *Hunter-Gatherer Foraging Strategies: Ethnographic and Archaeological Analysis*, B. Winterhalder and E. A. Smith (eds.), 36–65. Chicago: University of Chicago Press.

———. 1984. Anthropology, Evolutionary Ecology, and the Explanatory Limitations of the Ecosystem Concept. In *The Ecosystem Concept in Anthropology*. E. Moran (ed.), 51–85. Boulder: Westview Press.

———. 1988. Risk and Uncertainty in the 'Original Affluent Society': Evolutionary Ecology of Resource-Sharing and Land Tenure. In *Hunters and Gatherers*, vol. 1, *History, Evolution, and Social Change*, T. Ingold, D. Riches, and J. Woodburn (eds.), 222–51. New York and Oxford: Berg.

———. 1991. *Inujjuamiut Foraging Strategies: Evolutionary Ecology of an Arctic Hunting Economy*. New York: Aldine De Gruyter.

Smith, James G. 1978. Economic Uncertainity in an "Original Affluent Society": Caribou and Caribou-Eater Chipewyan Adaptive Strategy. *Arctic Anthropology* 15(1): 68–88.

Smolyak, Anna V. 1976. Predstavleniia nanaitsev o mire [Nanai Beliefs about the Universe]. In *Priroda i chelovek v religioznykh predstavleniiakh narodov Sibiri i Severa*, I. S. Vdovin (ed.), 129–60. Leningrad: Nauka.

Soffer, Olga. 1985. *The Upper Paleolithic of the Central Russian Plain*. Orlando, Florida: Academic Press.

Sokolov I. 1935. Struktura stada severnykh olenei i ee znachenie v olenevodcheskom khozyaistve [The Structure of a Reindeer Herd and Its Role in the Reindeer Economy]. *Sovetskii Sever* 1:63–67.

Sokolova, Zoia P. 1990a. S'ezd malochislennykh narodov Severa (vzgliad etnografa) [The Congress of the Small Peoples of the North; an Ethnographer's Perspective]. *Sovetskaia etnografiia* 5:142–46.

———. 1990b. Narody Severa SSSR: proshloye, nastoiashchee i budushchee [Peoples of the Far North of the USSR: Their Past, Present, and Future]. *Sovetskaia etnografiia* 6:17–32.

Solov'ev, Dmitrii K. 1927a. Belaia kuropatka v Pechorskom krae [Ptarmigan in the Pechora Area]. *Ural'skii okhotnik* 8–9:20–26.

———. 1927b. Na Pechore [Along the Pechora River]. *Ural'skii okhotnik* 1:23–27.

Sonntag, R. M., and G. C. Broadhead. 1989. Documentation for Revised Bowhead Whale Catch Data (1948–1987). *Report of the International Whaling Commission* 39:114–15.

Sosunov, P. I. 1925. Tobol'skii Sever [The Tobol North]. *Severnaia Aziia* 3–4. Leningrad.

Spencer, Robert F. 1959. The North Alaskan Eskimo: A Study in Ecology and Society. *Bureau of American Ethnology Bulletin* 171. Washington, D.C.

SS "Herman." 1909. SS "Herman" Trade Books. Manuscript. Old Dartmouth Historical Society, New Bedford, Mass. Copy provided to the author by J. Bockstoce.

Stager, John K., and Robert J. McSkimming. 1984. Physical Environment. In *Arctic*, D. Damas (ed.), 27–35. *Handbook of North American Indians* 5. Washington, D.C.: Smithsonian Institution.

Stanford, Dennis J. 1976. The Walakpa Site, Alaska: Its Place in the Birnirk and Thule Cultures. *Smithsonian Contributions to Anthropology* 20. Washington, D.C.

Stanley, Y. 1980. Paleoecology of the Arctic-Steppe Mammoth Biome. *Current Anthropology* 21(5): 663–66.

Starkov, Vadim F. 1986. Osvoenie Shpitsbergena i obshchie problemy russkogo arkticheskogo moreplavaniia [Settling of the Spitsbergen and General Issues in Russian Arctic Navigation]. Unpublished Ph.D. diss. Moscow: Institute of Archaeology.

Starokadomski, L. M. 1946. *Ekspeditsiia Severnogo Ledovitogo okeana (1910–1915 gg.)* [The Arctic Ocean Expedition, 1910–1915)]. Moscow: Glavsevmorput'.

Statistics. 1991. Statistics on the Economic and Cultural Development of the Northern Aboriginal People of the USSR (for the period of 1980–1989). *Circumpolar and Scientific Affairs* 91–02. Ottawa: Indian and Northern Affairs, Canada.

Steensby, Hans P. 1917. An Anthropogeographical Study of the Origin of the Eskimo Culture. *Meddelelser om Grønland* 53(2).

Stefansson, Vilhjalmur. 1921. *My life with the Eskimo*. New York: Macmillan.

Steller, Georg W. 1938. Opisanie strany Kamchatki, eye zhitelei, ikh nravov, naimenovanii, obraza zhizni i razlichnykh obychaev [Description of the Land of Kamchatka, of its Inhabitants, and of Their Customs, Names, Life Style, and Various Traditions]. Manuscript, F. K-I, op. 1, no. 304. Russian Translation from the German Edition of 1774. Archive of the Institute-Museum of Anthropology and Ethnography, St. Petersburg.

Stern, J. J. 1970. The Meaning of "Adaptation" and Its Relation to the Phenomenon of Natural Selection. In *Evolutionary Biology*, T. H. Dobzhansky (ed.), 4:39–66. New York: Appleton-Century-Crofts.

Stora, Nils. 1987. Russian Walrus Hunting in Spitsbergen. *Études/Inuit/Studies* 11(2): 117–38.
Stott, D. H. 1969. Cultural and Natural Checks on Population Growth. In *Environment and Cultural Behavior*, A. Vayda (ed.), 90–120. Garden City, N.Y.: Natural History Press.
Sturdy, David A. 1972. Exploitation Patterns of a Modern Reindeer Economy in West Greenland. In *Papers in Economic Prehistory*, E. S. Higgs (ed.), 161–68. Cambridge: Cambridge University Press.
———. 1975. Some Reindeer Economies in Prehistoric Europe. In *Paleoeconomy*, E. S. Higgs (ed.), 55–85. Cambridge: Cambridge University Press.
Sullivan, Robert J. 1942. *The Ten'a Food Quest. The Catholic University of America. Anthropological Series* 11. Washington, D.C.: The Catholic University of America Press.
Suslov, Innokentii M. 1930. Rashchioty minimal'nogo kolichestva olenei potrebnogo dlia tuzemnogo seredniazkogo khoziaistva [Estimates of the Minimal Number of Reindeer Adequate to Support an Indigenous Household]. *Sovetskii Sever* 3:29–35.
Suttles, Waine. 1968. Coping with Abundance: Subsistence on the North-West Coast. In *Man the Hunter*, R. Lee and I. DeVore (eds.), 56–68. Chicago: Aldine.
Suvorov, Evgenii K. 1912. *Komandorskie ostrova i pushnoi promysel na nikh* [The Commander Islands and Their Fur Industry]. St. Petersburg: Departament Zemledelia.
———. 1914. O promysle morzha i kita na Chukotskoi zemle [On Walrus and Whale Hunting off the Chukchi Land]. *Materialy k poznaniiu russkogo rybolovstva* 3(5): 189–98.
Svedeniia. 1939. Svedeniia o estestvennom dvizhenii naseleniia za 1939–1961 [Records on Natural Growth of the Population, 1939–1961]. Manuscript, F.15, op.1, no.12. State Archive of the Chukchi Autonomous Area, Anadyr.
Sverdrup Harald U. 1930. Plavanie na sudne "Mod" v vodakh morei Lapteva i Vostochno-Sibirskogo [A Voyage of Exploration of the Ship "Maud" in the Laptev and East Siberian Seas]. *Materialy Komissii po izucheniiu Iakutskoi ASSR* 30. Leningrad.
Svodnaia tablitsa. 1932. Svodnaia tablitsa o nalichii kochevogo naseleniia v 1 tunsovete v 1931 g. [Summary Register of the Nomad Population of the First Native Soviet in 1931]. Manuscript, F.197, op.2, no.10. State Archive of the Nenets Autonomous Area, Nar'ian-Mar.
Syroechkovskii, Evgenii E. 1974. *Biologicheskie resursy Sibirskogo Severa (problemy osvoeniia)* [The Biological Resources of the Siberian North (Issues in Management)]. Moscow: Nauka.
———. 1982. Dikii severnyi olen' v SSSR [Wild Reindeer in the USSR]. In *Promyslovaia teriologiia*, 53–71. Moscow: Nauka.
Syroechkovskii, Evgenii E., and Elena V. Rogacheva. 1974. Moose of the Asiatic Part of the USSR. *Naturaliste Canadien* 101(3–4): 595–604.
Taksami, Chuner M. 1976. Predstavleniia o prirode i cheloveke u nivkhov

[Ideas about Nature and Man among the Nivkhs]. In *Priroda i chelovek v religioznykh predstavleniiakh narodov Sibiri i Severa*, I. S. Vdovin (ed.), 203–16. Leningrad: Nauka.

———. 1984. Problema vzaimosviazi prirody i obshchestva (po materialam etnografii korennogo naseleniia Tikhookeanskogo poberezh'ia SSSR) [The Issue of Interrelationships between Nature and Society (Derived from the Ethnographic Data on the Indigenous Peoples of the Pacific Coast of the USSR)]. In *Rol' geograficheskogo faktora v istorii dokapitalisticheskikh obshchestv*, 167–81. Leningrad: Nauka.

Tanner, Adrian. 1979. *Bringing Home Animals: Religious Ideology and Mode of Production of the Mistassini Cree Hunters*. New York: St. Martin's Press.

Taylor, J. Garth. 1974. *Labrador Eskimo Settlements of the Early Contact Period. National Museum of Man. Publications in Ethnology* 9. Ottawa.

Taylor, William E., Jr. 1963. Hypotheses on the Origin of Canadian Thule Culture. *American Antiquity* 28(4): 456–64.

———. 1966. An Archaeological Perspective on Eskimo Economy. *Antiquity* 40(158): 114–20.

Terletskii, Petr E. 1930. Osnovnye cherty khoziaistva Severa [Main Features of the Economy in the North]. *Sovetskii Sever* 9–12:42–85.

———. 1932a. *Naselenie Krainego Severa (po dannym perepisi 1926–27 gg.)* [The Population of the Polar North (According to the Census Data of 1926–1927)]. Leningrad: Institut Narodov Severa.

———. 1932b. Severnoe olenevodstvo [Northern Reindeer Industry]. In *Sbornik po olenevodstvu, tundrovoi veterinarii i zootekhnike*, 11–52. Moscow: Vlast' Sovetov.

———. 1934. K voprosu o parmakh Nenetskogo okruga [On the "Parma" Groupings in the Nenets Area]. *Sovetskii Sever* 5:35–44.

———. 1967. Naselenie Krainego Severa SSSR [Population of the Far North of the USSR]. Manuscript. Institute of Ethnology and Anthropology, Moscow.

Testart, Allain. 1982. The Significance of Food Storage Among Hunter-Gatherers: Residence Patterns, Population Densities and Social Inequalities. *Current Anthropology* 23(5): 523–37.

Thomas, R. Brooke. 1973. Human Adaptation to a High Andean Energy Flow System. *Occasional Papers in Anthropology* 7. Pennsylvania State University, Department of Anthropology.

Thompson, Laura. 1949. The Relations of Man, Animals and Plants in an Island Community (Fiji). *American Anthropology* 51(2): 253–67.

Tikhomirov, Boris A. 1971. Osobennosti biosphery Krainego Severa [Biosphere Specifity of the Far North]. *Priroda* 11:30–42.

———. 1974. Izuchenie tundrovykh biogeotsenozov [Studies of the Tundra Biogeocenosis]. In *Programma i metodika biogeotsenologicheskikh issledovanni*, 251–66. Moscow: Nauka.

Titova, Zinaida D. (comp.). 1978. *Etnograficheskie materialy severovostochnoi geograficheskoi ekspeditsii, 1785–1795* [Ethnographic Data of the Northeast Geographical Expedition, 1785–1795]. Magadan: Knizhnoe Izdatel'stvo.

Tomilin, Avenir G. 1957. Kitoobraznye [The Cetaceans]. *Zveri SSSR i prilezhashchikh stran IX*. Moscow: Academy of Sciences.

Tomkovich, P. S., and A. G. Sorokin. 1983. Fauna ptits Vostochnoi Chukotki [Bird Fauna of the Eastern Chukotka]. In *Rasprostranenie i sistematika ptits*, 77–159. Moscow: Nauka.

Tremaine, Marie. 1953. Introduction. In *Arctic Bibliography*, 1:5–9. Washington, D.C.: U.S. Department of Defense.

Tret'yakov, P. N. 1936. Pervobytnaia okhota v Severnoi Evrazii [Primitive Hunting in Northern Eurasia]. *Izvestiia GAIMK* 106:220–262. Leningrad.

Tugolukov, Vladilen A. 1969. *Sledopyty verkhom na oleniakh* [Treckers on Reindeerback]. Moscow: Nauka.

———. 1979. *Kto vy, yukaghiry?* [Who are You, the Yukaghirs?]. Moscow: Nauka.

Turmanina, V. I. 1970. Vliianie na rastitel'nost' vnutrivekovykh ritmov uvlazhnennosti [The Impact on Vegetation of Intracentenary Rhythms of Humidity]. In *Ritmy i tsiklichnost' v prirode*, 168–81. *Voprosy geografii* 79. Moscow.

Turner, Christy G. II. 1985. The Dental Search for Native American Origin. In *Out of Asia: Peopling the Americas and the Pacific*, R. Kirk and E. Szathmary (eds.), 31–78. Canberra: Australian National University.

Turov, Mikhail G. 1990. *Khoziaistvo evenkov taiozhnoi zony Srednei Sibiri v kontse XIX-nachale XX v.* [The Economy of the Evenks in the Boreal Forest Zone of Central Siberia. Late 19th to Early Twentieth Century (Principles of Land Management)]. Irkutsk: Irkutskii Universitet.

Tuzemnoe Khoziaistvo. 1929. *Tuzemnoe khoziaistvo nizov'ev Amura v 1927–1928 gg. (po materialam obsledovaniia 1928 g.)* [The Native Economy of the Lower Amur River in the Years 1927–1928 (According to the Inventory of 1928)]. Khabarovsk-Blagoveshchensk: Izdatel'stvo Dal'okhotsoiuza i Dal'kraiispolkoma.

Usher, Peter J., and George Wenzel. 1987. Native Harvest Surveys and Statistics: A Critique of Their Construction and Use. *Arctic* 40(2): 145–60.

Uspenskii, Savva M. 1970. Osobennosti dinamiki chislennosti i ispol'zovaniia resursov okhotnich'ikh zhivotnykh v Arktike i Subarktike [Specifity of Population Dynamics and Game Population Management in the Arctic and Subarctic]. In *Proceedings of the Eleventh International Congress of Biologists and Game Managers*, 738–41. Moscow.

Uspenskii, Savva V., and Aleksandr A. Kishchinskii. 1972. Opyt aerovisual'nogo uchiota gnezdovykh populiatsii vodoplavaiushchikh ptits v tundre [An Attempt at Aerovisual Counting of the Nesting Waterfowl Populations of the Tundra]. In *Okhotovedenie*, 210–34. Moscow.

Ustinov, V. I. 1956. *Olenevodstvo na Chukotke* [Reindeer Economy on the Chukchi Peninsula]. Magadan: Knizhnoe Izdatel'stvo.

V. A. 1935. U chukoch v Chaunskoi gube (zapiski vracha) [Among the Chukchis around the Chaun Bay (A Doctor's Records)]. *Sovetskii Sever* 2:60–64.

Vaikmiaeh, R. A., T. A. Martma, Ya.-M. K. Punning, and K. R. Tyugu. 1984. Variatsii 8^{18}o i Cl^- v lednikovom kerne Zapadnogo lednikovogo polia na ostrove Severnaia Zemlia [Variations in 8^{18} o and Cl^- Content in the Ice-Kern from the Western Glacier Field, Severnaia Zemlia Islands]. *Materialy gliatsiologicheskikh issledovanii* 51:192–95.

Vaikmiaeh, R. A. and Ya.-M. K. Punning. 1982. Usloviia formirovaniia izotopno-geokhimicheskogo sostava lednikov Evraziiskoi Arktiki: gliatsioklimaticheskii aspekt [Formation Conditions for the Geochemical Isotope Content of Eurasian Arctic Glaciers: Glacio-Climatic Aspect]. In *Proceedings of the Eleventh INQUA Congress*, 2:32–33. Moscow.

Vainstein, Sev'ian I. 1972. *Istoricheskaia etnografiia tuvintsev. Problemy kochevogo khozyaistva* [Historical Ethnography of the Touvinians: Issues in the Nomadic Economy]. Moscow: Nauka. Translated as: *Nomads of South Siberia: The Pastoral Economies of the Tuva.* Cambridge: Cambridge University Press, 1980.

———. 1981. Voprosy rasprostraneiia olenevodstva u samodiiskikh narodov [On the Distribution of the Reindeer Economy among the Samoyed Peoples]. In *Congressus Quintus Internationalis Finno-Ugristarum*, 8:118–23. Turku, Finland.

Vakurov, A. D. 1975. *Lesnye pozhary na Severe* [Forest Fires in the North]. Moscow: Nauka.

Van-Linshotten, Ia. G. 1915. Niderlandskie ekspeditsii k severnym beregam Rossii v 1594–1595 gg [Dutch Expeditions to the Arctic Coastlands of Russia in 1594–1595]. *Zapiski po gidrografii* 39(3–4). Petersburg.

Van Stone, James W. 1974. *Athapaskan Adaptations: Hunters and Fishermen of the Subarctic Forests.* Arlington Heights, Ill.: Harlan Davidson.

Vasil'ev, Vladimir I. 1970. Siirtia—legenda ili real'nost' [Siirtia: Legend or Reality]. *Sovetskaia etnografiia* 1:151–57.

———. 1976. Vozniknovenie elementov chastnosobstvennicheskogo uklada u samodiiskikh narodov Obsko-Eniseiskogo Severa [On the Rise of Patterns of Private Property among the Samoyed Peoples of the Ob'-Enisei Far North]. In *Stanovlenie klassov i gosudarstva*, A. I. Pershits (ed.), 314–41. Moscow: Nauka.

———. 1979a. Ekologicheskii faktor i nekotorye problemy kul'turogeneza severnykh samodiitsev [The Ecological Factor and Some Issues in the Genesis of Culture among the Northern Samoyed Peoples]. In *Osobennosti estestvenno-geograficheskoi sredy i istoricheskie protsessy v Zapadnoi Sibiri*, 101–103. Tomsk: Tomskii Universitet.

———. 1979b. *Problemy formirovaniia severosamodiiskikh narodnostei* [Issues in the Formation of the Northern Samoyed Peoples]. Moscow: Nauka.

———. 1980. Problemy etnogeneza severosamodiiskikh narodov (nentsy, entsy, nganasany) [Studies in Ethnogenesis of the northern Samoyed Peoples (Nenets, Enets, Nganasan)]. In *Etnogenez narodov Sesera*, I. S. Gurvich (ed.), 41–67. Moscow: Nauva.

———. 1990. Teoreticheskie i istochnikovedcheskie problemy izucheniia etnicheskoi istorii (na materialakh narodov Severa SSSR) [Theoretical and Resource Issues in Studies of Ethnic History (Based on Data on the Northern Peoples of the USSR). *Sovetskaia etnografiia* 6:33–41.

Vasil'ev, Vladimir I., Zoia P. Sokolova, and Vladilen A. Tugolukov. 1987. Etnicheskie obshchnosti i etnicheskie processy nakanune oktiabria [Ethnic Groupings and Ethnic Processes before October (of 1917)]. In *Etnicheskoe razvitye narodnostei Severa v sovetskii period*, I. S. Gurvich (ed.), 32–61. Moscow: Nauka.

Vasil'ev, Vladimir I., and Vladilen A. Tugolukov. 1987. Natsional'no-gosudarstvennoe stroitel'stvo, sozialisticheskoe pereustroistvo khoziaistva, byta i kul'tury i etnicheskie protsessy. (1917–1940) [Administrative Development, Ethnic Processes, and Socialistic Transformation in the Economy and Everyday Life of Native Cultures (1917–1940)]. Ibid. 62–90.

Vasil'ev, V. N. 1936. Olen'i pastbishcha Anadyrskogo kraia [Reindeer Pastures of the Anadyr Area]. *Trudy Arkticheskogo Instituta* 62:9–104. Leningrad.

Vasilevich, Glafira M. 1969. *Evenki. Istoriko-etnograficheskie ocherki (XVIII-nachalo XX v.)* [The Evenks: Historico-Ethnographic Essays (from the 1700s to the early 1900s)]. Leningrad: Nauka.

Vasilevich, Glafira M., and Maksim G. Levin. 1951. Tipy olenevodstva i ikh proiskhozdenie [Patterns of Reindeer Breeding and Their Origin]. *Sovetskaia etnografiia* 1:63–87.

Vasil'evskii, Ruslan S. 1985. Stanovlenie i razvitie primorskoi sistemy khoziaistva v severnoi chasti Tikhookeanskogo basseina [The Rise and Development of Maritime Economic Patterns in the North Pacific Area]. *Kratkie soobshcheniia Instituta Arkheologii* 181:52–57. Moscow.

Vayda, Andrew P. 1969. An Ecological Approach in Cultural Anthropology. *Bucknell Review* 17(1): 112–19.

———. 1976. On the "New Ecology" Paradigm. *American Anthropologist* 78(3): 645–46.

Vayda, Andrew P., and Bonnie J. McCay. 1975. New Directions in Ecology and Ecological Anthropology. *Annual Review of Anthropology* 4:293–306.

Vdovin, Innokenti S. 1950. K istorii obshchestvennogo stroia chukchei [On the History of Chukchi Social Structure]. *Uchenye zapiski Leningradskogo universiteta* 115:73–100.

———. 1954. *Istoriia izucheniia paleoaziatskikh iazykov* [A History of the Study of Palaeoasiatic Languages]. Moscow and Leningrad: Academy of Sciences.

———. 1965. *Ocherki istorii i etnografii chukchei* [Essays in the History and Ethnography of the Chukchis]. Moscow and Leningrad: Nauka.

———. 1973. *Ocherki etnicheskoi istorii koryakov* [Essays in the Ethnic History of the Koryaks]. Leningrad: Nauka.

———. 1974. Koryaki-olenevody na Kamchatke v XVIII–XIX vv. [The Reindeer Koryaks of Kamchatka during the 1700s and 1800s]. *Kraevedcheskie zapiski* 5:104–20. Petropavlovsk-Kamchatskii.

———. 1975. Istoricheskie osobennosti formirovaniia obshchestvennogo razdelelniia truda u narodov severo-vostoka Sibiri [On the Formative Historical Conditions of Social Cooperation among the Native Peoples of Northeastern Siberia]. In *Sotsial'naia istoriia narodov Azii*, 143–57. Leningrad: Nauka.

———. 1976. Priroda i chelovek v religioznykh predstavleniiakh chukchei [Nature and Man in Chukchi Religious Beliefs]. In *Priroda i chelovek v religioznykh predstavleniiakh narodov Sibiri i Severa*. I. S. Vdovin (ed.), 217–53. Leningrad: Nauka.

Vecsey, C. 1980. American Indian Environmental Religions. In *American Indian Environments: Ecological Issues in Native American History*. C. Vecsey and R. W. Venables (eds.), 1–37. Syracuse.

Velichko, A. A., Yu. N. Gribchenko, A. K. Markova, and V. P. Udartsev. 1977. O vozraste i usloviakh obitaniia stoianki Khotylevo na Desne [On the Age and Conditions of Residence at the Khotylevo Site on the Desna River]. In *Paleoekologiia drevnego cheloveka*, I. K. Ivanova and N. D. Praslov (eds.), 40–50. Moscow: Nauka.

Verbov, Georgii D. 1939. Perezhitki rodovogo stroia u nentsev [Survivals of the Clan Society among the Nenets]. *Sovetskaia etnografiia* 2:43–66.

Vereshchagin, Nikolai K. 1967a. Primitive Hunters and Pleistocene Extinction in the Soviet Union. In *Pleistocene Extinctions: The Search for a Cause*. P. S. Martin and H. E. Wright (eds.), 365–98. New Haven: Yale University Press.

———. 1967b. Geologicheskaia istoriia losia i ego osvoenie pervobytnym chelovekom [Geological History of the Alces and its Exploitation by Prehistoric Man]. *Biologiia i promysel losia* 3:3–37. Moscow.

———. 1971. Okhoty pervobytnogo cheloveka i vymiranie pleistocenovykh mlekopitaiushchikh v SSSR [The Hunts of Prehistoric Man and the Extinction of Pleistocene Mammals in the USSR]. *Trudy Zoologicheskogo Instituta* 49:200–32. Leningrad: Nauka.

———. 1977. Berelyokhskoye kladbishche mamontov [Berelyokh Mammoth "Cemetery"]. In *Mamontovaia fauna Russkoi ravniny i Vostochnoi Sibiri*, A. O. Skarlato (ed.), 5–50. *Trudy Zoologicheskogo Instituta* 72. Leningrad: Nauka.

———. 1979. *Pochemu vymerli mamonty* [Why Mammoths Became Extinct]. Leningrad: Nauka.

Vereshchagin, Nikolai K., and Gennadij F. Baryshnikov. 1984. Quaternary Mammalian Extinctions in Northern Eurasia. In *Quaternary Extinctions: A Prehistoric Revolution*. P. S. Martin and R. G. Klein (eds.), 483–516. Tucson: University of Arizona Press.

Vereshchagin, Nikolai K., and I. E. Kuz'mina. 1977. Ostatki mlekopitaiushchikh iz paleoliticheskikh stoianok na Donu i verkhnei Desne [Remains of Mammals from Paleolithic Sites on the Don and Upper Desna Rivers]. In *Mamontovaia fauna Russkoi ravniny i Vostochnoi Sibiri*, A. O. Skarlato (ed.), 77–110. *Trudy Zoologicheskogo Instituta* 72. Leningrad: Nauka.

Vershinin, A. A. 1972. Rasprostranenie i chislennost' dikikh kopytnykh v

Kamchatskoi oblasti [Distribution and Numbers of the Wild Ungulates in the Kamchatka Province]. In *Okhotovedenie*, 109–27. Moscow.

Vibe, Christian. 1967. Arctic Animals in Relation to Climatic Fluctuations. *Meddelelser om Grønland* 170(5). Copenhagen.

———. 1981. Animals, Climate, Hunters, and Whalers. In *Proceedings of the International Symposium on Early European Exploitation of the Northern Atlantic, 800–1700*. 203–11. Groningen: University of Groningen.

Vincent, D., and A. Gunn. 1981. Population Increase of Muskoxen on Banks Island and Implications for Competition with Peary Caribou. *Arctic* 34(2): 175–79.

Vinogradov, Mikhail P. 1949. Morskie mlekopitaiushchie Arktiki [Sea-Mammals of the Arctic]. *Trudy Arkticheskogo instituta* 202. Leningrad.

Vishnevskii, Anatolii G. 1976. *Demograficheskaia revolutsiia* [The Demographic Revolution]. Moscow: Statistika.

Vitiugov A. 1923. Olenevodstvo [Reindeer Industry]. *Severnoe khoziaistvo* 3–5. Arkhangel'sk.

Vol'phson, Alexandr G. 1985. *Osnovnye ekologicheskie i sotsial'nye faktory stanovleniia kul'turno-khoziaistvennogo uklada olennykh chukchei i koryakov* [The Main Ecological Factors in Formation of the Cultural and Economic Pattern of the Reindeer Chukchis and Koryaks]. Report no. 8904–B85. Magadan, Moscow: VINITI.

Vol'phson, Alexandr G. (ed.). 1986. Whaling of Gray Whales (*Eschrichtius gibbobus*) and Its Significance in the Life of the Aboriginal Population on the Chukotka Peninsula. Special Report Submitted to the International Whaling Commission. Moscow.

Voprosy i otvety. 1787. Voprosy i otvety o sostoianii zemli obitaemoi samoedami i o ikh promyslakh [Questions and Answers on the Condition of the Land Inhabited by the Samoyeds and on Their Economies]. V. Krestinin (comp.). *Novye ezhemesiachnye sochineniia* 7–9. St. Petersburg.

Voronin, R. N. 1978. *Belaia kuropatka Bol'shezemel'skoi tundry. Ekologiia i khozyaistvennoe ispol'zovanie* [The Arctic Ptarmigan of the Bol'shaia Zemlia Tundra: Ecology and Management]. Moscow: Nauka.

Vorren, Ørnul'v. 1974/75. Man and Reindeer in Northern Fennoscandia: Economic and Social Aspects. *Folk* 16–17:243–52. Copenhagen.

Vrangel', Ferdinand P. 1948. *Puteshestvie po severnym beregam Sibiri i po Ledovitomu moriu, sovershennoe v 1820, 1821, 1822, 1823 i 1825 gg.* [Journey along the Northern Coasts of Siberia and across the Arctic Sea Undertaken in the Years 1820, 1821, 1822, 1823, and 1824]. 2d ed. Moscow: Glavsevmorput'.

Waisberg, Leo. 1975. Boreal Forest Subsistence and the Windigo: Fluctuation of Animal Populations. *Anthropologica* 17(2): 169–85.

Waldman, Carl. 1985. *Atlas of the North American Indian*. New York: Facts on File Publications.

Washburn, A. L., and G. Weller. 1986. Arctic Research in the National Interest. *Science* 233:633–39.

Watt, Kenneth F. 1971. *Ekologiia i upravlenie prirodnymi resursami* [Ecology and Resource Management]. Moscow: Mir. First Edition: *Ecology and Natural Resource Management*. New York: McGraw-Hill, 1968.

Weeden, Robert B. 1985. Northern People, Northern Resources, and the Dynamics of Carrying Capacity. *Arctic* 38(2): 116–29.

Weidick, Anker. 1982. Klima- og gletscherandringer i det sydlige Vestgrønland: di sidste 1000 år. *Grønland* 5–7:235–51.

Weiner, John S. 1964. Human Ecology. In *Human Biology: An Introduction to Human Evolution, Variation and Growth*, G. A. Harrison, J. S. Weiner, J. M. Tanner, and N. A. Barnicot (eds.), 401–508. New York and Oxford: Oxford University Press.

Welch, Harold E., et al. 1992. Energy Flow through the Marine Ecosystem of the Lancaster Sound Region, Arctic Canada. *Arctic* 45(4): 343–57.

Wenzel, George. 1986. Resource Harvesting and the Social Structure of Native Communities. In *Native People and Renewable Resource Management*, J. Green and J. Smith (eds.), 10–22. Edmonton: Alberta Society of Professional Biologists.

———. 1991. *Animal Rights, Human Rights: Ecology, Economy and Ideology in the Canadian Arctic*. Toronto-Buffalo: The University of Toronto Press.

Weyer, Edward. 1932. *The Eskimos: Their Environment and Folkways*. New Haven: Yale University Press.

Wheelersburg, Robert P. 1991. Uma Saami Native Harvest Data Derived from Royal Swedish Taxation Records 1557–1614. *Arctic* 44(4): 337–45.

Whittington, Stephen L., and Bennett Dyke. 1984. Simulating Overkill: Experiments with the Mosimann and Martin Model. In *Quarternary Extinctions: A Prehistoric Revolution*, P. S. Martin and R. G. Klein (eds.), 451–65. Tucson: University of Arizona Press.

Wilimovsky, Norman J., and John N. Wolfe (eds.). 1966. *Environment of the Cape Thompson Region, Alaska*. Oak Ridge, Tenn.: U.S. Atomic Energy Commission.

Wilkinson, P. F. 1972. Ecosystem Models and Demographic Hypothesis: Predation and Prehistory in North America. In *Models in Archaeology*, D. L. Clarke (ed.), 543–76. London.

———. 1975. The Relevance of Musk-ox Exploitation to the Study of Prehistoric Animal Economies. In *Paleoeconomy*, E. S. Higgs (ed.), 9–53. Cambridge: Cambridge University Press.

Williams, Nancy M., and Eugene S. Hunn (eds.). 1982. *Resource Managers: North American and Australian Hunter-Gatherers*. Boulder: Westview Press.

Winterhalder, Bruce. 1981. Foraging Strategies in the Boreal Forest: An Analysis of Cree Hunting and Gathering. In *Hunter-Gatherer Foraging Strategies*, B. Winterhalder and E. A. Smith (eds.), 13–35. Chicago: University of Chicago Press.

———. 1983. Boreal Foraging Strategies. In *Boreal Forest Adaptation:*

The Northern Algonkians, A. T. Steegmann (ed.), 201–41. New York: Plenum Press.
Wissler, Clark. 1917. *The American Indian: An Introduction to the Anthropology of the New World*. New York: Douglas C. McMurtrie.
Wolfe, Robert J., and Robert J. Walker. 1987. Subsistence Economies in Alaska: Productivity, Geography and Development Impacts. *Arctic Anthropology* 24(2): 56–81.
Woodby, D. A., and Daniel B. Botkin. 1993. Stock Size prior to Commercial Whaling. In *The Bowhead Whale*, J. J. Burns and J. J. Montague (eds.), 387–407. *Society for Marine Biology. Special Publication* 2.
Woods, Shelagh Jane. 1986. The Wolfe at the Door. *Northern Perspective* 14(2): 1–8.
Workman, William B. 1988. The Development of Sea Mammal Hunting among Prehistoric North Pacific Cultures. In *International Symposium on Human-Animal Relationship in the North*, 23–42. Abashiri, Japan.
Worl, Rosita. 1982. *A Synopsis of Alaska Native Subsistence Economies and Projection of Research Needs*. Anchorage.
Yesner, David R. 1980a. Caribou Exploitation in Interior Alaska: Paleo-ecology at Paxson Lake. *Anthropological Papers of the University of Alaska* 19(2): 15–31.
———. 1980b. Maritime Hunter-Gatherers: Ecology and Prehistory. *Current Anthropology* 21(6): 727–50.
Zabrodin, V. A. 1976. Problemy khoziaistvennogo osvoeniia i okhrany dikikh severnykh olenei tundrovykh populiatsii [Issues in Management and Protection of the Tundra Stocks of Wild Reindeer]. In Dikii severnyi olen', *Trudy Instituta sel'skogo khoziaistva Krainego Severa*, 12–13: 11–13. Noril'sk.
Zaitsev, A. N. 1970. Gigienicheskaia kharakteristika fakticheskogo pitaniia naseleniia Krainego Severa [Hygienic Review of the Actual Nutrition of the Population of the Far North]. *Problemy Severa* 14:198–203. Moscow.
Zaitsev, I. 1966. Dikii olen' na Chukotke [Wild Reindeer in Chukotka]. *Okhota i okhotnich'e khoziaistvo* 8:9. Moscow.
Zamiatnin, Sergei N. 1960. Nekotorye voprosy izucheniia khoziaistva v epokhy paleolita [Some Questions in the Study of Paleolithic Economy]. *Trudy Instituta etnografiii* 54:80–108. Moscow.
Zenkovich, Boris A. 1938. Razvitie promysla morskikh mlekopitaiushchikh na Chukotke [Development of Sea-Mammal Hunting on the Chukchi Peninsula]. *Priroda* 11–12: 59–63.
Zherebtsov, Liubomir N. 1982. *Istoriko-kul'turnye vzaimootnosheniia komi s sosednimi narodami* [Komi Historical and Cultural Relationships with the Neighboring Peoples]. Moscow: Nauka.
Zherekhova, Irina E. 1977. Opisanie i izmerenie zubov mamontov Berelyokha [Description and Measurements of Mammoth Teeth from the Berelyokh Site]. In Mamontovaia fauna Russkoi Ravniny i Vostochnoi Sibiri, A. O. Skarlato (ed.), 50–57. *Trudy Zoologicheskogo Instituta* 72. Leningrad: Nauka.

Zhigunov, P. S. (ed.). 1961. *Severnoe olenevodstvo* [Northern Reindeer Industry]. Moscow: Sel'khozizdat.

Zhilinskii, A. A. 1917. *Morskie promysly Belogo moria i Ledovitogo okeana* [Sea-Mammal Industries of the White Sea and Arctic Ocean]. Petrograd.

———. 1919. *Krainii Sever Evropeiskoi Rossii. Arkhangel'skaia guberniia* [The Far North of European Russia: Arkhangel'sk Gubernia]. Petrograd.

Zhilinskii, A. K. 1923. K voprosu o sporakh olenevodov Kaninskoi tundry [On the Conflicts among the Reindeer Herders in the Kanin Tundra]. *Severnoe khoziaistvo* 1:45–48 (Arkhangel'sk).

Zhitkov, Boris M. 1913. Poluostrov Iamal [The Yamal Peninsula]. *Zapiski Russkogo Geograficheskogo obshchestva (Otdelenie geografii)* 49. St. Petersburg.

Zimenko, Aleksei V. 1987. Proekt kompleksnoi mezhdistsiplinarnoi programmy "Komandory" ["The Commander Islands": An Outlook for a New Interdisciplinary Research Program]. In *Ratsional'noe prirodopol'zovanie na Komandorskikh ostrovakh*, V. E. Sokolov (ed.), 41–61. Moscow: Moskovskii Universitet.

Zolotarev, Aleksandr M., and Maksim G. Levin. 1940. K voprosy o drevnosti i proiskhozhdenii olenevodstva [On the Antiquity and Origin of Reindeer Breeding]. In *Problemy proiskhozhdeniia, evoliutsii i porodoobrazovaniia domashnikh zhivotnykh*, S. Bogoliubski (ed.), 1: 171–89. Moscow and Leningrad.

Zolotokrylin, A. N., A. N. Krenke, M. E. Liakhov, V. V. Popova, and M. M. Chernavskaia. 1986. Kolebaniia klimata Evropeiskoi chasti SSSR v istoricheskom proshlom [Climate Change over the European Part of the USSR during the Historical Past]. *Izvestiia Akademii Nauk SSSR (Series "Geografiia")* 1:26–36.

Zuev, Vasilii F. 1947. Materialy po etnografii Sibiri XVIII veka (1771–1772) [Data on Siberian Ethnography of the 1700s (1771–1772)]. *Trudy Instituta etnografii* 5. Moscow.

Index

UNIVERSITY PRESS OF NEW ENGLAND publishes books under its own imprint and is the publisher for Brandeis University Press, Brown University Press, University of Connecticut, Dartmouth College, Middlebury College Press, University of New Hampshire, University of Rhode Island, Tufts University, University of Vermont, and Wesleyan University Press.

Library of Congress Cataloging-in-Publication Data
Krupnik, I. I. (Igor ' Il 'ich)
[Arkticheskaîa ėtnoėkologiîa. English]
Arctic adaptations : native whalers and reindeer herders of northern Eurasia / Igor Krupnik ; translated by Marcia Levenson.
p. cm. — (Arctic visions)
A rev. and expanded translation of: Arkticheskaîa ėtnoėkologiîa.
Includes bibliographical references and index.
ISBN 0-87451-632-3. — ISBN 0-87451-633-1 (pbk.)
1. Human ecology—Arctic regions. 2. Arctic peoples—Social life and customs. I. Title. II. Series.
GF891.K78131993
304.2'0911—dc20 93-10996
∞